Career Counseling in Schools

—

MULTICULTURAL AND DEVELOPMENTAL PERSPECTIVES

Roger D. Herring, EdD, NCC, NCSC

CAREER COUNSELING IN SCHOOLS

10 9 8 7 6 5 4 3

American Counseling Association
5999 Stevenson Avenue
Alexandria, VA 22304

Director of Acquisitions
Carolyn Baker

Director of Publishing Systems
Michael Comlish

Copy Editor
Elaine Dunn

Cover design by Jennifer Sterling, Spot Color

Library of Congress Cataloging-in-Publication Data
Herring, Roger D.
    Career counseling in schools : multicultural and developmental
perspectives / Roger D. Herring.
        p.   cm.
    Includes bibliographical references and index.
    ISBN 1-55620-168-0 (alk. paper)
    1. Career education—United States.   2. Educational
counseling—United States.   3. Vocational guidance—United
States.   4. Multiculturalism—United States.   I. American
Counseling Association.   II. Title.
LC1037.5.H478   1998
371.4'25'0973—dc21   97-36620
                                                                                          CIP

Contents

PART IV: COGENT AREAS
OF CAREER DEVELOPMENT

PART V: PRACTICAL APPLICATIONS

Preface

THIS BOOK REPRESENTS a viable alternative resource for counselor educators, school counselors, and other helping professionals who have not discovered an appropriate multicultural approach to career development. Current theories of career choice and development have not addressed multicultural concerns, or they have addressed them inappropriately and superficially. As a result, providing school counselors and career counselors with an inclusive resource by which to enhance ethnic minority youths and other special populations with an appropriate multicultural and developmental career education represents the focus of this book.

The book is designed to enhance the school counselor's knowledge about cultural diversity and to provide appropriate career development interventions with special population students. The text provides counselors-in-training and in-service school counselors with direction for synergetic, multicultural, and developmental interventions with all of their students. To appropriately serve the career development needs of diverse students, these helping professionals may need to revisit and adjust their career counseling goals, to create expanded career guidance services, to generate different process skills, and to acquire more content knowledge.

Throughout the text, the term *school counseling* refers to both the profession and the program of services established by school counselors. The term *counseling* is not limited to remedial relationships or interpersonal relationships, but rather refers to a wide selection of services and activities that are chosen to help students prevent disabling events, focus on their overall development, and remedy existing concerns (Schmidt, 1996). The term *youths* applies to both children and adolescents.

Currently, the U.S. society is in a state of tremendous social change, contributing complexities, turbulence, and uncertainty to lifestyles and value systems (Goldenberg & Goldenberg, 1994). The United States reflects an increasingly diverse society, exemplified by the fact that one in every four citizens today is a person of color (Homma-True, Greene, Lopez, & Trimble, 1993). In fact, demographers project that European Americans will be an ethnic minority in every city with 50,000 or more people in this country by the year 2000 and in the entire nation by the year 2010 ("Demographer," 1992).

Therefore, an inherent purpose of this book exists as an assistance to those school counselors who will travel the multicultural road.

FOCUS ON THE TEXT

This book combines the themes of (a) the relation of changing demographics to sociocultural and psychocultural imperatives in schools; (b) the balance between universalism (e.g., recognizing commonalities among humans) and cultural pluralism (e.g., recognizing that distinct ethnic, cultural, religious, gender, conditions of disability, and class distinctions exist among students); (c) the resilience and adaptation of ethnic and cultural student groups; and (d) the ethnic and cultural status as stressors on the normal development of school-age youths (Herring, 1997b).

I review current career development and choice theories in light of their attention to multicultural concerns. The emphasis is to increase the career awareness of students and to convey the complex barriers they face in the world of work. This approach integrates content material and synergetic strategies, followed by experiential activities that integrate these variables in a practical manner.

ORIENTATION AND TERMINOLOGY

Readers who are familiar with my work understand my personal biases. For those who are not, a brief overview is necessary. First, I stress the need to acknowledge within-group differences that exist among individuals from the same ethnic or cultural background. For the record, more variance exists within groups than does between groups.

The second bias involves my proclivity to synergetic counseling approaches. The aim of school counseling is not to try to force a theoretical template on every counseling interaction. Rather, it is to analyze what strategy works best for each student at a particular time with regard to history and environment (Herring, 1997a). I support the "jack of all trades, master of none" analogy of eclecticism and admonish professionals of that orientation to take another step and become more synergetic.

A third bias concerns the use of the term *minority* without an appropriate adjective. I stated previously (Herring, 1997b) that different terms and definitions are applied to describe ethnic groups in the United States, including people of color, people from developing nations, racial minorities, linguistic minorities, the culturally different, the culturally diverse, oppressed minorities, disadvantaged people, and ethnic minorities.

The term *ethnic minority* is used as it subsumes three important elements: *Ethnicity* denotes cultural uniqueness; *minority* refers to individuals who are relatively powerless, receive unequal treatment, and regard themselves as objects of discrimination; and *therapeutic encounter* requires that school counselors learn from students about their cultural values, signs, and behavioral styles. Consequently, ethnic minor... than a categorical description of race, culture, or color ...flects the boundaries of separation and, in particular, how ...ries are managed, protected, ritualized through stereo... ...metimes violated—these are the primary areas of inter... ...n for school counseling (Ho, 1992).

...ias concerns ambiguous terminology and labeling. For ...rm *American* is often used by the media and in some lit... ...o the citizens of the United States. Such usage is insen... ...izens of this hemisphere who also consider themselves ...(e.g., Canadians or Mexicans). Similarly, confusion ...terms *Hispanic* and *Latino/Latina*. The ethnic label ...used by the Office of Management and Budget since ...person of Mexican, Puerto Rican, Cuban, Central or ...an or other Spanish culture or origin, regardless of race" (...Register, 1978, p. 19269). The Royal Academy of the Spanish Language further defines those individuals born in Spanish-speaking countries south of the Rio Grande as "*Hispanoamericanos*," lending credence to the appropriateness of the use of *Hispanic* as a referent to those individuals (Marin & Marin, 1991).

The label *Latino/Latina* is perceived as more accurately reflecting the political, geographical, and historical links present among the various Latin American nations, regardless of the language spoken, than other terms (Hayes-Bautista & Chapa, 1987; Trevino, 1987). A difficulty arises, however, in that the etymological history of *Latino/Latina* would force acceptance as Hispanics of those individuals who trace their cultural roots to all of European Roman/Latin influence (France, Italy, Rumania, Spain, and Portugal). In this book, I use *Hispanic* as the label for this ethnic group.

A fifth bias is the reluctance to use color designations for ethnic students. The error of presuming a connection between ethnic groups and skin color is obvious. For example, in the United States, the color *White* is most often used as a referent for non-people of color and commingled with *Caucasian*. In reality, White most appropriately reflects European Americans because all Caucasians are not white skinned.

My final bias is the reluctance to perpetuate the term *race* as a designator of groups of people. Race was originally used to distinguish between groups of people from external physical characteristics (Herring,

1997a). Contemporary society has become so genetically mixed over the centuries that the most appropriate distinguishing term should be *ethnic groups*.

OVERVIEW OF CONTENTS

The text is arranged in five major parts. **Part I: Background** discusses the central perspectives of career development from a multicultural developmental orientation. The more popular theories of career development and choice are reviewed in regard to their multicultural efficacy. **Part II: Developmental Career Program for Schools** describes the implementation of career development programs for school populations. The discussions emphasize a developmental approach to the dissemination of educational services to students, specifically elementary, middle/junior high, and senior high school distinctions. **Part III: Career Applications for Student Populations** presents discussion relevant to the major ethnic minorities. In addition, gender, lifestyle, and special populations are reviewed in regard to their career development. **Part IV: Cogent Areas of Career Development** involves discussions of how the family can assist or prevent appropriate career development for their children. In addition, chapters stress the delivery of appropriate information services and the need for unbiased appraisal resources. The section concludes with a discussion addressing the future direction of career development in the schools. **Part V: Practical Applications** presents several examples of practical application of the information presented in the text. Ten vignettes depicting students' career dilemmas challenge the reader to attempt appraisals of the presenting problems.

Chapters 2 to 13 each concludes with a section titled "Experiential Activities," which offers suggestions to implement within a school counseling setting and which may be adapted to various ages and grade levels as well as learning styles. These activities are designed to integrate environmental and cultural factors into career development interventions.

The future of career guidance and counseling in the schools, with regard to diverse student populations, is tied to the effectiveness of school counselors. As the twenty-first century approaches, school counselors must be ready to deliver career development to students from a range of socializations. The students must be adequately prepared for tomorrow's world of work. The challenges presented by the constantly changing field of technology exist as one example of the need for accurate career information. It is my hope that this book will facilitate the implementation of an efficacious multicultural and developmental career development program in schools.

Acknowledgments

———

I AM INDEBTED to a number of individuals for their contributions to, and assistance with, the development of this book. I gratefully acknowledge the dedicated support staff and faculty of the Department of Educational Leadership at the University of Arkansas at Little Rock: Ruba Musallum, for her invaluable computer, technical, and graphic arts contributions; David S. Spillers, Chair, and Keith Runion, Counselor Education Program Coordinator, for their continued support and encouragement. Sincere gratitude is also extended to the external reviewers (David Jepson and Michael Garrett) for their invaluable suggestions for the text. And, of course, none of this would have come to fruition without the support and encouragement (and sometimes devil's advocate) of my earth companion and soul mate, C.A.M. A final salute is due to the assistance provided by the staff of the American Counseling Association, especially Carolyn C. Baker, Director of Acquisitions, and to Elaine Dunn the copy editor and Marty Christy the proofreader.

About the Author

ROGER D. HERRING, ED.D., NCC, NCSC, is currently Professor of Counselor Education at the University of Arkansas—Little Rock. His background includes 20 years of experience in public school teaching, administration, and counseling. He has been the recipient of numerous research awards at the state, regional, and national levels. Dr. Herring has published over 50 professional articles and book chapters in journals and edited works, emphasizing counseling Native American Indian and genetically mixed youths. He is a major contributor to the synergetic counseling model. He is also the author of *Counseling Diverse Ethnic Youth: Synergetic Strategies and Interventions for School Counselors* (Harcourt Brace), *Multicultural Counseling in Schools: A Synergetic Approach* (ACA), and *Counseling Native American Indians* (Sage).

Part I

Background

PART I PRESENTS a background that provides a foundation for the remainder of the text. Chapter 1 discusses the central perspectives of career development from multicultural and developmental perspectives. This discussion presents a historical overview, contemporary issues, and future needs within career guidance and counseling. Chapter 2 surveys the major theories of career choice and development. Emphasis is placed on how these theories address multicultural issues in their orientation. If a viable multicultural component is not present, suggestions are offered to school counselors in relation to the efficacy of that particular theoretical orientation.

1

Multicultural Career Development: Central Perspectives

No one can make you feel inferior without your consent.

Eleanor Roosevelt

Herr and Cramer (1996) eloquently described the dynamic state of career guidance and counseling in the United States and in much of the rest of the world:

> Maturing theoretical perspectives; transitions to transnational and global economies, dramatic shifts in occupational structures; high unemployment rates among some groups of youths and adults; demands for higher levels of literacy, numeracy, flexibility, and teachability in the labor forces of industrialized nations; concerns about the quality of work life and worker productivity; and changes in the composition of the labor force have combined to change the content, processes, and consumers of career interventions and services. (p. xi)

These factors demonstrate the increasing importance of the appropriate delivery of career guidance, career counseling, and career education. Researchers generally agree that the goals of science include the understanding, prediction, and control of some kind of natural phenomena (Osipow & Fitzgerald, 1996). Career development represents one of those sciences. Embedded in the delivery of career guidance and career counseling as components of career education is the infusion of multicultural sensitivity into career delivery systems.

This chapter presents six perspectives representing current and future needs, traditions, and challenges to career guidance and career counseling. Commonly used terminology is also offered for the reader's use. Discussion begins with the interpretation and use of the terms *career guidance* and *career counseling*.

CAREER GUIDANCE AND CAREER COUNSELING: CHANGES ARE COMING

Career guidance and career counseling are both old and new terms (Herr & Cramer, 1996). They are old because they have been in use for 75 years and because of their role in the separation of counseling psychology from clinical psychology in the early 1950s (Herr & Cramer, 1987). Career guidance, the broader term, is new because it extends beyond earlier models of vocational guidance and embraces life span career development (Herr & Cramer, 1996). Pressures and emerging challenges such as those enumerated in the opening quote have increased the comprehensive nature of career guidance and career counseling and made them processes of international importance (Herr, 1990). Although the terms are old, they have become increasingly common in usage since the 1970s.

A HISTORICAL PERSPECTIVE OF CAREER GUIDANCE AND CAREER COUNSELING

The philosophies and practices of vocational guidance can be traced into antiquity (Capintero, 1994). In the United States, examples of vocational guidance were found in schools as early as the late 1800s. The more likely sources for these services, however, were philanthropic organizations, settlement houses, the Young Men's Christian Association, and private vocation bureaus (Herr & Cramer, 1996).

In 1909, Frank Parsons, considered the father of vocational guidance in this country, established the Vocations Bureau in Boston. His posthumously published book, *Choosing a Vocation* (1909), offered various strategies to aid adolescents in the identification of their capabilities and job options with reasonable expectations of success. Parsons's view of vocational guidance incorporated these steps:

> First, a clear understanding of yourself, aptitudes, abilities, interests, resources, limitations, and other qualities. Second, a knowledge of the requirements and conditions of success, advantages and disadvantages, compensation, opportunities, and prospects in different lines of work. Third, true reasoning on the relations of these two groups of facts. (p. 5)

Parsons's three steps have inspired considerable research and developmental efforts (Herr & Cramer, 1996). For example, the first step has stimulated research to identify and measure individual differences and to ascertain their influence on occupational satisfaction or success. The second step has encouraged more attention on the acquisition and use of occupational information sources. The third step has generated research into decision-making processes.

For most of its first 50 years, vocational guidance was concerned with predicting occupational choice or success from test scores prior to employment. This traditional view of vocational guidance has been challenged by many theorists since 1950. For example, Super (1951) recommended that the National Vocational Guidance Association's official definition be revised to emphasize the psychological nature of vocational choice. This revised definition blended the previously separate personal and vocational dimensions of guidance (Herr & Cramer, 1996).

Super's (1951) redefinition of vocational guidance generated paradigm shifts from occupational to career models in the literature. Career models have introduced new aspects into the concept of vocational guidance such as developmental career guidance. The use of career models has also placed concern for self-understanding equal to occupational understanding or task mastery.

The late 1950s and early 1960s witnessed a tremendous growth and expansion of school counseling. A critical outcome of this growth was the relationship of the process of decision making to school counseling (Boy & Pine, 1963). By the late 1960s, the term *career guidance* was appearing in the literature as often as the term *vocational guidance*. By the 1980s, career guidance had become comprehensive. In short, career guidance has absorbed vocational guidance techniques and expanded them to offer more discriminating strategies to a larger population (Herr & Cramer, 1996).

A LIFE SPAN PERSPECTIVE OF CAREER GUIDANCE AND CAREER COUNSELING

Many contemporary adults had few opportunities as adolescents to assess their personal characteristics or to have various career alternatives available to them. A survey of adults (National Occupational Information Coordinating Committee, 1990) found that nearly two thirds of the respondents would seek more information about career options if they were beginning their careers, with African Americans (79%) and Hispanics (75%) indicating the most interest in additional career data, followed by European Americans (63%). Only 40% of working adults followed a definite plan in mapping out their careers, with college graduates (62%) more likely than high school graduates (32%) to plan a career. Thirty percent got started through a series of chance circumstances (18%) or took the only job that was available (12%), and 23% were influenced by family and friends. See Something to Consider 1.1 for additional data.

Something to Consider 1.1
Working Adults With No Career Guidance as Adolescents

A 1989 telephone survey of adults was conducted by the Gallup Organization for the National Occupational Information Coordinating Committee and the National Career Development Association (National Occupational Information Coordinating Committee, 1990). They found the following:

- 27% of African Americans said they took the only jobs that were available to them, compared with 19% of Asian Americans, 17% of Hispanics, and 10% of European Americans.

- 27% of all respondents said they needed additional assistance in finding information about jobs, with African Americans reporting the highest need (44%) and European Americans the least (25%) among ethnic groups.

- 53% of the respondents said public high schools are not providing the training in job-seeking skills for students who are not going to college.

- 40% of the respondents said high schools are not providing enough help to students to choose careers.

- 7% (12.5 million) of U.S. adults needed help in 1989 in selecting, changing, or getting a job.

- 19% of Asian Americans and 15% of African Americans reported they needed assistance in the labor market. For European Americans, the figure was 6%, and for Hispanics 8%

- 25% of the respondents said job stress or pressure had interfered with their off-the-job relationships; 20% said job stress had affected their ability to do their jobs.

SOURCE: From *Almost Two Thirds of Americans Would Seek More Information About Career Options If They Had It to Do Over Again, New Survey Finds* (Press Release), by the National Occupational Information Coordinating Committee (NOICC), 1990. Copyright 1990 by NOICC. Adapted with permission.

The findings of the 1989 survey reinforced those of a 1987 survey on career development (Gallup Organization, 1987). Lester and Frugoli (1989, p. 69) suggested four particularly significant findings:

1. A strong need and interest exists for career information on the part of both youths and adults.
2. Individuals are extremely interested in career planning.
3. A perception exists that individuals need help in getting and using career information.
4. A need is apparent to target career information to the noncollege bound.

Essentially the same pattern of findings from data collected in 1980 was reaffirmed by 1993 data. Something to Consider 1.2 synthesizes the data.

Contemporary career education programs and comprehensive career guidance programs today may alleviate some of these problems

Something to Consider 1.2
Working Adults With No Career Guidance as Adolescents: Update

An analysis by Hoyt and Lester (1995) of 1993 data reported the following findings:

1. Ethnic differences continue to operate as a deterrent to equity of career development opportunities for African Americans as compared with European Americans (p. 74).

2. Significant differences in career development exist among adults with various kinds of educational experiences (p. 53).

3. Career development needs exist, significantly, among adults in all age categories (p. 88).

4. A high priority must be placed on meeting the career development needs of persons who drop out of 4-year colleges and universities before receiving a degree (p. 93).

5. Special attention must be provided to those youths who either drop out of high school or seek to enter the labor market with only a high school education (p. 94).

SOURCE: From *Learning to Work: The NCDA Gallup Survey*, by K. B. Hoyt and J. N. Lester, 1995, pp. 53–94.

among tomorrow's adult populations (Herr & Cramer, 1996). Students in educational settings, however, must receive adequate and appropriate career guidance and career education, and this need is not restricted to only college-bound students. The William T. Grant Foundation Commission on Work, Family, and Citizenship (1988) advocated fulfilling the needs of students not bound for college, for whom career guidance and counseling are unevenly available throughout the United States.

THE ROLE OF CAREER EDUCATION IN CAREER GUIDANCE AND COUNSELING

Career education is a phenomenon not only of the United States but also in other parts of the world. Australia, Great Britain, France, Canada, the Netherlands, the Scandinavian countries, the former Soviet Union, Spain, and what were previously East and West Germany, among other nations, have each initiated some version of career education since the late 1960s (Herr & Cramer, 1996). Obviously, approaches to career education by other nations reflect their own value systems and worldviews.

The term *career education* was initially used by James Allen, U.S. Commissioner of Education, when he addressed the National Association of Secondary Principals Convention in 1970. He said, "It is the renewed awareness of the universality of the basic human and social need for competence that is generating not only increased emphasis today on career education, but a whole new concept of its character and its place in the total educational enterprise" (Allen, 1970). Allen's successor, Sidney Marland, is given credit for the formal and comprehensive introduction of career education in 1971.

By 1987, career education's definition reflected goals established by the National Career Education Leaders' Communication Network (Hoyt & Shylo, 1989, pp. 5–6), which included the following:

1. To promote and implement private sector and education system partnerships
2. To equip persons with general employability, adaptability, and promotability skills
3. To help persons in career awareness, exploration, and decision making
4. To reform education by infusing a "careers" emphasis in classrooms
5. To make work a meaningful part of the total lifestyle
6. To relate education and work so that better choices of both can be made
7. To reduce bias and stereotyping and thus protect freedom of career choice

The total concept of career education embraces the systematic, coordinated implementation of all seven of these components (Hoyt & Shylo, 1989).

Evaluation in Career Education

Space does not allow for an in-depth analysis of the various resources that emphasize the outcomes of career education. Readers are referred to Herr (1978) and Bhaerman (1977) for their analyses. Evaluation studies clearly demonstrate that career education can provide students with general and specific skills, as well as improve their academic achievement (Hernandez, 1995; Hoyt, 1980; Trebilco, 1984). Students experiencing career education treatments would be expected to improve on outcome measures by about one half of a standard deviation above the mean as compared with students who do not receive treatment (Baker & Popowicz, 1983).

Ingredients of Effective Career Education Models

Empirical data have documented the basic components of effective career education models. A singular model that is congruent with every situation does not exist. Effective models of career education, however, do share several ingredients (Herr & Cramer, 1996, pp. 39–40):

1. They have visible and continuing administrative support.
2. The goals of career education are seen as major commitments of the mission.

3. Career education is a planned, integrative dimension, not a random add-on or by-product.
4. Resources are provided for planning and for systematic staff development.
5. Field experiences (e.g., internships, career shadowing, and others) are planned to extend and to reinforce curriculum infusion and other career education instruction.
6. Career education is not seen as something so different that one has to start from ground zero.
7. Career education and vocational education are not confused.
8. An evaluation process is built into the planning and implementation of career education so that its results can be examined and advocated as appropriate.

Relationship to Career Guidance and Counseling

Career education has established that no other group of specialists is more important to its goals than career guidance personnel (Hoyt, 1984, 1985). Thus, a central task of school counselors is to help students identify their career options, understand the implications thereof, plan how to integrate necessary educational experiences to achieve goals, and make wise, timely decisions (Herr & Cramer, 1996). Something to Consider 1.3 differentiates the terms *career education* and *career guidance* in a more profound way.

THE ROLE OF THE SCHOOL COUNSELOR IN CAREER GUIDANCE AND CAREER COUNSELING

The evolution of career guidance approaches and definitions has generated debate about the school counselor's role. The American School Counselors Association's (1985) position paper recommended school counselors to concentrate on the delivery of common, core experiences that lead to the acquisition of career maturity. These core experiences include:

1. Clarifying work values and developing coping and planning skills.
2. Assessing abilities, personality traits, and interests through formal and informal measures.
3. Providing occupational and career information, linking community resources with guidance.
4. Helping students learn interviewing and job-hunting skills.
5. Encouraging training, goal setting, and decision making related to a tentative career path.
6. Integrating academic and career skills in a school curriculum.

Something to Consider 1.3
Career Education and Career Guidance Differentiated

The terms *career education* and *career guidance* are often confused or interchanged. The similarities and differences of these terms are presented below.

Similarities

Differences

1. Both are rooted in the career education process and in the theory/research of career education.

Career education is also rooted in the teaching/learning process. Career guidance is not.

2. Both include longitudinal efforts that move developmentally, from career planning/decision making to implementation.

One of the basic reasons for the existence of career education is to serve as a vehicle for educational reform. Educational reform is not part of the basic charter of career guidance.

3. Both are intended to serve the developmental needs of all persons and are not limited to any one portion of the general population.

Although career education is pictured as a total community effort headed by several kinds of persons, career guidance efforts need to be headed by career guidance professionals.

4. Both are committed to protecting and enhancing freedom of career choice for all persons.

The most critical aspects of the maximum implementation of career education lie in efforts directed by classroom teachers. The most crucial aspects of the implementation of career guidance lie in efforts carried out by career guidance specialists.

5. Both emphasize education/work relationships at all levels of education.

Career education places great emphasis and a high priority on bringing an appropriate emphasis to the goal of education as preparation for work among all basic goals of education in the United States. Career guidance has not made this a priority for the movement.

6. Both include efforts that begin at the kindergarten level and continue well into the retirement years.

7. Both view the work values of persons as part of their total systems of personal values and so view work as an integral part of their total lifestyle.

8. Both recognize the importance of paid and unpaid work.

9. Both recognize, applaud, and seek to facilitate the key role parents play in the career development of their children.

10. Both support career development as an effort extending beyond the career counselor.

SOURCE: From Hoyt (1984) and Hoyt and Shylo (1989).

The most recent revision of minimum career counseling competencies by the National Career Development Association (1991) added four categories and updated the original six. Selected excerpts from these 10 competency categories include:

1. Ability to support and challenge clients to examine the balance of work, leisure, family, and community roles in their careers.
2. Knowledge about assessment variables such as ethnicity, gender, culture, learning style, personal development, and physical and mental ability.
3. Knowledge of information, techniques, and models related to computer-assisted career information delivery systems and career counseling.
4. Sensitivity toward the developmental issues and needs unique to ethnic/cultural minorities.
5. Ability to provide effective supervision to career counselors at varied levels of experience.
6. Ability to apply ethical standards to career counseling and consulting situations.
7. Ability to design evaluation programs that consider the needs of special populations, ethnic and cultural minorities, the elderly, persons with challenges, and women.

Developmental career guidance does not infer that school counselors will not continue to have responsibility for crisis counseling, remediation, or assisting students in other developmental and educational areas. A major assumption is that school counselors' career guidance functions are reflected in the skills taught and in a program that can ultimately be related to desired outcomes (Herr & Cramer, 1996).

The School Counselor as an Applied Behavioral Scientist

Work and career development holds an important place in human behavior. Consequently, the varieties of work and how men and women choose work in Western culture have attracted the interests of behavioral scientists (Osipow & Fitzgerald, 1996). The trend for a school counselor to be an applied behavioral scientist who practices synergetic counseling suggests approaches that extend beyond traditional models. For example, synergetic counseling suggests that no single theory can cover all of the career needs of students (Herring, 1997a, 1997b; Herring & Walker, 1993). Rather, this synergetic model suggests a more inclusive concept of career guidance and career counseling approaches. As a result of increasing diversity, students will have multiple presenting problems that will require multiple approaches, treatments, and experiences appropriately applied to his or her needs.

School counselors also serve as scientist–practitioners (Herr & Cramer, 1996). The school counselor needs to become more involved in research and evaluation of in-place career delivery systems. Familiarity with and contribution to the literature are also required. School counselors must do more to enhance their profession and rely on counselor educators in these arenas.

Based on their review of 164 empirical studies, R. E. Campbell, Connel, Boyle, and Bhaerman (1983) concluded:

1. Vocational guidance interventions achieve their intended outcomes primarily if guidance personnel provide structured interventions in a systematic developmental sequence.
2. Vocational guidance has demonstrated its effectiveness in influencing career development and adjustment of individuals in the five broad categories of improved school involvement and performance, personal and interpersonal work skills, preparation for careers, career planning skills, and career awareness and exploration.
3. Vocational guidance has been successful in assisting individuals representing a wide range of subpopulations and settings, including those in correctional institutions, vocational training centers, community colleges, and those susceptible to various challenges.

Additional reviews of empirical studies addressing the outcomes of career interventions (e.g., Oliver & Spokane, 1988) document that career education, career counseling, and career guidance yield positive results and reinforce the efficacy of such interventions. These reviews support the effectiveness of one-on-one counseling as compared with other styles in terms of amount of gain per hour of effort. They also support longer (minimum of 10 sessions) and more comprehensive sessions, which yield nearly twice the beneficial effects of briefer interventions.

The School Counselor as a Change Agent

School counselors will be increasingly involved in collaborative efforts with teachers, parents, administrators, community agency personnel, and employers (e.g., Herring & White, 1995). Examples of such activities include creating positive climates for learning, modifying curriculum content, and working with employers to provide work study or shadowing experiences.

School counselors have many possibilities for action both at student and at institutional levels. At the student level, they assist students to rid themselves of limits on career choice. Students frequently have internalized external projections, for example, that students of particular ethnicity, age, or gender or who are challenged should not consider certain job options. They may have also internalized the implied reasons for restricting such choices (Herr & Cramer, 1996). Action should also include promoting student interest in careers in which students of culturally diverse groups have been underrepresented (P. Lee, 1995).

At the institutional level, school counselors try to keep parents, teachers, potential employers, and other personnel from restricting equitable access to job opportunities on the basis of such stereotypes. The reduction of bias will involve the counseling program as well as resource, collaborative, and consultative roles.

The School Counselor as a Technologist

Career guidance has incorporated into the school counselor's professional repertoire forms of technology that extend the counselor's potential to effect behavioral change (Herr & Cramer, 1996). Games, work samples, problem-solving kits, videos, self-assessments, and computer interactive systems are but a few of the means developed recently to provide learning and stimulated experience designed to increase student exploration and planning.

Computer-assisted career guidance systems are rapidly becoming a core element in the delivery of career and educational guidance services. Technology applied to career guidance is likely to expand rather than recede, and thus the career guidance professional of the future will need to have a conceptual framework and personal competencies by which to use such resources effectively (Herr & Cramer, 1996; Peterson, Sampson, & Reardon, 1991).

Computers and technology, however, are valuable only to the degree that the outcomes they facilitate are appropriate to the program planning or counseling outcomes to be achieved. "Career counselors must learn to view the use of computer-assisted approaches to individual career development as part of a plan—as one of the treatment options—not the only, or even the preferred, approach for all counseling problems" (Herr & Cramer, 1996, p. 55).

A MULTICULTURAL PERSPECTIVE OF CAREER GUIDANCE AND CAREER COUNSELING

The demographics of the United States are changing at an increasing rate. No longer is the cultural portrait predominantly Western European. Nowhere are the demographic shifts better reflected than in the nation's public schools. For example, demographers predict that ethnic minorities will constitute nearly one third of the U.S. population and nearly half of the school-age youths by the year 2020 (Steinberger, 1991).

African Americans, Asian Americans, Hispanic (Latino/Latina) Americans, and Native American Indians constitute the major ethnic minority groups in the United States. Contrary to the uniformity suggested by their labels, each of these groups subsumes a highly heterogeneous mix of peoples and subcultures, and each is growing faster than the majority population, with the implication that the U.S. workplace is becoming increasingly diverse and will continue to do so (Osipow & Fitzgerald, 1996). Specific demographic summaries are presented in a subsequent chapter.

Changes in values accompany demographic shifts. Historically, the economic strength of the United States was based on the tenets of industrialization, with its emphasis on centralized authority, conformity, and standardization. Future success, however, is linked to organizational, diversity, and multiple perspectives.

This shift in values is perhaps most evident in this nation's school systems. Court-ordered desegregation in the 1960s and 1970s, the push for bilingual education, and the call for massive reforms during the past decade have brought multiculturalism to the forefront and cleared the way for changes that encourage respect for and appreciation of differences.

Nevertheless, in many communities, these changes are slow in coming. A national survey by the National Opinion Research Center at the University of Chicago recently revealed that many European Americans still hold negative stereotypes of ethnic minorities (Steinberger, 1991). A majority of the 1,100 European Americans who participated in the study see African Americans and Hispanics as being more likely to prefer welfare to work, more prone to violence, lazier, less intelligent, and less patriotic.

The task of eliminating racial stereotypes and prejudice has fallen squarely in the laps of public school systems in this nation. Policymakers, educators, and sociologists view education as the key to overcoming bias and discrimination, to fostering an appreciation for diversity. If this nation is to prosper in an increasingly competitive global economy, all communities must find ways to engage youths who feel disconnected in school and who no longer see themselves, nor others in their group, as having a shot at future success. Such mindsets are entirely incongruent with the European American value system that emphasizes individual success and competitiveness within the world of work.

One of the greatest challenges within career development is to determine how ethnic minority students and families "can gain access to the full range of careers commensurate with their abilities and equitable opportunities for promotion and economic reward" (Gelso &

Fretz, 1992, p. 385). By the year 2000, ethnic minorities will account for more than 25% of all U.S. workers and one third of all new entrants into the labor force (Tidwell, 1992).

Criticisms of Current Theoretical Models

Numerous criticisms have been voiced with regard to the inadequacy of theory to explain the career development of ethnic minority and special needs students. For example, Fitzgerald and Betz (1994) argued that gender and cultural factors have been ignored in theories of career development despite their important influences. Cultural factors are defined by these authors as those "beliefs and attitudes commonly found among group members—often these are socialized by society (i.e., occupational gender stereotypes, internalized homophobia)" (p. 107). Three themes are recurrent in this apparent lack of attention to multicultural concerns: The theories are based on erroneous assumptions, particular theoretical concepts are not applicable, and important career determinants are omitted from the theories (D. Brown, 1990a).

Erroneous assumptions.   One erroneous assumption, for example, is that students have an array of choices open to them; that is, they are free to choose among alternatives that are close to their interests, values, and abilities. Thus, the restrictions imposed by the sociopolitical environment are ignored (e.g., E. J. Smith, 1983). Also, the theories are viewed as exaggerating the role of personality characteristics (e.g., Osipow, 1983), a criticism that sociologists label the *psychological bias* of theories (D. Brown, 1990a).

In addition, traditional career theories have not addressed the needs of special populations. For example, the inability of students with challenges to compete adequately for jobs in their communities clearly indicates their need for more appropriate career and vocational preparation prior to leaving high school (Omizo & Omizo, 1992). At the other extreme, research suggests that gifted male and female youths may need different types of career education at different points in their educational careers (Gassin, Kelly, & Feldhusen, 1993). In addition, few studies have explored career choices of siblings of students with a developmental disability (Konstam et al., 1993).

The issue of gender equity is another example of the weakness of traditional career theories. For the year 2000, four in every five women ages 25 to 54 will be employed and will account for 47% of the total labor force (Kutscher, 1987). Yet, gender equity in the labor force has not been addressed by traditional career models. Women are still concentrated in low-paying, traditionally female-dominated occupations (e.g., clerical and retail sales), whereas the majority of jobs in the higher paying, and often math- and science-related fields, are held by men (Sadker, Sadker, & Donald, 1989). The majority of women and girls still plan to enter occupations that are traditionally dominated by women (Eccles, 1987; Gerstein, Lichtman, & Barokas, 1988). One important reason is the internalization of gender role stereotypes and cultural expectations of women and men (Bartholomew & Schnorr, 1994).

Lack of applicability. Current theoretical models were developed to explain the development of middle-class European American men, resulting in aspects that are inapplicable to ethnic minority populations. Numerous researchers (Arbona, 1990; Cheatham, 1990; Cook, 1991) have reinforced Osipow's (1983) earlier contention that the assumptions inherent in traditional theories of career development fail to accommodate non-Eurocentric perspectives (Gelso & Fretz, 1992). Despite a variety of documented ethnic differences in career development (Arbona, 1990; Leong, 1991), London and Greller's (1991) 20-year retrospective of vocational behavior research included the charge that research on ethnic and cultural groups and strategies for responding to these differences have represented an all-too-empty stage in the career development literature.

For example, Super's (1953) model of sequential and continuous developmental stages has been challenged as inapplicable to low-income African Americans, who, rather than having the luxury of the exploration stage, instead must find jobs in their early teens and then must take a series of unrelated jobs interspersed by unemployment (Osipow, 1975). Additional developmental tasks may be encountered as well, such as "coming to terms with the issue of race and what this means for . . . career development" in this nation's society (E. J. Smith, 1983, pp. 189–190). A final example is that the higher level occupational environments (e.g., Enterprising, in Holland's 1973 model) may not be equally available to ethnic minorities and the European American male middle class (D. Brown, 1990a).

Lack of sufficient determinants. The complaint that career theories omit variables that are important career determinants for ethnic minority students most frequently focuses on the constraining factors of mainstream society's sociopolitical system, particularly racism and the effects of the differential opportunity system (e.g., E. J. Smith, 1983). For example, parents are among the most important sociocultural factors influencing career development, especially in areas such as expectations for achievement and teaching about the world of work (Santrock, 1993). The more pervasive career theories neglect this influence. The under- and overrepresentation of ethnic minority groups in various occupational categories can be attributed to many factors present in a multicultural society (Axelson, 1993). Some of the

more obvious social conditions and personal issues that affect employment opportunities and occupational patterns include education,
poverty, regional differences, prejudice and special interest groups,
individual and group preferences within cultural diversity, and personal expectations.

Underlying all these criticisms is the notion that ethnic minority
students' career development process and outcomes are different from
those of European Americans. Unfortunately, at least two specific
problems preclude the synthesis of supporting research for these differences (D. Brown et al., 1990). First, much of the research has been
conducted with a "psychology of race differences" approach. This paradigm assumes that the "proper approach" to the study of ethnic
minority people is to compare them with European Americans, most
often from a middle-class perspective (Korchin, 1980). The underlying
message is that ethnic differences are the result of inherent and
unchangeable determinants (Korchin, 1980). A second problem with
the research is that ethnicity has often been confounded with social
class (D. Brown et al., 1990; Osipow, 1975). For example, a consistent
finding is that lower-class African Americans are less vocationally
mature than European American middle-class youths (D. Brown et al.,
1990).

Despite these difficulties with the research, certain observations
about the current status of ethnic minorities strongly support the following observations about the career development of ethnic minority
groups (E. J. Smith, 1983).

1. Ethnic minorities are overrepresented in certain occupational environments and underrepresented in others.
2. Some ethnic minorities—specifically, African Americans, Hispanics,
   and Native American Indians—have higher unemployment rates
   and lower incomes than European Americans do.
3. The career development process involves some differences, especially in career choices.

In an attempt to deal with some of these problems, L. S.
Gottfredson (1986) proposed that the barriers faced by special populations (including but not limited to ethnic minorities) can be conceptualized in an "at-risk" framework. In essence, Gottfredson's premise is
that special groups face varying degrees of risk that create career
choice problems. "Risk factors are attributes of the person or of the
person's relation to the environment that are associated with a higher-
than-average probability of experiencing the types of problems under
consideration" (p. 143). An inadequate education, for example,
decreases the probability of success.

L. S. Gottfredson (1986) postulated three categories of risk: (a) factors that cause students to be different from the general population (e.g., poverty, low intelligence, cultural segregation, low self-esteem); (b) factors involving differences within one's own social group (e.g., having nontraditional interests for one's gender, social class, or ethnic group); and (c) factors involving family responsibilities (e.g., being a primary caregiver or primary economic provider). Then, on the basis of either a review of the literature or her own estimates (in the absence of literature), she identified the degree to which each category of risk is faced by five ethnic groups, males and females, and six groups with challenges (e.g., students who are visually challenged). For example, African American males and females are at risk in all categories of difference from the general population (e.g., coming from a poor family, being culturally isolated or segregated) and African American females are at a higher than average risk with respect to caregiving and economic providing. This "at-risk" framework is essentially intended to identify the barriers to free career choice. Thus, the Hispanic male is estimated to be at risk regarding family responsibilities (with respect to fulfilling the role of economic provider), which means, for example, that he is less free to seek self-fulfillment in other roles that do not produce income.

One advantage of this framework is that it avoids the "different is deficient" implication that emerges when analysis is confined to the problems of ethnic groups. All groups (even European American males) are at risk in some areas. The areas of risk are simply different.

L. S. Gottfredson's (1986) framework is not a theoretical statement on ethnic minorities, but it does suggest some directions for future theorizing. If career development theory is to be adequately comprehensive, D. Brown et al. (1990, p. 389) purported that a framework is needed that will give sufficient attention to the reciprocal determinism of sociological variables (e.g., racism and the differential opportunity structure), established psychological variables (e.g., interests, values, and abilities), and nonestablished psychological variables (e.g., ethnic identity development).

Techniques useful in dealing with other types of special career problems experienced by different special needs populations are discussed elsewhere in this book. Of particular note is the growing recognition in the literature and in legislation that *special needs* populations comprise not only students who are denied equality because of historical discrimination based on ethnicity, gender, culture, class, or age, but also students who are at significant points of transition in their lives (e.g., death in the family or peer group and acts of nature) who become vulnerable, and thus, at least temporarily, students with special needs. Although such conditions may not be fixed as are ethnicity and gender, they can nevertheless cause problems for the student at school and in other parts of life; career guidance and counseling can be helpful in such situations. Helping ethnic minority students' career development is ultimately one of the most serious challenges facing the career counselor (Hoyt, 1989).

A TERMINOLOGICAL PERSPECTIVE OF CAREER EDUCATION, CAREER GUIDANCE, AND CAREER COUNSELING

Every profession has its own jargon and identifying characteristics. Career guidance and career counseling are no different. A central role of definitions is to translate the philosophical themes that give career guidance and career counseling coherence and common cause into more operational terms (Herr & Cramer, 1996). The following definitions represent the most commonly used terms in the career literature.

Avocation: An activity pursued for its own sake with an objective other than monetary gain, although it may incidentally result in gain (Super, 1976).

Career: Various definitions can be found. Most of the definitional variance is the result of divergent interpretations by career theorists. Super's (1976) definition is probably the most cited concept of career. He defined it as

> the course of events which constitutes a life; the sequence of occupations and other life roles which combine to express one's commitment to work in his or her total pattern of self development; the series of remunerated and nonremunerated positions occupied by a person from adolescence through retirement, of which occupation is only one; includes work-related roles such as those of student, employee, and pensioner together with complementary avocational, familial, and civic roles. Careers exist only as people pursue them; they are person centered. It is this last notion of careers, "they exist only as people pursue them," which summarizes much of the rationale for career guidance. (p. 4)

Career adaptability: Readiness for career decision making in adulthood.

Career awareness: The inventory of knowledge, values, preferences, and self-concepts that an individual draws on in the course of making career-related choices (Wise, Charner, & Randour, 1978).

Career counseling: A process in which a school counselor and student(s) are in an interpersonal process designed to assist individuals with career development problems; the process of choosing, entering, adjusting to, and advancing in an occupation (D. Brown et al., 1990).

A lifelong process focused on identifying and acting on the students' goals, in which the school counselor uses a repertoire of synergetic strategies (Herring, 1997a, 1997b), to help generate self-understanding, understanding of options available, and wise decision making in the student, who has the responsibility for his or her personal actions.

Career development: The total constellation of psychological, socio-logical, educational, physical, economic, and chance factors that combine to shape the career of any given individual over the life span (Sears, 1982). Career development proceeds whether or not career guidance and career counseling are used. Thus, career development is not an intervention but the object of an intervention (Herr & Cramer, 1996).

Career education: All experiences by which individuals acquire knowledge and attitudes about self and work and the skills by which to identify, choose, plan, and prepare for work and other options constituting a career; an effort aimed at refocusing education and the broader community in ways that will help individuals acquire and use the knowledge, skills, and attitudes necessary for each to make work a meaningful, productive, and satisfying part of his or her life (Hoyt, 1978).

Career guidance: McDaniels (1978) summarized numerous definitional concepts of career guidance as an organized program to assist an individual to assimilate and integrate knowledge, experience, and appreciation related to (a) self-understanding; (b) understanding of the work society and those factors that affect its constant change, including worker attitude and discipline; (c) awareness of the part leisure may play in a person's life; (d) understanding of the necessity for many factors to be considered in career planning; and (e) understanding of the skills and information necessary to achieve self-fulfillment in work and leisure (p. 17).

Career intervention: "Any direct assistance to an individual to promote more effective decision making, or more narrowly focused, intensive counseling to help resolve career difficulties; activity (treatment or effort) designed to enhance a person's career development or to enable that person to make more effective career decisions" (Spokane, 1991, p. 22).

Career ladder: "A succession of jobs available to an individual worker with each job successively offering increased responsibility and wages and more desirable working conditions" (R. N. Evans & Herr, 1978, p. 32).

Career lattice: A term typically used to portray the opportunities for workers to shift from one career ladder to another, vertically and horizontally.

Career management: The active and conscious participation in shaping one's career and accepting responsibility for the activities and choices made toward those ends (Hansen & Tennyson, 1975).

Career maturity: The repertoire of behaviors necessary to identifying, choosing, planning, and executing career goals available to a specific individual as compared with those possessed by an appropriate peer group; being at an average level in career development for one's age (after Super, 1957). Attitudinal and cognitive readiness to cope with the developmental tasks of finding, preparing for, getting established in, pursuing, and retiring from an occupation (Super, 1984, p. 34).

Career path: A term typically used in business and industry to describe a series of positions available in some occupational or specialized work area, ordinarily connoting possibilities (Herr & Cramer, 1996).

Employment: Time spent in paid work or in indirectly paid work such as homemaking (Super, 1976).

Job: A group of similar paid positions requiring some similar attributes in a single organization (Super, 1976).

Labor: Productive work for survival or support, requiring physical or mental effort (Super, 1976).

Leisure: Time free from required effort or for the free use of abilities and pursuit of interests (Super, 1976). Self-determined activities and experiences that are available depending on income, time, and social behaviors; they may be physical, social, intellectual, volunteer, creative, or any combination of the five (Sears, 1982).

Occupation: A group of similar jobs found in industries or organizations that exist independent of any person. Careers, on the other hand, exist only when people are pursuing them (Super, 1985, p. 1).

Play: Activity that is primarily recreational and relaxing; engaged in for its own sake; it may be systematic or unsystematic, without objective or with a temporary and personal objective; it may involve the expenditure of effort, but that effort is voluntary and easily avoided by the player (Sears, 1982, p. 142).

Position: A group of tasks to be performed by one person, usually for pay, that exist whether vacant or occupied. They are task and outcome defined, not person centered (Super, 1976).

Program: "An organized compilation of techniques or strategies with specific and well defined objectives that is designed to alter systematically the vocational behavior of a group of individuals in a specific behavior setting (e.g., school, work, or community) over time" (Spokane, 1991, p. 22).

Strategy: "A philosophy or plan of action, or a group of techniques intended to change the vocational behavior of an individual, group of individuals or an organization. Career counseling of an individual by a single counselor is an example" (Spokane, 1991, p. 22).

Technique: "A time limited application of career intervention principles designed to accomplish a focused goal or to alter a specific vocational behavior. A career life line and a vocational career sort are examples" (Spokane, 1991, p. 22).

Work: The systematic pursuit of an objective valued by oneself (even if only for survival) and desired by others, requiring effort. It may be compensated (paid work), uncompensated (volunteer work or an avocation), intrinsic enjoyment of the work itself, the structure given to life by the work role, the economic support that work makes possible, or the type of leisure that it facilitates (Super, 1976).

SUMMARY

To attain the desired goal of eliminating the barriers to successful career development will require multifaceted, multicultural interventions. Such interventions will entail improving counseling techniques (individual and group) and improving the current, inequitable career opportunity structure and poor educational system that created the disparity in achievement and the low expectations levels of certain ethnic minority groups. The reasons ethnic minority students may choose to explain or to justify a point of view are inextricably related to their assumptions about career knowledge and skills. Ethnic and cultural minority students, as well as other special populations, often enter career counseling and career decision making with ideas about the career development process that hinder their decision-making ability (Herring, 1990a). The reality that these populations do internalize the negative aspects of their historical and contemporary experiences deserves to become a primary concern of school counselors as well as other helping and service personnel in educational settings.

2

Theories of Career Choice and Development: How Multicultural Are They?

What treatment, by whom, is most effective for this
individual, with that specific problem, and under what set
of circumstances?

G. Paul (1967, p. 111)

A basic concern regarding career development is the assumption that society generally desires its members to want to work, to acquire the necessary skills for work, and to find satisfaction in the work they do; thus, students' objectives in their career development include finding work possible, meaningful, and satisfying (Isaacson & Brown, 1993). School counselors, regardless of developmental level, must understand students, their situations, and the career development process to provide effective career guidance, counseling, and education as students begin to make career decisions. This process is more likely to be effective when school and career counselors derive their career guidance and counseling strategies from a theoretical foundation.

This chapter presents brief discussions of the major theories of career choice and development. To comprehend these theories is to understand the priorities in career development at the time of their origin (Zunker, 1990). However, the reader is cautioned that these theories have generally evolved from research on European American males. This limitation severely restricts theoretical generalizations for many populations. Thus, the major emphasis is placed on drawing the reader's attention to this reality rather than providing an in-depth analysis of the theories.

A FRAME OF REFERENCE

School counselors, career counselors, and others involved in career development of students frequently overlook the significance of a fundamental principle: that a professional can perform effectively only when he or she has mastered the knowledge and theory on which his or her profession is based (Isaacson & Brown, 1993). School and career counselors must comprehend the theoretical premises that serve as the frames of reference with which they approach each student. Without this frame of reference, school and career counselors operate in a hit-and-miss fashion regardless of their skill level.

Shertzer and Stone (1980) identified four inherent functions of theories: (a) Theory summarizes and generalizes a body of knowledge; (b) theory facilitates understanding and explanation of complex phenomena; (c) theory serves as a predictive function by estimating what will occur under certain conditions; and (d) theory stimulates further research. School and career counselors rely on these functions as they endeavor to provide appropriate development needs.

Several researchers have challenged the appropriateness of existing career development theories. For example, Warnath (1975) described conditions in the workplace beyond the control of the individual, such as the effects of technological change, the increasing trend toward larger organizations to the detriment of small ones, and the general subservience of employee needs to those of the employer. Warnath encouraged counselors to help students seek alternatives to paid employment as sources of life satisfaction. His rationale was hinged on the number of uncontrollable factors that interrupt or impede personal career decisions.

Baumgardner (1977) contended that fully rational career decisions may be neither possible nor desirable. He concluded that counselors cannot change the rapidly changing workplace and therefore should help students to recognize that only minimal planning is possible because uncertainty and conflict will constitute a major portion of their relationship to work. In addition, researchers have found shortcomings in vocational choice theories (Carkhuff, Alexik, & Anderson, 1967), have emphasized a lack of comprehensiveness (Fitzgerald & Crites, 1980), and have stressed the lack of agreement on the definitions of career as well as the tendency to use an objective approach to career development (Collin & Young, 1986).

Other researchers have responded to these criticisms. Osipow (1977) concurred that numerous conditions are immune to personal intervention but suggested that students can make many choices that affect their career lives. In addition, Herr (1977) emphasized that most vocational theories allow for individual variation in choice-making style and that the aim of career counseling is not to eliminate all uncertainty but to reduce unnecessary uncertainty to a minimum.

As Isaacson and Brown (1993) have intimated, some readers may believe that consideration of career choice and development theories should be delayed until more justifiable and appropriate theories are available. Osipow (1983) responded that school counselors interact with students on a daily basis. Unless the counselor offers more than empathic listening, students will have no plans of action for their career decision making. Accordingly, an incomplete theory is an improvement over no foundation for action at all. Osipow emphasized that theory precedes and accompanies empirical evidence and guides this evidence to its fruition.

A classification of the various career choice and development theories can be difficult and often misleading. The theoretical positions often have certain degrees of commonality, slightly different interpretations of some basic assumptions, and often contradictory views of other data (Isaacson & Brown, 1993). The reader is cautioned to be alert to these nuances and overlappings as the discussion continues.

CURRENT THEORIES OF CAREER CHOICE AND DEVELOPMENT

In the early 1950s, Ginzberg, Roe, and Super published career development and occupational choice theories that have become landmarks in the development of the career guidance and counseling domain. These publications were instrumental in generating an increase in career guidance practices and support materials as well as numerous research projects and subsequent methods for delivering career guidance and counseling programs (Zunker, 1990). Other theorists who followed included Holland, Tiedeman, Gelatt, Krumboltz, and Bordin, who have also contributed to career development and choice theories.

Among early theorists on vocational counseling, Parsons (1909) maintained that vocational guidance is accomplished first by studying the individual, second by surveying occupations, and third by matching the individual with the occupation. This process, called *trait-and-factor theory*, became the foundation of many vocational counseling programs such as those of the Veterans Administration, the YMCA, the Jewish vocational services, colleges, and universities (Super, 1972).

The trait-and-factor approach has been the most durable of all theories of career guidance (Brown, 1990b; Zunker, 1990). An oversimplification of trait-and-factor theory might be "putting the right peg in the right hole" (Isaacson & Brown, 1993). In fairness, however, it means matching the individual's traits with requirements of a specific occupation. The key characteristic is the assumption that individuals

have unique patterns of ability (i.e., traits) that can be objectively measured and correlated with the requirements of various types of occupations (Zunker, 1990).

Williamson (1939, 1949) and A. J. Jones (1945) were prominent
advocates of trait-and-factor counseling during the years immediately
following World War II. A. J. Jones (1970), revised and updated by
Stefflre and Stewart, enumerated five assumptions basic to the trait-
and-factor approach:

1. Vocational development is largely a cognitive process in which individuals use reasoning to arrive at decisions.
2. Occupational choice is a single event.
3. There is a single right goal for everyone making decisions about
   work.
4. A single type of person works in each job.
5. There is an occupational choice available to each individual. (p. 182)

Loosely interpreted, these assumptions remain generally acceptable
today (Isaacson & Brown, 1993).

Williamson (1939, 1949) suggested that counseling involves six
steps: analysis, synthesis, diagnosis, prognosis, counseling, and follow-up.
He also viewed career counseling as usually presenting one of four types
of problems: no choice, uncertain choice, unwise choice, or a discrepancy
between interests and aptitudes. The diagnostic step in counseling focuses
on identifying which, if any, of these categories apply to the student.

Practical applications.   Trait-and-factor theory has been responsible for at least two major contributions to career counseling (Isaacson
& Brown, 1993). First, its emphasis on identifying individual characteristics such as attitude, ability, interest, and personality has influenced the development of numerous assessment and appraisal instruments and techniques. Second, the emphasis on knowledge and
understanding occupational possibilities has encouraged the development of occupational information. Even when integrated into other
theories of career guidance, the trait-and-factor approach has been of
inestimable value (Zaccaria, 1970).

Major criticisms.   Some of the basic assumptions of the trait-and-
factor theory have been challenged over the years. The limitations of
testing have been made apparent from two widely cited research projects (Ghiselli, 1966; Thorndike & Hagen, 1959). The dangers of over-
reliance on test results as predictors of a student's future career were
made clear by these research findings (Zunker, 1990). Another concern is its failure to deal adequately with the choice-making process
itself (D. Brown, 1990a). However, some advocates argue that trait-
and-factor theory has never been fully understood and that advocates
of trait-and-factor approaches never approved of excessive use of test-

ing in career counseling (D. Brown, 1990a). Other data, such as work experience and general background, are as important in the career counseling process (Williamson, 1939).

The following assumptions of the trait-and-factor approach also raise concerns about this theory: (a) There is a single career goal for everyone, and (b) career decisions are primarily based on measured abilities (Herr & Cramer, 1996; M. F. Miller, 1974). These assumptions severely restrict the range of options in career development and, in essence, narrow the consideration of the trait-and-factor theory as a major theory of career development (Zunker, 1990).

Multicultural concerns.   D. Brown (1990a) contended "that trait-oriented postulates apply equally well to men and to women, to non-minorities and to minorities, and are therefore comprehensive" (p. 345). However, this author also advised that "because in some instances the measurement devices used to assess traits discriminate against minorities and women, the methodology generated by trait psychologists may be of limited use for these groups" (p. 345). Valid assessment devices must be developed if trait-and-factor approaches are to be used with these populations.

Use by school counselors.   The most applicable component of the trait-and-factor model for school counseling rests in the practicality of Williamson's (1939) six-stage model of career counseling. The stages offer a rational approach to counseling outcomes and individual decision making. In addition, this model allows for multiple assessments and multiple sources of information that lessen the probability of "single-shot counseling." Multiple sources of information are vital to the appropriate counseling of ethnic and cultural minority youths. School counselors can even adapt this model for other types of counseling as well.

PERSONALITY-BASED THEORIES

The two most viable personality-based viewpoints are represented by Anne Roe's needs approach and John Holland's typology approach. Both advocated that the appropriateness of an occupation for a specific individual depends on that individual's personality, which in turn is primarily the product of early experience.

Roe's Theory of Career Choice

Roe's (1956) theoretical orientation is based primarily on Maslow's (1954) hierarchy of psychological need and the effects on career direction by childhood relationships within the family. The hierarchy of psychological need concept suggests that lower order needs, those essential for maintaining life, are so strong that higher level needs will not be addressed until lower order needs are reasonably well satisfied.

Moreover, the hierarchy suggests the order of priority of the basic needs, as follows:

1. Physiological needs
2. Safety needs
3. Need for belongingness
4. Need for importance, respect, self-esteem, and independence
5. Need for self-actualization
6. Need for information
7. Need for understanding
8. Need for beauty

Roe (1956) emphasized that early childhood experiences and parental styles affect need hierarchy and the relationships of these needs to later adult lifestyles. The need structure of the individual would be greatly influenced by early childhood frustrations and satisfactions. Roe proposed that the emotional climate in the home—the relationship between parent and child—is one of three types: emotional concentration on the child, avoidance of the child, or acceptance of the child. These emotional climates are thought to have a circular relationship with each type and its two subdivisions shading into the others. Figure 2.1 depicts this circular process.

Emotional concentration on the child includes subdivisions of overprotecting and overdemanding parents. *Overprotecting* parents encourage dependency and limit exploratory behavior; are indulgent, allow special privileges, and show affect; intrude and expect to be told everything that the child thinks or experiences; and limit friendships. *Overdemanding* parents set high standards for the child, enforce conformity to the standard, expect the child to be constructively busy, and select friends for the child in accordance with their own standards.

The avoidance parenting style includes two extremes: rejection and neglect. Emotionally *rejecting* parents tend to be more extreme in behavior compared with demanding parents. They express attitudes of coldness, hostility, derogation, and ridicule; may leave the child alone and may prevent contact with other children; and establish rules to protect themselves from intrusions by the child into their lives. *Neglecting* parents do not express hostility or ridicule—they simply ignore. They provide a minimum of physical care, no affection, and leave children to fend for themselves but make no effort to avoid them.

The acceptance climate includes the subdivisions of casual and loving. In *casual* acceptance climates, parents pay some attention and are mildly affectionate. They accept the child as part of the general situation and are responsive if not occupied with other matters. They are easygoing, make few rules, exert little effort to train the child, and do not enforce training rules. In *loving* climates, parents help with impor-

Figure 2.1
Hypothesized Relations Between Major Orientation, Occupational Choice, and Parent–Child Relations

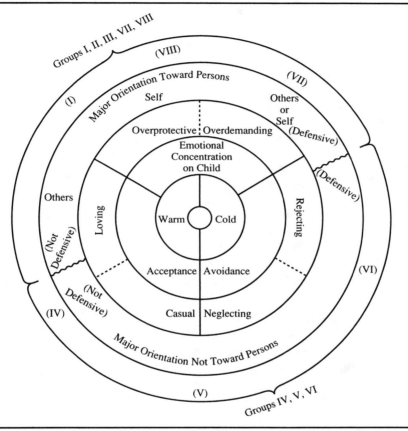

SOURCE: From "Early Determinants of Vocational Choice," by A. Roe, 1957, *Journal of Counseling Psychology, 4*, p. 216. In the public domain.

tant things without being monopolistic, tend to reason rather than punish, and give encouragement when warranted and try to help with problems. They invite the child's friends to the home, encourage independence, and allow the child to take chances in growing up.

Roe (1956, 1957) suggested that these six subdivisions produce two types of behavior. The categories of loving, overprotective, and overdemanding produce a major orientation toward people. The areas of casual, neglecting, and rejecting result in a major orientation away from people. Both of these range from defensive to nondefensive. Person-oriented occupational areas include service, business contact, organizations, general culture, and the arts and entertainment. Occupations that are not person oriented include technology, the outdoors, and science. Thus, individuals whose family climate reflects either of these two orientations are likely to seek an occupation reflecting that orientation.

Roe modified her theory after studies refuted her claim that different parent–child interactions result in different vocational choices (L. B. Green & Parker, 1965; D. H. Powell, 1957). She assumed the position that the early orientation of a child is related to later major decisions—particularly in occupational choice—but that other variables not accounted for in her theory are also important factors. The following statements express Roe's revised view on career development (Roe & Lunneborg, 1990):

1. The life history of any man and many women, written in terms of or around the occupational history, can give the essence of the person more fully than can any other approach.
2. Situations relevant to this history begin with the birth of the individual into a particular family at a particular place and time and continue throughout his or her life.
3. There may be differences in the relative weights carried by different factors, but the process of vocational decision and behavior do not differ in essence from any others.
4. The extent to which vocational decisions and behaviors are under the voluntary control of the individual is variable, but it could be more than it sometimes seems to be. Deliberate consideration of the factors involved seems to be rare.
5. The occupational life affects all other aspects of the life pattern.
6. An appropriate and satisfying vocation can be a bulwark against neurotic ills or a refuge from them. An inappropriate or unsatisfying vocation can be sharply deleterious.
7. Because the goodness of life in any social group is compounded of and also determines that of its individual members, the efforts of any society to maintain stability and at the same time advance in desired ways can perhaps be more usefully directed toward developing satisfying vocational situations for its members than any other. But unless the vocation is adequately integrated into the total life pattern, it cannot help much.
8. There is no single specific occupational slot which is a one-and-only perfect one for any individual. Conversely, there is no single person who is the only one for a particular occupational slot. Within any occupation there is a considerable range in a number of variables specifying the requirements.

Practical applications.   Another significant aspect of Roe's (Roe & Lunneborg, 1990) theory is an eight-group classification system of occupations: I = Service, II = Business Contact, III = Organization, IV = Technology, V = Outdoor, VI = Science, VII = General Culture, and VIII = Arts and Entertainment, represented in the outer circle of Figure 2.1. Each of these groups is further divided into six levels based on degree of skill, responsibility, and capacity. Practical applications of this classification system include the Career Occupational Preference System (COPS) Interest System (also known as the California Occupational Preference Inventory; Knapp & Knapp, 1977, 1984, 1985), the Vocational Interest Inventory (Lunneborg, 1981), the Ramak and Courses Interest Inventories (Meir, 1975; Meir & Shiran, 1979), and an interest inventory used in the fourth edition of the *Dictionary of Occupational Titles* (U.S. Department of Labor, 1977), all examples of practical applications of Roe's ideas.

Major criticisms.   Roe's proposal generated a considerable amount of research, but it never gained much support or became a major force in influencing practice (D. Brown, Brooks, and Associates, 1996; Osipow, 1983). The effect postulated by Roe of the parent–child interactions on later vocational choices is difficult to validate. Differing parental attitudes and subsequent interactions within families present numerous variables so that no study could be sufficiently controlled to be considered empirical. Isaacson and Brown (1993) also noted problems that contribute to this lack of research support. For example, an accurate evaluation would necessitate a longitudinal study following the individual through childhood into maturity. In addition, many of Roe's proposals reflect vague or ambiguous generalizations. Also, parental behavior is inconsistent, not only between parents but also within a specific parent. Finally, influences other than home environment affect the child.

Multicultural concerns.   Even though Roe has recognized the importance of sociodemographic variables in career choice, she still has not developed an adequate statement about how this interaction occurs and has failed to account for the actual decision-making process itself (D. Brown et al., 1990). One part of the problem is Roe's concentration on occupation choice rather than career development. Thus, a multicultural concern is reflected in the failure to provide insights into indecisiveness in career decision making.

Roe's classification of occupations appears to be satisfactory for men but it is not adequate for women, largely because of its omission of the homemaker–mother role (Roe & Lunneborg, 1990). No system exists for part-time activities outside the home or avocational pursuits if the homemaker has them, nor does the theory account for women who stay at home but assist their husbands in their work. In addition, Roe's apparent disinterest in the few practical applications of her theory and her reliance on personality theory and the importance placed on childhood environments offer meager, if any, application to multicultural populations.

Use by school counselors.   School counselors need to emphasize the importance of the various roles played by a wife and mother. For example, it is permissible to list the wife role as "domestic engineer" on resumes. Also, as many part-time jobs and hobbies often result as career choices, students need to be alerted to that probability as well as materialistic or intrinsic advantages. In addition, the importance of socialization within childhood environments is inalienable to the appropriate career counseling for ethnic and cultural minority youths.

Holland's Theory of Vocational Choice: A Typology Approach

In 1959, Holland set forth a comprehensive trait-oriented explanation of vocational choice that built on but extended the trait-and-factor model (D. Brown et al., 1996). He published an enlarged version of his theory in 1985 and was contemplating a third revision by 1995. Basically, Holland (1973) theorized that individuals are attracted to a given career by their particular personalities and numerous variables that constitute their backgrounds. Career choice is an expression of, or extension of, personality into the world of work followed by subsequent identification with specific occupational stereotypes. This comparison of self with the perception of an occupation and subsequent acceptance or rejection is a major determinant in career choice. Congruence of one's view of self with occupational preference establishes what is termed the *modal personal style.*

Modal personal style is a developmental process established through heredity and the individual's life history of reacting to environmental demands. Central to Holland's theory is the presumption that an individual selects a career that satisfies his or her preferred personal modal preference. For example, a socially oriented individual prefers to work in an environment that provides interaction with others (e.g., teaching). Holland stressed the importance of self-knowledge in the search for one's vocational satisfaction and stability (Zunker, 1990).

From this perspective, Holland developed six kinds of modal occupational environments and six matching modal personal orientations. These are summarized in Table 2.1, which also offers representative examples of occupations and themes associated with each personal style.

Holland (1973) proposed that personality types can be arranged in a coded system following his modal-personal-orientation themes. In this way, personality types can be arranged according to dominant

Table 2.1
Holland's Modal Personal Styles and Occupational Environments

Personal Styles	Themes	Occupational/Environments
Aggressive, prefers concrete vs. abstract work tasks, basically less sociable, poor interpersonal interactions	Realistic	Skilled trades such as plumber, electrician, and machine operator; technician skills such as airplane mechanic, photographer, draftsperson, and some service occupations
Intellectual, abstract, analytical, independent, sometimes radical and task oriented	Investigative	Scientific such as chemist, physicist, and mathematician; technical such as laboratory technician, computer programmer, and electronics worker
Imaginative, values aesthetics, prefers self-expression through the arts, rather independent and extroverted	Artistic	Artistic such as sculptor, artist, and designer; musical such as a music teacher, orchestra leader, and musician; literary such as editor, writer, and critic
Prefers social interaction, social presence, concerned with social problems, religious- and community-service-oriented, and interested in educational activities	Social	Educational such as teacher, educational administrator, and college professor; social-welfare-oriented such as social worker, sociologist, rehabilitation counselor, and professional nurse
Extroverted, aggressive, adventurous, prefers leadership roles, dominant, persuasive, and makes use of good verbal skills	Enterprising	Managerial such as personnel, production, and sales manager; various sales positions, such as life insurance, real estate, and car salesperson
Practical, well-controlled, sociable, rather conservative, prefers structured tasks and prefers conformity sanctioned by society	Conventional	Office and clerical worker such as timekeeper, file clerk, teller, accountant, keypunch operator, secretary, bookkeeper, receptionist, and credit manager

SOURCE: From *Making Vocational Choices: A Theory of Careers* (3rd ed.), by J. L. Holland. Reproduced by special permission of the publisher, Psychological Assessment Resources, Inc. Copyright 1973, 1985, 1992, 1997 by Psychological Assessment Resources, Inc. All rights reserved.

combinations. For example, a code of ASI would indicate that an individual is very much like people in Artistic occupations, and somewhat like those in Social and Investigative occupations. Holland's Occupational Classification system has corresponding *Dictionary of Occupational Titles* numbers for cross-reference purposes.

The four basic assumptions underlying Holland's (1973) theory are:

1. In [American] culture, most persons can be categorized as one of six types: realistic, investigative, artistic, social, enterprising, or conventional. (p. 2)
2. There are six kinds of environments: realistic, investigative, artistic, social, enterprising, or conventional. (p. 3)
3. People search for environments that will let them exercise their skills and abilities, express their attitudes and values, and take on agreeable problems and roles. (p. 4)
4. A person's behavior is determined by an interaction between his [or her] personality and the characteristics of his [or her] environment. (p. 4)

The relationships between Holland's personality types are illustrated in Figure 2.2. The hexagonal model provides a visual presentation of the inner relationship of personality styles and occupational environment coefficients of correlation. For example, adjacent categories on the hexagon such as conventional and enterprising are most alike, but opposites such as realistic and social are most unlike. Those of intermediate distance such as enterprising and artistic are somewhat unlike.

Figure 2.2
Holland's Hexagonal Model

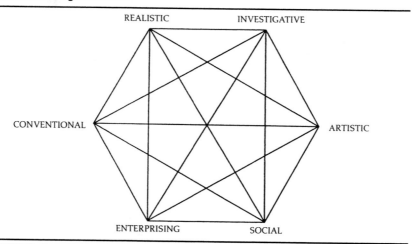

The hexagonal model introduces four key concepts, according to Holland. The first, *consistency of personality patterns*, is illustrated by a social individual who also expresses interests in the adjacent categories, artistic and enterprising. The second concept is the idea that personality types are *identified* and *differentiated*. Individuals who fit a pure personality type will express little resemblance to other types. Conversely, those individuals who fit several personality types have poorly defined personality styles. The third concept, *congruence*, occurs when an individual's personality type matches the work environment. Finally, Holland's model provides a calculus for his theory in which theoretical relationships between types of occupational environments can be empirically validated.

In the process of career decision making, Holland postulated that the hierarchy level or level of attainment in a career is primarily determined by individual self-evaluations. Intelligence is considered less important than personality and interest (Holland, 1966). Furthermore, the factor of intelligence is subsumed in the classification of personality types. For example, individuals who resemble the conventional type of modal personal orientation are generally intelligent and naturally have skills such as digital dexterity and ordering.

A plethora of research on person–environment fit in Holland's model suggests several conclusions. There is a consistent but moderate (ranging from $r = .15$ to $r = .54$) relationship between person–environment fit and job satisfaction (Spokane, 1996). Research results on the relationship of consistency and differentiation with career outcomes have been less positive. It is apparent that some of the research has reflected poor methodology and quality.

Practical applications.   School counselors have been enriched significantly as a result of Holland's work. Holland has developed four instruments: the Vocational Preference Inventory (VPI; 1953 and revised in 1985), the Self-Directed Search (SDS; 1971 and most recent revision in 1996), the Vocational Exploration and Insight Kit (VEIK; Holland, Daiger, & Power, 1980), and My Vocational Situation (MVS; Holland et al., 1980). The SDS is possibly the most widely used inventory (Holland, Fritzsche, & Powell, 1994). It contains an assessment booklet, an Occupations Finder, and an interpretive guide called "You and Your Career" (Spokane, 1996). Foreign language editions are available for most of the versions.

The *Professional Manual of the Self-Directed Search* (Holland, 1996) and the *Dictionary of Holland Occupational Codes* (G. D. Gottfredson, Holland, & Ogawa, 1982) list occupations and their corresponding Holland codes alphabetically. Numerous interest inventories based on his ideas are available (e.g., the Strong Vocational Interest Blank; Strong & Campbell, 1981). Numerous self-help books are also partly or entirely based on

Holland's ideas. Holland and Gottfredson's (1990) annotated bibliography listed over 500 publications relating to Holland's theory.

Major criticisms. Extensive testing suggests that Holland's modal-personal-orientation and occupational-environment models do indeed exist (Osipow, 1983). Individuals are products of their environments, which subsequently greatly influence their personal orientations and eventual career choices. However, weaknesses do exist, such as the following, as suggested by D. Brown et al. (1990):

1. Holland has failed to provide any real insight into the development of personality, except to suggest that types tend to reproduce themselves. (p. 348)
2. Holland has not commented on how problematic personality patterns can be altered. (p. 348)
3. Some of the basic constructs underpinning the theory are suspect, especially those of consistency and differentiation. (p. 348)
4. Holland has not addressed the psychological processes involved in choice making. (349)
5. Career development per se has also not been of major concern to Holland. (p. 349)

Holland (1985a, p. 119) enumerated the following weaknesses of his typology:

1. The hypotheses about the person–environment interactions have received support, but they also require more testing.
2. The formulations about personal development and change have received some support but they need a more comprehensive examination.
3. The classification of occupations may differ slightly for the different devices used to assess the types.
4. Many important personal and environmental contingencies still lie outside the scope of the theory, although an attempt has been made to include the role of education, sex, intelligence, social class, and other major variables.

Multicultural concerns. Several studies have shown the usefulness of Holland's theory with Native American Indians (Gade, Fuqua, & Hurlburt, 1988), African American males (Greenlee, Damarin, & Walsh, 1988; Sheffey, Bingham, & Walsh, 1986), and African American females (Walsh, Hildebrand, Ward, & Mathews, 1983; Walsh, Woods, & Ward, 1986). Holland himself (1985b) effectively summarized age, gender, and ethnic differences.

Some evidence suggests that Holland's theory is applicable to male and female nonprofessional workers (Salomone & Slaney, 1978). However, the widely used SDS and Holland's theory in general have been attacked as being gender-biased (Zunker, 1990). A major criticism centers on the claim that the SDS limits the career considerations for females and that most females tend to score in three personality types (artistic, social, and conventional; Weinrach & Srebalus, 1990). In defense, Holland suggested that females will display a greater interest in female-dominated occupations as a reaction to the contemporary sexist society (D. Brown et al., 1990; Zunker, 1990). Revisions of the VPI and the SDS have corrected items that may have exaggerated the sex differences commonly found in interest profiles (D. Brown et al., 1990; Spokane, 1996). Holland's theory has also generated research on bias-free career counseling (e.g., Holland, 1973; Zener & Schnuelle, 1972).

In addition, Holland has not offered any discussion on the impact of environmental and economic constraints on the process of career development (D. Brown et al., 1990). He also has not considered the possible validity of the developmental psychologists' positions related to the impact of aging on perceptions of the relative importance of life tasks (D. Brown et al., 1990).

Use by school counselors.   Holland's theory has provided the impetus for hundreds of studies, has had a tremendous influence on practice because of the instruments he has developed, and is the most influential model of vocational choice making currently in existence (D. Brown et al., 1996). Nevertheless, school counselors need to emphasize the expanded career choices for women and girls in contemporary society. Special attention needs to address historical and traditional career models for females and males in comparison to current nontraditional career options. School counselors especially need to be aware of the possible sex bias of some of the Holland appraisal instruments and to allow for this bias in their interpretations of the resulting codes.

DEVELOPMENTAL THEORIES

Developmental theories are less interested in explaining career choice than in describing the process of choice. These theories emphasize life stages and the career-related issues and concerns that occur at various developmental stages. In Super's (1953) theory, the focus is extended throughout the life span.

Super's Life Span Approach

Probably no single individual has written as extensively about career development or influenced its study as much as Donald Super (Isaacson & Brown, 1993). His theoretical propositions were highly influenced by research generated within the areas of differential psychology, developmental psychology, sociology, and personality theory. In fact, Super even refers to his perspective as a "segmented" theory consisting of related propositions, out of which he envisions an integrated theory will ultimately emerge (Super, 1972).

Super has restated his original postulates and has added postulates over the years. His latest postulates (Super, 1990) numbered 14 and are listed in the following order, with brief commentary: The original propositions are Numbers 1–6 and 9–12; Numbers 7, 8, 13, and 14 are later additions.

1. *People differ in their abilities and personalities, needs, values, interests, traits, and self-concepts.* The concept of individual differences is so universally accepted that few seriously challenge it.
2. *People are qualified by virtue of these characteristics, each for a number of occupations.* The range of abilities, personality characteristics, and other traits is so vast that each individual has the prerequisites for success in multiple occupations. Similarly, few occupations require a special ability, skill, or trait to the point that excludes many people.
3. *Each occupation requires a characteristic pattern of abilities and personality traits—with tolerances wide enough to allow both some variety of occupations for each individual and some variety of individuals in each occupation.* Because the patterns of abilities required in various occupations will rarely be unique, considerable overlapping can be expected. A number of occupations will exist in which a specific distribution of assets can result in satisfactory performance. The same case scenario is also true for a number of patterns of ability.
4. *Vocational preferences and competencies, the situations in which people live and work, and, hence, their self-concepts change with time and experience, although self-concepts, as products of social learning, are increasingly stable from late adolescence until late maturity, providing some continuity in choice and adjustment.* Super (1984) stressed that self-concept must be defined broadly so as to include both an internalized personal view of self and the individual's view of his or her existing situation. Super suggested that personal construct might be a more appropriate term than self-concept because of his broader definition.
5. *This process of change may be summed up in a series of life stages (a "maxicycle") characterized as a sequence of growth, exploration, establishment, maintenance, and decline, and these stages may in turn be subdivided into (a) the fantasy, tentative, and realistic phases of the exploratory stage and (b) the trial and stable phases of the establishment stage. A small (mini) cycle takes place in transitions from one stage to the next or each time an individual is destabilized by a reduction in force, changes in type of personnel needs, illness or injury, or other socioeconomic*

or personal events. Such unstable or multiple-trial careers involve new growth, re-exploration, and reestablishment (recycling). The formalizations of these vocational developmental stages are (Super, 1977, pp. 48–50):

1. *Growth* (birth–age 14 or 15): characterized by development of capacity, attitudes, interests, and needs associated with self-concepts;
2. *Exploratory* (ages 15–24): characterized by a tentative phase in which choices are narrowed but not finalized;
3. *Establishment* (ages 25–44): characterized by trial and stabilization through work experiences;
4. *Maintenance* (ages 45–64): characterized by a continual adjustment process to improve working position and situation; and
5. *Decline* (ages 65+): Characterized by preretirement considerations, work output, and eventual retirement.

6. *The nature of the career pattern—that is, the occupational level attained and the sequence, frequency, and duration of trial and stable jobs—is determined by the individual's parental socioeconomic level, mental ability, education, skills, personality characteristics (needs, values, interests, traits, and self-concepts), and career maturity and by the opportunities to which he or she is exposed.* All experiences in an individual's life development influence attitudes and behaviors. Factors over which individuals have no or little control often dictate limitations that may not be overcome regardless of one's efforts.

7. *Success in coping with the demands of the environment and of the organism in that context at any given life-career stage depends on the readiness of the individual to cope with these demands (that is, on his or her career maturity).* Super (1990) identified *career maturity* as a constellation of physical, psychological, and social characteristics that represent an individual's readiness and ability to deal with his or her development problems and challenges and that have both emotional and intellectual components. If the individual's maturity is equal to the problem, the problem is resolved with minimal difficulty. If the individual's maturity is not sufficient for the task, inadequate responses of procrastination, ineptness, and failure are likely to occur (Isaacson & Brown, 1993).

8. *Career maturity is a hypothetical construct. Its operational definition is perhaps as difficult to formulate as is that of intelligence, but its history is much briefer and its achievements even less definite.* Super's 25-year longitudinal study, called the Career Pattern Study, included the concept of maturity as related to career or vocational development problems (Fisher, 1989; Kleinberg, 1976; Super, Kowalski, & Gotkin, 1967; Super & Overstreet, 1960). Out of this and other research, Super and his associates developed the Career Development Inventory and Crites's (1978) Career Maturity Inventory.

9. *Development through the life stages can be guided partly by facilitating the maturing of abilities and interests and partly by aiding in reality testing and in the development of self-concepts.* Career counselors can guide students toward a successful vocational choice in two ways: (a) by helping them to develop abilities and interests and (b) by helping them to acquire an understanding of their strengths and weaknesses (Isaacson & Brown, 1993).

10. *The process of career development is essentially that of developing and implementing occupational self-concepts. It is a synthesizing and compromising process in which the self-concept is a product of the interaction of inherited aptitudes, physical makeup, opportunity to observe and play various roles, and evaluations of the extent to which the results of role playing meet the approval of superiors and fellows (interactive learning).* Super's (1980) description of a life-career rainbow illustrates the different roles played by each individual during his or her lifetime and the influences these roles have on lifestyle and career. For example, most individuals play roles that include child, student, citizen, worker, spouse, homemaker, parent, and retiree. Figure 2.3 depicts Super's rainbow.

Figure 2.3
The Life-Career Rainbow

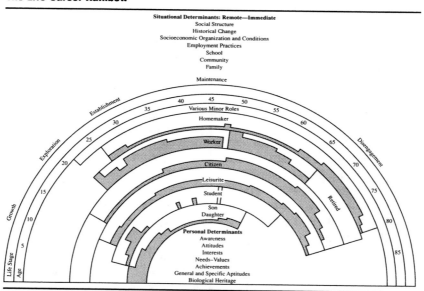

SOURCE: From "A Life-Span, Life-Space Approach to Career Development," by D. E. Super, 1990. In D. Brown. L. Brooks, and Associates (Eds.), *Career Choice and Development: Applying Contemporary Theories to Practice* (p. 212). Copyright 1990 by Jossey-Bass. Reprinted with permission.

11. *The process of synthesis of or compromise between the individual and social factors, between self-concepts and reality, is one of role playing and of learning from feedback, whether the role is played in fantasy, in the counseling interview, or in such real-life activities as classes, clubs, part-time work, and entry jobs.* An individual is constantly and abstractly modifying his or her self-concept to match what occupations have to offer in a situation.

12. *Work satisfactions and life satisfactions depend on the extent to which the individual finds adequate outlets for abilities, needs, values, interests, personality traits, and self-concepts. They depend on establishment in a type of work, a work situation, and a way of life in which one can play the kind of role that growth and exploratory experiences have led one to consider congenial and appropriate.* If the individual discovers pleasure and satisfaction with his or her occupation, a congruence has been established and the individual is contented. If the individual does not experience self-satisfaction and work satisfaction, he or she more often than not will seek another occupation.

13. *The degree of satisfaction people attain from work is proportional to the degree to which they have been able to implement self-concepts.* Super and Kidd (1979) explored career change and modification in adults, recognizing the increase in midlife career change. They suggested that *career adaptability* may be an appropriate term to identify an individual's ability to face, pursue, or accept evolving career roles.

14. *Work and occupation provide a focus for personality organization for most men and women, although for some persons this focus is peripheral, incidental, or even nonexistent. Then other foci, such as leisure activities, and homemaking, may be central. (Social traditions, such as gender role stereotyping and modeling, racial and ethnic biases, and the opportunity structure, as well as individual differences, are important determinants of preferences for such roles as worker, student, leisurite, homemaker, and citizen.)* Super's (1980) life-career rainbow basically depicts the reflection of an individual's occupation or major role. Super believed that his segmented theory is applicable to both men and women, allowing for women's childbearing role.

Super's five stages of vocational development (Proposition 5) provide the basis for an individual's vocational behavior and attitudes, which are evidenced through five vocational developmental tasks. These developmental tasks are shown in Table 2.2.

Super (1957) also addressed the concept of career patterns, particularly their determinants. He modified the six classifications developed by D. C. Miller and Form (1951) from their research of career patterns for men into four classifications, which are depicted in Table 2.3. Super also described seven categories of career patterns for women.

Table 2.2
Super's Vocational Developmental Tasks

Vocational Developmental Tasks	Age (years)	General Characteristics
Crystallization	14–18	A cognitive process period of formulating a general vocational goal through awareness of resources, contingencies, interests, values, and planning for the preferred occupation.
Specification	18–21	A period of moving from tentative vocational preference toward a specific vocational preference.
Implementation	21–24	A period of completing training of vocational preferences and entering employment.
Stabilization	24–35	A period of confirming a preferred career by actual work experience and use of talents to demonstrate career choice as an appropriate one.
Consolidation	35+	A period of establishment in a career by advancement, status, and seniority.

SOURCE: From *Career Counseling: Applied Concepts of Life Planning,* by V. G. Zunker. Copyright 1998, 1994, 1990, 1986, 1981 Brooks/Cole Publishing Company, Pacific Grove, CA 93950, a division of International Thomson Publishing Inc. By permission of the publisher.

Super (1974) identified six dimensions that he thought were relevant and appropriate for adolescents:

1. *Orientation to vocational choice*: An attitudinal dimension determining if the individual is concerned with the eventual vocational choice to be made.
2. *Information and planning*: A competence dimension concerning specificity of information individuals have concerning future career decisions and past planning accomplished.
3. *Consistency of vocational preferences*: An individual's consistencies of preferences.
4. *Crystallization of traits*: Individual progress toward forming a self-concept.
5. *Vocational independence*: Independence of work experience.
6. *Wisdom of vocational preferences*: Dimension concerned with individual's ability to make realistic preferences consistent with personal tasks.

Zunker (1990) provided examples of how the translation of these dimensions into occupational terms can generate directions for pro-

Table 2.3
Super's Career Patterns for Men

Classification of Pattern	Classification of Typical Career	Characteristics
Stable	Professional, managerial, skilled workers	Early entry into career with little or no career pattern
Conventional	Managerial, skilled workers, clerical workers	Trial work periods followed by entry into a stable pattern
Unstable	Semiskilled workers, clerical and domestic workers	A number of trial jobs that may lead to temporary career pattern, followed by further trial jobs
Multiple trial	Domestic workers and semiskilled workers	Nonestablishment of career pattern marked by continual change of employment

SOURCE: From *Career Counseling: Applied Concepts of Life Planning*, by V. G. Zunker. Copyright 1998, 1994, 1990, 1986, 1981 Brooks/Cole Publishing Company, Pacific Grove, CA 93950, a division of International Thomson Publishing Inc. By permission of the publisher.

gram implementation. For example, the attitudinal dimension of orientation to vocational choice may translate for one student to mean "I don't know what I'm going to do and haven't thought about it" and for another to mean "I really want to decide, but I don't know how to go about it" (p. 29). The variance in levels of career maturity development, as illustrated by both student comments, indicates to the school counselor a career development weakness that deserves attention.

Practical applications. Life-span, life-space theory has been widely accepted and creatively applied within career counseling (D. Brown et al., 1996). Super has developed several instruments, including the Career Development Inventory (Super et al., 1971), which assesses key elements of career maturity, and the Guided Career Exploration (Super & Bowlsbey, 1979) program for high school students. Super has commented on the counseling process and made contributions to career development programs at all educational levels (D. Brown et al., 1990).

Major criticisms. The original statement of the model (Super, 1953) appeared at a time when many men spent a career in a single company and many women worked as homemakers or in sexually segregated occupations (Siltanen, 1994). The Career Pattern Study investigated only the career patterns of men and focused on just the exploration stage (Super, Savickas, & Super, 1996). As a result, the model suffered much criticism for emphasizing European American men to the neglect of women and ethnic minorities. The original theory would seem to have validity for only sections of the current population, but since its introduction, the theory has been refined, elaborated, and renamed to more completely address issues related to gender and culture (Super et al., 1996).

Research on postadolescent male development appears to support Super's life stages approach (R. Gould, 1978; D. J. Levinson, Darrow, Klein, Levinson, & McKee, 1978). Both of these research efforts, however, focused on later age periods than Super theorized. Murphy and Burck (1976) suggested that the increasing frequency of midlife career changes may indicate that an additional stage, the renewal stage, be inserted between the establishment and maintenance stages. In addition, failure to integrate the main aspects of his theory (e.g., self-concept, developmental tasks, and developmental stages) into a unified theory has resulted in segments of a metatheory that are not unified (D. Brown et al., 1990).

Multicultural concerns.   The addition of the life-space segment to the original theory more fully addresses women's careers. Life-span, life-space theory currently addresses multiple roles and their demands more comprehensively and concentrates on how individuals negotiate their roles and increase their happiness with them and in them (Super et al., 1996). Current research clarifies when family and career create interrole conflicts for women and when the two roles provide complementary opportunities for the fulfillment of personal values (Claes, Martin, Coetsier, & Super, 1995; Nevill, 1995).

Regardless of Super's recognition of the variables of sex, race, and socioeconomic status as variables to be considered in career development, he has failed to construct propositions that can account for differences in career patterns observed in low socioeconomic groups (D. Brown et al., 1990). In addition, "propositions regarding the processes that propel women into career patterns similar to and different from men's" and the variable of "discrimination, regardless of where the process begins" need to be developed (p. 355). The applicability of current data on career maturity to ethnic minorities, especially disadvantaged groups, has been researched but results remain largely inconclusive.

Use by school counselors.   The application of any of Super's concepts and derived appraisal instruments should be considered within the limitations of his hypotheses. School counselors need to emphasize the inadequacies of his model in relation to the influences of classism. Students deserve to be informed of potential effects of discrimination in the workforce and be prepared to deal with such incidences in an appropriate way. Students also deserve to understand that they are not limited, necessarily, by their class status. Commitment and perseverance can overcome most obstacles.

A "culturally-appropriate career counseling model" (Fouad & Bingham, 1995) has been devised for career counseling that includes establishing a culturally appropriate relationship, attending to culturally specific variables during the appraisal—for example, by use of the Multicultural Career Counseling Checklist (Ward & Bingham, 1993)—and collaborating with students in performing culturally sensitive interventions. School counselors must realize, however, that one role of culture is to organize individual variation among its members and that many individuals belong to and form identities from elements belonging to a mixture of ethnic minorities (Super et al., 1996).

Ginzberg and Associates

Ginzberg, Ginsburg, Axelrad, and Herma (1951; an economist, a psychiatrist, a sociologist, and a psychologist, respectively) presented a "radical new psychologically based theory of career development that broke with the static trait and factor theory of occupational choice" (D. Brown et al., 1990, p. 3). On the basis of research results comparing male youths from high socioeconomic backgrounds with male youths with unskilled or semiskilled fathers, and a second group of female college students, these researchers concluded that occupational choice is a developmental process that occurs over time. This process is basically irreversible and is characterized by compromise because an individual must balance interests, aptitudes, and opportunity. Originally, the theory purported that occupational choice culminated in early adulthood. They identified four variables that influence vocational choice: a reality factor, the educational process, emotional factors, and personal values. These authors projected three primary periods that they called fantasy, tentative, and realistic.

In later writings, Ginzberg (1972, 1984) included three modifications: (a) The decision-making process is parallel to the individual's work life; (b) decisions are not always irreversible and can be delayed or even modified; and (c) the worker continually attempts to optimize the work situation, seeking changes and adjustments that improve the fit between worker and job.

Major criticisms.   The theory developed by Ginzberg and his associates had an initial influence on career development theory. That influence has decreased to the point that this theory is of primarily historical interest. However, their introduction of the concept that career choice occurs developmentally remains as a landmark contribution (D. Brown et al., 1990).

Multicultural concerns. Ginzberg's theoretical precepts have weak, if any at all, multicultural application. Variables such as gender, ethnic group membership, socioeconomic status, and environmental influences are too influential not to be included in any theory of career development or decision making. The lack of empirically driven support weakens an already immature proposition.

Use by school counselors. School counselors will not discover many opportunities to implement Ginzberg's ideas. Considering all the limitations and weaknesses of this model, its applicability for school settings is practically nonexistent.

David Tiedeman's Individualistic Developmental Perspective of Decision Making

Tiedeman (1961), Tiedeman and O'Hara (1963), and Miller-Tiedeman and Tiedeman (1990) suggested that career development is a process of organizing an identification with work through the interaction of one's personality with society. According to these theorists, career development develops within the general process of cognitive development as one resolves ego-relevant crises. Tiedeman (1961) referred to the evolving self-in-situation from the earliest awareness of self to the point at which the individual becomes capable of evaluating experiences, anticipating and imagining future goals, and storing experiences in memory for future reference.

Within this context, the path of career development parallels Erikson's (1963) eight psychosocial crises stages: (a) trust, (b) autonomy, (c) initiative, (d) industry, (e) identity, (f) intimacy, (g) generativity, and (h) ego integrity. Self-in-situation, self-in-world, and the orientation of work develop as the individual resolves the psychosocial crises of life. As the ego identity develops, career-relevant decision-making possibilities also develop; one can contemplate broad career fields and specific occupations, taking all situations into consideration.

In this paradigm, decision is extremely crucial in vocational development. Every decision, as well as the total lifetime process, includes two periods or aspects, each of which has several substages. The anticipation period is subdivided into exploration, crystallization, choice, and specification. The period of implementation and adjustment is divided into induction, transition, and maintenance. Vocational development is viewed as the sum of a complex series of decisions made over considerable time, with each previous decision having an impact on later choices and each experience affecting later choices as well (Zunker, 1990).

Practical applications. A major contribution of Tiedeman and O'Hara's (1963) theory is the focus on increased self-awareness as important and necessary in the decision-making process (Zunker, 1990). Adaptation to a working environment for meaningful peer-group affiliation and work performance is stressed. The model has been adapted to apply in four general modalities. Tiedeman (1979) and colleagues first used their decision-making model as the core design for a computer-involved Information System for Vocational Decisions (ISVD). Then, Dudley and Tiedeman (1977) designed the Information System for Educational Research Decisions (ISERD). A third application (Peatling & Tiedeman, 1977) generalizes the design of ISVD and ISERD into an Information System for Life Decisions. A fourth application is evidenced by Miller-Tiedeman's (1980) curriculum model involving the components of ego development, values development, and decision-making strategies.

Major criticisms.   While self and context develop simultaneously, the impact of the individual on context is neglected in this paradigm (D. Brown, 1990a). School and career counselors need more insight into this process. They also need to understand how they can experience the personal realities of students, so that they can be of assistance in the life-career dimension. In addition, although this theory has had an important impact on the career decision process, it is limited by lack of empirical data.

Multicultural concerns.   One concern exists in this model's denigration of race and ethnic group. The model presumes that racial differences are negligible in the career decision-making process. D. Brown et al. (1990) stated that career counselors need more insight into the process of how self and context develop than what the Tiedeman model offers. In addition, they need to understand and experience the personal realities of individuals, so they can assist on the life-career dimension.

Use by school counselors.   Students require understanding within their own personal and social environments. The effects of ethnicity and its interactions with social institutions are required to complete the total picture of the individual student. School counselors must ensure that the personal realities of their students, as well as the influences of these realities on their career options and career personalities, are understood.

Circumscription and Compromise: Gottfredson's Model of Occupational Aspirations

L. S. Gottfredson's (1981) theory described how individuals become attracted to certain occupations. She believed that self-concept in vocational development is a key factor to career selection because people desire jobs that are congruent with their self-images. The key determinants of self-concept development are social class, level of intelligence, and experiences with sex-typing. Individuals progress through four developmental stages:

1. *Orientation to size and power* (ages 3–5): Thought process is concrete; children develop some sense of what it means to be an adult.
2. *Orientation to sex roles* (ages 6–8): Self-concept is influenced by gender development.
3. *Orientation to social valuation* (ages 9–13): Development of concepts of social class contributes to the awareness of self-in-situation. Preferences for level of work develop.
4. *Orientation to the internal, unique self* (beginning at age 14): Introspective thinking promotes greater self-awareness and perceptions of others. An individual achieves greater perception of vocational aspirations in the context of self, sex role, and social class.

L. S. Gottfredson's (1983) original intention was to explain "how the well-documented differences in aspirations by social group (e.g., race, sex, social class) develop" (p. 204).

Practical applications.   Gottfredson's theory suggests that students with indecision problems either do not have clear awareness of their sex types, prestige needs, abilities, interests, and values or are unaware of how these self-concepts match the occupational world (D. Brown et al., 1990). The school or career counselor may use interest inventories, ability tests, and vocational card sorts to clarify students' vocational priorities. In addition, reading occupational literature work experience can be useful for students who are clear about their self-concepts but unaware of occupations that match their self-concepts.

Major criticisms.   Gottfredson's model has been criticized for its conceptualization of self-concept (Pryor, 1985), its conceptualization of the compromise process (Taylor & Pryor, 1985), its philosophical foundation (Betz & Fitzgerald, 1987), and its operationalized weaknesses that have limited empirical studies to a handful (D. Brown, 1990a).

Use by school counselors.   The self-concept and self-esteem of students affect their career choices. Low self-images are particularly prevalent among ethnic and cultural minority youths and lower income youths. School counselors should be alert to the potential of these influences on students' career plans, or lack thereof. Special attention must be given to students who display poor decision-making skills and strategies suggested to help them improve their task approach skills, including career decision making.

KRUMBOLTZ'S SOCIAL LEARNING THEORY OF CAREER CHOICE

The social learning theory of career decision making (Krumboltz, 1979; Krumboltz, Mitchell, & Jones, 1976) derived from the social learning theory of behavior (Bandura, 1977). This theory addresses the questions of why individuals enter specific occupations, why they change occupations at selected times, and why they may express various preferences for different occupational activities at selected times in their lives. According to this theory, four categories of factors influence the career decision-making journey for any individual.

1. *Genetic endowment and special abilities*: Genetic endowment and special abilities are inherited qualities that may restrict educational and occupational preferences and skills. Examples include ethnic group membership, sex, physical characteristics, and irreversible physical disabilities. The assumption is that special abilities (e.g., intelligence and artistic ability) result from the interaction of inherited predispositions and exposure to selected environmental activities.

2. *Environmental conditions and events*: These factors of influence are beyond the control of the individual. For example, governmental policies may restrict or limit certain occupational opportunities. Natural disasters, such as floods and tornadoes, are additional examples of influences beyond the control of individuals.

3. *Learning experiences*: Learning experiences consist of instrumental and associative learning experiences. Instrumental learning experiences include those the individual learns through reactions to consequences, through direct observable results of actions, and through the reactions of others (Krumboltz et al., 1976). Associative learning experiences include negative and positive reactions to pairs of previously neutral situations (Krumboltz et al., 1976). These associations may also be learned through observations, written materials, and media sources. For example, the statement "doctors are all rich" influences an individual's perceptions of that career area.

4. *Task approach skills*: The fourth factor includes the sets of skills the individual has developed, such as problem-solving skills and work habits. These sets of skills influence the outcome of problems and tasks confronted by the individual.

Krumboltz et al. (1976) emphasized that each individual's unique learning experiences over the life span develop the primary influences that lead to career choice. These influences include (a) generalization of self derived from experiences and performance in relation to learned standards, (b) sets of developed skills used in coping with the environment, and (c) career entry behavior such as job and college applications.

Practical Applications

The determination of an individual's problematic beliefs and generalizations is of major importance in the social learning model (L. K. Mitchell & Krumboltz, 1990). Assisting individuals to fully understand the validity of their beliefs is a major component of the social learning model. Specifically, the counselor should address the following problems (Krumboltz, 1983):

1. Persons may fail to recognize that a remedial problem exists (individuals assume that most problems are a normal part of life and cannot be altered).
2. Persons may fail to exert the effort needed to make a decision or solve a problem (individuals exert little effort to explore alternatives; they take the familiar way out).
3. Persons eliminate a potentially satisfying alternative for inappropriate reasons (individuals overgeneralize from false assumptions and overlook potentially worthwhile alternatives).
4. Persons may choose poor alternatives for inappropriate reasons (the individuals are unable to realistically evaluate potential careers because of false beliefs and unrealistic expectations).
5. Persons may suffer anguish and anxiety over perceived inability to achieve goals (individual goals may be unrealistic or in conflict with other goals).

The social learning theory is both descriptive and explanatory because the process of career choice is described and examples of factors that influence choice are given. The model also provides several observations for career counseling (Krumboltz, Mitchell, & Gellat, 1975, pp. 11–13):

1. Career decision making is a learned skill.
2. Persons who claim to have made a career choice need help too (career choice may have been made from inaccurate information and faulty alternatives).
3. Success is measured by students' demonstrated skill in decision making (evaluations of decision-making skills are needed).
4. Students come from a wider array of groups.
5. Students need not feel guilty if they are not sure of a career to enter.
6. No one occupation is seen as the best for any one individual.

Major Criticisms

Krumboltz has adapted and extended Bandura's (1977) social learning theory. The theory is not developmental so it does not account for job change. D. Brown (1990a) contended that this may be the theory's greatest weakness. Social learning theories have generated a plethora of research studies, but few researchers have tested the propositions as they are related to the career development of individuals. Krumboltz's theory is presently not a major influence on either career development research or the practice of career counseling (D. Brown, 1990a).

Multicultural Considerations

The social learning theory posits that all individuals are born with certain inherited characteristics into certain environments and are exposed to various learning experiences. They cannot control their heredity, but they can exert some influence on their environments and on the nature of some of their learning experiences. The specific nature of the learning experiences to which one is exposed and the environmental conditions and events that influence career choice are heavily influenced by such factors as race, ethnicity, gender, class, and culture. Similarly, physical characteristics, in addition to gender, will have an effect on what learning experiences are available to individuals. The cultural environment into which one is born has an effect on the kinds of role models with which one can come in contact as well. The social learning theory of career choice suggests that maximum career development of all individuals requires each individual to have the opportunity to be exposed to the widest possible array of learning experiences, regardless of race, ethnicity, gender, or class.

Use by School Counselors

Students from ethnic and cultural minority groups and low-income families will frequently mirror the role models to which they have been exposed. These reflections will often be negative to the improvement of their financial status as adults. School counselors can play pivotal roles in the enhancement of these students' future lives by exposing them to more accurate career role models and encouraging strategies such as guided imagery and fantasied futures. In addition, students need to be encouraged to consider a number of nontraditional career choices before making a final decision.

ADDITIONAL MODELS

Some career theories have been, and continue to be, more influential than others, in terms of career development research and counseling practice (D. Brown et al., 1990). Space constraints prevent the presentation of all theories of career development. The reader is advised to check the citations for additional and more profound discussions of the various models. Career models that were not presented in this chapter include Bordin, Nachmann, and Segal's (1963) psychoanalytical theory of career development; Blau, Gustad, Jessor, Parnes, and Wilcox's (1956) relationships of process of choice and process of selection; the learning theory applications of O'Hara (1968) and A. W. Miller (1968), and Gelatt's (1962) decision-making model. These models may be included in the category of less influential career development models.

More recent models that have potential for becoming more multi-culturally centered theories include a cognitive information-processing approach to career problem solving and decision making (Peterson et al., 1991; Peterson et al., 1996); a model of career development from a social cognitive perspective (Lent, Brown, & Hackett, 1994); a values-based, holistic model of career and life-role choices and satisfaction (D. Brown, 1995, 1996); and a revised work adjustment theory (Dawis, England, & Lofquist, 1964; Scott, Dawis, England, & Lofquist, 1960), currently labeled the theory of work adjustment and person–environment correspondence counseling (Dawis, 1996).

SUMMARY

Most of the major theories of career development were first articulated in the 1950s and 1960s. The labor force of that era was predominantly male and European American. During the last 20 years, there has been a large influx of both women and ethnic groups. The reader quite naturally may ask questions relating to the appropriateness of the various career development theories for women and ethnic groups.

To date, research on women and career choice has been meager and generally emphasized their preparation in work and family activities. Research on ethnic minority groups and career development has been even more limited. Some of the available research appears to reveal group differences in career choices and developmental patterns (e.g., Astin, 1984). Other research suggests that the differences between European American male workers and both female and ethnic minority workers are great enough to justify and require separate career development theories (Isaacson & Brown, 1993).

The most important task for career counselors is to be fully aware of the uniqueness of every individual student (Isaacson & Brown, 1993). The counselor can then address the psychological and sociological factors that are central to each of the career development and choice theories. This approach ensures that personal characteristics such as gender, culture, class, ethnic group membership, alternative lifestyle, and conditions of disability are considered.

EXPERIENTIAL ACTIVITIES

1. Defend the statement: Career development is a continuous process.
2. Apply a career development theory to your own career development.
3. Which career development theory reflects the most multiculturalism?
4. Develop your own theory of career development. Identify the components of other theories you agree with and why you agree with them.

Part II
Developmental Career Programs for Schools

PART II DESCRIBES the implementation of career guidance and counseling programs for typical school populations. The discussions emphasize a developmental approach to the dissemination of career educational services to students. Chapter 3 presents the appropriate parameters of career guidance and counseling programs for elementary schools. The career focus for this developmental stage is ensuring that students become aware of occupations and the world of work. Chapter 4 stresses the need for middle and junior high school students to become oriented to careers and learn appropriate sources of information relating to careers. Chapter 5 addresses the need for high school students to acquire good decision-making skills as they begin to consider their futures in relation to employment and its accompanying prerequisites.

3

Career Development in the Elementary School: Awareness of Occupations

What the best and wisest parent wants for his [her] own child
that must be what the community wants for all its children.

John Dewey

Schools have the responsibility to help students use their knowledge and skill to develop realistic and self-satisfying career goals. School counselors assist with this process by (a) providing students with accurate information about the world of work and existing career opportunities; (b) appraising students' interests and abilities and sharing these findings to enable students to make appropriate career choices; and (c) encouraging students to broaden their options as a precaution to future changes in career opportunities and the job market (Schmidt, 1996). In addition to these responsibilities, school counselors have the obligation to acknowledge the influences of multicultural issues and concerns, such as gender, ethnic-group membership, classism, and conditions of exceptionality. This recognition is vital to the appropriate delivery of career counseling and education to diverse student populations.

To some educators and parents, career information and development seem out of context with the elementary curriculum of learning basic skills and nurturing personal development. In elementary schools, career development may get only "a cursory glance with a unit on career exploration taught in some grades, or a Career Week planned for students to learn about occupations in their community" (Schmidt, 1991, p. 110). Although students at early ages should not be exposed to occupational information or formal presentations about career choices, they nevertheless are influenced by family, media, and other events that lead them toward career decisions. School counselors can help with this decision-making process by "infusing career information, self-interest activities, and illustrations of the relationship between work and education into daily instruction" (p. 37). At the same time, the school curriculum "should guard against gender stereotyping in materials, information, and activities that it presents to these young, impressionable minds" (p. 37).

CAREER DEVELOPMENT IN ELEMENTARY SCHOOLS

The perspective on career guidance has shifted from a focus on vocational development during adolescence and early adulthood to a broad view of career development throughout the various life stages of the individual. This evolution has occurred over the past 25 years. Gysbers and Moore (1975) conceptualized career development as self-development of the person over the life span through the synthesis of roles, settings, and events of his or her life. These authors also expanded the concept of career to encompass (a) the various roles that an individual assumes at each life stage; (b) the settings in which he or she lives, learns, works, and engages in leisure activities; and (c) the significant events over one's lifetime, such as entering school, moving from one occupational field to another, getting married, and retiring.

Acceptance of these definitions of career development and careers has resulted in recognition of the importance of providing career development programs in the elementary schools (J. V. Miller, 1984; Walz & Benjamin, 1984). The American School Counselor Association (1984b) issued a career development policy statement calling for school counselors to assume leadership in implementing developmental career guidance programs for all students, beginning no later than kindergarten.

The importance of the elementary school years as a foundation for children's later career decisions underscores the necessity of planned attention to the elementary student's career development. Although the responsibility for career education planning rests primarily with classroom teachers, the elementary school counselor can make a major contribution as a coordinator and consultant in developing a continuous, sequential, and integrated program (R. L. Gibson & Mitchell, 1995). As a coordinator, the elementary school counselor has a responsibility for the coordination of the various guidance and counseling activities aimed at developing career awareness. As a consultant, the elementary counselor may confer directly with teachers, parents, administrators, and other helping professionals to help an identified third party, such as a student, in the school setting. In this role, the counselor helps others assist the student in dealing more effectively with career awareness needs.

Career Developmental Theories

Chapter 2 presented discussions of the various career development and choice theories. In this chapter, I will simply emphasize the basic theoretical perspectives of career development regarding an elementary school population. The discussion is intended to be selective rather than inclusive.

A developmental approach.   A developmental approach to career guidance is highly consistent with the developmental philosophy of contemporary elementary school counseling programs and their goal of helping all children to experience healthy intellectual, social, emotional, and career development for success in the present and future (Hoffman & McDaniels, 1991). The current perspective of career development is one of self-development and that of career is one of subsuming all roles, settings, and events in the life of a person. Thus, in reality, the overall elementary guidance and counseling program may well be perceived as a life-career development program (Hoffman & McDaniels, 1991).

Developmental theory proposes that human development occurs in stages over the life of an individual, with specific developmental tasks to be mastered in the intellectual, social, emotional, vocational, and physical domains during each stage (Havighurst, 1964). A developmental task is described as being midway between an individual's need and a societal demand, defining it as "a task which arises at or about a certain period in the life of an individual, the successful achievement of which leads to his [or her] happiness and to success in later life, while failure leads to unhappiness in the individual, disapproval by society, and difficulty in later tasks" (Havighurst, 1972, p. 2).

By the age of 9 or 10 years, children generally have a relatively clear and differentiated concept of themselves (P. P. Minuchin, 1977), with most in this age group relatively free of the self-doubts and anxieties common during adolescence. Erikson (1963) labeled the crisis of the middle childhood years *industry versus inferiority.* Self-confidence and the learning of new skills and tools have developmental importance during these years, with significant implications for the child's maturation into a productive and self-assured adult worker (Seligman, Weinstock, & Heflin, 1991). The foundation for future achievement seems to be established during these years, and by fifth grade, future high and low achievers can be differentiated (Solomon, Scheinfeld, Hirsch, & Jackson, 1971).

Career development theories.   The beginning stage of vocational development outlined by Havighurst's (1964) theory, which starts at age 5 and ends at age 10, is called *identification with a worker* (p. 216). The child's central task is to identify with significant adults and to integrate the concept of work into his or her idea of self. A critical antecedent of Havighurst's initial stage is mastery of the task of projecting oneself into the future and conceiving of oneself as eventually achieving adult status. Once that is completed, the task of identifying with significant adult workers can begin (M. J. Miller & Stanford, 1987; S. I. Vondracek & Kirchner, 1974). School and career counselors need to provide appropriate interventions for elementary students to be exposed to diverse and differentiated adult workers.

Most development theorists view the elementary school age period as vital in beginning career exploration. For example, Super (1953, 1980) identified specific vocational development tasks to be accomplished at each life stage. During the *growth* stage (birth to age 14), these tasks include forming a picture of the kind of person one is, developing an orientation to the world of work, and acquiring an understanding of the meaning of work. According to Super, the self-concept during this stage is developed through identification with key persons in the family and at school. He further posited that from ages 4 to 10 years, during which children are in the *fantasy* substage of the growth stage, children's needs are dominant, and role playing in fantasy is important to their vocational development. In essence, Super viewed the development of increased self-awareness, awareness of the value of many kinds of work in their world, feelings of competency, and satisfaction from their own work as critical to children's sound career development and as the tentative period in which children start thinking about careers and themselves. Super also purported that children will use fantasy in their play and act out career roles. They become more aware of their interests, and by the age of 11 and 12, their interests are strong determinants of the activities they choose and the aspirations they consider.

By 10 years of age, most children have passed through the fantasy stage of career development when career preferences typically are linked to a desire for mastery and move into the interest stage, in which enjoyable activities provide the basis for career aspirations (Super et al., 1957). Career goals tend to be more realistic than are those of younger children and begin to reflect values as well as interests (Seligman et al., 1991). Children in the latency or preadolescent years tend to be less rigid and stereotyped in their thinking about appropriate sex role behavior than are both younger and older children, and this contributes to a broadening of occupational options and a receptivity to new ideas (Seligman, 1980).

Others also have characterized the childhood years as a developmental stage of career awareness. Hummel and McDaniels (1982) identified the period from birth to 11 years of age as the awareness stage; during this period, children believe they can do the things they like to do and transform needs and desires into occupational preferences. J. V. Miller (1984) also portrayed the years from birth to 12 years of age as an awareness stage, and the American School Counselor Association (1984a) policy statement on career guidance cited the elementary school years as a period for children to develop awareness of self and careers. Ginzberg, Ginsburg, Axelrad, and Herma (1951) labeled the age period from birth to age 11 as the fantasy period; it is valuable for children's participation because they can visualize themselves in a variety of adult career roles without any risk and have fun doing it.

More than 40 years ago, Roe (1956) hypothesized that parent–child interaction and family dynamics had an impact on children's occupational preferences. In the years since Roe's initial work, numerous studies have focused on the relationship between family background and career development, adding another dimension to the study of career development (Brooks, Whiteman, Persach, & Deutsch, 1974; Marjoribanks, 1984, 1985; Otto & Call, 1985; Schrock, 1981; Splete & Freeman-George, 1985; Weeks, Wise, & Duncan, 1984).

Additional perspectives.   Some additional perspectives on the ability of elementary school students to conceive of themselves in occupational terms, the gender differences in such behavior, and the knowledge of elementary students about occupations and related issues can be obtained from the findings of the National Assessment of Educational Progress's Career and Occupational Development Project. This national study included over 28,000 nine-year-olds (J. T. Miller, 1977). Selected findings from this assessment include the following:

1. Nine-year-olds can describe things they do well and things they cannot do well, although for the most part they are too young to relate these directly to occupational activities. It is harder for them to state their limitations than their strengths.
2. Nine-year-olds have limited methods of evaluating their own abilities or are unable to do this. Girls more often judge by what others say or by tests and grades, whereas boys more often judge by personal comparison or comparison with a piece of data.
3. Most 9-year-olds are able to state strong and weak interest activities but fewer are able to state weak interests than are able to state strong interests.
4. Nine-year-olds generally have much knowledge of the duties and requirements of visible occupations, although there is evidence of gender differences in the knowledge of specific occupations.
5. When given a list of 26 household skills and maintenance-building skills that are work related and done without assistance, most 9-year-olds indicated that they had done many of the activities (e.g., babysat, repaired a toy, shopped at the store, planted vegetables or flowers, painted an object).

6. About 60% of 9-year-olds have participated in out-of-school learning experiences, such as special training and lessons. Boys, African Americans, and children whose parents have less than a high school education have had fewer such experiences than other groups.

7. Most 9-year-olds can give acceptable responses to exercises that measure their skills in working effectively with peers, coworkers, and others.

8. Most 9-year-olds do not perceive themselves as being responsible for their own behavior.

9. Most 9-year-olds show resourcefulness in completing a task assigned to them when the instructions are clear. Fewer, however, are able or willing to take the initiative to seek assistance in completing a task that is unclear to them.

10. About 60% of 9-year-olds see the responsibility for selecting what work they will do for a living as belonging to someone other than themselves. African Americans and those whose parents do not have high school diplomas are less apt to see their future work as their own decision than are European Americans or those whose parents have more than a high school education.

Research on the national level generates important information. Elementary school counselors and other career-focused school personnel need to keep abreast of research findings such as these. Such data certainly have relevance for effective career guidance program planning.

The solution.   To meet children's career development needs, the elementary career development program should consist of a systematic sequence of guidance and counseling experiences appropriate to the children's various developmental ages as they proceed through the childhood years (Hoffman & McDaniels, 1991). Hoffman and McDaniels suggested that these experiences should be tailored to help children accomplish the following career development tasks: (a) develop self-understanding and a realistic, positive self-concept; (b) acquire the knowledge, understanding, attitudes, and competencies to function effectively in their current life roles, such as son or daughter, family member, sibling, student, classmate, worker at home and at school, friend, peer-group member, team member in sports and games, and "leisurite"; and (c) develop an awareness of the career development options available to them in school and the community.

Awareness of the World of Work

Career development in elementary schools emphasizes awareness of the world of work for the primary grade levels and orientation for the upper grade levels. Elementary school children are aware of the many different careers that contribute to their growth and their safety.

Beginning with observations of people at work and continuing with concerns about how best to spend their allowances, students become gradually and developmentally aware that just about everyone contributes to a functioning world. An important function of the guidance program is to help students understand that paid and unpaid work both contribute to a better world. Often the contributions of homemakers, Peace Corps workers, and volunteers are overlooked in the study of careers—an omission the career component should correct.

Besides developing an awareness of the world of work, elementary school students also need to become aware of themselves. Self-awareness fosters the ability to make good decisions about the labor market based on knowledge of strengths, weaknesses, values, interests, and other factors.

The major notion at the awareness level is to expand the students' perspectives about the world of work and to promote an ongoing process of self-discovery. The awareness level lays the foundation for the exploration and decision-making stages, but it does not stop when exploration begins. Developing self-awareness is a lifelong process (VanZandt & Hayslip, 1994).

CHARACTERISTICS OF ELEMENTARY SCHOOL STUDENTS

In addition to Havighurst's (1964) previously mentioned *identification with a worker* stage, elementary school students display several additional characteristics in relation to their career awareness. Several of these characteristics are described in the following discussions. For example, Drummond and Ryan (1995) advised that

- Children's self-concept is determined by what others say about them and expect of them—parents, teachers, and counselors are highly influential in the development of children's self-esteem
- Children begin to develop their ability to show empathy and move through several stages of moral development during this period
- Some experts think that television inhibits the social development of children and encourages them to be passive recipients of information rather than to be actively involved in the discovery of knowledge
- In this developmental period, children decrease their involvement in free play and replace it with hobbies, reading, organized team sports, and other activities
- Some children are mastery oriented and accept the responsibility for their actions and for the outcomes of their behavior, whereas others are helpless and attribute their successes and failures to factors over which they have no control and tend not to change their estimates of their capabilities when presented with success.

J. H. Evans and Burck (1992) investigated the effects of career education interventions on academic achievement. In their meta-analysis of 67 studies (1st- through 12th-grade levels) of the impact of career education on academic achievement, they found a small positive effect. Career education interventions improved student academic achievement levels an average of 0.16 standard deviation over alternative or control conditions. Their results supported the value of career education as a contributor to academic achievement.

Elementary students of average ability seemed to profit the most in their academic achievement. This effect was particularly true in the following situations:

1. If they were randomly assigned to groups.
2. If the career intervention was coupled with math and language arts subject matter.
3. If the intervention averaged 151–200 hours per 9-month school year.
4. If the program was concluding its second year with the same students.

Sex role stereotypes. The elementary school student may still choose only occupations traditionally associated with his or her own sex even when allowed to choose any career area (M. J. Miller, 1989; M. J. Miller & Stanford, 1987). Kohlberg (1966) made a strong case for his belief that children have well-developed universal sex role stereotypes by age 4 or 5 years, and by 5 or 6 years those stereotypes have become stable and constant regardless of variations in parental behaviors. Weeks and Porter (1983) studied the effects of a 10-week intervention strategy with 24 kindergarten children. The treatment group was exposed to nontraditional, vocational role models and curriculum materials. A control group was exposed to a curriculum unconnected to vocational or sex roles. The results suggested that children in the treatment group were only slightly (and not significantly) less traditional in their vocational preferences at the end of the intervention than were the control group children. The implication is that efforts to influence kindergarten children's role stereotypes and preferences through educational curricula and limited exposure to nontraditional models may be a case of "too little, too early" (M. J. Miller, 1989). Perhaps, the development of more flexibility in the children's cognitive structure is a prerequisite for these efforts. See Research Emphasis 3.1 for additional research data regarding sexist-oriented vocational preferences.

Parental influence. During the elementary school years, students become oriented to sex roles (L. S. Gottfredson, 1981). Leifer and Lesser's (1976) comprehensive review and integration of the literature on young children's knowledge about the developmental nature of career awareness concluded that parents are the primary determinants of children's career choices. Thus, the phrase "ask your parents"

Research Emphasis 3.1
African American Elementary Students: Sexist-Oriented Vocational Preferences

---

M. J. Miller and Stanford (1987) studied sex differences among 387 African American children from a rural elementary school in northern Louisiana. The sample included 71 first graders (46 boys and 25 girls), 84 second graders (44 boys and 40 girls), 81 third graders (35 boys and 46 girls), 74 fourth graders (36 boys and 38 girls), and 77 fifth graders (29 boys and 48 girls). School officials identified the children as being from a low socioeconomic class on the basis of their families' eligibility for reduced lunch prices.

Students were interviewed individually in a small room in their school building for about 5 minutes. After a brief, informal conversation, designed to put students at ease, they were asked the following question: "A (boy, girl) could be all sorts of things when (he, she) grows up. What are some things you would like to be when you grow up?" The interviewers were European American.

Results indicated the following:

1. Boys and girls did not differ appreciably in their abilities to project into the future.
2. Significant differences between sexes in Grades 1, 3, and 4 on quantity of occupational preferences and the significance in Grade 3 on range of occupational preferences indicate that boys mentioned more occupations and a wider range of occupations than did girls.
3. Both boys and girls tended to respond according to traditional sex role stereotypes.

SOURCE: From "Early Occupational Restriction: An Examination of Elementary School Children's Expression of Vocational Preferences," by M. J. Miller and J. T. Stanford, 1987, *Journal of Employment Counseling, 24,* 115–121. Copyright 1987 by the American Counseling Association. Adapted with permission.

---

appears to belong in the elementary career development curriculum (M. J. Miller, 1989).

Birk and Blimline (1984) studied the role parents' occupational fantasies have on their children's development. The participants included students enrolled in kindergarten, third grade, and fifth grade, along with their parents. Parents and children were given a short questionnaire to complete. A sample item from the parent's questionnaire was: "Think of five jobs you'd like your child to enter as an adult and rank order them." A sample item from the child's questionnaire was: "If you can't be what you most want to be, what would be your next choice?" Holland's (1973) classification of occupations was used.

Results revealed that, when parents indicated jobs they would like their child to enter, their choices were consolidated in two broad areas from Holland's (1973) system: Social (S) and Investigative (I). Analysis of the children's questionnaires indicated that their first career choices tended to be either Realistic (R) or S. The R choices were accounted for mainly by the boys (48% chose R occupations), but 69% of the girls chose S occupations. These data appear to reconfirm the relatively restrictive pattern in parental fantasies regarding their children's future career areas as well as the somewhat narrow perception children hold about their future career choices. The authors suggested that for parents to encourage expansive thinking about career alternatives in their children, parental imaginations might need to be stimulated and their concepts of appropriate options broadened.

COUNSELING AND GUIDANCE IMPLICATIONS FOR THE ELEMENTARY SCHOOL

The scope and sequence of career preparation activities is hinged on the priority the program has within a school district as well as the availability of appropriate materials and trained personnel (Drummond & Ryan, 1995). Program goals need to include objectives relating to awareness of self, awareness of decision making, and awareness of necessary competencies. Such goals for three career preparation programs for K–3 students in three states are compared in Table 3.1.

Improving self-esteem is a necessary overall goal for career development interventions, especially during the elementary grades. Elementary school counselors should be assisting students to increase their awareness of self, their sense of autonomy (i.e., internal locus of control; Super, 1983), their level of aspirations, and their belief in becoming what they wish to become (Leonard, Jeffries, & Spedding,

Table 3.1
Comparison of Goals of Three Career Preparation Programs for K–3

Portland, OR	Iowa City, IA	Riverside, CA
Identify and develop attitudes toward the world of work	Develop interpersonal relationships	Develop self-awareness
Acquire knowledge about world of work	Discover relationship between education and life planning	Develop occupational awareness
Identify their individuality and relate it to occupational roles	Learn educational competencies necessary to survive in changing world	Attitude development
Develop decision-making skills	Develop appreciation and positive attitude toward work	Develop economic awareness
Develop physical and mental skills related to occupational goals	Be actively involved in the career development process and get family involved in student's career decision making	Learn basic life and survival skills

SOURCE: From Drummond and Ryan (1995).

1974). Understandably, some school counselors may think that such an emphasis may raise a student's expectations to a level from which the "tumble" may be harmful to the ego (M. J. Miller, 1989). However, reality factors such as aptitudes and abilities have relatively little relevance for elementary school students (L. S. Gottfredson, 1981; Leonard et al., 1974). The words "you can't" or "that's not possible" are inappropriate in elementary school career development and guidance activities.

The initial stage of career development is self-awareness. Without self-awareness, the stages of career awareness and career decision making become moot. Perls, Hefferline, and Goodman (1951) postulated that everything is grounded in awareness and that awareness alone can be both curative and nourishing. The introductory stage of career development should include activities that address an elementary student's (a) awareness of self, (b) feelings of autonomy and control, (c) need for playful behavior, and (d) desire for exploration (M. J. Miller, 1989). Something to Consider 3.1 presents sample K–6 career goals and competencies for developmentally focused school counseling programs.

Characteristic Activities

Although educators agree that career exploration should be introduced early in a child's academic education (Neukrug, Barr, Hoffman, & Kaplan, 1993), to include this dimension in the required academic curriculum of the classroom is extremely challenging. School counselors often have little time to explore careers with younger children, and what time they do spend on careers needs to be focused. Elementary school counselors should not use activities such as (a) disseminating highly specific information about occupations, (b) having students project themselves in some occupation in the future, and (c) inviting dynamic speakers and career role models to the school to discuss various jobs. These activities may simply waste the counselor's time while not addressing the elementary student's needs (M. J. Miller, 1989).

The cornerstones of career guidance programs at the elementary school level should include (a) improving self-awareness, (b) promoting self skills needed later in life (e.g., cooperation), and (c) providing general information about the world of work (M. J. Miller, 1989). In other words, at the elementary school level the introductory stage of career development should include activities that target students' awareness of self, feelings of autonomy and control, need for playful behavior, and desire for exploration.

School and career counselors will note that students in this age group prefer concrete experiences and active participation. Passive listening and lectures are ineffective with these students. The developmental objective of occupational awareness is to have students learn about different jobs in the community, the working conditions, and the functions, duties, and titles of the workers (Drummond & Ryan, 1995).

Something to Consider 3.1
Sample K–6 Career Goals and Competencies

Overall Goals

- Become aware of personal characteristics, interests, aptitudes, and skills
- Develop an awareness of and respect for the diversity of the world of work
- Understand the relationship between school performance and future choices
- Develop a positive attitude toward work

Competencies

Kindergarten students will be able to:
- Identify workers in the school setting
- Describe the work of family members
- Describe what they like to do

First-grade students will be able to:
- Describe their likes and dislikes
- Identify workers in various settings
- Identify responsibilities they have at home and at school
- Identify skills they have now that they did not have previously

Second-grade students will be able to:
- Describe skills needed to complete a task at home or at school
- Distinguish which work activities in their school environment are done by specific people
- Recognize the diversity of jobs in various settings

Third-grade students will be able to:
- Define what the term future means
- Recognize and describe the many life roles that people have
- Demonstrate the ability to brainstorm a range of job titles

Fourth-grade students will be able to:
- Imagine what their lives might be like in the future
- Evaluate the importance of various familiar jobs in the community
- Describe workers in terms of work performed
- Identify personal hobbies and leisure activities

Fifth-grade students will be able to:
- Identify ways that familiar jobs contribute to the needs of society
- Compare their interests and skills to familiar jobs
- Compare their personal hobbies and leisure activities to jobs
- Discuss stereotypes associated with certain jobs
- Discuss what is important to them

Sixth-grade students will be able to:
- Identify tentative work interests and skills
- List elements of decision making
- Discuss how their parents' work influences life at home
- Consider the relationship between interests and abilities
- Identify their own personal strengths and weaknesses

SOURCE: From *Developmental School Counseling Programs: From Theory to Practice*, by P. O. Paisley and G. T. Hubbard, 1994, pp. 218–221. Copyright 1994 by the American Counseling Association. Reprinted with permission.

Infusion Into the Curriculum

Elementary school children need exposure to an academic curriculum that infuses self-concept, self-awareness, and career/technological awareness activities. School and career counselors cannot be solely responsible for the career development of their students. As classroom teachers see their students everyday, they should be on the frontline of career development implementation. Classroom teachers in the language arts, social studies, mathematics, or science areas can easily infuse career awareness into these subjects.

School counselors can serve as consultants and facilitators to the classroom teacher (Drummond & Ryan, 1995). The counselor can help the classroom teacher infuse occupational preparation activities into the curriculum. For example, if the objective of social studies classes were to focus on multiculturalism, a unit emphasizing nontraditional and nonstereotypical career areas could be infused. Students could write a story or a paragraph describing a female doctor or a male nurse. In math classes, students count the number of roles certain careers require. For example, a nurse may be required to dispense medicine, give shots, file records, answer phones, and so forth.

Kiser (1996) suggested that school counselors may initiate a study of careers that may be integrated across the curriculum with the help of the classroom teacher and a classroom "travelmate." The concept of the travelmate—a teddy bear or other stuffed animal—was originally designed to introduce children to world geography (McCarty, 1993). Through air travel, this travelmate was flown with a journal to various countries, where those people who hosted the travelmate would record in its journal details of the area it was visiting. By bringing the travelmate concept closer to the classroom, school counselors may initiate a project in which children use the travelmate to study careers in their community or city, in conjunction with the classroom teacher's using the travelmate to study geography, math, and language (Kiser, 1996). The reader is referred to this source for additional input and examples of the implementation of this idea.

Appraisal Resources

Appraisal instruments provide a structured approach to facilitate counselors' understanding of the interests, self-concept, and attitudes of elementary school students. These instruments can be used effectively with individual students, small groups, and intact classes to facilitate planning or informing school personnel about an appropriate appraisal of students. Table 3.2 gives examples of such instruments. The reader should note potential biases of these appraisal instruments (see Chapter 12).

Table 3.2
Career Development Appraisal Instruments for K–6 Students

Category/Instrument Interests/Attitudes Level	Beginning Grade	Description	Publisher
Wide Range Interest Opinion Test	5	Assesses perceptions of ability, aspiration level, and social conformity for use in vocational and career planning and counseling	Jastak
Career Maturity Inventory Attitude Scale and Competency Test	6	Assesses students' attitudes and competencies regarding career decisions	CTB/McGraw-Hill
COPSystem Interest Inventory Farm R COPSystem Intermediate Inventory	6	Assesses interests related to occupational clusters	Educational and Industrial Testing Service
Explore the World of Work	4	Assesses vocational interests	CFKR Career Material, Inc.
Hall Occupational Orientation Inventory (Intermediate)	3	Assesses psychological needs related to worker's traits and job characteristics	Scholastic Testing Service
Individual Career Exploration	3	Assesses general career areas of interests	Scholastic Testing Service
Safran Students Interest	5	Measures occupational interests and school subject interests	Nelson Canada
Career Awareness Inventory, Level 1	3	Measures how much students know about careers and their own career choices	Scholastic Testing Service
Arlin-Hills Attitude	K	Measures attitudes toward teachers, learning, language, and arithmetic	Psychologists and Educators
Survey of School Attitudes	1	Measures student's attitudes toward reading and language arts, science, social studies, and mathematics	The Psychological Corporation

(continued)

Table 3.2   (continued)

Category/Instrument Interests/Attitudes Level	Beginning Grade	Description	Publisher
Values Inventory for Children	1	Assesses values of children and their relations to other children, parents, and authority figures	Sheridan Psychological Services
The Affective Perception Inventory	1	Measures students' attitude toward self and school and specific school subjects	Soares Associates
Martinek-Zaichkowsky Self-Concept Scale for Children	1	Assesses global self-concept and physical, emotional, and behavioral aspects of self-confidence	Psychologists and Educators
SCAMIN: A Self-Concent and Preschool-Motivation Inventory	K–3	Early elementary forms Assesses achievement investment, role expectations, achievement needs, and self-adequacy	Person-Ometrics
Coopersmith Self-Esteem Inventory—School Form	3	Assesses attitudes toward self, school, family, and peers	Consulting Psychologists Press
Culture Free Self-Esteem Inventory	3	Measures general self-esteem, school	Special Child Publications
Piers–Harris Children's Self-Concept Scale	4	Assesses student self-concept in six areas: behavior, intellectual and school status, physical appearance and attributes, anxiety, popularity, happiness, and satisfaction	Western Psychological Service

Career Guidance Techniques

Career guidance and counseling programs in schools are based on seven processes: classroom instruction, counseling, assessment, career information, placement, consultation, and referral (National Occupational Information Coordinating Committee, 1988). The issue is not these processes but rather what kind of content they will include. In addition to the career guidance techniques suggested in this chapter, Herr and Cramer (1996) offered numerous examples of techniques that might be integrated with one of these seven processes. The reader is encouraged to consult this resource.

Career guidance techniques are of little value unless they are planned for and integrated into a systematic manner (Herr & Cramer, 1996). In addition, some students will not respond to either curricular or group guidance activities. Problems involving personal relationships, decision making and problem solving, adjustment to one's failures and successes, and meeting the demands of everyday living are best handled in an individually focused activity (R. L. Gibson, 1972).

SUMMARY

Luchins's (1960) primary effect—that information obtained first carries the most weight in ultimate decisions—has relevance for elementary school populations. Career guidance and development for elementary school students must concentrate on helping them to understand the general nature of the world of work. In addition, these students need to understand how their perceptions of work can affect both the quantity and range of their occupational preferences. Children in this age group have clearly given thought to their futures, have some clear goals and interests, and are not too young to benefit from career education and information (Seligman et al., 1991).

Elementary school counselors should seek to become familiar with the home and family situations of the children they counsel and should reach out to troubled families, making referrals as needed. Concurrently, school counselors should not push children to make early occupational decisions. Most elementary students have not made enduring career plans; therefore, the verbalizations of career goals should be emphasized rather than commitments to career choices.

EXPERIENTIAL ACTIVITIES

The following activities, taken from Herr and Cramer (1984), are worthy of consideration because of their proven ability to generate meaningful and fruitful discussions among elementary school students.

Curriculum Infusion—Career Units
- Have students create and then discuss "I wish" poems.
- Analyze short stories based on characters portraying different interests or values.

- Do oral reports on different occupations with the student pretending to be the worker.
- Build interest careers around different career clusters.
- Select a career cluster requiring competence in a particular subject matter (e.g., math, science, language) and identify occupations related to it.

Group Activities

- Play "Let's Pretend" or "What's My Line" using occupations as the content.
- Students may keep a log of examples of occupational stereotyping that they see on TV.
- Have students describe 10 different workers who built, maintain, or operate the school.
- Have students produce a cartoon strip about some aspect of the world of work that went wrong.
- Have students identify two commonly used tools in each career cluster.

Community Involvement—Career Surveys

- Take field trips to sites that allow students to see how subject matter is applied to solve work problems or is necessary to facilitating work activity.
- Develop and organize lists of resource speakers and field trips to observe the workers' roles in various occupations.
- Visit a local factory and observe the entire production process. Assign small groups to study one aspect of the process thoroughly, make a display of it, and present it to the class.

Several activities M. J. Miller (1989) suggested include these:

This Feels Like a Peach

A series of Gestalt theory-based classroom or small-group exercises designed for groups through the sixth grade (Remer & Schrader, 1981). The exercises focus on learning how to be aware of oneself and one's environment.

What Do Your Parents Do?

Students can interview their parents and discover what they do, where they work, what kinds of clothing are required, what they like or dislike most about their occupations, how they decided on the type of work, and what other types of jobs they would like to attempt.

How Does McDonald's Affect My Life

Students are asked to identify all the workers that affect their lives between the time they arise in the morning to the time they go to bed at night, such as the mail carrier, paper carrier, radio disc jockey, breakfast food manufacturer, and so on. Groups could be formed to determine whether one category of workers was more important than another and discuss their reasons for this choice.

I've Got a Great Plan

The class or small group can be involved in real situations as well as imaginary or simulated situations in planning and decision making. Planning skills are needed to plan class parties and other school activities. Activities that reinforce students' ability to plan and use decision-making competencies are beneficial.

Hey! It's Story Time!

Guided reading or bibliotherapy can be used to help students gain an understanding of themselves and their environment but also can be used to accomplish career development objectives.

Selected activities as presented by Drummond and Ryan (1995) include:

- Outside speakers and career role models, especially ethnic and cultural minority parents.
- The students dress or use pantomime or use pictures or role playing to depict occupations and have the other students guess. Emphasize nontraditional career roles.
- Identify and use tools. A variety of either pictures of tools or real tools could be used and discussed regarding typical and atypical occupations in the area. The students could be asked to identify what occupations use each tool.
- Dramatic presentations. The students could dress up as workers or family members and demonstrate the roles, responsibilities, or duties of that person.
- Puppets can be used to role play duties and responsibilities of school personnel or family members. Emphasize nonstereotypical career roles.
- Videos or other visuals, worksheets. Activities could include experiences in which students have to describe the worker, classify the job, or some features of nontraditional job environments.

4

Career Development in the Middle/Junior High School: Orientation and Exploration

In the final analysis our most common basic link is
that we all inhabit this small planet. We all breathe
the same air. We all cherish our children's future.
And we are all mortal.

John F. Kennedy

In the 1970s there was a trend from the elementary, junior, senior high school organizational concept to the elementary, middle, senior high school concept. A rationale for the middle school concept is based on data indicating that modern youths reach physical, social, and intellectual maturity at a younger age than did previous generations and that the junior high school may no longer meet their developmental needs (R. L. Gibson & Mitchell, 1995). Regardless of which type of intermediate school exists, either institution will reflect such characteristics as providing for (a) the orientation and transitional needs and (b) the educational and social–developmental needs of their students (R. L. Gibson & Mitchell, 1995).

From a career development perspective, the grade levels of any intermediate school are crucial. Whereas the traditional junior high school concept (Grades 7, 8, and 9) is congruent with the career developmental task of career exploration, the middle school concept (Grades 4–8) would require school counselors to deal also with career orientation with the lower grade levels. Other grade combinations are also possible with intermediate schools. For this chapter's discussion, career orientation will be emphasized for Grades 4 to 6 and exploration will be emphasized for Grades 7 to 9.

CAREER DEVELOPMENT IN
MIDDLE/JUNIOR HIGH SCHOOLS

The middle/junior high school is a transition period between childhood and adolescence as well as between general and specialized education (Herr & Cramer, 1996). The processes and goals of this transition period reflect either solutions or further exacerbations of what J. S. Coleman (1974) perceived as the gap between "youth and adulthood" or what other observers see as the gap between "education and work" (Herr, 1994). This period is also a time of particular vulnerability, a time when young adolescents may adopt self-damaging behavior patterns that can sometimes shorten their lives or diminish their prospects for the future (Hamburg & Takaniski, 1989).

J. T. Gibson and Associates (1991) studied what 13- to 15-year-old adolescents in disparate cultural and socioeconomic environments in 17 nations, including the United States, perceive to be their most pressing problems and what they do to cope. They found that *family, schooling,* and *personal identity/self-concept* were the three most frequently cited (69.1%) classes of problems. Within the category of *schooling,* the categories of *academic failure* and *academic achievement* accounted for 18.6% of all responses, and within the *personal identity/self-concept* category, *growing up* and *self-confidence* consistently ranked first or second when all groups were considered.

Individual problem solving was the most frequently reported class of coping strategy. The categories of *trying harder* and *planning a solution* ranked first or second in all groups. Gender differences were not generally found in these rankings.

The findings of the study led J. T. Gibson and Associates (1991) to conclude that (a) "Adolescent concerns are age-related and remarkably similar regardless of national background, socioeconomic grouping, or gender," and (b) "Although adolescent concerns are more similar than different, the Disadvantaged/Poverty populations have a greater variety of problems than their more advantaged peers and at a higher percentage of some problems" (p. 214).

Middle Grades School

Middle grade students are guided to focus on the same general themes as the K–3 students—self-awareness, occupational awareness, attitude toward work, educational awareness, economic awareness, and learning basic life and survival skills—but at a higher level (Drummond &

Ryan, 1995). Typical objectives for middle grade career guidance strategies are included in Figure 4.1. In addition, Something to Consider 4.1 explores the career development needs of typical 10-year-olds.

Junior High School

Career development for junior high students has been addressed by several career theorists. For example, Ginzberg (1972) identified the age between 11 and 17 years as the tentative period, which is divided into four stages: interest, capacity, value, and transition. The interest stage appears around ages 11 and 12; the capacity stage, between 12 and 14. The value stage usually evolves during middle or late adolescence. The transition stage occurs approximately at age 18. For the junior high student, according to this model, interest and capacity are the primary stages of career development. Early adolescents enter the tentative stage; Super (1980) placed junior high students in the tentative stage in which they explore their interests and aptitudes. Most career theories concur that orientation and exploration are the essential career tasks for this age group.

Figure 4.1
Career Guidance Goals for Middle Grade Students

Decision Making
- See the need to establish goals
- Use decision-making skills in working with school-related problems

Self-Awareness
- Be aware of individual strengths and weaknesses
- Relate strengths and weaknesses to job choices
- Be aware of ethnic group or cultural group membership

Educational Awareness
- Investigate the relationship between educational skills and individual success

Economic Awareness
- Understand the process of production and distribution of products and services
- Understand the law of supply and demand
- See the relationship between economic conditions and jobs available
- See the relationship between ethnic-cultural group and jobs available

Occupational Awareness
- Be able to classify occupations according to several types of systems
- Recognize how careers influence one's roles in life
- Discuss the advantages and disadvantages of jobs considered

Work Attitudes
- Learn the rights and responsibilities of a worker
- Recognize the role of work in society
- Understand the work attitude of own ethnic/cultural group membership

---

Something to Consider 4.1
The Career Development of 10 Year Olds

Seligman, Weinstock, and Heflin (1991) examined the career development of preadoles-cent children and assessed how the children's career development was related to their perceptions of their families, their self-image, their career awareness, their interests, and their work/family aspirations. Participants were 24 children (17 girls and 7 boys) between the ages of 9 years 6 months and 10 years 6 months. Of the children, 16 were in fourth grade, 7 were in fifth grade, and 1 was in sixth grade. Participants included African American, European American, and Asian American children, selected from both private and public school settings, with most coming from a middle-class socioeconomic back-ground. One child lived with a single parent; the others were in two-parent households.

The data from this study suggest that, by the age of 10 years:

1. Children have done quite a bit of thinking about their future.
2. Children can articulate clearly their career and family aspirations.
3. Most children are knowledgeable about their parent's or parents' careers as well as about the nature and entry requirements for their own career aspirations.
4. Career goals are increasingly determined by interest as the children mature.
5. Parental influence on career development declines as the child is exposed to other influences.
6. The importance of the child's relationship with the father declines, perhaps because the children are less influenced by power and mastery needs and have become more self-aware and introspective.
7. Maternal influence on self-image and children's plans for their own families increase.

SOURCE: From "The Career Development of 10 Year Olds," by L. Seligman, L. Weinstock, and E. N. Heflin, 1991, *Elementary School Guidance and Counseling, 25*, 172–181. Copyright by the American Counseling Association. Reprinted with permission.

Orientation and Exploration

In most career education models, programs for middle grade students involve orienting them to the world or work. For Grades 7 through 9, the emphasis is on exploration and planning. This does not imply that the elementary school foci of self-awareness and career awareness have been completed, but rather that as children mature, they face new demands (Herr & Cramer, 1996).

Orientation. Too frequently career preparation for middle grade students consists of a single, brief unit once a year. The Iowa State Department of Education (1986) suggested five developmental outcomes emphasizing personal and social development for middle grade students.

1. Be able to demonstrate concern and respect for feelings and inter-ests of others.
2. Be able to distinguish between self-characteristics and group char-acteristics.

3. Be able to demonstrate tolerance and flexibility for interpersonal relationships in group situations.
4. Be able to demonstrate contributing competencies in group situations.
5. Be able to relate values to interpersonal communication.

In addition, Pugh (1986) presented numerous objectives on a middle grade unit on occupations. For example, after learning about occupations, students will be able to match personal attributes with them, will be able to set short- and long-term personal goals and be able to revise them, and will be able to name qualities of a good worker. In addition, in class discussions, students will be able to state their determination to accomplish their life goals.

Middle grade students are expected to realize the influence of their educational planning for living a responsible and self-fulfilling life. They are expected to be able to (a) discuss a variety of occupations and jobs; (b) develop an appreciation for and a positive attitude for work; (c) develop skills for locating, evaluating, and interpreting information about career opportunities; (d) start to develop job-seeking skills; and (e) be familiar with the occupations in their area (Drummond & Ryan, 1995).

Exploration and planning. The need for preadolescents and young adolescents to acquire knowledge and skills important to exploration and planning derives from their opportunities to engage in activities farther from home and independent from the family as well as from the nature of the school itself (Herr & Cramer, 1996). The exploration stage of career development encourages students to make some tentative choices about areas of particular interest and to investigate those choices more thoroughly before making commitments. Typical exploration activities include job shadowing, computer searches, employer interviews, and volunteering. This is also a time for exploring educational opportunities and choices related to personal, family, and social development. Individuals need to explore career opportunities that interest them. If these exploration opportunities happen at school, students will be more likely to understand the relationship between their academic programs and the world of work. However, career exploration should help individual students make informed choices about career directions. Although every student does not have to make a final choice of careers, most are encouraged to do so, and they are able to if they have developed a thorough awareness of self and the world of work and have carefully explored the options of greatest interest (VanZandt & Hayslip, 1994).

Characteristics of Middle/Junior High Students

Kimmel and Weiner (1985) suggested that the primary developmental tasks of early adolescents are adapting to mental and biological changes, accepting how one looks, and learning to use one's mind and body effectively. Lefstein and Lipsitz (1986) summarized the needs of this age group as follows:

- Diversity
- Self-exploration
- Meaningful participation
- Positive interaction with peers and adults
- Physical activity
- Competence and achievement

Gender differences.   Bartholomew and Schnorr (1994, p. 246) contended that expanding career options for young women through career counseling programs requires:

- Enhanced counselor awareness of gender role stereotyping
- Breaking down women's gender role and occupational stereotypes
- Helping women overcome math and science stereotypes
- Improving young women's self-concepts
- Enhancing young women's self-esteem and self-confidence
- Addressing fear of success issues
- Helping female students formulate realistic family and life-planning goals
- Examining their peer influences
- Developing support systems

Each of these elements of a career program can be manifested by particular activities (Herr & Cramer, 1996, p. 389, including the following:

- Mentoring
- The use of selected videotapes and other media about gender role possibilities and stereotypes
- The provision of female role models in mathematics and science occupations
- The use of processes that encourage self-awareness, confidence, risk taking, and perseverance
- The reading of biographies and autobiographies about notable women and then discussing the kinds of choices the women made and the consequences and obstacles that were involved
- Helping young women to consider ways to balance and integrate various career and family life roles
- Promoting parental involvement with their child's career planning and exploration of opportunities
- Creating ways to reinforce the importance for young women of planning their own life rather than allowing others to define it for them

Additional proven strategies by which school counselors can attempt to facilitate realistic exploration of career aspirations in young female adolescents include exposing them to nontraditional role models (i.e., stereotype debunking; Cramer, Wise, & Colburn, 1977), role clarification and decision-making workshops (Wilson & Daniel, 1981), semester-long group sessions (Vincenzi, 1977), and using women in nontraditional careers as guest speakers (Herr & Cramer, 1996). School counselors can assist classroom teachers and parents to support enthusiastically career exploration that is free from traditional sex biases.

Miller's characteristics.   M. J. Miller (1988) described five characteristics of middle grade and junior high students in the following manner.

1. *It's Time to Start Deciding.* Cognitively, students are still—at least in the earlier middle grade years—in the stage of concrete operations whereas vocationally, their choices pass from the general, fantasy stage into the tentative stage; that is, they begin to make meaningful choices based on their current self-knowledge (Tuckman, 1974). In reality, the eighth and ninth grades are the first instances in the typical student's life in which official choice points are an actuality (e.g., specific courses; Herr & Cramer, 1996).
2. *Just What Are My Abilities?* Throughout the middle grades, the incremental development of formal operational thought emerges, along with the ability to concentrate on one's capabilities as a basis for tentative vocational choices (Tuckman, 1974). Because students at this stage are becoming increasingly self-focused, they should be encouraged to examine their own uniqueness (e.g., how their abilities differ from those of others; Tuckman, 1974). "Ability" starts to become an important determinant of social behavior and expectations between the ages of 9 and 13 (M. J. Miller, 1988). "Just what are my abilities?" appears to be a widespread concern throughout the middle grade experience.
3. *I Want a Job With Some Status.* Occupational prestige begins to awaken for the first time during middle or junior high school. Generally irrelevant to the average first grader, prestige among adolescents (and later adults) becomes a critical determinant of occupational choices (Reeb, 1974). As these students develop an awareness of prestige differences among jobs, their aspirations start to reflect a concern with prestige level (L. S. Gottfredson, 1981).
Boys' occupational preferences seem to shift away from blue-collar work toward major professional and executive jobs. Girls' preferences seem to shift toward lower level jobs, from lesser professional to semiprofessional and clerical work. Although the trends differ as a function of gender, the same growing awareness of prestige exists

(L. S. Gottfredson, 1981). Prestige, however, is defined differently according to one's perceived ability and social class membership; that is, more able students aspire to higher level jobs, and within all ability groups, the higher social class students have higher aspirations (Della Face, 1974; Sewell & Shah, 1968).

4. *Just Who Am I; What Do I Value?* The middle or junior high school years are transition years; self-exploration appears to be a natural occurrence, regardless if the school fosters such exploratory behaviors (Stamm & Nissman, 1973). Career concepts such as compromise and consistency (or lack thereof) between aspirations and expectations become operational as realities, and idealistic fervor and naiveté get their first temperings in the reality testing of curricular, athletic, and part-time work experiences (Herr & Cramer, 1996). In addition, values begin emerging with enough continuity to be measurable, thus justifying the use of value clarification strategies with this school population (Herr & Cramer, 1996).

5. *I Feel More Comfortable With My Peers.* The middle or junior high school years reflect the greatest variance of maturity levels of any student population, and individual differences begin to become dominant (M. J. Miller, 1988). Because the young adolescent is experiencing such rapid changes emotionally, physically, and cognitively, he or she becomes self-centered and generalizes his or her self-centeredness to others, assuming that others are as immersed with them as they are with themselves (Elkind, 1980). This "imaginary audience" creates in adolescents an aversion to individualized contact with a counselor because most adolescents believe everyone will know that they have been to a "shrink" and believe that others will think of them as "crazy" (Elkind, 1980). Group counseling or group activities centered around developmentally relevant issues (e.g., work values) may be preferred over individual counseling with this population (M. J. Miller, 1988).

The most important characteristics a school counselor should remember as they interact with junior high students include (Drummond & Ryan, 1995) the following:

- Early adolescents are egocentric and concerned about the reaction of others to them.
- Personal appearance becomes extremely important.
- Early-maturing boys tend to have higher self-esteem and self-confidence than late-maturing boys.
- Most students arrive at the formal cognitive stage although formal thinking may not be used in all subjects.
- The rapid rate of development in girls as compared with boys is

evident in the marked differences in the social orientation and maturity of the sexes.

- Cognitive subabilities (e.g., spatial, verbal, memory, induction, and deduction) begin to become more acute.
- Students will desire autonomy.

COUNSELING AND GUIDANCE IMPLICATIONS FOR THE MIDDLE/JUNIOR HIGH SCHOOL

Just as with the elementary school years, school counselors have a specific mission in providing appropriate career guidance and counseling endeavors for middle grade and junior high students. Although the foci are different, these students still deserve and need the most effective career development efforts possible. This section will provide the reader with numerous implications for these school counselors.

Characteristic Activities

The American School Counselor Association (1977) stated that "orientation to junior and senior high schools, educational placement, career self-direction, and group activities to promote self-direction, particularly in value formation and decision-making, are all areas with special implications for the middle/junior high school counselor" (p. 3). The need for early intervention in the career development of students is clear. Early intervention ensures that school counselors will recognize the all-too-common reality of students becoming trapped (O'Key, Snyder, & Hackett, 1993). Ideally, career development interventions should be integrated throughout the school years, but the need is particularly great during the eighth grade, when the students set their sights on high school. Many elementary and middle school counselors create and implement brief classroom guidance units addressing the world of work (e.g., Sandler, 1989). Unfortunately, many elementary and middle school counselors lack either the administrative support or the specific training in career development to successfully create and implement such a vocational guidance unit (O'Key et al., 1993).

As the discussion previously mentioned, middle and junior high school students prefer small-group and class-group counseling activities over individual counseling sessions. Career exploration activities appear to be the most efficacious strategies for counselors to use. In addition, school counselors need to be constantly sensitive to the developmental tasks applicable to this age population. See Something to Consider 4.2 for samples of Grades 6–9 career goals and competencies for developmentally focused school counseling programs and Research Emphasis 4.1 for supplemental data.

Something to Consider 4.2
Samples of Grades 6–9 Career Goals and Competencies

Overall Goals

- Become aware of personal characteristics, interests, aptitudes, and skills
- Develop an awareness of and respect for the diversity of the world of work
- Understand the relationship between school performance and future choices
- Develop a positive attitude toward work

Competencies

Sixth-grade students will be able to:

- Identify tentative work interests and skills
- List elements of decision making
- Discuss how their parents' work influences life at home
- Consider the relationship between interests and abilities
- Identify their own personal strengths and weaknesses

Seventh-grade students will be able to:

- Identify tentative career interests and relate them to future planning
- Recognize the connection between school performance and related career plans
- Identify resources for career exploration and information

Eighth-grade students will be able to:

- Identify specific career interests and abilities using the results of assessment instruments
- Consider future career plans in making educational choices
- Describe their present skills, abilities, and interests
- Use resources for career exploration and information

Ninth-grade students will be able to:

- Recognize positive work habits
- Refine their knowledge of their own skills, aptitudes, interests, and values
- Identify general career goals
- Make class selections on the basis of career goals
- Use career resources in goal setting and decision making

SOURCE: From *Developmental School Counseling Programs: From Theory to Practice*, by P. O. Paisley and G. T. Hubbard, 1994, pp. 218–221. Copyright by the American Counseling Association. Reprinted with permission.

The following discussion will present additional activities for students in middle and junior high school. They are not intended to be inclusive. Rather, they are provided as examples to encourage school counselors to be more creative and multicultural in their career development activities with this population.

Research Emphasis 4.1
Career Development Needs of 13-Year-Olds

Aubrey's (1978) monograph—one in a series of publications developed by the Commission on National Assessment of the National Vocational Guidance Association for Measurement and Evaluation in Guidance, with support from the National Advisory Council on Career Education and National Assessment Project—reported the following information on the career development needs of 13-year-olds:

1. Most can state two things they can do well (strengths) and two things that they cannot do well (limitations).
2. Although almost all can identify something they would like to do better, only about three fourths have actually tried to find out how to do it better.
3. Boys more often judge by a personal comparison while doing an activity, whereas girls tend to judge more by what others say.
4. When asked to state their strong and weak interest activities in terms of self-improvement, 13-year-olds' answers cluster in the group sports, school, and academic areas.
5. Thirteen-year-olds score low on identifying the earning power of highly visible occupations. Overall, however, boys and girls are equally knowledgeable about highly visible occupations.
6. Nearly 70% of 13-year-olds are interested in a current hobby, sport, game, or activity that they feel would be of use in obtaining a job.
7. When asked to list 10 things to be considered in choosing a job or career, most 13-year-olds can list 2 things and less than half can list more than 5 things.
8. The first choices of 13-year-olds for future jobs tend to be occupations generally requiring college degrees or lengthy training periods beyond high school.
9. More than 94% of 13-year-olds can give two or more acceptable reasons why people who wish to work cannot find a job.
10. Three fourths of 13-year-olds feel they eventually should make the final decision as to what job they would take to make a living.

SOURCE: From *Career Development Needs of Thirteen Year Olds: How to Improve Career Development Programs,* by R. F. Aubrey, 1978. pp. 1–15. Copyright by the National Advisory Council for Career Education. In the public domain.

M. J. Miller (1988) suggested the following specific activities that have proved to be effective in getting students at the middle/junior high level to think about career exploration.

Just how important is prestige? Given the relative importance of occupational "prestige" during this age period, activities that require students to explore their thinking about prestige are essential. Small groups of 6 to 10 members, for example, can define *prestige* (or *status*), rank order any list of 10 occupations in terms of prestige/status, or discuss the impact of family and socioeconomic status on occupational prestige. Such activities result in intensified awareness of how others' standards can affect occupational outlooks and decision making.

Let's play cards.   The Occ-U-Sort (L. K. Jones, 1983) can be used effectively to grasp the students' thoughts and perceptions of occupational prestige and to help explore with students the standards of others that they might be attempting to fulfill. The Occ-U-Sort is also a direct, easily comprehensible way of introducing to the student how the world of work is organized (i.e., according to Holland's, 1973, typology).

The Occ-U-Sort has a set of 60 cards, each of which has the name of an occupation on the front and a description of it on the back. The cards are resorted in several ways that encourage students to consider and articulate their motivations and values in thinking about career options. Card sorts require the student's active participation in the assessment process, are readily adapted to almost any population (aged, young, disabled, ethnic minority), and are strongly recommended.

What is important to me?   Students need to become aware of the numerous factors that will affect their future lifestyle: income, education, class, ethnicity, and prestige. Students can explore these factors through the compiling of a Life Style Album (Hansen, Klaurens, & Tennyson, 1972). In small groups, students find examples of each factor in newspapers, television, commercials, and other literature that reflect the influence of each factor on life pattern. Students will then compile an album, describing how these factors relate to the life pattern of their own family.

The world outside of school.   M. J. Miller (1988) suggested that the school counselor should provide students with relevant and current vocational information. Holland's (1984) typology of classifying environments and occupations is recommended as the most appropriate format. Holland's model can be demonstrated through field trips, interviews, and written and oral presentations.

Debunking occupational myths.   During the discussion section of any activity, the counselor must listen carefully to ascertain among students the possible existence of commonly held myths about occupations. See Something to Consider 4.3 for a list of common myths. M. J. Miller (1988) suggested that a productive idea is to administer a quiz that addresses common myths about career development. Such a quiz permits the school counselor to use a cognitive behavioral approach to challenge irrational beliefs. This approach is also worthwhile when school counselors are interacting with ethnic and cultural minority youths (e.g., Herring, 1990a).

Infusion Into the Curriculum

Career development concepts need to be infused into the school's curriculum at all developmental levels. For middle and junior high school levels, this infusion should concentrate on orientation and explo-

Something to Consider 4.3
What's a Myth Quiz?

An extremely productive activity for middle and junior high school students is one called "Debunking Occupational Myths: A Quiz." To challenge and perhaps to change faulty beliefs and misconceptions are at the core of many vocational concerns. Below are the 10 true (T) or false (F) items, arranged in no particular order. The counselor using them may elect to discard or add others. Correct responses are in parentheses.

1. The goal of career counseling is to find the one perfect occupation (F).
2. Once a decision has been made it should be pursued to the end (F).
3. Although most youngsters are not sure of what they want to do vocationally, most are fairly sure of what they do not want to do or be when they grow up (T).
4. Certain "types" of people seem to be employed in certain "kinds" of work (T).
5. The main purpose of an interest test is to be able to tell a student what occupation he or she should choose (F).
6. Occupational prestige is one factor to consider when selecting an occupation (T).
7. Your worth as a person should be determined by the type of occupation you have (F).
8. Talking with someone actually employed in a job that you find interesting is a good way of finding out about the work world (T).
9. The process of making a decision many times causes feelings of anxiety and self-doubt (T).
10. Deciding on a college major or some type of occupation should be complete by your junior year in high school (F).

SOURCE: From "Career Counseling for the Middle School Youngster," by M. J. Miller, 1988, *Journal of Employment Counseling, 25,* 177–178. Copyright 1988 by the American Counseling Association. Adapted with permission.

ration. The most commonly found example of career orientation and exploration infusion at this level is the presence of a required course for students. This course may be one semester or two semesters. It may be titled "Introduction to Vocations," "Orientation to Careers," or some other title. Depending on the school system, this course may be offered at any level from Grades 7 to 9. Such courses supplement school counselors in their task.

The inclusion of such introductory courses can be greatly enhanced by the classroom teacher. By incorporating career orientation and exploration topics in subject matter classes, teachers expose students to more practical applications of career clusters. The math teacher, for example, can allow students to apply fractions in the preparation of pizzas. Students will learn how to divide the pizza into eighths or sixteenths. At the same time, the classroom teacher can interject commentary about career opportunities in math as well as in the pizza industry.

Another practical activity is found in the development of a career portfolio. This process assists students to prepare for the high school experience and aids them in setting goals for the future (Drummond

& Ryan, 1995). This project can be adapted for any of the middle/ junior high grade levels. The objectives of such a portfolio programs are the following.

- Students will gather information regarding their learning styles, personal competencies, present and future vocational interests, and their parents' expectations.
- Students will evaluate the data gathered and formulate choices through instruction on decision making, use of decision trees, and group discussions.
- Students will design and build an actual portfolio stating learning strengths and weaknesses, academic and vocational interests, social interests, and immediate and possible future goals. (p. 103)

Appraisal Resources

The purpose of appraisal resources in the middle/junior high grades is to assist students in discovering their interests, values, abilities, and aptitudes. Other purposes could be to ascertain self-concept and self-esteem, career maturity, and irrational beliefs. The following discussion will emphasize some of the more commonly applied appraisals for this population.

Self-report instruments, such as the Vocational Awareness Scale (VAS, Helwig, 1984), can provide valuable information for individual students. The VAS assesses career awareness and the use of internal information in career decision making. The VAS can be useful with junior high students to focus their concentration on aptitudes, self-reported abilities, and self-expressed interests. Helping students translate their abilities into occupational clusters is the responsibility of the school counselor. Table 3.2 in the previous chapter lists some of the more commonly used standardized instruments for middle and junior high grades. The reader is cautioned to consider the use of these appraisal tools in light of the discussion presented in Chapter 12 on multicultural concerns.

Numerous other tests are available to the school counselor for measuring abilities and aptitudes. In fact, any activity or appraisal tool that attempts to compare a student's ability against his or her peers is potentially beneficial. L. S. Gottfredson (1981) suggested the use of an ability test rather than a vocational maturity instrument for measuring career maturity because of the cognitive development of this age group.

Information About the World of Work

Middle and junior high school students need to be presented with a broader range of occupations within contemporary and future society.

Realistic career goals cannot be set without appropriate, current, and multiple exposures to the world of work. The school counselor bears ultimate responsibility to provide students with relevant educational and vocational information (Perrone, 1973).

Holland's typology.   Holland's (1973) typology is an excellent avenue of providing information about the world of work. For example, students can interview individuals in or write a report on an occupation represented within each of Holland's six personality types. Field trips can be arranged to introduce each of Holland's types. For example, visiting a hotel manager would introduce an Enterprising type of occupation. Activities generated by the school counselor that use vocational information while enhancing a student's self-image are productive (M. J. Miller, 1988).

Broadening Horizon Project (BHP).   The BHP represents a joint venture between the Arizona Department of Education and Arizona State University to expand the career aspirations of eighth-grade female students, ethnic minority students, and disabled students to careers involving math and science (O'Key et al., 1993). Both data-based and anecdotal indexes (i.e., pre- and postproject career self-efficacy surveys, student interview sheets, and student reaction sheets) were examined in evaluating the appropriateness and effectiveness of the project.

The BHP curriculum uses a foundation of experiential learning to increase confidence among the student participants. The construct of self-efficacy (i.e., the degree of confidence in one's ability to successfully compete in a specific career) has shown promise in recent years as a means of explaining career development patterns (Lent & Hackett, 1987). The curriculum is designed to be presented by co-facilitators to groups of approximately 20 to 25 eighth graders over the course of four 80-minute sessions. The structure requires students to work in pairs on computers.

Students completing pre- and posttest surveys ($N = 41$) indicated a marked increase in career and academic self-efficacy, significant at the .001 probability level. Thus, preliminary results indicate the curriculum is quite successful in its primary objective: increasing students' confidence in their ability to aspire to careers in math and science.

Career Guidance Techniques

In addition to the career guidance activities and techniques previously suggested in this chapter, additional examples are presented for the reader's consideration. Once again, these examples are not intended to be inclusive. The intent is to inspire the reader to be creative and generate additional interventions and strategies.

Involving business and industry.   Pinson (1980, p. 138) synthesized from various documents and statements recommendations from business and industry about how they can be useful in career guidance. Selected examples are the following:

1. Using the business and industry community to validate civic and social outcome measures as well as the work competency indexes developed by schools as exit requirements.
2. Using community work stations as frequently for observation and exploration by elementary and middle school students as for actual work experience at the secondary school level.
3. Involving business and industry in ways that further curriculum objectives in all subject areas (i.e., assisting students to conduct a job search in the yellow pages could indirectly increase their reading achievement levels)

Using simulations.   Simulations have been extremely popular techniques in many areas of guidance and counseling. One example of a simulation applicable to career guidance is evidenced in the Making of Life Decisions, or MOLD, model described by R. H. Johnson and Myrick (1971). In this strategy, each student follows six basic steps:

1. Completes a personal profile sheet describing abilities and interests.
2. Becomes involved with small-group sessions that assist in self-appraisal.
3. Explores career fields and makes a tentative career choice based on abilities and interests.
4. Plans on paper the next year of life, making decisions about education, job, home life, and leisure activities. The student selects from alternatives available in the local community, not fictional or fantasized options.
5. Receives feedback on decisions, such as grades earned in each course and whether or not a job is acquired. This feedback is gained from probability tables, which include such variables as ability, study time, and chance.
6. Uses the results and plans the following year. In this way, contingency plans and consequences of immediate decisions can be recognized.

The field trip trap.   Children have little direct opportunity to go behind the scenes and see how and where many types of work are performed (Isaacson & Brown, 1993). Thus, middle and junior high school counselors are challenged to satisfy the career awareness needs of their students in creative and action-oriented ways. One avenue has traditionally been the field trip. Generally, field trips tend to be limited to firehouses, banks, bakeries, zoos, or newspapers (Hoppock, 1976). These visitation sites can become uninteresting and worthless traps for the students. R. L. Gibson, Mitchell, and Basile (1993) differentiated between a worthwhile field trip and a get-out-of-school excursion. The primary requirement for meaningful field trips rests in careful attention to the planning, conducting, and follow-up phases of the trip.

Because pizza is an immediate attention getter with students, a field trip to a pizza restaurant can provide an entertaining learning experience. The Project Pizza Connection is designed for fourth and fifth graders, but the suggested format and activities for parents and children may be adapted as needed (Beale & Nugent, 1996). A carefully planned field trip to a pizza restaurant can help accomplish two important goals: (a) Students are provided an excellent opportunity to witness myriad workers cooperating to provide a service, and (b) students observe a work setting as an organization of people doing work. The reader is encouraged to access this resource and learn how to plan and implement an effective field trip involving the components of getting ready, the actual visit, and following up the visit.

The career academy.   Another innovative idea is the concept of a career academy. The counselors of Memphis, Tennessee, joined with neighborhood Boys Clubs and the Shelby County Chapter of Links, Inc., an international service organization, to provide a career academy for 40 students in Grades 4–9 (Young, Thomas, Hilliard, Shaw, & Epstein, 1996). The Career Academy, conducted on three consecutive Saturdays, was designed for the students (known as Career Cadets) to master six objectives.

1. Reflect self-awareness by listing five personal examples of each awareness factor (interests, needs, wants, values) that are important in making career choices.
2. Reflect career awareness by (a) identifying five career information tools and resources; (b) specifying five top career choices; and (c) listing the training, education, experience, and entry requirements for the specified five favorite careers.
3. Reflect academic and vocational awareness by (a) listing the total credits needed for graduation, (b) identifying 10 required courses in the academic-college path, and (c) identifying 10 required courses in the vocational-work path.
4. Reflect awareness of career synthesis (correlation of self-awareness information, academic or vocational preference information, and career awareness information) by listing five careers compatible with those three aforementioned information areas.

5. Reflect awareness of problem-solving and decision-making strategies for academic and career planning by (a) listing five steps for effective problem solving, (b) listing five steps for effective decision making, and (c) choosing either the academic-college path or the vocational-work path for career planning purposes.
6. Reflect awareness of peer leadership role and responsibility by (a) identifying the peers for mentoring, (b) listing the career-related peer leader activities initiated, and (c) listing the career education activities in which they assisted school counselors and teachers.

Career Cadets were expected to complete three Career Academy assignments that reflected the Career Academy objectives and complemented the miniworkshops. First, cadets were to maintain a notebook with Career Academy activities. Second, cadets were to design and implement a personal success action plan. Third, cadets were to help educators motivate other students with career guidance activities through peer leadership and mentoring.

Additional guidance techniques.   Herr and Cramer (1996, pp. 406–409) offered numerous examples of ideas that have been tried in career education or career guidance settings across the nation. A few of those ideas are given here:

Curriculum Infusion

- Display posters in each subject matter area illustrating the contributions of workers in related occupations.
- Teach students good study habits and relate these to good work habits.
- Divide class into small groups and have the students compete in naming the most occupations in goods-producing or service-producing occupations.
- Set up career cluster explorations in industrial arts classes that give pertinent hands-on experience in each cluster.
- Following group discussion on the effects of technology on the world of work, have students identify six occupations that existed 29 years ago and have now been combined with other occupations or have ceased to exist.

Decision Making and Acquisition of Career Information
- Provide role models who not only have nontraditional careers but also are raising children to help both female and male students understand ways in which career and lifestyle decisions can be integrated.

- Have students list major decisions regarding their future that they must make:
  a. Within 2 years (e.g., high school course selection)
  b. Within 5 years (e.g., trade school, college, occupation)
  c. Within 10 years (e.g., where to live, work, marriage).
- Use a variety of simulated decision-making games and compare the steps they portray (e.g., life career game, consumer, economic system).
- Play match-up games in which students are expected to choose the correct types of educational requirement for various occupations.
- Have students solve a scrambled letters puzzle based on decision-making terminology.

Community Involvement

- Develop a Youth Employment Service to bring students seeking part-time work together with employers having short-term or odd jobs.
- Develop performance contacts with students in relation to community projects that would help them acquire career awareness.
- Develop a directory of entry-level jobs in the community, including job descriptions, requirements, contact persons, and procedure for applying.
- Have students engage in volunteer community service work in hospitals, nursing homes, orphanages, and other settings. Discuss their experiences in helping others in class and explore the potential occupations related to them.
- Invite local employment service counselors to talk with students about jobs available in the community.

SUMMARY

This chapter examined the implications of career guidance and development for students in middle and junior high schools, as well as the implications for career guidance and career counseling of preadolescents and young adolescents in the primary areas of orientation, exploration, and planning. To some extent, the issue of identity formation was identified and described. Concrete examples of activities and strategies were provided for school counselors working at these levels. The chapter is intended to serve as an impetus for school counselors to become actively involved in the career development needs of those they serve.

EXPERIENTIAL ACTIVITIES

1. On one side of an 8½ × 11-in. piece of paper, describe your life from the time you were born until today. Use any technique you wish. Do not describe something that you are unwilling to share. When you have completed this lifeline, share your description with a classmate.

   On the other side of the paper, create a description of your life from now until the time when you will be 100 years old—not an unreasonable expectation. Again, use any technique you wish, but do not describe something that you are unwilling to discuss. Share this description, also with a classmate.

   How are you different from your partner? What are some common themes? Did you find any surprises about yourself? What other observations or questions do you have?

2. Have students construct an individual educational career plan that includes goals for the senior high school, postsecondary education, and the entry to work.

3. Have students role-play a decision situation involving the need for compromise.

4. Generate career guidance and career counseling interventions that are applicable for your school and community.

5. Prepare and complete a resource list of available nontraditional workers for potential guest speakers.

6. In your role as a school counselor, what can you do to ensure the appropriate career development for your students?

5

Career Development in the High School: Decision Making

―――

When I chose to pursue technical skills instead of college, people thought
I was very foolish. Today I am a fully qualified heavy equipment mechanic
working for a good company with a good future. Since leaving high school
I have never been unemployed. I feel that college is important,
but technical skills are the backbone of America.

—Journeyman heavy equipment mechanic

Senior high school students differ significantly in their individual career development and career maturity. Possible reasons for these variances include inconsistent exposure to career developmental tasks in previous grades, inappropriate or inaccurate information delivery service experiences, and the confounding variables of socioeconomic status (SES), class, and minority ethnic group membership. In addition, 30% of senior high school students have had work experience and have developed attitudes toward work and different career areas (Drummond & Ryan, 1995). High school counselors are too often external to the success of adolescents in the world of work. Rather, vocational education, career education programs, and work experience programs are often the primary resources for high school students by providing technical and career counseling.

This chapter presents the primary career developmental tasks of high school populations. In addition, selected aspects of career counseling for these students are included. High school students need to be prepared for the world of work as they enter a period of transition from secondary student to adult citizen.

THE HIGH SCHOOL YEARS: A PERIOD OF TRANSITION

One mission of career guidance and counseling in high schools is to prepare students for their future lives. Secondary education continues the integration of career guidance into the curriculum and provides direct services to help students narrow their career interests and choices. Whereas in middle/junior high schools, students are exposed to activities that enable them to explore current trends in different careers, in senior high schools, school counselors offer numerous services including career interest inventories, aptitude testing, and current occupational information to help students decide about their careers (Schmidt, 1996). During high school years, students' decisions about career choices connect to future educational plans about entering the job market, enrolling in vocational schools for technical training, or attending college after graduation.

Career Development Theories

Ginzberg, Ginsburg, Axelrad, and Herma (1951) identified the period from 11 to 18 years as the tentative period, consisting of the stages of interest, capacity, value, and transition. During their sophomore year, most high school students evolve through the value stage. One of the dominant values in this period is altruism—thinking about the idea of service to society rather than their own needs. Other changes include beginning to be aware that they might choose a career that would use their special skills.

The transition period appears in the junior and senior years. These students begin to realize that they have to make timely, concrete, and realistic vocational decisions. Students are increasingly autonomous and begin to consider the practical aspects of career preparation and decision making.

Super (1969, 1990) labeled this period from 14 to 25 years the exploratory stage with three substages: tentative, transitional, and trial. Adolescence represents the tentative and transitional stages. The developmental tasks during this period are crystallization, specification, implementation, stabilization, and consolidation. Crystallization, the primary career development task of adolescence, is characterized by high school students formulating ideas about work that might be appropriate for them.

High school students begin to explore resources to help them in their decision making and give less time to their hobbies; in short, they develop a realistic self-concept (Super, 1990). The implementation, stabilization, and consolidation stages usually are implemented after high school completion and during the early adulthood period.

The goal of career guidance and career counseling programs is to have individuals attain the proper position on the continuum of vocational development as to their life stage of development and age (Super, 1990). Crites (1978) developed a model to understand the variables affecting a student's degree of career development. He included factors such as the consistency, content, realism, competencies, process, and attitudes of career choice.

Decision Making

The high school years are concerned with making sure students make well thought-out career decisions. This educational stage has been labeled preparation or placement, based on sound decision making. All in-school experiences, not just vocational programs, and out-of-school experiences, such as delivering papers, baby-sitting, and working in restaurants, are preparation for life and career. Many hobbies and sports activities provide valuable career lessons. Students need to be able to make the connection between their studies and their part-time work with their future life or career plans. High school counseling programs that spend disproportionate amounts of time on college admissions to the exclusion of preparation services for work-bound youths are not serving the preparation needs of a large group of students (VanZandt & Hayslip, 1994). In addition, accommodations become necessary for the rapidly changing demographics in this nation. By the year 2030, it is projected that Hispanic youths will have increased by almost 80% to 10 million, African American youths will increase by 14%, and European American youths will decline by 10% (Brindis, 1997).

Characteristics of High School Students.

Adolescence represents a period of rapid changes frequently confounded by confusion and uncertainty (Eccles et al., 1993). High school students experience many transitions, including changing from dependency on parents to autonomous activities and from confiding in parents and significant others to their peers. To become responsible adults, this population must understand their roles and responsibilities in society.

Most adolescents become capable of formal thought, form hypotheses and problems, and engage in complex mental operations (Ginsburg & Operr, 1988). Yet these same adolescents tend to concentrate more on possibilities than realities, and egocentrism (in the form of introspection) continues. Erikson (1968) labeled adolescence *identity versus role confusion*, which is characterized by development of inner assurance and reinforcement by recognition from significant others.

Cosse (1992) concluded that the development for female adolescents is based on interpersonal, empathic relatedness and is driven by both qualities; therefore, they develop empathic understanding. Male adolescents, on the other hand, develop their autonomy by learning to think and stand alone and follow an internalized set of rules applicable to all situations. The differential treatment of male and female adolescents by parents and educators influences their role expectations and career choices

Erikson (1968) stated that occupational choice has a tremendous impact on teenagers' sense of identity—more than any other single factor. The decision is one of the biggest commitments the adolescent has to make, and rapid changes in the job market and technology make this decision even more difficult. Erikson also found that career choice presents such a threat to many adolescents' personal identity that, instead of making a firm commitment and then feeling overwhelmed and unable to act, they may need to take a psychosocial moratorium. The moratorium is a period in which the adolescent does not make a commitment but postpones this decision to a later time. The experience can be positive or negative. If the adolescent uses this time for exploration of possibilities, it might lead to a good choice and positive results. If adolescents cannot resolve their inner conflict, they may develop negative identity and become involved in defiant and destructive behaviors.

CAREER GUIDANCE GOALS FOR HIGH SCHOOLS

The goals of a career guidance program rest on the priority and support the program receives within the state and school district (Drummond & Ryan, 1995). Some high schools support formal and rigid career guidance, whereas others may reflect an informal and voluntary approach. The generating impetus, as in most educational endeavors, is the availability and amount of financial support. An example of one state's commitment to career guidance competencies is seen in the Florida State Department of Education's (1988) Florida Career Guidance Competencies for Grades 9–12. These competencies include the following:

- Developing a marketable skill
- Making decisions and choosing alternatives in planning and pursuing educational and career goals
- Understanding the interrelationship of life roles and careers
- Understanding the continuous changes in male and female roles and how they relate to career decision

- Applying skills to revise the students' career plan
- Understanding the relationships between educational achievement and career planning, training, and placement
- Using positive attitudes toward work and learning
- Researching, evaluating, and interpreting information about career opportunities
- Locating, obtaining, maintaining, and advancing in a job
- Understanding how societal needs and functions influence the nature and structure of work

High school students need to be encouraged to compile a career portfolio during their secondary experience. The portfolio should contain the following items (adapted from Drummond & Ryan, 1995):

- School activities: all clubs, offices held, honors and awards received, and athletic participation
- Hobbies and leisure activities
- Abilities, skills, and/or special talents (out of school). Profiles from the Armed Services Vocational Aptitude Battery (ASVAB), Pre-Scholastic Achievement Text (PSAT), Scholastic Achievement Test (SAT), American College Test (ACT), and other tests
- Work experience: type of part-time jobs held during summer or during school hours—paid, volunteer, or credit
- Educational courses completed
- Career plans and information received about vocational programs at the high school level, business education, work study programs, and so on
- Record of interviews held with the school counselor and nonconfidential topics discussed
- Brochures, catalogs of postsecondary schools reviewed
- Completed resume

Another necessary goal of an effective secondary career guidance program is the implementation of a career education needs assessment. Needs assessments are more reliable and informative if they are considered before sampling student needs. In addition, these needs surveys should be conducted annually to ensure the reflection of current career opportunities. School counselors also need to concentrate on the career areas available within the local community as most students stay in or return to their home areas. Community and parents need to be involved in any needs assessments for schools their children attend. Figure 5.1 presents some sample items that are typically included on a career education needs assessment for high school students.

Figure 5.1
Career Guidance Needs Assessment

Directions: Circle the number of the item you would like to know more about or have more experience in doing. If a parent or community leader, respond according to your thoughts relative to the career needs of students in your community.

1. Learn how to function more effectively in small groups.
2. Learn appropriate social skills needed for group activities.
3. Improve students' ability in self-control.
4. Show respect for others.
5. Learn to modify my value system based on feedback from interpersonal relationships.
6. Learn to demonstrate knowledge and skills of societal interdependence.
7. Locate and use available resources for reaching students' potential.
8. Learn how to improve students' educational performance so that they will able to attain their educational and career plans.
9. Learn strategies on how to cope with success as well as failure.
10. Acquire knowledge of steps necessary for entry into postsecondary educational and training programs.
11. Evaluate personal assets and limitations for meeting requirements for postsecondary education and training programs.
12. Understand how education relates to entering the job market.
13. Accept lifetime learning as a way of life.
14. Attain skills to change and adapt to constantly changing requirements for occupations.
15. Learn general skills that can apply to a variety of occupations.
16. Study the positive contributions all occupations make to society.
17. Understand the relationship between occupational roles and lifestyles.
18. Learn how the requirements of entry-level occupations are related to students' high school program of study.
19. Understand and make use of available handbooks and materials published by national, state, and local agencies and commercial publishers on jobs, careers, and so forth.
20. Learn the different clusters/systems of classifying jobs and know what jobs are included in each cluster.
21. Design a workable guide for beginning the formulation of goals and plans that reflect the ability to locate, evaluate, and interpret information about career/ vocational opportunities.
22. Learn more effective time management skills.
23. Identify alternative courses of action in a given decision-making situation.

School counselors should remember to be alert to the variables of ethnicity, class, gender, and conditions of disability in both their career guidance competencies and career guidance needs assessments. These factors are too often overlooked in the process of implementing a career guidance program. School counselors need to be proactive rather than reactive in their career guidance program endeavors.

COUNSELING IMPLICATIONS
FOR THE HIGH SCHOOL COUNSELOR

High school counselors are mandated to address students' career education and development through the 12th grade. In some instances, they may even continue beyond. Moreover, they must accomplish this task from developmental perspectives. Something to Consider 5.1 presents samples of Grades 10–12 career goals and competencies for a developmentally focused school counseling program.

Studies of the high school counselor's role indicate that career planning is a vital component of secondary programs. This function includes guidance and counseling processes to help students assess their strengths, weaknesses, and interests and choose educational and

---

Something to Consider 5.1
Sample of Grades 10–12 Career Goals and Competencies

Overall Goals
- Become aware of personal characteristics, interests, aptitudes, and skills
- Develop an awareness of and respect for the diversity of the world of work
- Understand the relationship between school performance and future choices
- Develop a positive attitude toward work

Competencies
Tenth-grade students will be able to:
- Clarify the role of personal values in career choice
- Distinguish educational and skill requirements for areas or careers of interest
- Recognize the effects of job or career choice on other areas of life
- Begin realistic assessment of their potential in various fields
- Develop skills in prioritizing needs related to career planning

Eleventh-grade students will be able to:
- Refine future career goals through synthesis of information concerning self, use of resources, and consultation with others
- Coordinate class selection with career goals
- Identify specific educational requirements necessary to achieve their goals
- Clarify their own values as they relate to work and leisure

Twelfth-grade students will be able to:
- Complete requirements for transition from high school
- Make final commitments to a career plan
- Understand the potential for change in their own interests or values related to work
- Understand the potential for change within the job market
- Understand career development as a life-long process
- Accept responsibility for their own career directions

SOURCE: From *Developmental School Counseling Programs: From Theory to Practice*, by P. O. Paisley and G. T. Hubbard, 1994, pp. 218–221. Copyright by the American Counseling Association. Reprinted with permission.

career plans that are compatible with these characteristics. Schmidt (1996) recommended that school counselors use individual and group conferences at each grade level so students have the opportunity to check their progress, evaluate life goals, and set new objectives. They are preventive services planned to help students stay on track and in school. These services also urge students to seek higher goals than what they may have planned initially. Frequently, the information they have about themselves, the world of work, future employment patterns, and educational opportunities is limited, outdated, or simply inaccurate. Holding annual conferences with counselors is one way to acquire current, accurate information. Something to Consider 5.2 offers a sample planning form to use with students.

In the effective and appropriate delivery of career development to high school students (and to a lesser extent other grade levels), two important areas of concerns can negatively affect a smooth process: dropout prevention and teenage pregnancy. These subjects deserve some comment in this chapter.

Dropout Rates

Another role that school counselors play involves the identification and prevention of dropouts, or as many knowledgeable educators prefer, pushouts. High dropout rates are differentiated by ethnic group, culture, and SES. For example, the percentage of Hispanic dropouts is almost double that of African Americans (34% to 18%), and 40% of all female school dropouts cite pregnancy or marriage as the reason for leaving (Brindis, 1997). Most of the career development strategies by school counselors can also serve as dropout preventive measures. For example, high dropout rates for students with Realistic interests is consistent with Holland's (1996) hypothesis that students with Realistic codes have a greater difficulty adjusting to the typical school environment, which is often dominated by an emphasis on cognitive achievement.

Findings from Hurlburt, Schulz, and Eide's (1985) study with Native American Indian high school students, using Holland's (1970) Self-Directed Search, showed that Native American Indian female high school students were at a higher risk of leaving school than were the male students, especially female students with Realistic and Social interests. School counselors suggest that many female students with outdoor and mechanical preferences seemed out of place with the curricula offerings and the social climate. Furthermore, many female students with high Social interest seemed to perceive pressure to pursue domestic and family activities and leave school early. Research Emphasis 5.1 offers additional insights into preventing dropout rates for Native American Indian high school students.

Something to Consider 5.2
Sample Student Career Planning Form

Littlefield High School

Student Planning Form

Student _____   Date _____

My Career Interests:

1. _____

2. _____

My Long-Term Educational Goal: _____

Course Work Needed to Realize My Goal:

	Courses Taken	Year Completed	Final Grade
Communication Skills	_____	_____	_____
Technical Reading	_____	_____	_____
Literature	_____	_____	_____
Foreign Language	_____	_____	_____
Mathematics	_____	_____	_____
Statistics and Logic	_____	_____	_____
Sciences	_____	_____	_____
Social Studies	_____	_____	_____
Art/Music/Drama	_____	_____	_____
Vocational Courses	_____	_____	_____
Other Courses	_____	_____	_____

Extracurricular Experience _____

My Planning Conferences With Counselor(s) (or Teacher/Advisors):

Date	Decisions/Plans	Counselor or Teacher
_____	_____	_____
_____	_____	_____
_____	_____	_____
_____	_____	_____

Postsecondary Tasks I Need to Accomplish (college applications, scholarship applications, entrance exams, job interviews, resume writing, etc.)

Task	Date Completed
_____	_____
_____	_____
_____	_____

SOURCE: From *Counseling in Schools: Essential Services and Comprehensive Programs* (2nd ed.), by J. J. Schmidt, 1996, p. 231. Copyright 1996 by Allyn & Bacon. Adapted with permission.

Research Emphasis 5.1
Dropout Prevention and the Self-Directed Search: Native American Indian Students

Gade, Hurlburt, and Fuqua (1992) using Holland's (1970) Self-Directed Search, studied 596 (321 female, 275 male) Native American Indian high school students in eight high schools in the province of Manitoba, Canada. This sample included 103 female and 65 male dropouts. The sample represented three typical models of Native American Indian education in this region: four residential board attending with European Canadian students from the area; two provincial controlled schools; and two locally controlled. Both gender groups had a 10th-grade median grade level with a mean age of 16.2 years for female students and 16.4 years for male students. The faculty ranged from 50% with Native heritage in the locally controlled schools to 10% in the residential schools.

Results:
- Overall dropout rates were 32.1% for female students and 23.6% for male students over one year only
- Above-average dropout rates were recorded for female students with Realistic and Social interest preferences
- Both female and male students with Enterprising preferences had above-average dropout rates
- Almost half of all female students with Realistic preferences dropped out
- The lowest dropout rates were recorded for female students with Investigative preferences (21.1%) and male students with Conventional preferences (0.0%)

Suggestions to Increase Retention Rates:
1. Female students, in general, are a higher risk than male students to leave school. School counselors can help female students to identify interests as early as possible.
2. The total student body in these schools had a narrow concentration among the six categories. School counselors can use exploratory career units, more elective courses, work study programs, and job shadowing experiences.
3. Small-group guidance programs need to emphasize self-exploration and values clarification.
4. Exit and follow-up interviews are encouraged for all school leavers (Larsen & Shertzer, 1987).

SOURCE: From "The Use of the Self-Directed Search to Identify American Indian High School Dropouts," by E. M. Gade, G. Hurlburt, and D. Fuqua, 1992, *The School Counselor, 39*, 311–315. Copyright by American Counseling Association. Adapted with permission.

Whelage and Rutter (1986) used data from High School and Beyond, a longitudinal survey of approximately 30,000 sophomores from 1,105 public and private high schools nationwide, to study student alienation and rejection of school. One of the variables in their analysis was teacher interest in students.

When those who eventually became dropouts were asked to rate Teacher Interest in Students on a 4.0 scale, marks of fair to poor were given by 56% of the Hispanics, 50% of the Blacks, and 59% of the whites. Non-college-bound students were not much more positive, in view of the fair-to-poor ratings given by each racial group (Hispanics 49%, Blacks 47%, and whites 49%). (p. 380)

Whelage and Rutter (1986) also looked at the locus of control and self-esteem of students before and after they dropped out and compared these attributes with those of peers who continued on to graduation and beyond. They found that dropouts began with slightly higher self-esteem than the non-college-bound who stayed in school and that the dropouts actually increased the differential over time. The overall increase in self-esteem in dropouts matched that of the highest group, the college-bound. For at-risk students, it seems, school can actually inhibit personal growth. Dropping out of school apparently had beneficial effects on the self-images of these students. Almost certainly, such school-related contributors as lack of positive, cooperative relationships involving students, staff, parents, and administrators affect students' school performance and their decision to drop out (Testerman, 1996).

To combat school dropout, Brindis (1997, pp. 8–9) suggested several intervention programs:

1. Implement transition programs to assist students between elementary to middle school and middle school to high school.
2. Increase efforts to identify students at risk of leaving school prematurely.
3. Work closely with families to increase the overall number of students who stay in traditional schools or who are enrolled in other meaningful educational and job-training opportunities.
4. Develop outreach programs in work sites, recreational programs, churches, and through the media to reach dropouts to promote access to educational, counseling, and employment services.
5. Develop or expand programs that provide access to postsecondary education.
6. Develop community partnerships among businesses, schools, churches, community-based organizations, and parents.
7. Promote skills in decision making and goal setting to enable youths to explore an expanded range of life opportunities.

The dropout data presented in this discussion may appear overly negative to those who purport that dropout rates are decreasing. In fact, the U.S. Department of Education and various education commentators maintain that dropout rates have been decreasing for African Americans and the school population as a whole (National Center for Educational Statistics, 1995). Unfortunately, multiple definitions of the term *dropout* among states and school systems, inaccurate reporting, and a lack of standardized reporting procedures make it difficult to know for sure whether this assertion is true. In fact, there is disturbing evidence that, in some settings at least, dropout rates are higher than are generally acknowledged and may be rising (Fossey, 1996). Indeed, as a whole, the United States has made virtually no progress in improving on-time graduation rates since the 1970s (National Center for Education Statistics, 1995). To ensure more efficacious dropout information, public education needs a single, easily understood, and reliable indicator of student attrition, one that would allow comparisons to be made among school districts in different states (Fossey, 1996).

Teenage Pregnancy

"I never expected to have a baby at 15," says a high school Native American Indian sophomore. "It just sort of happened." After her boyfriend broke up with her, she briefly considered abortion but decided to keep her baby. Now she struggles to care for her 11-month-old son and to finish school.

This story is not rare or unusual. Each year in the United States, 10% of girls ages 15 to 19 years conceive (Yawn & Yawn, 1997). Slightly more than one third of these teens choose elective abortions, 13% miscarry, and 56% deliver their children. Of those who do deliver, 95% choose to keep their child within its family of origin. Adolescent pregnancy is not new, but teen marriage and parenting are not consistent with many of today's expectations such as high school graduation and postsecondary education for both young men and women. Adolescent pregnancy is not unique to any ethnic group or geographic area.

The rate of sexual activity in unmarried teenagers is affected by SES, ethnic factors, parental education level, family support, perceived life choices, and strength of religious beliefs in the community (Brindis, 1997; MacFarland, 1993; Yawn & Yawn, 1997). These factors and ethnic illustrations warrant brief attention.

SES. Poverty is the factor most strongly related to teen pregnancy (Yawn & Yawn, 1997). Where youths live is important in determining the age and the circumstances of initiation of sexual intercourse. The poverty rate among Hispanic youths ages 6 to 17 years is 35.2%, compared with 41.9% among African Americans and 13.5% among European Americans (Brindis, 1997). African American, European American, or Hispanic young women with below-average academic skills coming from families with below-poverty incomes are about five times more likely to be teenage mothers than those with solid skills and above-average family incomes (Brindis, 1997).

Parental education.   Only 40% of Hispanic teens live in families headed by a parent with a high school diploma, compared with 66% of African American adolescents and 80% of European American adolescents (Brindis, 1997). The more years of education a mother completes, the older her daughter is likely to be at her first sexual intercourse (Postrado, Weiss, & Nicholson, 1997).

Family support.   Two reports have indicated that family support for teenage mothers is very different for African American and Hispanic American youths (Brindis, 1997). African American girls generally are encouraged to return to school, whereas Hispanic girls are viewed as having entered the realm of motherhood with primary responsibilities for the home rather than finishing their education.

Among adolescents who became pregnant purposely, researchers have delineated one subtype that tends to be influenced by a culture that accepts and may even reward early pregnancy. Interviews with African American adolescent mothers in a low-income section of the Washington, D.C., area revealed that their pregnancies were almost always intended and desired (MacFarland, 1997). In this group, early pregnancies were common and were modeled by mothers, aunts, and peers; and it was generally assured that extended families would help in caring for the children. Early childbearing among Hispanics appears to be strongly related to limited perceived life options.

Perceived life choices.   Studies suggest that pregnant adolescents differ from nonpregnant adolescents in lower educational motivation and a tendency to be more impulsive (MacFarland, 1997). Female teenagers with high educational expectations are less likely to initiate sexual intercourse and the least likely to "go steady" (Postrado et al., 1997). Although African American teenage girls have higher educational aspirations than their peers of other ethnicities, they also have a more positive attitude toward teen pregnancy (Postrado et al., 1997). For example, the career options listed by African American women are fewer than those of European American women at all socioeconomic levels and may influence desire for earlier motherhood. Rural communities often have the fewest visible career options for all adolescents. Increasing the awareness of career and educational choices may help in delaying sexual intercourse.

Religious values.   The presence of strong religious beliefs (not merely church attendance) has been shown to delay the age of initiation of sexual activity (Yawn & Yawn, 1997). These beliefs and perceived career opportunities may influence the ethnic variations in onset of sexual activity.

An estimated 513,000 teenagers in the United States gave birth in 1995. Public officials, clergy, educators, parents, and policymakers have explored the controversial question of why so many teenage girls end up pregnant. Actually, the rate of teenage pregnancies in this nation, though still among the highest in the industrialized world, is declining, according to the National Center for Health Statistics (Chassler, 1997). In 1995, about 57 of every 1,000 teenage girls gave birth—down from 68 per 1,000 in 1970 and an even higher number in the 1950s. "Many more teenagers were having babies back in the Ozzie and Harriet days," says Susan Newcomer of the Center for Population Research at the National Institutes of Health. "The difference is that, back then, pregnant teens got married. Now most don't" (Chassler, 1997, p. 4). Teenage girls give birth to 13% of the babies born in this nation, representing almost a third of all unmarried mothers. Research Emphasis 5.2 presents additional ethnic demographic data.

Of particular concern to career development, a recent survey offered responses from 720 girls ages 12 to 19 years about what unwed teens should do if they get pregnant (Chassler, 1997). More than half (55%) said that unwed teenage girls should keep their babies; 36% said

---

Research Emphasis 5.2
Adolescent Pregnancy: Sociocultural and Ethnic Factors

- African American teens are twice as likely to be sexually active as European American teens.
- Birth rates are higher among African American teens than European American teens.
- Isolated African American communities have a higher proportion of teenagers who have engaged in sexual intercourse than well-integrated, ethnically mixed communities.
- African American adolescents initiate intercourse at a younger age than European American adolescents irrespective of socioeconomic status.
- African American young women are twice as likely as their European American counterparts to use prescription contraceptives.
- Hispanic American adolescents are more likely to be sexually active than European American teens, but they are also more likely to be married.
- Almost half (49%) of never-married Hispanic American girls ages 15–19 years report they had experienced sexual intercourse, compared with 61% of African American girls and 52% of European American girls.
- Fifty-four percent of both Hispanic and African American teens ages 15–19 who become sexually active use contraception at first intercourse, compared with 69% of European American teens.
- Only 27% of young Hispanic Americans who gave birth during their teen years completed high school by their mid-20s compared with 67% among African Americans and 55% among European Americans.
- European American adolescents report the use of coitus interruptus three times as often as African American adolescents.

SOURCE: From Yawn and Yawn (1997) and Brindis (1997).

they should marry the father. If unwed teens do not want their babies, 82% said these girls should put their babies up for adoption; 24% said they should have abortions. About 90% said the fathers of these babies should be forced to pay child support. But 60% disagreed with the statement "unmarried teen mothers should not be allowed to get welfare." The majority of the girls felt this way, regardless of their race, income, or educational level or whether they came from a single-parent or two-parent family.

These data have important implications for high school counselors in their career development programs. Regardless of the students' SES, high schools have to include in their career development delivery services opportunities for these young girls to plan for a future in the world of work. Many urban, comprehensive high schools already provide pre- and postnatal health and child-care services for this population. In some situations, the fathers have access for parenting and child-care classes as well. Such programs allow these teen parents to attend regular classes and not have to worry about babysitters and nursery school expenses. Nevertheless, smaller schools cannot afford such services and their students may be the ones who "fall through the cracks."

Chassler (1997) cited sociologist Kristin Luker's astute analogy:

> Having a baby is a lottery ticket for many teenagers. It brings with it at least the dream of something better, and if the dream fails, not much is lost. If America cares about its young people, it must make them feel that they have a rich array of choices, so that having a baby is not the only or most attractive one on the horizon. (p. 5)

Research Emphasis 5.3 presents survey results relating to what teenage girls say about preventing teen pregnancy.

Military Options

The role of the school counselor in working with high school students interested in a military service career and the role of military recruiters in schools have been researched (Ciborowski, 1978, 1980). What have been obscured by the career and employment emphases of in-school military recruiter are three fundamental issues: (a) the basic role of the military, (b) discriminatory recruitment policies of the military in regard to gay and lesbian soldiers, and (c) sexual harassment of women (Ciborowski, 1994).

The American School Counselor Association's (1984a) position statement recognized that "the relationship between the military recruiter and the school counselor is a potential source of conflict" (p. 73) and suggested that counselors "explore both positive and negative aspects of military . . . options" (p. 74). Counselors have the re-

---

Research Emphasis 5.3
What Teenage Girls Say About Preventing Teen Pregnancy

This survey was conducted among girls ages 12 to 19 in March 1996. The overall sample was selected to conform to the latest available U.S. Census data for the nine geographical divisions and within each division by annual household income and size. Of the 1,148 questionnaires mailed, 720 were completed and returned, representing a response rate of 62.7%. The results are accurate to within ±3.7% at the 95% level of confidence.

- 97% said "having parents they can talk to" could help prevent pregnancies and 93% said "having loving parents" reduces the risk.

- 96% said "having self-respect" and "being informed about sex, pregnancy and birth control" are critical to preventing pregnancy.

- 96% said the most influential deterrent was "being aware of the responsibility of caring for a child."

- 93% said knowing how condoms were used and being satisfied with life lower the risk; 91% cited carefully choosing boyfriends and always using contraceptives.

- 86% said they knew a teen who had been pregnant; 9 out of 10 girls had the baby.

- 80% said having a baby would have a negative effect on a girl's life.

- 66% said pregnancy among unmarried teens was a problem in their community; 87% said more had to be done to prevent adolescent pregnancy.

- 52%, among those age 12 to 15, said not dating older men reduces the risk.

- 6% said they have been pregnant. Most (69%) kept it, whereas 22% had an abortion. None gave up the baby for adoption and 9% did not respond to the question.

SOURCE: From "What Teenage Girls Say About Pregnancy," by S. Chassler, 1997 (February 2), *Parade Magazine*, pp. 4–5. Copyright 1997 by Parade Publications. Reprinted with permission.

sponsibility to explore all issues as part of any student's decision to enter military service. Group settings, in particular, are an ideal vehicle for raising such lifestyle issues (Ciborowski, 1994; Jepsen, Dustin, & Miars, 1982). Counselors provide a balance between the needs of the recruiters to have access to students and the students' needs to have unbiased facts for making informed decisions (Ciborowski, 1994).

Easing the Transition

Graduating seniors continue to reflect the developmental tasks of seeking autonomy and developing a personal identity. Undecided about further schooling, college, or employment, seniors seek much of their advice from one another instead of from adults (Hoppock, 1976). During this period of transition between high school and college or work life, many senior students, especially cultural and ethnic minority students, need career-oriented programs that address not only the need for factual information but also their emotional needs (O'Dell & Eisenberg, 1989).

High school counselors are also cautioned to remember that many high school students do not display difficulty in making appropriate career decisions. For example, L. K. Jones (1993) studied 221 11th graders (48% male, 52% female) with a mean age of 16.5 years. This sample's ethnic composition was 68.1% European American, 30% African American, and 1.9% other. The students were administered the self-scoring version of the Career Decision-Making System (CDMS; Harrington & O'Shea, 1982) and the Career Key (CK; L. K. Jones, 1990). The majority of the students reported that they had learned about occupations, developed a clearer idea about possible occupations for themselves, learned about themselves, and been encouraged to learn about occupations. Neither the CDMS nor the CK stimulated career development. This result might indicate that the students were apparently already quite active in seeking out vocational information. Nevertheless, this study indicated that the use of these instruments can help school counselors determine how well they are meeting their program objectives and make necessary adjustments.

Parker (1992) suggested a series of informal sessions for senior students only. These sessions are co-led by college professors and business professionals. The college professors provide insight on programs of study for particular majors; the business professionals discuss the need for a solid educational foundation. For example, a seminar on financial aid information is provided by each college, university, and business school participating in the career day at the close of the seminars.

Several goals may be at least partially met through Parker's (1992) Career Seminars for Seniors intervention concept:

1. Factual information is provided on desired occupations.
2. Students are assisted in matching postsecondary education programs to their goals.
3. Motivation is provided for decision making and process guidelines are supplied.
4. Anxiety over new social and academic rules is reduced.
5. Channels of communication are opened between students and school counselors.

Personality Type and Educational Satisfaction

Holland (1996) hypothesized that satisfaction with an educational environment is related to specific personality types. The more congruence there is between a student's personality type and the educational environment, the more satisfying student–teacher interactions will be. Holland's hypothesis has been tested with high school students and has yielded mixed results. For example, Hearn and Moos (1978) found support for the characteristics attributed to the environmental models with Investigative classes emphasizing teacher control and a task orientation while deemphasizing involvement and affiliation. Likewise, Werner (1974) found congruence with school environments related to satisfaction for male students but not for female students. For selected definitions of the environment, Cole (1975) found that student satisfaction with the high school environment was correlated in a weak positive direction with actual school satisfaction.

Holland's (1970) Self-Directed Search (SDS) is one example of the incorporation of Holland's typology for appraisal use. The SDS is a self-administered, self-scored, and self-interpreted vocational counseling tool. A three-letter occupational code is obtained to match with suitable occupations. Scores are totaled for activities, competencies, occupations, and self-estimates. These scores are totaled for a summary of six personality types: Realistic, Investigative, Artistic, Social, Enterprising, and Conventional. The SDS has been found useful across age, gender, class, and ethnic variables.

For example, Native American Indian students need considerable career and vocational guidance. In general, Native American Indian students appear to aspire to occupations visible on or near their reservations (Hurlburt, Schulz, & Eide, 1985). Substantial studies have indicated that tests and assessment tools normed on non-Native American Indians may be unreliable for Native American Indian students. For example, Haviland and Hanson (1987) found that the Strong–Campbell Interest Inventory (D. P. Campbell & Hanson, 1981) has only adequate validity for Native American Indian college students. In addition, academic achievement deficit in reading may influence ability to answer questions on tests. Listening and reading skills have been found to handicap academic progress in many Native American Indian students. For example, in one school system 43.4% of the students were functioning at one or more years below expected grade level. Research Emphasis 5.4 presents a study of Native American Indian students and vocational counseling.

Employment and the Job Search

Many high school students do not consider postsecondary education as a viable option. For whatever reason, these students desire immediate employment. School counselors must meet these students' needs just as unbiasedly as the concerns of students opting for postsecondary educational experiences are addressed. Realistically, however, students must be informed of the potential vertical movement and advancement limitations inherent in employment not requiring some technical training. Frequently, these students express irrational expectations in the job-

Research Emphasis 5.4
Using the Self-Directed Search With Native American Indian High School Students

Research was conducted on 75 Treaty Indian high school students from Manitoba and Ontario in Canada. They attended local public high schools and were administered the Self-Directed Search (SDS). Cree was the first language for 60% and English for 20%. Ages ranged from 15 to 22 years. The SDS was administered separately to male and female students. Students scored and found their code in the Canadian Edition of the Occupational Finder. Retesting occurred 3 months later for the 52 students who had not dropped out of school.

Significant stability occurred on all scales except for Social for female students. The median retest reliability of the SDS was .72 for male and .61 for female students. The absence of English as the first language did not appear to influence retest reliability. The researchers did recommend additional testing with larger samples.

SOURCE: From "Using the Self-Directed Search With American Indian High School Students," by G. Hurlburt, W. Schulz, and L. Eide, 1985, *Journal of American Indian Education, 25*(1), pp. 34–41. Copyright by the Center for Indian Education, College of Education, Arizona State University, Tempe. Adapted with permission.

search process (Liptak, 1989). The following irrational expectations must be addressed, and students must be taught to defeat these expectations.

The perfect plan. One irrational expectation may be the belief that an individual must have a "perfect" job-search plan. The school counselor should challenge the student to develop a plan, stress that no one best method exists, and explain that people seldom if ever obtain everything they desire.

A one-time activity. A second irrational expectation may be the belief that the job-search process is a one-time event. The counselor should stress that the job search is an ongoing developmental process and teach the student job-hunting skills that will be used again.

Counselors as expert job finders. Many students have the expectation that the counselor is an expert who will find them a job. The school counselor demonstrates to the student that they teach job-hunting skills and help appraise the student's skills and abilities. The counselor must also stress that the student is the one in control.

Rejection blues. Students often expect that it will be catastrophic if they get rejected for a job opportunity. The counselor intervenes by acknowledging that being rejected is unpleasant but not catastrophic unless students think it is and by showing students that they can allow themselves to get upset and depressed. The counselor explains that rejection is a reality and cannot be changed. The student can talk with employers that rejected them for feedback and to understand that the rejection is not personal.

Job-search nerves.   Some students also expect the job-search process to be nerve-racking and filled with anxiety. In this case, the school counselor stresses that the worst thing about being unemployed is exaggerated beliefs of unemployment. The counselor demonstrates that worrying about finding a job only aggravates the problem. The student needs to explore satisfaction in another life role.

An excellent resource recommended for high school and career counselors is *Getting It Together, The Practical Job Search* (Munch, 1993). This resource is an updated collection of pertinent materials for students to consider before they even look for a job. A good job search involves numerous areas: application resume, letter of application, interview skill development and practice, thank you letter, and the process of a job search. This guide is presented in a working three-ring binder, allowing for individual personalization.

Appraisal Resources

Numerous strategies and interventions are available for the high school counselor to consider. One valuable resource is *Helping Your Child Choose a Career* (Otto, 1996). This revised edition is written in easy-to-read style while reporting accurate, current findings on both educational and occupational trends bearing on the kinds of career options available to today's youths. The many subtopics in each chapter will be helpful to both parents and students who have questions about the present and projected picture of factors affecting the occupational society. The discussion of occupations and jobs provides a helpful set of ways to consider "work" as part of total lifestyle. This resource also presents a well-organized set of recommendations for high school youths planning to attend a 4-year college or university. Perhaps, most important, Otto confronts the fact that most high school youths seeking to compete in the emerging information-oriented, high-skills career society must seriously consider enrolling in some form of postsecondary education. Table 5.1 lists the more commonly used appraisal instruments for high school students. The reader is cautioned to select multicultural appraisal tools that meet the criteria of Chapter 12.

SUMMARY

As this chapter has demonstrated, numerous ethnic youths believe life has nothing to offer them other than a dead end and no where to go. In addition, things will probably get worse. These youths express feelings of futility, and their voices are filled with a tone of sorrow. In short, they have reached a sense of apathy. To counter these negative perspectives, school counselors need to help these students discover

Table 5.1
Appraisal Instruments to Measure Aptitudes, Interests, and Values

Title	Description	Publisher
Armed Services Vocational Aptitude Battery	Evaluates vocational interests and aptitudes	Department of Defense
ACT Assessment Program	Measures academic achievement and used to help students develop postsecondary plans	American College Testing Program
Differential Aptitude Test	Assesses aptitude in eight areas for educational vocational guidance purposes	Psychological Corporation
COPSystem Aptitude Battery	Quick measure of eight aptitudes	Psychological Corporation
Career Maturity Inventory	Measures attitudes and competencies related to career decisions	CTB/McGraw-Hill Career
Orientation Placement and Evaluation (COPES)	Assesses personal values related to work	Educational Testing Service
Work Values Inventory	Measures 15 intrinsic and extrinsic values inherent to work	Riverside Publishing
Career Assessment	Contains 22 interest scales and 91 occupational scales	National Computer Systems
COPSystem Interest and Inventory	Assesses interests in professional and skilled job clusters	Educational Industrial Testing Service
Harrington–O'Shea Career Decision Making	Measures interests and abilities of students	American Guidance Service
Jackson Vocational Interest Survey	Gives a profile of interest in 10 areas	Research Psychologist Press
Kuder Preference Record, Vocational	Assesses interests in 10 general areas	Science Research Associates
Occupational Aptitude Survey and Interest Schedule	Measures aptitudes and interests of high school students for various occupations	PRO-ED
Ohio Vocational Interest Survey	Measures vocational and occupational interests	Psychological Corporation

some personal meaning in life to cultivate dreams and develop the means to turn those dreams into reality (Nystul, 1993). In conjunction with social and personal counseling, the school counselor needs to ensure that these youths are provided the most appropriate career development interventions possible. This focus, together with positive academic and career experiences, will go far to help alleviate the hopelessness and helplessness manifested by this population.

Testerman (1996) stated the situation most astutely when she wrote:

> A high school may provide the best instruction in the world, but if a segment of the school population is not present physically or is feeling alienated or absent mentally, of what value is excellent pedagogy? Secondary schools can no longer limit themselves to the cognitive realm and ignore the affective domain. They must attend to both head and heart, especially with those students who find school a less-than-appealing place to learn. (p. 365)

And, of course, these comments can also include school counselors and their career development programs.

EXPERIENTIAL ACTIVITIES

1. Collect career guidance guidelines and models from your state and local school systems. Compare the goals and objectives and the type of activities suggested. What are the common features? What are the unique features?
2. Interview several high school teachers at your school and find out if they infuse career education into their teaching. What are some of their innovative ideas?
3. Interview high school students who are currently employed part time or full time. What are their thoughts about their working experience? What do they see as the advantages and disadvantages of their work experience? How have their educational experiences prepared them for the world of work?
4. What are your experiences relating to military recruiters in schools?

Part III
Career Applications for Student Populations

PART III ADDRESSES CAREER DEVELOPMENT and its applicability to various multicultural groups. Chapter 6 presents discussion relevant to major gender issues in career development. Chapter 7 emphasizes the appropriateness of career development when considering ethnic minority students. Chapter 8 highlights career development issues among a rising student population: gay, lesbian, bisexual, and transgender students. Chapter 9 discusses career development concerns among special needs populations. Chapter 10 concludes this part with a perspective on the family and its influences on the career development of students.

6

Gender Issues in Career Development

We make too much of it;

we are men and women in the second place,

human beings in the first.

Olive Schreiner

Gender, a final dimension of diversity, also affects learning and career development. Visit any kindergarten class and observe how students' choices of toys are influenced by gender. Enter a junior-or senior-level math class, and the likely scene will depict a disproportionately low number of female students. Although awareness and sensitivity are changing some of these trends, some researchers continue to believe that schools shortchange girls (Sadker & Sadker, 1994).

Title IX of the Education Amendments Act of 1972 was designed to correct the biased treatment male and female students received in school. Some provisions that protect students from gender bias also restrict the rights of educators to decide for themselves how to respond to certain gender issues. Title IX requires schools to provide equal educational opportunities to all students regardless of gender and serves as the main legal basis for efforts to eliminate gender-discriminatory educational practices. Fischer and Sorenson (1991) noted some specific aspects of this act:

- Students may not be denied admission to schools or subjected to discriminatory admissions practices on the basis of their gender.
- Once admitted, students may not be excluded from participation in, be denied benefits of, or be subjected to discrimination while participating in any academic, extracurricular, research, occupational training, or other educational program or activity.

- All courses and activities, except human sexuality courses, must be open to all students regardless of their gender. If offered, human sexuality courses must be available to all students, but they can be taught separately to male and female students.
- Standards for student participation in physical education activities and ability groupings within these activities must be objective and applied equally to all students regardless of gender. Separate athletic teams may be provided for male and female students for contact sports or for other sports when the separation is justified by differences in skills. However, if a school has a contact sport for male students only, a noncontact alternative team sport for female students must be provided.
- Dress codes must be applied equally to male and female students.
- Graduation requirements must be the same for both genders.
- Textbooks and other instructional materials are exempted from Title IX regulations because of potential conflicts with freedom of speech rights guaranteed by the First Amendment and other legislation.

GENDER DISPARITIES

A great deal of individual variability exists within any group; nevertheless, a few *average* differences between groups do occur with some consistency. Male and female students are similar in terms of academic and physical ability, but they differ somewhat in terms of achievement, motivation, self-esteem, explanations for success and failure, and expectations for themselves (Ormrod, 1995). Gender disparities are probably largely environmental in origin. Teachers and school counselors should hold equally high expectations for both genders and ensure that both genders have equal educational opportunities.

Numerous factors contribute to the gender differences observed in career development interventions in school settings. For example, male and female students are exposed to gender-biased career information. In addition, gender bias exists in textbooks, the unequal amounts of attention and different kinds of feedback and encouragement they receive from their teachers, the gender segregation they experience, and so on. Bias against students in school also occurs as a result of the interplay between the ways in which teachers and counselors relate to students in terms of ethnic groups, socioeconomic classes, and gender groups. Because schools play a significant role in creating and maintaining gender differences, school personnel need to be committed to the view that bias against any student for any reason is undesirable and needs to be eliminated. This chapter examines the school's role in the creation and maintenance of gender differences in students' achievement and participation in school settings. The primary emphases are administrative imbalance, curriculum materials, teacher instructional style, courses and activities, gender segregation and separation, encouragement of behavior differences, and intolerance of male behavior patterns. Something to Consider 6.1 provides three examples of gender disparities in schools.

Administrative Imbalance

Although women comprise the majority of classroom teachers, they are grossly underrepresented in administrative positions (H. Grossman, 1995). In 1990, 83% of the nation's school principals and superintendents were male and the majority of these, 75%, were European American men ("SUNY study," 1990). This situation conveys the message to students that men, especially European American men, are and should be authorities. Concurrently, a potential career area is inappropriately maligned.

Curriculum Materials

Although curriculum materials that students currently use are not as sexist as the materials used in classes in the 1960s and 1970s, they continue to introduce society's gender biases into the school's structure

---

Something to Consider 6.1
Gender Disparities in Schools: Examples

It is not always easy to apply a set of principles to a real-life situation when some of the principles that apply to a specific situation appear to lead to apparently contradictory solutions to the problem. Note the following examples.

1. After raising her hand repeatedly to volunteer answers to her math teacher's questions without being called on, a sixth-grade student complains that her teacher is unfair because the teacher always calls on the boys to answer the difficult questions. The teacher does not believe she is correct.
2. A male Native American Indian 10th grader in a predominantly poor neighborhood school tells his counselor in no uncertain terms to get off his case and stop telling him about the value of a high school diploma. He insists that a high school diploma does not help Native American Indians. The counselor tells the student he is wrong. The next day the student brings in some articles that confirm that Native American Indian male students who graduate high school do not earn significantly more than those who do not.
3. A counselor overhears two African American seniors say they plan to protest the prejudice they experienced in school by wearing some outlandish clothes to the graduation ceremony rather than the conservative clothes and cap and gown prescribed by the school administration.

SOURCE: From *Teaching in a Diverse Society*, by H. Grossman, 1995, p. 200. Copyright 1995 by Allyn and Bacon. Adapted with permission.

(Heinz, 1987; Purcell & Stewart, 1990). Many problems still exist. For example, authors and publishers continue to use male pronouns to describe individuals whose gender is unknown and the term *mankind* for all people. In most of the material students read, fathers still work and mothers stay at home doing domestic chores. When parents work outside the home, they are still described as involved in gender-stereotypic jobs, but to a lesser degree. Men are depicted as engaged in three times as many different occupations as women, and fathers are the executives, professionals, scientists, firefighters, and police officers. Men participate in a variety of different athletic activities; women are involved primarily in sports that have traditionally been considered female sports.

Computer software is also biased against women. Woodill (1987) claimed, "Much of computer software has been designed by males for males, as shown by the predominance of male figures in programs, computer ads, and on the software packaging" (p. 55). Although changes have occurred, curriculum materials remain quite sexist.

Student Expectations and Career Aspirations

Even preschool students are aware that men and women tend to hold different kinds of occupations: doctors, police officers, and truck drivers are usually men, whereas nurses, teachers, and secretaries are usually women. By the time they enter elementary school, students have formed definite stereotypes about the careers that are appropriate for men and women, and these gender stereotypes influence their own career aspirations (Deaux, 1984; A. Kelly & Smail, 1986; Nemerowicz, 1979). As they move into the high school years, students are more likely to recognize that both men and women can hold virtually any job; nevertheless, they continue to aspire to careers consistent with male–female stereotypes (J. Smith & Russell, 1984). Women also tend to choose careers that they believe will not interfere with their future roles as wives and mothers, thus even further limiting their aspirations (Eccles [Parsons], 1984). Men set higher expectations for themselves than women do, especially when a task is stereotypically masculine (e.g., Deaux, 1984; Durkin, 1987; Lueptow, 1984). Something to Consider 6.2 describes several career patterns of women.

Teacher Attention, Feedback, Evaluation, and Expectations

Both male and female teachers treat male and female students differently. Teachers tend to create and maintain gender differences in school through the attention and feedback they give students, how they evaluate them, and the expectations they communicate to them (H. Grossman & Grossman, 1994). This section focuses on the harm

---

Something to Consider 6.2
Career Patterns of Women

Wolfson (1976) identified several patterns that appear to be characteristic of women's occupational experience. A range of individual variation undoubtedly exists within each of these, and none represents a "normal" or particularly desirable pattern. The identified patterns were:

1. **The stable homemaking career pattern:** The woman marries during or soon after completing her formal education and has little or no significant work experience outside of the home.
2. **The conventional career pattern:** The young woman, after completing formal education, works in a traditional female occupation for a few years. Upon marriage or childbirth, she exits the paid labor market permanently.
3. **The stable career pattern:** The woman completes formal education and enters full-time work on a permanent basis. This entry marks the onset of a permanent commitment to work that is not markedly affected by marriage or childbearing.
4. **The double-track career pattern:** The woman enters the labor market after formal education, then marries and combines the work and homemaking experiences. Work may be interrupted for short periods by childbearing, but she continues a linear progress within her career as a parallel activity to marriage and family life.
5. **The interrupted career pattern:** Work begins after formal education but with marriage and childbearing a long interruption occurs, often 8 to 10 years. After children become relatively independent, the woman reenters the labor market in the same field.
6. **The unstable career pattern:** The woman combines work, marriage, and childbearing in a sporadic and unsystematic way. Entering and leaving jobs may reflect economic necessity or other personal circumstance. The nature of the work may vary widely, reflecting the nature of job opportunities rather than personal desire.
7. **The multiple-trial career pattern:** The woman tries, almost randomly, a series of unrelated jobs, persisting and progressing in none.

SOURCE: From "Career Development Patterns of College Women," by V. P. Wolfson, 1976, *Journal of Counseling Psychology, 23,* 119–125. Copyright 1976 by the American Psychological Association. Reprinted with permission.

done to students by gender bias in teacher attention and feedback. See Something to Consider 6.3 for additional suggestions in eliminating gender bias in the classroom.

Teacher attention. Beginning in preschool, male students receive more attention from their teachers (e.g., Brophy, 1985). Teachers interact with male students more often and ask them more questions, and those questions are more conceptual and abstract. One reason male students receive more attention is that teachers spend more time disciplining them for misbehavior (Grant, 1985). Much of the difference, however, is because teachers demonstrate a clear bias in favor of male students' participation in their classes. For example, teachers view male students as more independent thinkers and more likely to do better in math and science because they are "male" sub-

---

Something to Consider 6.3
Eliminating Gender Bias in the Classroom

---

1. Be sensitive to the possibilities of unconscious gender bias.
   - A teacher checks her interaction with her students by periodically videotaping one of her classes. She checks the tape to ensure that male and female students are called on equally, are asked the same number of high-level questions, and receive the same quality of feedback.
   - Another teacher consciously deemphasizes sex roles and differences in her classroom. She has male and female students share equally in chores, and she eliminates gender-related activities such as competition between male and female students and forming lines by gender.
2. Actively attack gender bias in teaching styles.
   - At the beginning of the school year, a teacher explains how gender bias hurts both sexes, and he forbids sexist comments in his classes. As classes study historical topics, he emphasizes the contributions of women and how they have been ignored by historians and points out the changes in views of gender over time.
   - A teacher selects stories and clippings from newspapers and magazines that portray women in nontraditional roles. She matter-of-factly talks about nontraditional careers with the students in reference to "when you grow up."

---

jects. Female students, in contrast, are viewed as more submissive and conforming (Fennema & Peterson, 1986). This pattern is especially clear in science and math classes (H. Grossman, 1995).

Teacher feedback.   Teachers also provide male and female students different kinds of attention. Again the differential treatment favors male students. Teachers give male students more praise and attention for high levels of achievement and correct responses (e.g., Brophy, 1985). In fact, teachers give high-achieving female students the least amount of attention, praise, and supportive feedback and the largest number of disparaging statements compared with low-achieving female students and all male students (e.g., Purcell & Stewart, 1990).

Teacher expectations.   Research, which needs updating, suggests that teachers have different academic expectations for female and male students (e.g., Hallinan & Sorensen, 1987). Although they do not expect male and female students to have different achievement levels in school, they view high achievement as a masculine characteristic and low achievement as feminine. These differences can affect students' self-confidence about their academic ability and their motivation to succeed in school and the world of work.

Evidence exists that students' access to teachers is sometimes influenced by students' gender and race. Damico and Scott (1988) reported that although the achievement of European American male students and African American female students was comparable, teachers were more likely to reinforce the academic behavior of European American male students. Teachers were also more likely to encourage and support the academic behavior of European American female students but to pay more attention to and provide support for the social behavior of African American female students. Some teachers were more likely to call on African American female students to help peers with nonacademic tasks and to ask European American female students to help peers with academic tasks. Apparently some teachers may perceive African American female students to be socially, but not cognitively, mature. In addition, African American female students are likely to be perceived as responding inappropriately to teachers and are sometimes perceived by teachers as being "overactive" (Herring, 1997a). They are actively attempting to participate in the class but do not understand teachers' rules for taking turns.

Effects on students.   Female students interpret their teachers' apparent disinterest in them differently. Boudreau's (1986) conclusion may be correct: "The idea conveyed to girls is, although subtle, quite clear. What boys do matters more to teachers than what girls do" (p. 18). Some evidence indicates that these biases are more characteristic of European American teachers than African American teachers (e.g., Simpson & Erickson, 1983). This finding may be one more example of the fact that "Blacks are less gender-typed and more egalitarian than whites" (Meece, 1987, p. 61).

The message African American female students receive is even more destructive (e.g., Grant, 1985). Teachers, especially European American teachers, perceive and treat African American female students in an even more biased manner than European American female students (Grant, 1985). Their teachers seem to be telling them that all they are good for is the stereotypic roles such as housekeepers, maids, child-care providers, and so on, that European Americans have historically assigned to African American women.

Courses and Activities

Many teachers and counselors believe that some courses belong in the male domain and others in the female domain. For example, teachers and counselors may encourage female students to enroll in lower math classes and male students to enroll in more advanced math courses. Many teachers and counselors also believe that higher education and certain careers and occupations are more appropriate for one sex or another, and vocational education teachers often harass female students enrolled in nontraditional vocational courses.

Academic courses.   In high school, where students have the opportunity to select their courses and activities, male and female students make somewhat different choices (e.g., American College Testing, 1989; Horn, 1990; K. R. Kelly & Cobb, 1991). This variance also occurs among gifted and talented students (Leung, Conoley, & Scheel, 1994; see Chapter 8). Generally, Hispanic American, Southeast Asian American, and poor European American male students are more likely than female students to plan work outside the home and to aspire to professional careers that require at least a bachelor's degree. These gender differences may be less true of European American female students who live in areas where gender-stereotyped perceptions of education are not as prevalent and of female students who prefer competitive rather than cooperative environments.

King (1989) studied 318 (156 male, 162 female) 10th-, 11th-, and 12th-grade students who averaged 16.5 years of age. The majority were from middle- and upper-middle-class families and 90% were European American. Results support the belief that the development of career maturity differs for male and female students if only in subtle ways. For male youths, the single most important determinant of career attitudes was age: the older, the more ready to make career decisions. Female youths reflect the same tendency as well. However, age is not as important for female youths as are a sense of family cohesion and an internal locus of control.

Vocational courses and career aspirations.   Differences in students' views of gender-appropriate careers appear as early as kindergarten (Kochenberger-Stroeher, 1994). Significantly, when the children chose nontraditional roles for women or men, their choice was based on personal experience (e.g., "One of my friend's dad is a nurse"). These gender-stereotypic views influence career decisions. In 1980, 30% of college-bound high school girls, compared with 50% of comparable boys, planned to study science and engineering in college. At the doctoral level, the differences were even greater: Only 25% of the doctoral degrees in science and engineering were awarded to female students (National Research Council, 1980). More recent research shows that this trend continues: Female students were less than half as likely as male students to pursue careers in engineering and physical and computer sciences (Eggen & Kauchak, 1997).

Although some shift is evident since the 1970s, male and female students continue to choose different vocational education courses and aspire to different careers and occupations (Hyde & Fennema, 1990; Karraker, 1991; K. R. Kelly & Cobb, 1991). Female students constitute more than 90% of the students in cosmetology, clerical, home economics, and health courses and less than 10% of the students in courses that deal with agriculture, electrical technology, electronics, appliance repair, auto mechanics, carpentry, welding, and small-engine repair.

One reason why male and female students select different academic and vocational courses is that they aspire to different careers (H. Grossman & Grossman, 1994). Female students are less likely to aspire to mathematics, science, or engineering careers. In comparison with African American, Hispanic American, Southeast Asian American, and working-class European American male students, female students, including those who are gifted and talented, aspire to less prestigious and lower paying occupations that typically do not require a college degree. This tendency is especially true of female students who have more traditional views of gender roles. It is also more likely to be true of younger children because female students' career aspirations become less gender stereotypical as they advance from kindergarten through high school (Canale & Dunlap, 1987). Case Study 6.1 illustrates an ethnic perspective in relation to a high school diploma.

These gender differences appear not to apply to the same extent to female students raised in rural areas, Filipino American female students, and middle-class European American female students, especially if their mothers have nontraditional high-paying occupations (C. C. Lee, 1985; Odell, 1989; Ruhland, Brittle, Norris, & Oakes, 1978). "The most powerful set of predictors of whether young women are aspiring to nontraditional, high status careers is the socioeconomic background of their family" (Ruhland et al., 1978, p. 22).

Participation in extracurricular activities. During the early 1980s, male and female students participated differently in their school's extracurricular programs (National Center for Educational Statistics, 1984; Stockard et al., 1980). Stockard et al. (1980) described these differences in the following terms:

Case Study 6.1
Gender and Ethnic Influences

One of a teacher's best students, an eighth-grade Hispanic American girl, informs the school counselor that she is not going to continue in the program in high school because she is not planning to go to college. When the counselor asks why, she replies that in her family and culture college is for boys. She says her plans are to finish high school, find a temporary job, get married, have four or five children, and stay home. The counselor believes that girls should be encouraged to go on to college so they can have the career and other opportunities a college degree provides.

SOURCE: From *Teaching in a Diverse Society,* by H. Grossman, 1995, p. 214. Copyright 1995 by Allyn & Bacon. Adapted with permission.

Males more often belong to chess, science, and lettermen's clubs and
females more often belong to dance teams and aspire to be cheerleaders
on the rally squad. Even though both sexes play in the band, they generally play different instruments (girls on the flutes, boys on the tubas) and
have different responsibilities (drum majors who lead the band and ma-
jorettes who twirl batons). Jobs on school newspapers and in student government are typically sex segregated. Boys are more often sports editors,
girls are feature reporters. Boys are often presidents of student bodies,
while girls are often secretaries. (p. 40)

Additional and more recent research is needed to determine
whether these patterns continue to exist today. The types of activities
in which students participate and the roles they assume in the activities
they are involved affect the career choices they make and their eventual lifestyles (H. Grossman & Grossman, 1994). See Case Study 6.2 for
an example of gender bias on the playground.

Gender Segregation and Separation

Studies conducted during the late 1970s and middle 1980s revealed
that some teachers discourage male–female interaction (e.g., Lockheed
& Harris, 1984). Instead of encouraging mixed-gender groups, some
teachers assigned different chores to male and female students. For
example, female students straightened the classroom and male students moved the furniture. Teachers separated students when assign-
ing seats or areas to hang clothes and when forming study and work
groups and committees. Lockheed and Harris (1984) reported a particularly pernicious management approach:

In classrooms, assignment to mixed-sex seating adjacencies or groups often
is used as punishment designed to reduce student interaction instead of as
a learning technique designed to foster cooperative interaction. (p. 276)

Research is needed to determine whether these segregation and
separation practices continue and if they are pervasive in contemporary school settings.

Case Study 6.2
Playground Bias?

Johnny attended a private school where the playgrounds were segregated by gender. In
one playground the girls skipped and jumped rope, in the other, the boys played football.
Johnny often stood on the sidelines and chatted with several other nonathletic boys.
Johnny's teacher was concerned and arranged privately with several of the male athletes
to include Johnny and his friends in the daily football game. The teacher warned that if
they failed to do so, all of the boys in the class would be punished.

Encouragement of Behavior Differences

Although all teachers desire well-behaved students, they appear to have different standards for male and female students (H. Grossman, 1995). Beginning in preschool, teachers tend to encourage gender-stereotypic behavior (e.g., Boudreau, 1986). Teachers praise male students more than female students for creative behavior and female students more than male students for conforming behavior. Male students are rewarded for functioning independently, whereas female students are rewarded for being obedient and compliant. Boudreau (1986) believed this form of discrimination harms female students: "The pattern of reinforcement that young girls receive may lead them to stake their sense of self-worth more on conforming than personal competency" (p. 25).

Research is needed to determine whether these types of teacher encouragement remain in school settings. Teachers and counselors who encourage these gender differences can certainly cause problems for female students in situations that require creativity, assertiveness, or independence (H. Grossman, 1995). Concurrently, numerous potential career opportunities for female students continue to go unexplored by these students.

Intolerance of Male Behavior Patterns and Biased Classroom Management Techniques

Classroom teachers contribute to the perpetuation or discontinuance of student behavior, positive and negative. Their decision to be either tolerant or intolerant of student behavior creates the mold for future student–adult interactions. Their judgment is inherent to the future success or failure of their students.

Intolerance of male behavior patterns. Educators, especially female educators, tend to be less tolerant of "male-typical" behaviors. African American male students are especially likely to suffer the consequences of teachers' intolerance. Many African American male students, and female students as well, express their emotions much more intensely than most European American students. When European American teachers and counselors observe African American male students behaving aggressively and assertively, they tend to assume that the students are much angrier or upset than they actually are (Herring, 1997a). Attributing a level of anger to African American students that would be appropriate for European American students who behaved in a similar way, teachers and counselors become uncomfortable, even anxious, and concerned about what they incorrectly anticipate will happen next. As a result, they intervene when no intervention is necessary. If teachers and counselors appreciated the cultural context of African American male students' seemingly aggressive behavior toward others and understood that such behavior is unlikely to cause the physical fight or whatever else they expect to occur, they would be less likely to have to intervene to make themselves feel more at ease in the situation. This, in turn, would lessen the likelihood that African American male students would get into trouble needlessly. In addition, suspensions and expulsions of this population would decrease and their exposure to appropriate career education would increase.

Biased classroom management techniques.   Teachers tend to reprimand male students more often than female students and differently as well (e.g., Boudreau, 1986). They tend to speak briefly, softly, and privately to girls but publicly and harshly to boys. With younger children, they tend to use physical methods, such as poking, slapping, grabbing, pushing, squeezing, and so on, with male students, and negative comments or disapproving gestures and other forms of nonverbal communication with female students (H. Grossman, 1995). Teachers are more likely to use even harsher disciplinary techniques, such as corporal punishment and suspension, with lower-class, African American, and Hispanic American male students than with middle-class European American male students (National Black Child Development Institute, 1990; Richardson & Evans, 1991).

This classroom management style is unfortunate because public and harsh reprimands and physical forms of discipline and severe punishments can cause students to react rebelliously to punishments that they believe are too harsh for their "crimes." This may help to explain why male students get into trouble in school and why male students from lower-class backgrounds and some non-European American backgrounds tend to get into even more trouble than European American middle-class students (National Black Child Development Institute, 1990).

COUNSELING IMPLICATIONS

Most of the knowledge that is known about career development has been derived from theories and research dominated by the experiences of men. When research has been done using men and women and separate data analysis is conducted, important differences have been found (e.g., Maccoby & Jacklin, 1974). In addition, the reality is that despite the existence of sex discrimination, male chauvinism, and archaic ideas about the roles of women, thousands of women are attaining high levels of career actualization and are successfully integrating them into personally productive and satisfying lifestyles (Blocher, 1989). The easiest way to use available career behavior data about women is to dispel the pervasive myths that continue to persist.

Special Emphasis 6.1 identifies the most common myths about women's career development and offers several propositions about barriers to their career actualization. Special Emphasis 6.2 illustrates the influences of gender stereotypes on career development. Special Emphasis 6.3 illustrates how subtle messages can affect gender and ethnic perceptions. Something to Consider 6.4 describes what it means to be male or female in contemporary society.

Gender Stereotypes

In making use of popular and traditional cultural symbols (e.g., Superman or Cinderella), children may position themselves within stories that reveal dominant ideological assumptions about categories of individuals and the relations between them: boys and girls, adults and children, rich and poor people, and people of varied heritages, physical demeanors, and societal powers (P. Gilbert, 1994). These assumptions about human relations are reductive fictions—fictions that remove the ambiguity and ability of everyday experience in the articulation of more unified selves, defined in opposition to unified "oth-

---

Special Emphasis 6.1
Myths and Propositions About Women's Career Development

Myths	Propositions
1. Women can be neatly classified as either career oriented or family oriented.	1. Women generally experience a decline in academic self-confidence during the later high school and college years.
2. "Career women" are different, or strange, or maladjusted.	2. Women generally experience some "fear of success."
3. Women work only because they are bored or restless, or for "pocket money."	3. Women are more motivated to help others than to achieve for themselves.
4. Women do not want high-level managerial or professional careers.	4. Home-career conflict is a prevalent and significant limiting factor in the career actualization of women.
5. Women will gladly give up education and higher levels of employment for a home-making role.	5. Sex discrimination in education and the workplace inhibits the career success of women.
	6. The career success of women tends to be limited by lower risk-taking ability than that of men.

SOURCE: From Blocher (1989) and Farmer (1978).

Special Emphasis 6.2
Gender Stereotypes and Career Development

Students absorb many rigid ideas about gender-stereotyped occupations. The following suggestions might provide incentives for school counselors and related professionals to generate additional ideas and strategies to reduce these ideas.

1. **Wise men.** Assess awareness of one common stereotype by asking students to draw a picture of a doctor. After they are finished, discuss the similarities and differences among the drawings. What conclusions can be reached about the image of a doctor? Discuss characteristics of ethnicity, gender, dress, age, and so on. Do their answers represent a generalized idea or a stereotype?

2. **Take Daughters to Work Day.** Contact businesses in the community and invite successful women to address the students. Survey parents for suggestions of women who have interesting careers. Feature photographs, articles, and biographies of diverse career women. Use students' stereotypes to generate discussion. Pose questions that connect careers with early education and training.

3. **Influential women.** Women have been omitted from most accounts of history. They are rarely seen as developers of ideas, initiators of events, or inventors of technology. Have students generate a list of women's achievements. Groups of students can research each woman's life and accomplishments. Offer students biographies of women's roles, from politics to science to sports.

4. **Women in folklore.** Positive models and stories of successful women can help overcome obstacles. Folktales often reflect stereotypical gender roles. Present tales of strong women to counteract folklore images of passive women who need a man to rescue them (e.g., Cinderella, Sleeping Beauty).

5. **Featuring women artists.** Show that art is not the sole product of dead European men.

6. **Countering gender stereotypes in children's literature.** Stereotyped thinking and behavior are found frequently in the books available in classrooms. Over 75% of the characters in children's books are male. In addition, male characters tend to take action, whereas female characters remain passive. Practice critical thinking skills by identifying stereotypes and evaluating sexism in textbooks. Could the characters' gender be reversed? An alternative is to retell the story from another perspective.

7. **Gender-typed play.** Children's toys and games perpetuate ideas of gender role stereotypes. Ask students to list examples of boys' toys and girls' toys. Discuss why certain toys and games are presumed to be gender specific. This discussion should result in increased options for gender-typed play and decreased negative response to gender role behaviors.

SOURCE: From *Multicultural Teaching: A Handbook of Activities, Information, and Resources*, by P. L. Tiedt and I. M. Tiedt, 1995, 78–82. Copyright 1992 by Allyn & Bacon. Adapted with permission.

ers" (James, 1993). The "us" and the "them" thus constructed have both textual and social ramifications (A. H. Dyson, 1996).

Many male students bring in popular car magazines (e.g., *Lowrider*), which they had learned about from their older brothers (A. H. Dyson, 1996). C. C. Lee (1995a) observed fourth graders fantasizing in a Chinese American neighborhood, describing the children's dominant use of Asian animation.

MODIFYING STUDENTS' STEREOTYPICAL BELIEFS ABOUT COURSES AND CAREERS

Until fairly recently, most people believed it was desirable for men and women to have different roles in society. However, with the advent of

---

Special Emphasis 6.3
The Mighty Morphin' Power Rangers: Hidden Messages?

The Mighty Morphin' Power Rangers (based on the original U.S. cast) are a multiracial group of five high school students who are picked by Zordon, a benevolent alien being, and his robot servant Alpha 2, to regularly save the earth from destruction by the evil aliens, Lord Zed, Rita Repulsa, and their earth-minions, the Putties.

In their daily lives, they are normal high school students who hang out together. They all happen to know karate as well. Though their super hero identities are secret, at school they wear their Ranger colors anyway (e.g., Jason, the Red Ranger, wears red). Jason and Tommy are the "leaders" of the team, the ones contacted by Zordon; they alert the others of an impending battle. They are European American boys who also run the school's Karate Club. They are portrayed as the "toughest" Rangers and also the most desirable (e.g., Kimberly, the Pink Ranger, has a crush on Tommy). Billy (the Blue Ranger), also European American, is the "smart" one, portrayed as slightly nerdy; he is usually working on some scientific gadget for the Rangers' secret hideout. Zack (the Black Ranger) is African American and runs the school's "Hip-Hop Dance Club." Trini and Kimberly are the only girls on the team. Trini (the Yellow Ranger) is Asian American and runs the Volleyball Club, and Kimberly (the Pink Ranger) is European American and runs the Gardening Club. At school, there are two peripheral but ever-present characters that serve as the witless, bumbling school bullies that taunt the Rangers and cause problems that need to be resolved by the end of the episode. They are named Bulk and Skull, both European American; they cause trouble just because they are bad tempered and stupid.

While in their Power Ranger uniforms, the team fights the Putties and the monsters equally, male alongside female, with equal powers. But when they are portrayed as average high school students, gender stereotyping is rampant. The girls are usually portrayed with stereotypically female interests, like shopping, gardening, and boys, whereas the boys are more interested in fighting and are more cerebral and less emotionally preoccupied. But this gender-stereotyping pales in light of the racial stereotyping in terms of the colors they wear: Zack wears black, Trini wears yellow, Kimberly wears pink.

Since the original cast was replaced in 1994, the colors have switched so that the African American Ranger no longer wears black, and the Asian American Ranger no longer wears yellow. However, gender roles remain highly stereotyped, and the plot structure is still simple.

Adapted from "Cultural Constellations and Childhood Identities," by A. H. Dyson, 1996, *Harvard Educational Review, 66,* 477. Copyright 1996 by *Harvard Educational Review.* Adapted with permission.

Something to Consider 6.4
What It Means to Be a Male or a Female in U.S. Society

The following exercise can be adapted for any age group to open communication about sex roles. Participants are divided into same-sex groups of three or four and asked to answer four questions on large sheets of newsprint to be displayed to the whole group. The four questions are:

For Girls' Groups:
1. What is good about being a girl?
2. What is bad about being a girl?
3. What do boys like about girls?
4. What don't boys like about girls?

For Boys' Groups
1. What is good about being a boy?
2. What is bad about being a boy?
3. What do girls like about boys?
4. What don't girls like about boys?

Each group is given a half hour to answer the questions by listing all the ideas suggested. No attempt is made to come to a consensus about the items listed. After the groups complete their assignment, the newsprint is displayed for everyone to see. The discussion focuses on the differences in perceptions between girls' and boys' groups.

Possible questions to be posed by the teacher/group facilitator are:
1. Do girls/boys like the same things about themselves that the other sex likes about them?
2. Are there differences between what girls/boys think the other sex likes and doesn't like about themselves?
3. How do these thoughts relate to careers and the world of work?

SOURCE: From *Group Processes in the Classroom*, by R. A. Schmuck and P. A. Schmuck, 1997, pp. 169–170. Copyright 1997 by McGraw-Hill. Adapted with permission.

the women's movement during the 1970s came the realization that traditional gender roles unnecessarily limit the options of both men and women (Huston, 1983). Gender stereotypes persist nevertheless; even preschoolers are aware of them (Ruble, 1988). Something to Consider 6.5 lists some of the common components of traditional gender stereotypes. School counselors and teachers have used a variety of approaches to encourage students to alter their gender stereotypical attitudes and behaviors about courses and careers. H. Grossman and Grossman (1994) suggested some that have been quite helpful.

Students are most likely to model behaviors that they believe are appropriate for their gender (with different students sometimes defining "gender appropriate" somewhat differently; Ormrod, 1995). Exposure to numerous examples of people in "nontraditional careers" can help broaden students' perceptions as to what behaviors are gender appropriate, broaden their academic choices, and possibly enhance their career aspirations. Effective models are likely to be attractive and prestigious; they are also likely to behave in traditionally gender-appropriate ways (Ormrod, 1995).

Several researchers have presented empirical support for sex differences in efficacy for occupations classified as traditionally male or traditionally female (Bonett, 1994; Clement, 1987; Hackett & Betz, 1981; Layton, 1984). Interventions may have optimal impact if they are introduced early in the career decision-making process. School counselors might encourage female students to enroll in those academic subjects related to many traditionally male careers (Bonett, 1994). If self-efficacy in these areas can be strengthened, female students may be less likely to eliminate careers that require math and science-related skills (Siegel, Galassi, & Ware, 1985).

Hackett and Betz (1981) postulated a causal model of career development with perceived self-efficacy functioning as a major mediator. Research has documented the different ways in which the influences of socialization contribute to the beliefs individuals develop regarding per-

---

Something to Consider 6.5
Male and Female Stereotypes

MALE		FEMALE
	Characteristics	
Aggressive		Affectionate
Ambitious		Sensitive
Competitive		Sympathetic
Courageous		Emotional
Independent		Talkative
Self-confident		Gentle
Dominant		Passive
Strong		Submissive
Unemotional		Weak
	School Subjects	
Mathematics		Art
Science		Music
Mechanics		Reading
Athletics		Literature
	Occupations	
Police officer		Librarian
Electrician		Model
Computer operator		Child-care worker
Car mechanic		Cleaner
Engineer		Secretary
Repairman		Hairdresser
Business manager		Nurse
Airline pilot		Ballet dancer
Scientist		Seamstress

SOURCE: From A. Kelly and B. Smail (1986); Lueptow (1984); Nash (1975); Stein (1971); and Stein and Smithells (1969).

sonal competencies and how such beliefs can influence the future course of lives by affecting the choices made and the accomplishments realized. These authors suggested (a) that career self-efficacy may be of particular importance in understanding and influencing women's career development; (b) that underutilization by women of their career talents and their underrepresentation in many higher status, higher paying, male-dominated occupations may be a direct result of social-ization-based differences between the sexes for traditionally male and traditionally female career domains; and (c) that men perceive them-selves to be equally capable to pursue either traditional male or female careers but women's efficacy expectations were strong for those occu-pations traditionally held by women but weak for the traditionally male vocations.

Use Nonstereotypical Role Models for Guest Speakers, Tutors, and Mentors

The severe shortage of female science and math teachers and male English and art teachers gives students little reason to question their gender-stereotypical concepts. The same is true of school counselors, who are primarily female. To counteract these student perspectives, counselors and teachers can invite nonstereotypical role models to participate in courses and activities that are traditionally viewed as feminine or masculine (e.g., male artists and female scientists). In the use of nontraditional role models needs to include African American and Hispanic American men and women because of their serious un-derrepresentation among school faculties (Herring, 1997a). The lim-ited research about the effectiveness of this approach indicates that exposing students to same-sex models improves female students' par-ticipation in math and male students' academic achievement in a vari-ety of courses (T. Mitchell, 1990).

Recruit Nontraditional Students Into Stereotypically Viewed Courses

Numerous forces dissuade female students from enrolling in math, com-puter, and science courses. Their parents often do not expect them to do well in these classes, perpetuating the stereotype. They have less confi-dence than male students in their math, computer, and science ability. They believe these courses are less valuable to them, and they are anx-ious about taking such courses (Eccles, Adler, & Meece, 1984). However, science activities that actively involve female students in designing and carrying out science experiences help combat gender stereotypes that the sciences are a male domain (Eggen & Kauchak, 1997).

SUMMARY

This chapter's discussion clearly indicates that schools play an important role in the formation and maintenance of students' stereotypic views of gender roles. As Meece (1987) interpreted it,

> Schools have been slow in adapting to recent changes in the social roles of men and women. As a result, schools may be exposing children to masculine and feminine images that are even more rigid and more polarized than those currently held in the wider society. Furthermore, the school setting does not seem to provide children with many opportunities to perform behaviors not associated with their gender. Therefore, schools seem to play an important role in reinforcing rigid gender distinctions. (p. 67)

School counselors and teachers have reason to be optimistic about the reduction of gender-stereotypical behavior in school settings. To accomplish this goal, educators can begin by examining and eradicating their own beliefs, attitudes, and behavior for possible gender bias (H. Grossman & Grossman, 1994).

Several techniques and strategies have been discussed in this chapter for expanding students' gender awareness. Interventions for changing students' stereotypical beliefs and behavior patterns can also have positive effects if they are used thoughtfully. Exposing students to alternative models of behavior, perspectives, and values without expecting, rewarding, or pressuring them to change may prove to be the best way to relate to students whose beliefs and attitudes about gender role stereotypes are different from what teachers and counselors prefer them to be (H. Grossman & Grossman, 1994).

EXPERIENTIAL ACTIVITIES

1. Discuss and generate examples of media-perpetuated (e.g., cartoons) gender role stereotypes.
2. Refer to Case Study 6.1. Disregard the description of the teacher's point of view. Instead, imagine what your viewpoint would be and how you would deal with the problem. If you prefer a number of different approaches, try to determine the factors that led you to select the particular approaches you would use.
3. Refer back to Case Study 6.2. How do you feel about the gender separation that existed on the playgrounds? What is your opinion about the way the teacher responded to Johnny and his friends' behavior? What might have been the teacher's reason for responding in that manner? How would you have responded?
4. If you are a preschool teacher/counselor, observe the extent to which students select toys and activities that conform to gender

stereotypes and the degree to which they attempt to get their way with others in gender-stereotypical ways.

5. If you are an elementary or middle school teacher/counselor, describe your students' learning styles and decide whether they conform to the gender patterns reported in this chapter.

6. If you are a secondary teacher/counselor, obtain the names of the students who are enrolled in higher level science and mathematics, foreign language courses, and so on. Review the list to determine whether the student make-up follows the gender patterns that researchers have reported. Do the same for student enrollment in the various vocational courses available in your school.

7. Refer to Something to Consider 6.1 and 6.3. Describe how you think teachers and counselors should handle each of the examples.

8. Which of the women's career patterns in Something to Consider 6.2 most reflects your own or your mother's if you have not begun a career? How have these patterns changed since 1976 or have they?

7

Career Development
With Ethnic Minority Students

—————

Modeling is not the best way to teach,
it is the only way to teach.

Albert Schweitzer

The culture and ethnic group of individuals directly influences the development of the constructs they use to form their identities, their knowledge structures of the world of work, the meanings they derive from work, the thought processes they use to derive career options and evaluate their prospects, and their views of personal success (Peterson, Sampson, & Reardon, 1991). No specific theory links the growth and development in cultural and ethnic perspectives directly to career development, but I propose the use of the *synergetic model* to demonstrate how the emergence of these perspectives influences career problem solving and decision making (e.g., Herring, 1997a, 1997b, Herring & Walker, 1993).

The career development literature on specific ethnic minority students is sparse and is not generally well-grounded. This chapter synthesizes the available literature to present an appropriate portrait of the career needs of ethnic and cultural minority youths. This chapter focuses on African American, Native American Indian, Asian American, and Hispanic American youths. Although comparisons may be made across these groups, within-group variances also need to be recognized. Sociocultural conditions, mental health problems, and some of the issues involved in addressing these concerns are discussed.

DEFINITIONS, DEMOGRAPHICS, AND THEORIES

In addition to the terminology discussion of Chapter 1, additional aspects of career development and counseling need to be defined. Furthermore, demographic data are needed to establish the rationale for serving the career developmental needs of ethnic minority youths. School counselors must also be cognizant of the degree of ethnic awareness displayed by the potential student counselees.

Definitions

From a career development perspective, *culture* is defined as a system of beliefs, values, customs, and institutions shared and transmitted by members of a particular society, from which individuals derive meaning for their work, love, and leisure activities (Peterson et al., 1991). An *ethnic group* is a group of people who regard themselves as distinct from other groups on the basis of shared social or cultural characteristics such as ancestry, history, language, religion, and politics (Christensen, 1989; Farley, 1982) and continue to identify themselves with the nation from which they or their ancestors came (Gollnick & Chinn, 1994). *Ethnicity* is the social characteristics of culture, including its common language, religious beliefs, customs, and politics (Farley, 1982). *Multicultural career development* is defined by Stone (1984) as "an intervention and continuous assessment process that prepares institutions and individuals to experience the realities of life, work, and leisure in a culturally diverse environment. In particular, multicultural career development considers the effect of and relationship among career options, ethnic-cultural demographics, and psychosocial factors that impact an individual's occupational choices in a pluralistic society" (p. 272).

Cross-cultural counseling is the study, research, and practice of the counseling process that occurs when counselor and student are from different cultures and are mutually affected by their different cultural experience (Stone & Brooks, 1979).

Demographics

Kinloch (1979) provided several methods of looking at minority groups. One way is to differentiate a group by physiological type (e.g., females, the aged, students). Another way is by ethnicity (e.g., European American, Asian American). A third method is by culture (e.g., Japanese, German, Amish). A fourth way is to classify economic types (e.g., poor, lower class, upper class). The fifth way is by behavioral type (e.g., mentally ill, delinquents, and criminals). This chapter emphasizes ethnic and cultural aspects of youths in the United States.

More than 100 ethnic groups and 170 Native American Indian groups currently reside in the Unites States, with the largest ethnic groups of school-age population being African American (15%), Hispanic (10%), and Asian (3%; U.S. Department of Education, 1994a). More than 7 million people immigrated to the United States during the 1970s, and another 7 million came during the 1980s. Between 1980 to 1990, the ethnic and cultural minority population increased by over 9%. The fastest growing were Asian (almost 100%) and Hispanic (53%). Estimates are that ethnic minorities in the school-age population will increase to 40% by the year 2000 (Villegas, 1991).

In addition, the population of bi- and multiethnic individuals, thought to include 1 to 2 million of mixed-race descent, is swiftly changing. A 1967 Supreme Court ruling legalized and spawned a sharp increase in interracial marriage. Interracial marriage rates have doubled each decade since 1970, from 310,000 that year to 1.2 million in 1992. The number of multiracial youths has grown accordingly: from 31,200 born in 1968 to four times that number, 128,000, in 1991 (Gross, 1996). As this population increases, career development programs may need to adapt to their unique needs.

Ethnic and cultural minority youths are the largest growing segment of the U.S. population. By the year 2000, ethnic minority youths will constitute nearly 30% of the population (U.S. Bureau of the Census, 1992). This change will be due primarily to increased birth rates among Hispanic Americans and rising immigration rates among Asians. The rate of growth of African American youths has been stable over the last decade, constituting 34% of the African American population; and the Native American Indian population has the largest percentage of children and adolescents, with 37.4% under 18 years of age (U.S. Bureau of the Census, 1992).

From a career developmental perspective, ethnic and cultural minority youths deserve a more appropriate and ethnic-specific perspective. Some particular concerns include the following characteristics.

African Americans.   The career development of African Americans historically was influenced by slavery: Men were employed primarily as agricultural workers and women as domestic workers (Drummond & Ryan, 1995). Today, about 80% of African Americans live in urban areas and slightly over 50% live in the South (U.S. Bureau of Census, 1992). Currently, the majority of African Americans are employed as blue-collar workers. Although African Americans are increasingly entering professional and technical careers, their numbers remain small in relation to their percentage of the total population in this nation.

Hispanic Americans.   Three major subgroups comprise 80% of the Hispanic American population: Mexican Americans (62%), Puerto Ricans (13%), and Cubans (5%). Sixteen other Spanish-speaking countries are represented from South and Central America and 8% of the population is from Spain (U.S. Bureau of the Census, 1992). Hispanic Americans have a higher unemployment rate than European Americans but lower than African Americans. Contrary to the migrant seasonal stereotype, only 5% of Hispanic American men work in farm occupations, with 58% in blue-collar jobs, 24% in white-collar occupations, and 13% in service occupations (U.S. Department of Education, 1994a).

Native American Indian/Alaska Native.   Native American Indians/Alaska Natives have the lowest living standards of any ethnic group in this nation. Approximately 24% live below the poverty level (U.S. Bureau of the Census, 1991). Unemployment on some reservations is reported to be as high as 90% (Herring, 1997b). The pattern is one of bare subsistence, with some of the worst slums in the United States existing on federal reservations (Rice, 1993). Currently, over 50% of Native peoples reside off reservations, with large enclaves in urban areas (Herring, 1997a). This ethnic population also has several cultural traits or values that conflict with mainstream society (e.g., time orientation and collectivism).

Asian Americans.   Outside of the Indo-Chinese refugees, Asian Americans have accommodated and adapted well to the existing mainstream society and are viewed as hard workers and skilled in mathematical and scientific fields. Most Asian subgroups (except for the Vietnamese) immigrated voluntarily. They have maintained ties with their home countries, have retained most of their cultural heritage, and have maintained their families as a unit (Drummond & Ryan, 1995). Many Asian Americans have been able to use their educational attainment to experience vertical career movement. Asian Americans also possess one of the lowest unemployment rates.

Mayhovich (1976) concluded that successful career development among Asian American individuals is influenced by their traditional culture. They tend to view education as a means of acquiring a salable skill and major in business administration, engineering, or science, not in the liberal arts. Leong (1993) cautioned that not all Asian Americans have Asian values, however.

Theories of Ethnic Awareness

To appropriately serve ethnic and cultural minority youths, school counselors will need to be aware of their personal ethnic awareness. Two theories of the development of ethnic awareness are briefly discussed.

Sue's model.   Sue (1978) and Sue and Sue (1990) postulated that an individual's worldview includes two dimensions of personality:

(a) internal and external locus of control (IC & EC; Rotter, 1966), and (b) internal and external locus of responsibility (IR & ER; E. E. Jones et al., 1971). These dimensions are represented in combinations, which divide individuals into four distinct quadrants. Individuals in Quadrant I (IC-IR) are associated with middle-class values and believe that they have control over their decisions and the ability to implement them (e.g., mainstream society). Individuals in Quadrant II (EC-IR) are associated with the sense of being a scapegoat and believe that they are held responsible for events over which they have little control (e.g., reservational Native American Indians). Quadrant III (EC-ER) individuals are associated with an inflexible approach to life and often blame "the system" for their fate (e.g., low-income African Americans). Quadrant IV (IC-ER) is composed of individuals who believe that they are able to control their destiny if given the opportunity (numerous cultural and minority group members). An individual's quadrant, shaped by culture and ethnicity, can affect how the individual develops career alternatives in the career counseling process (Peterson et al., 1991).

Christensen's model.   Christensen (1989) advanced a five-stage model of ethnic awareness. In Stage 1 (unawareness), individuals have given no thoughts to cultural, ethnic, or racial differences; nor are they aware of how these differences affect their opportunities in society. In Stage 2 (beginning awareness), individuals begin to question why different groups, including their own, possess different statuses in society. In Stage 3 (conscious awareness), individuals experience disequilibrium, preoccupation, and pain as they become more aware of the injustice, inequality, and oppression experienced by culturally disadvantaged groups. In Stage 4 (consolidated awareness), individuals become fully aware of how cultural differences affect social status and opportunity and begin to establish a sense of acceptance of themselves and dissimilar ethnic groups. In Stage 5 (transcendent awareness), individuals of both majority and minority cultures attain a sense of peace with themselves and are able to perceive transcendent, unifying, human qualities that span cultures. They feel comfortable within other ethnic groups as well as their own, whether it be a dominant or a minority group (Peterson et al., 1991).

Effective cross-cultural and multicultural career counseling involves an understanding of the degree of cultural-ethnic-racial awareness not only of the student but also of oneself as a career counselor. Communication may be difficult when a school counselor and student have differentiated levels of ethnic awareness, especially when the school counselor is unaware of his or her own level of development (Peterson et al., 1991). For example, a Stage 3 (conscious awareness) ethnic minority student and a Stage 5 (transcendent awareness) ethnic majority school counselor discussing the prospect of going to professional school may have different perceptions of the opportunities and risks of such a choice. The student may have fears and doubts that need to be acknowledged and appreciated by the school counselor, even though the school counselor may have progressed beyond this level of functioning.

Ethnic Awareness and Synergetic Theory

Information-processing theory contends that two domains are interactive in the internalization of external data: self-knowledge and occupational knowledge. Culture and ethnic perspectives are the foundations of each domain (Peterson et al., 1991). This interaction reflects a basic premise of the synergetic model (Herring, 1997b). In the self-knowledge domain, the essential constructs for forming one's identity are received from one's cultural-ethnic environment, again a synergetic tenet (Herring, 1997b). Whether students see themselves as the primary unit, whether independence and autonomy are valued, whether they believe that they can control their environment, whether the seeking of power and status is a life-orienting goal, what value is placed on competency and on winning rather than losing—these are examples of values that are derived from students' cultural-ethnic backgrounds and that form the core of their value systems and identities (Herring, 1997a, 1997b; Katz, 1985).

In the occupational knowledge domain, students' cultural-ethnic backgrounds provide the essential constructs and attributes needed for determining relationships among occupations, particularly in terms of their relative worth and status. The culturally differentiating status of teachers and those from the clergy illustrate this point. In some cultures, the perceived status of the clergy is considerably higher than in other cultures. The teaching profession reflects a similar shift from culture to culture. Consequently, in career decision making, cultural-ethnic environments influence the degree to which a career choice is determined by students or their families.

At the executive processing level, culture influences the choice of reasoning process: rational, intuitive, or dependent (Maruyama, 1978). The synergetic paradigm provides a framework for understanding how a student's cultural and ethnic identity influences his or her development of knowledge structures and thought processes through which information is transformed into career decisions.

SOCIOCULTURAL FACTORS

Ethnic minority youths present unique career development issues because of their developmental status and membership in their ethnic cultures. Some of the issues are related to sociocultural conditions (e.g., poverty, prejudice, and racism), whereas others are developmental issues faced by all youths. Developmental tasks, however, are also influenced by cultural factors. Most children are reared within the context of a family, whose members bear primary responsibility for the socialization of the children. Thus, understanding the culture's concept of family is vital to effective career interventions.

Sociocultural factors often interfere with the ethnic minority student's mastery of developmental tasks. Poverty, language barriers, and negative stereotypes restrict perceived as well as real access to environmental resources (Rivers & Morrow, 1995). The effective school or career counselor must appraise the youth's environment. Such practical issues may include developing transportation options to school, arranging tutorial services for youths, providing educational resources for parents, and openly discussing the impact of daily exposure to discrimination, conflicting values, ethnic stereotypes, and career mythologies. School and career counselors who directly observe diverse minority students in classrooms and home environments acquire more accurate data of peer relationship skills, attitudes toward authority, study habits, and the degree to which primary needs (e.g., safety, shelter, hygiene, and nutrition) are being met. The effective counselor must address sociocultural issues as well as intrapsychic concerns.

Poverty, Low Socioeconomic Status, and Class

Socioeconomic concerns are frequently the least discussed, and therefore the least addressed, multicultural issue. Economic deprivation and workplace discrimination are only two of the issues faced by less-advantaged youths. The effect of unemployed and underemployed parents on ethnic youths is tremendous. A central issue is a tendency for male counselors to dominate female and minority students and direct them into stereotypical career choices (Cayleff, 1986; E. E. Jones, Krupnick, & Kerig, 1987). For example, the median income for Hispanic American families is $20,306, compared with $31,610 for all other ethnic families; and nearly 26% of Hispanic American families have income below the poverty line, compared with 11% for the total population (U.S. Bureau of the Census, 1991). Hispanic Americans are generally clustered in blue-collar and semiskilled jobs (58%) or are unemployed (Marin & Marin, 1991).

The high rates of poverty in ethnic minority families have been well established in the census data and in the literature (U.S. Bureau of the Census, 1990). However, variations in poverty rates within ethnic minority groups need to be recognized (Liu, Yu, Chang, & Fernandez, 1990). Perhaps the most direct effect of poverty is restricted access to environmental resources with which to combat substandard housing, lack of comprehensive health care, and inadequate nutrition (Rivers & Morrow, 1995). Several studies lend strong support to the relationship of low socioeconomic status (SES), its concomitant stressors, and high rates of psychological maladjustment among ethnic youths (e.g., H. F. Myers, 1989).

Classism represents another variable in the appropriate delivery of services to students. Classism is not often presented as a viable variable in discussions of the educational and career development of students. Nevertheless, classism does have an important influence on students, perhaps to a greater extent than race or ethnicity. For example, one study indicated that the lower the parents' income and education, the less likely a child is to acquire a bachelor's degree or even enter college (Reinolds, 1996). Research Emphasis 7.1 offers additional interesting, and somewhat perplexing, insights into the effects of a student's class membership on his or her career development, in addition to some ethnic and gender considerations.

Another interesting observation is the relationship between a student's membership in a certain class structure and perceived parental

---

Research Emphasis 7.1
Income, Not Race, Fuels Educational Gap

The National Education Longitudinal Study of 1988 by the National Opinion Research Center at the University of Chicago, contracted by the U.S. Department of Education, tracked 25,000 teenagers from eighth grade in 1988 through their early college years in 1994. This research study indicated the following:

- 36% of those in the lowest income group entered postsecondary education.
- 63% of those in the middle income group entered postsecondary education.
- 88% of those in the most affluent group entered postsecondary education.

In 1988:
- 66% of 8th graders expected to earn at least a bachelor's degree.
- 23% of 8th graders expected to have some form of postsecondary education.

In 1994:
- Nearly 63% had some postsecondary education.
- Of those, 57% attended a 4-year institution, 36% attended a 2-year institution, and 7% attended a trade or technical school for fewer than 2 years.
- More women than men reported in 1992 that they expected to obtain at least a bachelor's degree.
- Asians and Pacific Islanders, more than any other ethnic group, expected to earn college degrees. And more of these groups than in any other group in the sample had graduated from high school and enrolled in postsecondary education in 1994.

SOURCE: From "Study: Income, Not Race, Fuel Education Gap," by C. Reinolds, June 20, 1996, p. 1A, *Arkansas Democrat Gazette*. Copyright 1996 by the Arkansas Democrat Gazette. Adapted with permission.

warmth. Several speculations might explain this characteristic. Rohner, Hahn, and Koehn (1992) agreed with W. M. Hurh (personal communication, October 21, 1988) that downwardly mobile parents may "extend closer attention and care to their children by making highly visible sacrifices (e.g., labor-intensive jobs not commensurate with their education and experiences) than the middle class parent, because the former would like to make sure their children will succeed in what they have failed." K. S. Newman (1988) provided other clues when she wrote "children in downwardly mobile [middle-class American] families find themselves drawing closer to their families because they feel they cannot 'desert a sinking ship' and because their parents lean on them for emotional support" (p. 104). Additional research is suggested to yield subsequent data on this question.

However, other issues also complicate factors in studying ethnicity in relation to career development. One reflects the confounding of race and ethnicity. Considerable disagreement exists regarding what is meant by *race* and whether or not that concept is useful even if an acceptable definition can evolve (Yee, Fairchild, Weizmann, & Wyatt, 1993). Another issue is the "overlap between being economically disadvantaged and being culturally disadvantaged, because poverty tends to cross racial and ethnic boundaries" (Herr & Cramer, 1996, p. 272). In addition, attitudes by European Americans toward ethnic minorities play a vital role in the education of all youths.

Language Issues

Children generally learn second languages more easily and more quickly than do adults. As a result, the language skills of bilingual children may threaten the traditionally strict hierarchical role of monolingual parents and children, particularly for first-generation Asian and Hispanic families (Curtis, 1990; Ho, 1992; Huang, 1994). Language issues may also interfere with academic achievement. For example, traditional learning styles for Native American Indian children rely heavily on nonverbal communication, observation, and enactment, as well as linguistic structures that are entirely different from those of the English language (Herring, 1997a). As a result, the English language skills of Native American Indian children are among the poorest of any group in the United States, which partially explains their historical academic underachievement (Ho, 1992).

African American children may experience the least difficulty in learning standard English. However, many African American children develop two forms, a "Black English" (also called African American Language) and the more standard English (Herring, 1997a; Russell, 1988). In fact, many African American youths intentionally oscillate between them ("code switching") in an attempt to regulate distance and emotional intimacy (Rivers & Morrow, 1995).

Stereotypes

Stereotypes are transmitted through overtly negative images and attitudes as well as in covert omissions of the positive aspects of ethnic minority cultures. These pervasive messages can become internalized if not countered by evidence to the contrary (Rivers & Morrow, 1995). When they are internalized, identity exploration may be restricted and a dichotomous mode of thinking can result (e.g., White is "good," ethnic minority is "bad"). One must choose between identifying with dominant values in order to achieve, thereby fulfilling the prophecy and acting out the negative stereotype. Such dichotomies are represented in the derogatory slurs that ethnic minority youths sometimes use to refer to one who has "sold out" to the dominant culture. For example, "oreo" refers to an African American who is considered "Black on the outside but White on the inside." Similarly, the terms "banana," "coconut," and "apple" refer to Asian Americans, Hispanic Americans, and Native American Indians, respectively.

Academic Underachievement and School Dropout

A primary concern of school personnel is lowering the dropout rates of students. The frequency of school dropout for the general population ranges from 5% to 30%, whereas ethnic minority students have a much higher rate, especially in inner cities (U.S. Bureau of the Census, 1991). Their value orientations, difficult SES, and familial conditions are not conducive to continuing education (Rice, 1993). Despite improvements in the high school completion rate, however, this nation is still losing 1,375 teenagers every day to the dropout or pushout cycle (Haycock, 1991).

During 1988, 4.3 million students older than age 14 (11%) dropped out of school. Of this number, 81% were European American, 16% were African American, and 2% were Hispanic American (U.S. Bureau of the Census, 1990). Liu et al. (1990) reported lower dropout rates for Asian American adolescents. In general, however, the academic plans of qualified ethnic minority students do not diverge greatly from those of European American students (G. Kerr & Colangelo, 1988). Exceptions exist in the proportion of African American students (35.4%) interested in engineering and the preference of Asian American students (29.5%) for health science.

G. Kerr and Colangelo's (1988) research provided additional insights. Overall, high-scoring ethnic minority students express higher degrees of preference for various services and special programs compared with European American students. African American students express higher levels of desire for study skills, personal counseling, independent study, honors programs, financial aid, and employment compared with other ethnic groups. Hispanic American students exceed European American students mainly in their desire for financial aid, independent study and honors, and employment. Asian American students exceed European American students mainly in their desire for educational, career, and personal counseling.

Ethnic Career Myths

Most ethnic minority students display less satisfaction with program choices and give lower ratings on receiving help with job choice and career decisions than do European American students (Richmond, Johnson, Downs, & Ellinghaus, 1983). These weaknesses contribute to a lack of self-awareness when these students contemplate career options. Research also indicates that ethnic minority students exhibit differences from European American students in background experience, values, and orientation that occur even though ethnic minority students' aspirations may equal or surpass those of middle-class European American students (Hispanic Research Center, 1991). These differences also tend to restrict an ethnic minority student's awareness of available careers and of the skills required. As a result, disproportionate numbers of ethnic minority students enter traditional career areas or remain unemployed. For example, Hispanic men are more likely to be employed in operator, fabricator, and laborer occupations than in any other occupational group, whereas non-Hispanic men tend to be employed in managerial and professional occupations (del Pinal & DeNavas, 1990).

Irrational beliefs held by ethnic minority students are referred to as *career myths* that are most often generated from historical, familial patterns of career ignorance and negative career developmental experiences (Dorn, 1987; Herring, 1990a). An example of a career myth is the belief that a career choice must be made before senior high school. Irrational career beliefs generally result in dysfunctional cognitive schema when ethnic minority students contemplate career decisions (Herring, 1990a).

School counselors are reminded, however, that many ethnic and cultural minority youths, as well as low-income European American youths, will display what the counselor may interpret as a career myth or irrational thinking. In reality, the youth may be presenting an important example of a "family rule," or shared belief within a subculture. For example, tenant farming tends to be a generational occupation. Youths are socialized that this is the family's way of making a living and to do something else does not indicate loyalty to the family. This tendency can be also be found in middle- and upper-income levels (e.g., the banking family, the lawyer family, the "Mom and Pop store").

Drummond and Hansford (1992) examined the career aspirations of 94 ethnic minority, pregnant teenagers enrolled in a dropout prevention program and found several trends:

1. Many of the participants had unrealistic assumptions about wanting to be in a profession even though they do not have the academic and economic resources necessary to be successful.
2. Occupational choice was not the immediate concern of the pregnant teens. They have other basic needs (e.g., physical, safety, and self-esteem) that they need to address first.
3. Schools do not address the career development and career maturity issues adequately.
4. Teens are not aware of the labor market and the types of available high-demand jobs.
5. Teens do not aspire to high technological jobs requiring advanced education but choose many types of jobs in which they will only be able to earn a marginal salary.
6. Pregnant teens are representative of at-risk youths who tend to wind up in occupations for which there is an oversupply of workers.

Research has also substantiated the relationship between irrational cognitions and indecisiveness in an ethnic minority student's career development experiences (Haase, Reed, Winer, & Bodden, 1979). In addition, irrational thinking has been found to be the basic component of ethnic minority students' career mythology (Slaney, 1983). Finally, research has demonstrated that traditional career theorists neglect to emphasize ethnicity and culture in their concepts (June & Pringle, 1977).

Chronic poverty and inappropriate education contribute to the persistence of career myths and low career aspirations among ethnic youths (Herr & Cramer, 1996). The lack of positive career role models also limits career choices of these youths. Such limitations continue the cycle of disproportionate employment and restrict the potential of ethnic minority youths, as well as low-SES youths in general.

MAJOR PSYCHOSOCIAL FACTORS

Ethnic and cultural minority youths also face numerous psychosocial obstacles in their attempts to participate in the world of work. This section emphasizes the major psychosocial factors affecting these youth:

identity conflicts, substance use and abuse, teenage pregnancy, suicide, and delinquency. The impact of these factors has been, and continues to be, counterproductive to successful career development for these youths.

Identity Conflicts

Ethnic identity is conceptually separate from personal identity and ethnicity. Ethnic identity is thought to be achieved through a process of crisis (exploration of alternatives) followed by commitment (decisions that reflect personal investment; Phinney & Alipuria, 1990). One simple approach to operationalizing ethnicity is to ask students what ethnicity they consider themselves to be.

For example, immigrating first-generation Asians are not identical to the people they left "back home," even though they may be identified as "traditional" immigrants (Sodowsky, Kwan, & Pannu, 1995). Asian families may have difficulty maintaining their sense of ethnic identity in a dominant culture that is vastly different from their own. The school counselor will need to be aware of the interplay of ethnic and nonethnic factors on the internal and external level as Asian American students develop their ethnic and personal identities (Huang, 1994). Ethnic identity constitutes a major issue among Hispanic American students as well (Comas-Diaz, 1990).

Substance Abuse

The problem of alcohol and other drug abuse in the United States continues to be of great concern. Three factors need to be recognized in this problem: physiological, sociological, and psychological (Lawson & Lawson, 1989). Physiological studies have indicated a genetic factor for some forms of substance abuse, sociological research has demonstrated the influence of family and peers, and psychological factors have been found to play a role. Although substance experimentation is relatively common among all adolescents, additional characteristics are reflected among ethnic minority youths. Diversity within ethnic minority groups makes it difficult to generalize from a particular subgroup to the larger group. For example, differences exist between reservation and non-reservation Native American Indians, among tribes, and even within tribes.

Native American Indian youths.   Results from 4 years of survey data conducted on over 200,000 eighth- and twelfth-grade students indicated that Native American Indian, Mexican American, and European American youths had higher lifetime prevalence rates for a number of substances compared with African American and Asian American youths. One in every seven Native American Indian eighth graders is currently using inhalants (Beauvais, 1992). Recent research has cited the following contributing reasons: use by peers, weak family bonding, poor school adjustment, weak family sanctions against drugs, positive attitudes toward alcohol use, cultural values, low educational achievement, low employment opportunity, and risk of school dropout (Swaim, Oetting, Thurman, Beauvais, & Edwards, 1993; Swaim, Thurman, Beauvais, Oetting, & Wayman, 1993).

African American youths. National surveys indicate that African American youths between 14 and 17 years of age use alcohol to a lesser degree than their European American counterparts and have fewer alcohol-related consequences (F. Brown & Tooley, 1989). African American youths age 12 to 17 reported use of alcohol at least once in 38.8% of the sample compared with 60.7% of European Americans and 44.1% of Hispanic American youth; African American girls reported lower use rates (17.9%) than did African American boys (National Institute on Drug Abuse, 1988). Contributing factors to abuse include poverty, unemployment, discrimination, and inadequate housing.

Hispanic American youths. Most studies of alcohol use indicate that rates of use among Hispanic American youths are either similar to or slightly below those of European Americans, but higher than rates for African Americans or Asian Americans (M. J. Gilbert, 1989). Chavez and Swaim (1992) found that the rate of use was higher for 8th-grade Mexican Americans. This pattern was reversed, however, among 12th-grade students, with European American seniors reporting higher rates than their Mexican American peers. The reversal is likely due to the higher rate of drug use among school dropouts and the higher rate of school dropout among Mexican Americans (Chavez, Oetting, & Swaim, 1994; Chavez & Swaim, 1992). Risk factors include quality of familial relationship, parental drinking, peer alcohol, and interactive effects (Felix-Ortiz & Newcomb, 1992).

Asian American youths. Little research literature is available on alcohol and drug use by Asian Americans. An important factor is the extreme diversity of this ethnic group. In fact, more than 20 Asian American groups have been identified by the U.S. Bureau of the Census (Zane & Sasao, 1992). More research is needed given this diversity and the increasing growth of this population.

Teenage Pregnancy

Whereas teenage mothers account for 12% of all births among European Americans, comparable proportions among Hispanic Americans, African Americans, and Native American Indians are 18%, 25%, and 22%, respectively (Malone, 1986). Approximately 40% of European Americans and 60% of African Americans become pregnant at least once by age 20 (McGowan & Kohn, 1990). Teenage pregnancy and parenthood are associated with educational setbacks, unemployment, family problems, and welfare dependency (Herring, 1997a, 1997b). Given the lack of role models, skills, and self-confidence necessary to pursue alternative paths, many ethnic minority girls, especially those from low-SES families, may actively seek the traditional role of mother as the only rite of passage by which to enter into adult womanhood (Rivers & Morrow, 1995).

Suicide

Native American Indians have the highest rate of completed suicide of any ethnic group (Herring, 1997a). Suicide is the second leading cause of death for Native American Indian youths, with 23.6 deaths per 100,000 in the 15–19-year cohort (U.S. Congress, 1986). For both Japanese and Chinese American adolescents, the suicide death rate has been reported to be consistently higher for foreign-born than for U.S.-born adolescents and for a much larger proportion of deaths than among European American youths (Liu et al., 1990). Suicide rates for African American youths are much lower than for European American youths (Gibbs, 1990). Little consistent data are available regarding recent suicide rates for Hispanic American adolescents (Heacock, 1990); however, the general consensus is that the Mexican American rate is approximately half that of European Americans (Hope & Martin, 1986).

Delinquency

Youths under the age of 21 account for about 30% of police arrests in the United States (U.S. Department of Justice, 1991). Factors related to chronic delinquency include low verbal intelligence, poor school performance, peer rejection in childhood, and membership in antisocial groups. A consistent factor is a family environment low in warmth, high in conflict, and characterized by lax and inconsistent discipline. Nonpeer and nonfamilial factors also influence the adolescent's choice of gang membership and delinquency (e.g., schools that fail to meet appropriate developmental needs).

Chavez et al. (1994) investigated delinquent behavior among Mexican American and European American adolescents. They found a consistent relationship between academic status and every type of delinquent behavior studied for both groups. Results suggest that Mexican American dropouts are no more delinquent than European American dropouts. Proportionally, however, there are more of them.

Impact of Psychosocial Factors

In summary, school counselors must understand how sociocultural and ethnic group contexts influence the development of mental health problems in ethnic minority youths. Concurrently, the negative influences of these problems on ethnic minority students' career development must be understood. Some researchers (e.g., Phinney, Lochner, & Murphy, 1990) contend that the common element among ethnic youths at risk for future psychological maladjustment is the maintenance of a foreclosed or diffused identity status. In addition, cultural marginality and the stress associated with acculturation result in heightened anxiety, lowered self-esteem, and aggressive acting-out or withdrawal behavior, which can contribute to such problems as substance abuse, academic underachievement or dropout, teenage pregnancy, delinquency, and suicide and homicide among ethnic minority youths (Rivers & Morrow, 1995).

CAREER COUNSELING WITH ETHNIC MINORITY YOUTHS

Several trends can be gleaned from the research on ethnic career counseling. One evolving and persistent theme involves values. Katz (1985) described a variety of culturally determined values that directly influence the career counseling process. Some of these values are the following: the status and power of the school counselor (i.e., authority figure vs. facilitator); communication (e.g., reflecting feelings vs. providing knowledge or advice); framing the problem in terms of cause-and-effect (i.e., degree of emphasis on family history, learned behavior, search for meaning); goals (insight oriented vs. change oriented); emphasis of scientific method (degree of emphasis on testing, appraisal, linear problem solving, and labeling problems); and time orientation (structured vs. unstructured). In each of these dimensions, students will possess personal value orientations, which may differ from that of the school counselor. School counselors should develop a sensitivity to student values that influence the counseling process and should be able to adopt counseling goals and treatment strategies that are consistent with the student's cultural and ethnic orientation or environment.

A second theme is that more than half the adults in this country who have enough information to express an opinion support increasing the emphasis placed on career development by public schools (D. Brown, Minor, & Jepson, 1992). School counselors who do not incorporate career development activities in their programs run the risk of losing public support for their program. Effective programs operate on the basis of carefully conceived plans predicated on the needs of their students (Wiggins & Moody, 1987). Support of African Americans for this increase in career development activities appears to be especially strong (National Career Development Association, 1991).

Another tendency is that African American students prefer social occupations more than do European American students; this tendency begins to appear as early as junior high school (M. J. Miller, Springer, & Wells, 1988). In addition, to survive the effects of dual discrimination in the workplace, many African American women have developed a coping system in which they avoid potentially discriminatory harmful work environments (K. M. Evans & Herr, 1991). See Something to Consider 7.1 for additional information on this concept.

The degree of acculturation also affects ethnic minority students' career plans. Ethnic minority students displaying higher degrees of acculturation tend to have higher occupational aspirations and expectations than do less acculturated ethnic minority students (Mahoney, 1992; Manaster, Chan, & Safady, 1992). Table 7.1 presents multiple career developmental needs of ethnic and cultural minority students.

Biracial Students

Gibbs and Hines (1992) studied the psychosocial adjustment of a sample of nonclinical biracial adolescents and their parents over 2 years. For biracial teens who identify with European American middle-class culture, academic achievement may be a way to gain acceptance and demonstrate values that they share with European American peers. However, awareness of prejudice and fear of failure in the academic realm may lead some of these adolescents to impose limitations on their academic achievement and ambitions. For those identifying with the minority culture, academic aspirations and studious behavior may invite ostracism or provoke ridicule. Because of fear of rejection by their peers, these teens may become involved in truancy, deliberately fail their courses, or engage in other self-defeating behaviors.

Something to Consider 7.1
African American Females' Coping System

To survive the effects of dual discrimination (i.e., gender and racial) in the workplace, African American females have developed (and perhaps perfected) a coping system, consisting of two components.

1. The avoidance of potentially harmful work environments where they perceive or anticipate a pattern of gender or ethnic discrimination.
2. A process of lowering or altering career goals (e.g., Savage, Stearns, & Friedman, 1979) that evaluates her perception of the opposing structure in a selected career field that may modify her goals to avoid prejudice, discrimination, and disappointments.

SOURCE: From "The Influence of Racism and Sexism in the Career Development of African American Women," by K. M. Evans and E. L. Herr, 1991, *Journal of Multicultural Counseling and Development, 19,* 130–135. Copyright 1991 by the American Counseling Association. Reprinted with permission.

Table 7.1
Career Developmental Needs for Ethnic and Cultural Minority Students

---

1. Need for systematic programs that emphasize self-awareness and career awareness to start in early childhood.
2. Need to use a broader model to look at skills and abilities (e.g., Gardner's, 1987, types of intelligence).
3. Need to relate academic skills to everyday life and career fields.
4. Need to reinforce achievement in mathematics and quantitative thinking.
5. Need for greater occupational awareness.
6. Need for more accurate occupational information on the local, state, and national levels.
7. Need for good role models.
8. Need for role models in nontraditional and diversified fields.
9. Need for fewer environment constructs that limit career development.
10. Need for fewer constraints that limit career development of ethnic/cultural minority students.
11. Need to be cognizant of current labor market trends.
12. Need to help ethnic/cultural minority students to diversify their interests and choices.
13. Need to develop and use more ethnic-cultural appropriate assessment resources.

In the realm of conflicts over educational and career aspirations, 75% of these biracial teens were performing above average academically and were planning to go to college and graduate school. However, fewer than half had made specific plans about careers or future lifestyles. Their educational aspirations appeared to be influenced primarily by their parents, whose average educational and occupational level was high, rather than by specific occupational goals. Thus, their biracial identity did not appear to have had a negative impact on their future aspirations, which seemed realistic and congruent with their academic performance.

International Youths

In a study of 789 Portuguese and 489 French students, the impact of nationality was significant on the determinants of salary, prestige, promotion, and "intellectual-manual" (Mullet, Neto, & Henry, 1992). Portuguese students, more than French students, tend to prefer jobs that they judged to provide the highest possibilities for promotion. The intellectual-manual dimension evidenced the greatest impact on Portuguese, but in the opposite direction, that is, toward manual jobs. Further research was advised to clarify whether Portuguese students more than French students perceive manual jobs as the most prestigious and the most likely to command high salaries. In addition, students of higher SES tended to prefer jobs judged by them to be the most prestigious and the most difficult to enter or the least accessible.

Need for Ethnic Career Counselors

Insufficient numbers of ethnic minority school counselors prevent students' contact with ethnic-similar counselors. A significant percentage of students, especially African American students, prefer ethnic-similar counselors (Herring, 1997a, 1997b). To significantly increase the number of ethnic minorities in the field of career planning and placement, however, requires multiple strategies. A short-term alternative can be found in a secondary school guideline developed by N. K. Campbell and Hadley (1992):

1. To design, implement, and evaluate a training program that allows ethnic minority staff to explore the field of career planning and placement as a career possibility.
2. To provide opportunities for selected staff to acquire a theoretical knowledge of career development concepts and issues and a core of career development skills.

Planning, implementing, and evaluating career development programs for diverse students are important roles for school counselors. A culturally responsive school counselor should orient students to the world of work within the context of values, interests, and abilities developed in diverse cultural contexts. Such orientation would include promoting interest in careers in which ethnically diverse groups have been underrepresented (C. C. Lee, 1995a). Chart 7.1 suggests 13 ways to convey career information to students in an appropriate manner.

A national study, focusing on potential barriers to higher education choice and access, found that parental income and education influence students' academic and career goals more than do ethnic factors (National Opinion Research Center, 1995). This study tracked 25,000 teenagers from the eighth grade in 1988 through their early college years in 1994 and showed that they tended to form aspirations and shape their futures before they reached high school.

The evidence suggests that youths coming from more privileged backgrounds, regardless of ethnicity or gender, have achieved uniformly well with their opportunities. The findings indicate that the lower the parental income and education, the less likely a student is to acquire a bachelor's degree or even enter college. The study showed that only 36% of those in the lowest income group went into post-secondary education. In contrast, 63% of students in the middle income group and 88% of the most affluent students attended college or vocational programs.

Chart 7.1
13 Better Ways to Pass Along Career Information

1. **Tailor the message:** Be sensitive to the student's exact informational needs.
2. **Resist the "loading down" syndrome:** Most students learn best with a single career placement task to accomplish.
3. **Don't leap over goal setting:** Thinking and speaking clearly about goals is significant.
4. **Promote career knowledge:** Differentiate job title, job function, work environment, and industry.
5. **Avoid jargon:** Discuss career planning in down-to-earth terms.
6. **Go easy on clichés:** Encouraging words and actions need to be combined with clear instructions.
7. **Get student feedback:** Ask if information was useful or whether the student can follow up.
8. **Use anecdotes for affect:** Stories about real students influence more than statistics or urging.
9. **Help students visualize career messages and jobs:** Use functional language with the students.
10. **Explain both sides of the job:** Explain the challenges of a job as well as a "bad day."
11. **Start by destroying career myths:** It is always helpful to mention a few myths that students believe and ask for reactions. The student needs to relate to them as well as refute them.
12. **Enhance learning with visuals:** Pictures, diagrams, and charts, plus humor, can make career planning procedures and steps more understandable.
13. **Help students find positive connections:** We use the term transferable skills but usually only to mean from job to job, not education to job, or college to career.

SOURCE: From "13 Ways to Pass Along Real Information to Students," by T. Bachhuber, 1992, *Journal of Career Counseling and Development, 52*, pp. 66–69. Copyright 1992 by Plenum Publishing Corporation. Adapted with permission.

To discern how students perceived their futures, eighth graders in the study were asked how much they expected to earn at age 30. Those in the highest income group said they expected on average to earn almost $63,000 in a year, whereas those in the lowest income group said they would earn an average of $46,000. Differences along ethnic lines were much smaller. African Americans on average estimated they would earn about $67,000 at age 30, whereas European Americans expected to earn an average of about $53,000.

Reinolds (1996) offered an excellent example of how state governments can intervene and increase ethnic minority students' access to higher education. For example, the state of Arkansas has done a good job of funneling students into higher education. The Arkansas Academic Challenge Scholarship (AACS) provides eligible students up to $9,000 to attend any Arkansas public or private college or university. To qualify for an AACS, students must have maintained a minimum high school grade point average (GPA) and scored at a certain level on their ACT/SAT exams. In addition, there are also financial need requirements, and students must certify that they are drug-free and pledge to stay that way. In addition, for each academic year that a student completes 24 credit hours and maintains a 3.0 cumulative GPA, they will receive $500 above the award received in the previous year. Another influence has been the Arkansas Student Loan Authority, which offers federally guaranteed loans at 1% less interest than the federal government. Arkansas's college-going rate—63% of high school graduates—is slightly above the national average of 62%, even though its average family income is one of the lowest in the nation.

Counseling Orientations to Consider

The initial decision for the school counselor is which theoretical model should be selected for their interventions. Frequently, available models can be confusing, overlapping, or redundant. The school counselor must make a wise choice. In review, models available for consideration include cross-cultural counseling, minority group counseling, multicultural counseling, and synergetic counseling.

Cross-cultural counseling.   Any counseling relationship in which two or more of the participants are culturally different is called *cross-cultural counseling*. Atkinson, Morten, and Sue (1993) defined this relationship as "situations in which both the counselor and student(s) are ethnic minority individuals but represent different racial/ethnic group . . . or the counselor is a racial/ethnic minority person and the student is European American . . . or the counselor is European American and the student is a minority" (p. 15).

Minority group counseling.   Any counseling relationship in which the student is a member of an ethnic minority group, regardless of the status of the school counselor, is considered minority group counseling. The research literature has concentrated on ethnic minorities and has examined the relationship between the European American school counselor and the ethnic minority student without recognition of other possibilities. This limited view of minority group counseling has resulted in some criticism because it ignores the special conditions of a counseling relationship in which the school counselor is also an ethnic minority person. Furthermore, concern exists that the term *minority group counseling* suggests a minority pathology; this is, perceived as analogous to "Black pathology," an attempt to explain African American behavior in terms of European American norms (Atkinson et al., 1993, p. 6).

Multicultural counseling.   Multicultural counseling encompasses all the facets of the diverse ethnic and cultural environments in contemporary society. In some respects, all school counseling is multicultural, taking into account the infinite number of possible school counselor–student combinations (Axelson, 1993). School counselors need to create a "cultural environment wherein two people can communicate with and relate to each other" (p. 12).

Synergetic counseling.   I suggest the use of synergetic counseling precepts. Stated simply, this model encourages the use of the most appropriate intervention for the student or students at the moment with considerations for historical and environmental influences. Additional influences on the counseling session would include issues of gender, age, sexual orientation, and conditions of medical, mental, physical, and/or emotional challenge.

Loganbill, Hardy, and Delworth (1982) classified interventions into five categories.

1. *Facilitative interventions* provide the basis of counseling relationships and involve the use of unconditional regard and warmth, respect, and empathy.
2. *Confrontive interventions* involve a comparison of students' functioning with their oral statements.
3. *Conceptual interventions* are designed to offer a cognitive understanding of issues that are important to a student's unique situation. The school counselor provides relevant information and encourages the student to use other perspectives when viewing particular circumstances.
4. *Prescriptive interventions* provide the student with a specific plan of action to use in a particular situation when immediate action is required or when a student needs clear directions to lower anxiety.
5. *Catalytic interventions* promote change or movement with a minimum of direct counselor involvement. The school is able to focus attention on key issues by assuming a low profile and using skillful questioning, probing, or exploring techniques. Caution is needed, however, when intrusive probing may be perceived as insensitive to certain ethnic and cultural minority groups (e.g., Native American Indians).

School and career counselors who use a synergetic approach with ethnic and cultural minority students may consider the following examples of concepts, activities, and techniques (Axelson, 1993; Herring, 1997b; Herring & Walker, 1993):

1. Identifying and reinforcing self-perceived qualities and self-movement.
2. Blocking negative thoughts.

3. Practicing positive visual imagery.
4. Validating self through identification with others.
5. Learning self-assertion skills.
6. Understanding and using the system.
7. Acquiring knowledge and information through career guidance and education.

The initial counseling session must begin with conceptual and facilitating interventions to ensure a shared understanding of what the sessions are about. The counselor must gain an understanding of the ethnic or cultural group membership of the student. Counselors have to exert time and effort to gain data (e.g., an assessment of class, acculturation, language, education, and subgroup membership) before addressing the problem and not assuming a generic ethnic personality.

Students, on the other hand, have to understand the limits of the counseling and be encouraged to be creative and persistent in their job search experiences by learning effective job-seeking techniques (Drummond & Ryan, 1995). Learning activities should include supervised practice, support services, and debriefings after they receive feedback from potential and actual employees. As in all areas of counseling, school and career counselors are required to engage in follow-up activities on their students periodically and systematically.

SUMMARY

Contemporary and future society is and will be even more reflective of ethnic and cultural heterogeneity. Current ethnic minority groups will evolve into the ethnic majority groups of tomorrow. School and career counselors must recognize the career development needs of diverse minority students and the types of interventions that are successful with these students (Drummond & Ryan, 1995). Concurrently, counselors must become more culturally sensitive and competent (Mahan & Rains, 1990).

A multicultural perspective is a vital viewpoint because of the more diverse student population that exists and the rapidly changing demographics in the United States (Swanson, 1993). The need for an enhanced awareness of the importance that culture and ethnicity play in the career development process is needed. Angry youths will remain as such until, within educative systems, people of all heritages and differences are valued and permitted to empower themselves through an egalitarian allocation of socioeconomic resources (Hernandez, 1995).

EXPERIENTIAL ACTIVITIES

1. Try the following exercises to enhance students' understanding and awareness of ethnic stereotypes in the world of work, as adapted from Aronson (1994, p. 31).

    1. Ask students to close their eyes for a moment and imagine a lawyer, then a police officer, then a doctor, then a criminal. Ask them to raise their hands if they saw a female lawyer, an Asian American police officer, a Hispanic American doctor, or a European American criminal. Explain that stereotypes operate so subtly sometimes that we don't even notice them.

    2. List the following "types of people" on the board and ask students to assign each a race or nationality on the basis of stereotypes. Have them fill in details about how each type of person dresses, how they talk, where they live, and what they value most in life.

        - chemistry professor
        - rap musician
        - gang member
        - bank president
        - hair stylist
        - political terrorist

        Now ask students to imagine the rap musician matching the description of the chemistry professor or the hair stylist fitting the description of the political terrorist. Discuss why it seems easy to think in terms of stereotypes. Consider the harm done by stereotypes when they are applied to entire groups of people.

    3. Do a sociogram (survey) of the class to find out the degree of interaction among students of different ethnicities: "If your mother would only let you invite two kids to your birthday party, which two from one class would you choose?" Or ask a similar question about getting help with homework.

    4. Survey career choices of students in the junior high, senior high, or community college. Compare the choices by ethnic or cultural group membership. Write a report of the results from your study.

    5. Participate in a dyadic encounter with an individual from a different ethnic or cultural group, or a recent immigrant. Describe your experiences.

8

Career Development With Gay, Lesbian, Bisexual, and Transgender Students

Come out, come out, whoever you are.

Adolescents have many problems centered around their emerging sexual drives and sexual orientation. However, educators and parents often disagree whether these topics are appropriate for school discussions. In general, sexuality and especially sexual orientation are forbidden topics in many schools, and many individuals and community groups demand that they remain so (H. Grossman, 1995). Yet many educators believe that these subjects are necessary components for school curricula. For example, only 1 out of 28 school district boards in the New York City public school system voted to include the approved elementary school curriculum that deals with homosexual orientation in their schools (Columbia Broadcasting System, 1993). To ignore adolescent sexuality is to ignore an aspect of student development that is often left fragmented from other areas of development, brings tremendous conflicts for students, and is unfortunately an area these students often cannot find help for elsewhere (Street, 1994).

This chapter addresses career development concerns of gay, lesbian, bisexual, or transgender (GLBT) youths. The main objective is to discuss, from a career guidance perspective, what it means to grow up as a GLBT youth in a homoprejudiced society. The uninformed reader will note that many authors have reappropriated the formerly pejorative word *queer*, radically using the term to include a range of sexualities, including but not limited to lesbian, gay, and other gender identities (Eisen & Hall, 1996). In addition, whereas the term *transsexual* defines those individuals who believe that they are really a member of the other gender trapped in bodies of the wrong gender, the term *transgender* refers to "individuals who do not comply with the either/or, female/male construction in society" (Ormiston, 1996, p. 201).

OVERVIEW OF THE PROBLEM

To accept the widely quoted estimate that 10% of the U.S. population is gay would indicate that approximately 3 million youths between 10 and 20 years of age are predominantly or exclusively homosexual (Deisher, 1989). When bisexual and transgender students are added, this population represents a significantly large minority within the school counselor's purview that warrants attention. These students come from every ethnic, religious, and class background. What they share is the experience of growing up being alienated from, yet shaped by, the social institutions, roles, and norms of their larger society (Gerstel, Feraios, & Herdt, 1989).

GLBT students are reared in a homophobic society and have little access to information that portrays alternative lifestyles in a positive way. Many suffer from homophobia and believe they are sick, evil, inferior, and disgusting. These self-perceptions can result in emotional problems such as depression, shame and guilt, low self-esteem, and self-hatred or at least ambivalence toward their sexual orientation (H. Grossman, 1995). In turn, their emotional problems can cause them to drop out of school, abuse substances, and commit suicide.

Children of GLBT parents can also experience many problems both in and out of school. Students who are reared by openly GLBT parents are exposed to the same homoprejudiced attitudes as GLBT students. Their parents' sexual orientation can expose them to prejudiced treatment in school. Like GLBT students, children of GLBT parents need appropriate education and support in and out of school.

As Herr and Cramer (1996) so aptly stated, "That sexual preference should have an impact on career development and choice is, in may ways, repugnant" (p. 292). Yet the reality is that GLBTs are barred from certain careers and find vertical mobility negligible because of their sexual orientation. The negative bias against GLBTs is often more intense than that directed at any other minority group, from both institutional and individual perspectives (Goleman, 1990).

CAUSATION OF SEXUAL ORIENTATION DIFFICULTIES

Both students who are worried about their sexual orientation and GLBT students need assistance and understanding. However, many counselors believe that the school is not the place to deal with or even discuss differences in sexual orientation. Dunham (1989) described the situation in the schools as follows:

> While mental health professionals have worked to create positive and meaningful programs for the gay and lesbian population, educational systems have been considerably less eager to recognize and respond to the needs of this minority group. Public schools have continued to treat homosexuality as a forbidden subject. (p. 3)

As a result of such attitudes within schools, this population continues to face a plethora of difficulties. In this section, eight of the causative factors of sexual orientation difficulties are briefly discussed. These main areas of causation are misunderstanding and misinformation, invisibility, identity development, lack of support systems, family problems, violence, sexual abuse, and sexually transmitted diseases.

Misunderstandings and Misinformation

Some segments of society continue to argue that a teenager lacks the maturity to determine his or her sexual orientation to be gay, lesbian, bisexual, or transgender. These critics contend that a nonheterosexual orientation is merely an adolescent fantasy that the youth will outgrow. Such assumptions reflect a gross misunderstanding of the sexual orientation and perpetuate the flow of misinformation.

Most high school counselors recognize that there are students in their schools for whom issues of sexual orientation may be of utmost concern, yet few programs address those needs. Rather, school counselors avoid confronting sexuality issues because of numerous internal and external factors. These factors may be grouped under two broad categories: homophobia and institutional discrimination.

Homophobia. Homophobia, or the irrational fear of GLBTs (Gramick, 1983), is the leading cause of the lack of services to GLBT persons of all ages. A school counselor's homophobia may seriously cloud his or her clinical assessment and interventions. Research suggests that counselors tend to view sexual orientation as the cause of problems in GLBTs, rather than viewing some more typical explanation as causative (Davidson & Friedman, 1981).

Institutional discrimination. Institutional discrimination occurs against GLBT students on two levels: within graduate school curricula and at the professional level (K. E. Robinson, 1994). First, school counselors are not educated regarding the special concerns of GLBT students as a minority group. Second, school counselors work within an educational system that programmatically ignores this population. Schools regularly fail to confront controversial matters, especially in the area of adolescent sexuality (Rofes, 1989). Questions regarding sexual orientation are not asked, general information about sexual identity is not offered, and referrals for individual counseling or group support are not made (K. E. Robinson, 1994). Such avoidance is clearly institutional denial of the existence of GLBT students.

Invisibility   Gay and lesbian youths are an isolated silent population that has generally been abandoned by society and overlooked by the counseling professionals (K. E. Robinson, 1994). "Gay and lesbian adolescents continue to be socialized to conceal their identities—educated to be invisible within the school community and the community at large" (Dunham, 1989, p. 5). Various causes of the current invisibility of GLBT students in schools have been identified: a reflection of society's justifiable desire to keep sexual orientation out of the school curriculum, homoprejudiced attitudes among educators, educators' lack of courage to advocate for the rights of GLBT students, and the failure of school personnel to correct many educators' misinformation about the causes and "cures" of homosexuality (H. Grossman, 1995).

The American School Counselor Association's (1980) statement titled "Human Sexuality and Sex Education" supports the establishment of developmental programs on human sexuality. In reality, school counselors can provide numerous supportive services to address sexuality issues as an adjunct to more specialized services (Street, 1994). However, few school districts have developed innovative projects such as Project 10 in Los Angeles and the Harvey Milk School in New York City that offer special services to GLBT students or students with GLBT parents (Friends of Project Inc., 1991; Ross-Reynolds, 1982). Project 10 provides help to students who remain in their local schools. The Harvey Milk School offers an alternative school setting for those who wish to escape the difficulties inherent in being openly GLBT in a regular high school setting. Both programs have their share of critics who believe that GLBT students need be counseled to convert to heterosexuality, but the Harvey Milk School has also been criticized by supporters of GLBT rights for capitulating to discrimination and homophobia—"ghettoizing" non-heterosexual students, removing them from the mainstream, and providing them with inferior educational opportunities (H. Grossman, 1995, p. 217). Because these programs are rare, most GLBT students are forced to rely on the assistance and understanding of individual teachers and counselors.

Gender-Identity Disorder and Identity Development

Research studies continue to confirm that adult homosexuality is strongly related to childhood gender-identity disorder, which is often apparent by the age of 2, usually by the age of 4, and almost always by the age of 6 (Coates, 1985; R. Green, 1987). Study results indicate that the first 3 years of life are critical for the development of gender identity (Money &

Ehrhardt, 1972). For example, the *Diagnostic and Statistical Manual of Mental Disorders'* (4th ed.; American Psychiatric Association, 1994) criteria for the male childhood gender-identity disorder include a strong wish to be a girl or insistence that one is a girl; rejection of one's own uniquely male anatomical features; and preoccupation with stereotypical female activities. Other research suggests that most boys who experience cross-gender identity in childhood develop into a homosexual orientation or otherwise atypical orientation (R. Green, 1987; Zucker, 1990). Longitu-dinal research on 50 feminine boys documented that most feminine boys acknowledge themselves as being homosexual, or at least bisexual, by late adolescence (R. Green, 1987). Other studies have found that the entire available sample of feminine boys had become homosexual by the time they reached their 20s (Money & Russo, 1979).

Numerous variables contribute to this pattern (Coates, 1985; R. Green, 1987). Some of these factors are an absent or inattentive father and an overprotective mother who expresses hostility toward men and toward typically masculine behavior. Such modeling tends to reinforce a boy's quiet, unobtrusive play (Street, 1994).

Lack of Support Systems

Isolation is the biggest factor for any minority group struggling to become accepted in a larger society (K. E. Robinson, 1994). A. D. Martin and Hetrick (1988) identified unique problems that homosex-ual youths face related to isolation and separated these into three main categories: cognitive, social, and emotional. The cognitive isolation reflects the almost total lack of accurate information available, as well as a predominance of inaccurate, negative, and stigmatic information about GLBTs. The social isolation of homosexual youths is evident in comparing them with other minority groups. An adolescent who is African American, Jewish, or Hispanic is not at risk to be thrown out of his or her family, to be expelled from his or her peer group, or to lose his or her religious social identity because of his or her minority status. The most serious factor to consider is the emotional isolation of the homosexual adolescent, who believes that he or she is abnormal, has no one to talk to, and suffers from feelings of being totally alone. This aspect of isolation is illustrated by the high incidence of attempted suicide among young gays and lesbians—they are two to six times more likely to attempt suicide than are heterosexual adolescents (Harry, 1991).

Family Problems

Family problems of homosexual adolescents range from feelings of alien-ation and fear that the family will discover the adolescent's homosexual-ity to actual violence and expulsion from the home (K. E. Robinson,

1994). Unlike other minority groups, homosexual youths are unique in that their parents almost never have the same sexual orientation as they do. Even parents who are aware and supportive of teenagers' developing homosexual identities lack personal experience of, and strategies for responding to, related problems (A. D. Martin, 1982; Muller, 1987).

Another concern is the reaction of parents if the school were to confront sexual orientation issues openly. Schools, however, must focus on the needs of their students rather than on the demands of parents or the larger community (Rofes, 1989). School counselors must remember that their primary clients are not the parents or the community, but the students (K. E. Robinson, 1994).

Violence

Violence is another issue that homosexual youths face every day. A. D. Martin and Hetrick (1988) found that more than 405 of their clients have suffered some form of violence because of their sexual orientation. Furthermore, 49% of that violence occurs within the family, usually from parents, but sometimes from siblings. See Case Studies 8.1 and 8.2 for practical examples of violence against homosexual students.

Sexual Abuse

The incidence of sexual abuse of homosexual students is also becoming more evident. A. D. Martin and Hetrick (1988) reported that 22% of their clients have been sexually abused. Homosexual adolescents, isolated and having no one to confide in, lack therapeutic intervention and are vulnerable to repeated attacks. This trend is especially frequent in families where a stepfather is present in the home.

Sexually Transmitted Diseases

The incidence of sexually transmitted diseases among homosexual adolescents presents a significant risk. For example, younger (22 years

---

Case Study 8.1
Harold

Harold is a middle-class African American 15-year-old boy who ran away after experiencing years of abuse from his father because of a gay relationship. He worked in a grocery store in the evenings and attended high school during the day, resolving to complete high school. Instead of a supportive environment at his new school, Harold found his peers hostile and harassing. Openly gay to his classmates and teachers, Harold was teased during class by other students and received no support from teachers. After he was physically assaulted at the bus stop after school, Harold felt pushed to the point of either quitting school or demanding action.

Case Study 8.2
Mary

Mary is an African American 15-year-old girl from Harlem. She had difficulty coping with the rejection she found in her inner-city high school because she was openly a lesbian. Name calling, harassing notes, and verbal threats of violence, including rape, began to turn an upbeat, cheerful girl into one of dysfunction and misery. As Mary faced the unpleasant task of 2 more years of such reactions, she found herself moving toward the idea of quitting school.

of age and younger) gay men have been shown to be significantly more likely to contract gonorrhea, as compared with older (23 years of age and older) gay men (Centers for Disease Control, 1990). So far, there is no evidence that suggests a similar trend in the contraction of the acquired immune deficiency syndrome (AIDS); the importance of such research, however, adds an even greater urgency to our efforts to identify the health and human service needs of gay youths and to respond appropriately (K. E. Robinson, 1994).

SOLUTIONS TO SEXUAL ORIENTATION DIFFICULTIES

R. Green's (1987) 15-year study with 50 gay boys inferred the "apparent powerlessness of treatment (i.e., counseling). . . (to effect any) major impact. . . on sexual orientation" (p. 318). Additional data from longitudinal studies indicate that counseling for change is not likely to produce lasting results; rather, much evidence indicates that sexual orientation is probably determined from early childhood and may even include genetic and hormonal predispositions (Street, 1994). School counselors would be wise to forego attempts to counsel these adolescents to "change" their sexual orientation (E. Coleman & Remafedi, 1989; K. E. Robinson, 1994). These youths are dealing with a trait that they cannot change, even as much as those who are heterosexual cannot change being heterosexual (Street, 1994).

In a survey of 46 homosexual adolescents, only 15% stated that they believed school counselors would be "helpful" in working with their homosexuality issues; 43% stated that they believed counselors would be "unhelpful" (Mercier & Berger, 1989). A concern often expressed by school counselors is that they are uncomfortable offering services to this population because they believe this is an area requiring specialized training (Street, 1994). This attitude is simply rationalization. Homosexual adolescents need the assistance of accepting themselves and of feeling good about themselves, when they feel so different from those around them (Krysiak, 1987; R. Powell, 1987).

The climate in most school settings is not conducive to offering homosexual support groups, although this is exactly what these youths need. Social acceptance and awareness that they are not alone are major issues for this population. Classroom-based developmental guidance is an effective format for educating students about individual differences in lifestyle choices (Street, 1994). Education about homosexuality may also be appropriate in this setting, particularly for students among the student population who are homosexual or bisexual but who would not approach the counselor (Remafedi, 1987). It is further incumbent on the school counselor to inform and educate the student body about safe sex, regardless of sexual orientation.

Textual Orientations

Malinowitz (1995) asserted that gay and lesbian students have been consistently silenced in school classes where, despite acknowledgment of gender, ethnic, and class differences, sexual identity is assumed to be universally heterosexual, a norm that is vigorously displayed by individuals' verbal and nonverbal homophobia. Because the discourse of sexual difference is deemed irrelevant by otherwise well-intentioned educators, these students feel powerless to construct their own knowledge or to author their lives in textually authentic ways.

Textual orientations are about shifting the terrain of epistemic privilege to create a "queercentric environment" (Malinowitz, 1995, p. 26) for GLBT students. "Queercentric" does not mean exclusively for GLBT students, but, rather, means acknowledging that "homophobia and the silencing of lesbian and gay discourse do have a significant impact on students who do not define themselves as lesbian or gay insofar as the silencing of any social group creates cognitive gaps for the whole community" (p. 28). Textual orientations thus describe attempts to bridge these gaps by inviting students to explore the tensions, complexities, and contradictions of sexual identity and the world of work.

Suggestions From Research Efforts

K. E. Robinson (1994) surveyed the research on counseling GLBT youths and synthesized some suggestions regarding how the school counselor can implement interventions toward addressing the needs of this student population in a subtle yet effective manner. The list is not exhaustive and serves only as an introduction to the possibilities of the creative and concerned school counselor.

Practice self-awareness.   School counselors need to explore their feelings and attitudes about homosexuality honestly. If a counselor is unaware of his or her own countertransference issues, he or she may be unable to provide an appropriate environment for the adolescent to explore both positive and negative feelings and beliefs about sexuality (Benvenutti, 1986).

Be informed of the available resources. The school counselor should have practical knowledge of the available resources that exist within the gay community and the community as a whole. These resources should include local support groups, gay community publications, and national organizations, as well as gay-affirmative therapists, physicians, and therapy groups when referrals for specialized services are required (Dulaney & Kelly, 1982).

Accept the student as a whole person. The school counselor should not assume that every GLBT student's problems are related to his or her sexuality (Dulaney & Kelly, 1982). Most problems of GLBT students are basically the same as those of other adolescents—self-esteem concerns, developmental issues, and family problems—not necessarily from being gay (K. E. Robinson, 1994). The primary developmental task for GLBT students is adjustment to a socially stigmatized role (Hetrick & Martin, 1987).

Use broad, open-ended assessments. School counselors should include questions about sexuality issues in the initial interview. This strategy conveys that the counselor considers sexuality an important aspect to be openly discussed (Dulaney & Kelly, 1982). Questions should be open-ended, such as "Are you involved with anyone?" or "Do you have any other special, close friends?" rather than "Do you have a boyfriend/girlfriend?" (Dillon, 1986).

Provide information. The school counselor should display referral materials on bulletin boards as a nonthreatening means of reaching the student body (Benvenutti, 1986). These materials should include sexual health information, telephone help lines, and community mental health seminars. In addition, school counselors should have an ample supply of free informative handouts about issues of sexuality for student use.

Facilitate an in-service training session. The school counselor can improve attitudes toward homosexuality by providing in-service training sessions for faculty and staff, as well as community members. Education can improve awareness and attitudes related to homosexuality (B. Newman, 1989). These sessions should be designed for the dissemination of information as well as for feedback from the participants.

Start a focus or support group. If the school counselor has several self-identified GLBT students, a focus or support group could prove helpful, regardless of whether the students are having any emotional or academic problems (K. E. Robinson, 1994). Support groups offer students the opportunity to develop social skills, learn about others beyond familiar stereotypes, and gain nonbiased information (K. E.

Robinson, 1991). Something to Consider 8.1 provides additional information on support groups.

Share your experiences.   School counselors need to expand the literature and knowledge about homosexual adolescents. They can contribute to this knowledge base by sharing their experiences with others. Many questions about sexual orientation can be answered by the students themselves (K. E. Robinson, 1994). School counselors have the opportunity to ask and subsequently convey the answers to others. Case Study 8.3 offers examples of GLBT students' thoughts.

Additional research offers the following suggestions for helping students who are concerned about their sexual orientation (e.g., E. Coleman & Remafedi, 1989; H. Grossman, 1995; Krysiak, 1987; Ross-Reynolds, 1982).

- Resist community pressure to avoid relating to the needs of students who are concerned about their sexual orientation.
- Refer students to community agencies and resources where they can obtain assistance.

Something to Consider 8.1
Support Groups for GLBT Youths

Many GLBT youths do not have parents or family members with whom they can discuss sexual issues, or they attend schools where they could be harmed or ostracized for "coming out." For many of these teenagers, social support groups play a vital role because they are able to interact with other youths like themselves. The following list is not inclusive of available support groups for this population.

Boston Association of Gay
   and Lesbian Youth (BAGLY)
Box 814
Boston, MA 02103
(800) 42-BAGLY (422-2459) or
   (617) 43-PROUD
TTY: (617) 983-9845
http://www.bagly.org/bagly

Parents, Friends, Families of Lesbians
   and Gays (PFLAG)
Box 18901
Denver, CO 80218
(303) 333-0286
or
1101 14th Street, Suite 1030
Washington, DC 20005
(202) 638-4200

Growing American Youth (G.A.Y.)
c/o Our World Too
11 South Vandeventer
St. Louis. MO 63108
(314) 533-5322

National Advocacy Coalition on Youth
   and Sexual Orientation
1025 Vermont Avenue, Suite 200
Washington, DC 20005
(202) 783-4165 FAX: (202) 347-2263

!Outproud! http://www.cyberspaces.com/outproud

Case Study 8.3
GLBT Youth Voices

Young people face much pain and alienation when they are forced to live a secret life. In the following synopses from their writings, young people (ages 14 to 18) share about their lack of power in schools and family lives. These comments offer insights into the variety of experiences and responses that youths have when they, a friend, or a family member is gay, lesbian, bisexual, or transgender (GLBT).

1. Joy wishes that her mother will realize that her lesbianism is just one part of her—something that has contributed to her identity and expanded her horizons. She believes that coming out to her parents has taught her to respect the strength it takes to be herself and to tolerate homophobics.
2. Kathryn opens herself to her schoolmates and teachers. By raising questions and confronting issues, she appeals to them to look inwardly at their fears, ignorance, and indifference toward homosexuality, and challenges them to confront both their personal beliefs and their part in creating the larger school culture.
3. Mandy uses her poetic ability as an outlet to understand why people do hurtful things to dissimilar people. She emphasizes how slow healing is and asks readers to think about their actions toward others.
4. Megan conveys that homophobia affects not only GLBT youths, but also youths who have a family member or friend who is. Judy is the daughter of a lesbian mother and shares the many dimensions of her own coming out process—a coming out not about her own sexuality but rather her attempts to speak truthfully about her two mothers.
5. Paul challenges everyone to question the use of labels such as "gay," "lesbian," and "bisexual." He acknowledges that while these labels may help some people identify who they are, they are also problematic in that they may make people feel trapped. Billy uses the more inclusive term "queer," a word that has historically been used against GLBTs but has been reclaimed by the gay community to acknowledge their diversity. Billy also talks about the difficulties of affirming oneself as both queer and Christian.
6. Rachel describes an incident that forced her to confront her silence about her lesbianism. She does so because the world lacks stories she cares about. She shares what it's like to long for a place where a person doesn't have to lie about who he or she is.
7. Schuyler, a heterosexual, shares his experiences and photographs as a member of a photography project about lesbian, gay, bisexual, and transgender youths. He learned about the rich diversity of the GLBT youth community and came to deplore their too common experience of not feeling safe to be themselves at school or at home. He believes the main lesson he learns is to change the topic of sexual orientation from something seen as dirty and shameful to something that needs to be openly discussed in schools and other places where learning occurs.

SOURCE: From "Youth Voices," edited by V. Eisen and I. Hall, 1996, *Harvard Educational Review*, 66(3), 173–197. Copyright 1996 by *Harvard Educational Review*. Adapted with permission.

- Protect students from harassment, criticize such incidents when they occur, and express disapproval of jokes about gays.
- Modify homoprejudiced attitudes. Oppose censorship of texts and library material that demonstrate respect for GLBT rights and lifestyles. Dispel myths about people with nonheterosexual orientations. Advocate for students rights. Include homosexual role models.

Gonsiorek (1988) stated the situation as this:

> A healthy socialization process involves positive role models. Ideally, the socialization experiences for gay and lesbian adolescents will include learning from competent gay and lesbian adults. Observing how successful adults develop productive and ethical lifestyles, resolve problems of identity disclosure, obtain support, manage a career and build relationships can be extremely valuable for teenagers. (p. 121)

It will not be easy for school counselors and other educational personnel to carry out these suggestions. As Rofes (1989) noted:

> Because many educators believe that homosexuality is sick, sinful, or criminal, it is tremendously difficult for them to truly adopt an objective stance when addressing gay and lesbian issues in the classroom. . . . By allowing positive treatment of homosexuality in the classroom, teachers are vulnerable to witchhunts by parents and school committees attempting to root out homosexual teachers. In certain parts of the nation, laws have been proposed and successfully passed that forbid positive discussion of homosexuality in public school classrooms. (p. 451)

ALTERNATIVE LIFESTYLES AND CAREER DEVELOPMENT

Given that the choice to live an openly GLBT lifestyle may well lead to discrimination, ostracism, and even violence, career counseling and lifestyle planning represent special challenges to school counselors working with these students. Careful vocational and lifestyle planning might include, for example, preparing while still young for an occupation or profession in which there is a maximum of freedom from constraints imposed by other people (Shannon & Woods, 1991). Or it might involve restructuring one's income-producing activity later in life to enable such freedom (Berzon, 1979).

Available Resources

For students who are exploring career job choice per se, school counselors need to be aware of special resources (Schmitz, 1988). These could include professional networks (e.g., National Lawyers Guild Gay Caucus, Association of Gay Social Workers, Gay Airline Pilots Association, and gay business and professional organizations in major cities); viable corporate climates (e.g., organizations recognized as possessing nondiscriminatory policies toward gays; see National Gay Task Force for listing); legal codes and statutes that protect the rights of GLBTs in the job setting (i.e., legislation that prohibits discriminating practices on the basis of sexual orientation); and printed materials that provide information relevant to the job search. For example, the *Gayellow Pages* provides an annual listing of networks, professional associations, and businesses and can be purchased at gay bookstores

(Shannon & Woods, 1991). School counselors also need to educate their GLBT students about careers that continue to discriminate on the basis of sexual orientation (Herek, 1990). For example, many federal government positions requiring a security clearance are not open to GLBTs.

Effects of "Coming Out"

Lifestyle planning might mean "coming out" to family and friends early in life so that deception does not have to become a painful habit to be broken later. Sifting one's values may also be necessary so that projects and goals would yield greater personal affirmation and freedom (versus material reward, for example). Coming out as a GLBT person also influences career decision. A lesbian may realize early that she will never depend on a male partner's salary (Hetherington & Orzek, 1989) and may, therefore, choose a male-dominated occupation to maximize her earning potential (Browning, Reynolds, & Dworkin, 1991). Because women, however, are still not widely supported in pursuing nontraditional occupations (Wilcox-Matthew & Minor, 1989), lesbians who have chosen these occupations may experience discrimination and other difficulties. A lesbian will need to decide if she wants to work in an occupation in which her sexual orientation need not be hidden, because self-disclosure in many occupations will result in overt or covert discrimination (Hetherington & Orzek, 1989). In addition, many gay and lesbian youths may remain "closeted" in order to enter careers such as teaching, child care, and child psychology because of the myth that they recruit children to the gay or lesbian lifestyle. A lesbian woman may choose to live in a large city or become involved in national gay/lesbian professional organizations to decrease feelings of isolation. In addition, occupational harassment and negative stereotypes are as real for lesbians as they are for heterosexual women.

The interdependence of careers and relationships is also important for many lesbians (Berzon, 1988). Lesbian couples face the same dual-career issues as nongay couples, but because their relationship is not validated by society, they usually cannot get support or assistance in dealing with these issues (Hetherington & Orzek, 1989). School counselors can help these youths explore their career options and distinguish between realistic and unrealistic fears; they also can provide information and support (Browning et al., 1991; see Case Study 8.4).

Career Counseling With GLBT Students

Problems of career counseling with GLBT students can arise from the low self-concept and poor emotional stability of the students as well as from the homophobia of the school counselors (Drummond & Ryan,

---

Case Study 8.4
Canary

Canary is a 17-year-old, confident, assertive lesbian student in the 11th grade. She enjoys the outdoors and wants to earn a good salary. She decided to become a park ranger and obtained a part-time job as a student intern with her state's park service. Canary decided to see her school counselor when the sexist remarks of the male interns and employees began affecting her self-esteem. Canary was one of only two female interns in the program. Some of the male interns frequently alluded to the fact that women should not become park rangers and that any woman who is interested in this career must be "queer." Canary was terrified that they would discover that she was a lesbian.

When Canary came to her counselor, she was depressed, and not eating or sleeping well. She did not want to give up her career choice and yet was unsure if she could continue to handle the hostile attitudes. Canary was involved in the local lesbian community and received support from them for her interests. The school counselor's counseling with Canary during her senior year included providing a safe environment to express her anger and frustration, cognitive disputations of irrational beliefs, role-playing ways to approach men, assertiveness, training to express discomfort with community and family expectations for her, and rehearsal of behavioral response to potential problems.

1995). Super (1990) noted the importance of self-concept to career development. In addition, GLBT students are often harassed, discriminated against, and the target of slurs and violence. This population may also have double or triple minority status when homosexuality is combined with other minority characteristics such as ethnic/racial membership, gender, and class (Hetherington & Orzek, 1989).

Career counseling can be effective with this population if school counselors are committed to eliminating their homoprejudiced attitudes (Hetherington & Orzek, 1989). The school counselor must become aware of gender issues and models of homosexual identity development. Helping students with self- and career awareness and knowing job-seeking strategies are common competencies for all students. School counselors working with this population need to be aware of the cultural heritage of the students, be comfortable with their differences, and be sensitive to their personal circumstances (Elliott, 1993). If these minimal conditions cannot be attained, the school counselor is obligated to refer the student to someone who can meet these conditions.

The National Gay and Lesbian Task Force maintains a list of companies that have a stated policy on sexual orientation. Counselors need to know which businesses and industries have nondiscrimination policies. Information on the attitudes of managers and workers toward

GLBTs is also important. Elliott (1993) found that gender discrimination exists within this group as lesbian workers earn less than gay workers.

The self-concept and identity integration of gays and lesbians may be related to their coming-out stage (House, 1991). In this process, GLBTs pass through stages of identity confusion to eventually identity integration. They move from a stage of being aware that they are different but confused, alienated, and defensive to a stage in which they have a healthy self-view and focus on age-appropriate issues and developmental plans (House, 1991).

With downsizing of companies and the downturn in the economy, many gay and lesbian students are in a quandary about coming out and remain in the closet and keep their lifestyle secret. Drummond and Ryan (1995, p. 350) offered some of the successful approaches counselors have used in working with this group.

- Help them network with the gay/lesbian community.
- Provide successful role models with the same sexual preference.
- Arrange for them to job shadow gays/lesbians in the career field in which they are interested.
- Get them involved in support groups of individuals with the same sexual preference.
- Help them arrange interviews with gay/lesbian workers in companies in which they are considering employment.
- Have them role-play problem situations on how to handle antigay and lesbian attitudes and homophobia.
- Find mentors for them.

Hetherington, Hillerbrand, and Etringer (1989) addressed the career issues of gay men, who are reputed to have more uncertainty about their career choices and less job satisfaction than either heterosexual men and women or lesbians. Sensitive counselors need to be aware of the three central issues identified by these authors.

One issue is *negative stereotyping* (e.g., equating homosexuality with mental disturbance or assuming that certain occupations are dominated by gay men). A second issue is *employment discrimination*, because the legal status of those who have a different affectional preference from the majority appears to be nonexistent and still evolving. A third issue concerns *limited role models*, which appear to have the same effect on gay men as the absence of appropriate role models has on any minority group.

Diamant's (1993) book on homosexual issues in the workplace discussed concerns in such occupational areas as the military, the church, the helping professions, education, and athletics. Orzek (1992) considered identity as a central factor affecting the career development and counseling of gays and lesbians. Most of the recent literature related to counseling gays and lesbians focuses on identity development models (e.g., Croteau & Thiel, 1993; McFarland, 1993; Walters & Simoni, 1993).

The school counselor must not limit or convey that there are limited career fields that gays and lesbians can enter (Drummond & Ryan, 1995). Lesbians may be more open to seeking nontraditional employment because they do not conform to the traditional gender role. In addition to their unique problems in career decision making and job discrimination, gay and lesbian couples also face conflicts that heterosexual couples face. For example, dual-careers couples may have conflicts when the partner is going to be relocated or wants to change career fields.

Counselor Sexual Orientation

Liddle's (1996) research suggested that gay and lesbian clients benefit from having a gay or lesbian therapist/counselor. Liddle collected data from 392 gay and lesbian volunteers who described their experiences with 923 therapists. She also examined 13 therapist practices as they related to client rating of therapist and failure to return for the second session.

Liddle concluded that (a) qualified support exists for therapist–client matching on sexual orientation for gay and lesbian clients; (b) heterosexual women therapists are seen as more helpful than heterosexual men and no less helpful than gay, lesbian, and bisexual therapists; and (c) the fact that heterosexual women therapists were no less helpful than gay, lesbian, and bisexual therapists also demonstrates that heterosexual therapists can be helpful with this client population.

Positive results have been found with gay/lesbian/bisexual support groups that were cofacilitated by heterosexual counselors (Chojnacki & Gelberg, 1995; Holahan & Gibson, 1994). These support groups were originally started with a gay counselor and a heterosexual female counselor cofacilitating. After the departure of the gay counselor, the only option was heterosexual counselors. The support groups continued and reported positive results for the group members.

The cited research and other studies indicate that sexual orientation of a school counselor could enhance the counseling relationship with similarly oriented students. The research also indicates that heterosexual women counselors do no worst than lesbian or bisexual counselors. It is probably unrealistic to suggest sexual orientation matches be employed in school settings. However, another reality is that there are gay, lesbian, and bisexual school counselors who have not "come out." It is hoped that these counselors are playing an authentic role with their GLBT students.

Inclusion or Exclusion

A controversial issue that needs some discussion is whether GLBT individuals should be included in a definition of multicultural counseling. One group of professionals contend that multicultural counseling should only refer to interactions between helping professionals and clients of diverse ethnic/racial backgrounds. Instead of expanding the definition, these individuals would prefer to use the words *counseling diverse populations* when dealing with issues related to gender, lifestyle, age, and disability.

The other side favors an inclusive definition of multiculturalism that includes sexual orientation. Pope (1995) argued that (a) sexual minorities must face identity-formation tasks similar to those of ethnic minorities, (b) multicultural skills are also important for dealing with sexual minorities, (c) a lesbian and gay culture exists, and (d) lesbian and gay oppression is evident and dehumanizing. I tend to align with the inclusionists.

SUMMARY

The most important thing to remember about GLBT youths is that they are just as diverse as heterosexual, or "straight," youths in terms of ethnicity, belief, and identity. These youths need a safe environment in which to grow and express themselves. The undeniable truth, however, is that many schools are still not safe for GLBT youths. Nor do they provide appropriate counseling services for these youths. For example, the suicide rate for GLBT youths is significantly higher than for heterosexual youths, and 30% of teenage suicides are among GLBT youths (P. Gibson, 1989). Many more live life in deep depression.

While it is wonderful that organizations such as the Boston Association of Gay and Lesbian Youth exist for GLBT youths, it is a sad commentary that so many teens have to move to big cities from surrounding smaller cities and towns to be able to find a place to be honest about their full identities. It is unfortunate that in schools and families such issues cannot be discussed (Eisen & Hall, 1996). Educators must modify their own homoprejudiced attitudes and those of their students, protect students from harassment, advocate for homosexual students' rights, include GLBT role models and issues and topics that affect GLBT students in the curriculum, oppose censorship of texts and library material that demonstrate respect for GLBT rights and lifestyles, and dispel myths about people with nonheterosexual orientations

(H. Grossman, 1995). In addition, many questions remain for research considerations.

EXPERIENTIAL ACTIVITIES

1. Should sexual orientation issues be included in the curriculum? Should counselors discuss their students' sexual orientation problems with students?
2. What should counselors and other educators do when community agencies and parents prefer or demand policies that conflict with their views of whether and how to deal with sexual orientation issues and problems?
3. How knowledgeable are you about Title IX?
4. How does your school respond to the career development needs of GLBT students?
5. Begin collecting resource materials about GLBT issues and concerns so when the time comes you will not have to postpone discussions.

9

Career Development
With Special Needs Students

The test for whether or not you can hold a job
should not be the arrangement of your chromosomes.

Bella Abzug

Most of the major theories of career choice and development have not addressed specifically the career developmental needs of students with disabilities or vocational disabilities. The theories provide an understanding of career choice or career development but have severe theoretical and practical limitations for working with this population (Drummond & Ryan, 1995). In addition, few studies, in comparison with studies addressing the general student population, have explored the career education, career guidance, and career counseling needs of special student populations. For this chapter's discussion, special student populations include students with a challenging characteristic that prevents a normal delivery of career guidance and counseling services. This chapter suggests these students can contribute to and participate in the world of work. This population simply requires appropriate accommodation to ensure their success. The discussion begins with an overview of the developmental issues among students with disabilities.

DEVELOPMENTAL ISSUES

The Division of Career Development of the Council for Exceptional Children (1987) stated that career development is a sequential process designed to assist youths and adults in achieving meaningful work roles, such as student, consumer, citizen, family member, and employee. A key issue is evidenced in the age at which the disability occurred. If the disability occurred at birth or early in the students' development, the students could be impaired in their ability to accomplish the developmental tasks at the appropriate time (Drummond & Ryan, 1995). Disabilities could influence their cognitive, intellectual, interpersonal, and communication development and subsequently their psychosocial development.

Lombana (1992) reported that the earlier a person becomes disabled, the less traumatic is the adjustment process. She emphasized that life stage is extremely important in the acceptance of a disability. For example, adolescents tend to be more introspective and insecure and might have a difficult time accepting their physical self. Super (1957) believed the time of onset of disability, whether in precareer or mid-career stages, influences the effects the disability will have on the individual's vocational self-concept. In addition, type of disability is also an important variable.

Super (1990) did not envision a need for a specialized career development theory for individuals with disabilities but did see a special application for a more general vocational theory. Super's assumption was that all youths without cognitive-functioning deficits of one kind or degree should parallel nondisabled development (Clark, Carlson, Fisher, Cook, & D'Alonzo, 1991). The age range and stages might vary some, but Super felt that growth and development of an individual can be facilitated and enhanced for those with disabilities.

Hershenson (1974) argued that a study of disabilities can aid career development theories in understanding all students and brings attention to disjunctions and nonmodal career patterns. He concluded that the experiences of the disabled are a valuable asset to be considered in extending the range of career development theories.

ATTITUDES TOWARD THE DISABLED

Perhaps those barriers most significant and most difficult to initially identify are those originating in attitudes of school personnel toward students with disabilities. If these attitudes are based on myths, stereotypes, fears, or ignorance, it is likely that substantial barriers to full participation of students with disabilities will be present in school settings (Hoar, 1992; Parette, 1992). Public attitudes are generally positive toward individuals with disabilities. This positive attitude, however, does not imply that misconceptions and stereotypes are not still quite pervasive. A Louis Harris poll found that 98% of the respondents believed that all individuals, regardless of ability, should have the chance to participate in mainstream society, and 92% believed that employment of individuals with disabilities would be economically beneficial (Wehman, 1993). However, Parette (1992) described three types of barriers that result from unintentional but nevertheless significant discrimination against individuals with disabilities: physical barriers, policy and procedural barriers, and attitudinal barriers.

The Conference Report of the Americans With Disabilities Act of 1990 (Pub. L. No. 101-336) stated that discrimination toward individuals with disabilities "continues to be a serious and pervasive social problem . . . and individuals with disabilities continually encounter various forms of discrimination" (p. 3). A *disability* is defined as "a physical or mental impairment that substantially limits one or more of an individual's major life activities." This act prohibits discrimination by employers against qualified individuals with disabilities in terms of the job application procedures; the hiring, advancement, and discharge of employees; job training; employee compensation; and the conditions and privileges of employment.

Lombana (1992) concluded that available research indicated that gender, age, race, and teaching experiences have relatively little impact on teacher attitudes toward students with disabilities. Teachers with greater knowledge of disabilities have more positive attitudes toward students with disabilities compared with teachers with lesser knowledge. Regardless, classroom teachers do not favor mainstreaming for students who are seriously disabled. Lombana also found that students with the least severe or visible disability appear to be more accepted or preferred. Emotionally disturbed or mentally retarded students are generally the least preferred.

School counselors and helping professionals need to have a broad understanding of the attitudes, knowledge, stereotypes, and beliefs that employers, peers, parents, and teachers have toward students with disabilities. Examples of individuals having responsibility for educating students with disabilities include vocational education teachers (e.g., home economics teachers) and technical education teachers. Nevertheless, classroom teachers play a major role in these students education.

RELATIONSHIP BETWEEN INTELLIGENCE AND OCCUPATIONAL SUCCESS

In the relationship between intelligence and occupational success, the debate over genetic or environmental influences on intelligence is not the primary focus of this chapter and therefore will not be discussed at length. However, the debate does deserve some attention. Research efforts directed toward premises integrating genetics, the nature of human intelligence, and the concept of race remain controversial (Fraser, 1995; S. J. Gould, 1994). Perhaps the strongest evidence against a genetic basis for intergroup differences in intelligence is that the average level of mental test performance has changed significantly for European American populations over time; moreover, particular ethnic groups have changed their relative positions during a period when there was little intermarriage to alter the genetic makeup of these groups (Sowell, 1995) . "When all is said and done, intelligence predicts neither later success in life nor job performance. It does not predict income disparities later in life" (Wolfe, 1995, p. 117).

Intelligence has been correlated with educational attainment and training program success as far back as the 1930s (Super & Crites, 1962). The work of L. S. Gottfredson (1984) has addressed significantly the study of intelligence and occupational success. Some relationship appears to exist between intelligence and occupational/vocational functioning (Morris & Levinson, 1995). Intelligence does have a substantial correlation with level of educational attainment and occupational prestige. In addition, mean intelligence levels can be assigned to occupations although considerable overlapping occurs. Intelligence seems to predict training and performance in clerical jobs best and can be correlated with vocational maturity and self-knowledge. Also, a relationship exists with type of vocational interest and a willingness to pursue selected vocations. High intelligence also seems to be associated with an increased likelihood that expressed and realistic interests will be congruent.

SPECIAL NEEDS POPULATIONS

Although specific group characteristics may change, students will continue to exist who have special needs for career development. Historically, these groups have been denied access to educational and occupational opportunities because of racial, sexual, age, cultural, or disability discrimination and bias. Ethnic/racial and sexual concerns are presented in other chapters in this book. For the purpose of this discussion, *special needs populations* include those student groups who are appraised as students with disabilities or other conditions that prevent them from being included in mainstream school curriculums.

Students With Disabilities

One population whose human potential is often underdeveloped is students with disabilities. Terminology describing students with disabilities changed during the 1980s from the *handicapped, mentally retarded,* or *handicapped students* to a more humanistic and less dehumanizing term reflecting that they are students first and that they have a disability second (Brolin & Gysbers, 1989). Yet, the terms *disability* and *handicapped* continue to be used interchangeably without recognition of another important distinction. A *disability* is "an impairment or functional limitation in one or more bodily systems" and a *handicap* refers to "an inability to perform work required by a particular job or to function in a work environment" (Daniels, 1981, p. 170). Herr and Cramer (1996) defined the *disabled* as

> a population that has a disability or several disabilities that may or may not be a vocational handicap. The disability may be *physical* (such as amputations, birth defects, cancers, heart problems, burns, deafness, blindness, multiple sclerosis, muscular dystrophy, orthopedic, spinal injury), *intellectual* (mental retardation, learning disability, brain damage, speech and language disorders), *emotional* (mental illness, substance abuse, alcoholism, obesity and other eating disorders), or *sociocultural.* In any case, best estimates are that in the United States over ten percent of the population have chronic physical, mental, or emotional conditions that limit their activity sufficiently to make a substantial career difference. (p. 294)

In school settings, the term *handicap* generally identifies students who have a physical or mental condition or limitation that prevents them from succeeding in a regular school program. More specifically, students who are mentally retarded, learning disabled, emotionally disturbed, orthopedically or visually disabled, and hearing, speech, or health impaired (with chronic problems such as diabetes or heart condition) are classified as *handicapped* (Zunker, 1990, p. 448). As a result of the Carl D. Perkins Vocational Education Act of 1984 (Pub. L. No. 98-524), schools are required to obtain both career-vocational interest and aptitude information on all students with disabilities who participate in career development and vocational education and training programs. The following discussion highlights several of the most common disabilities found in student populations.

Students with personality disorders. The relationship between personality and career development has played an important role in many career theories, beginning with Parsons's (1909) trait-and-factor theory of career choice. A student's personality affects career decision making, on-the-job performance, occupational success, and occupational functioning (Kjos, 1995). Zunker (1994) highlighted the importance of identifying behavior patterns that can interfere with a student's work role. He organized patterns around selected personality disorders.

The personality of the student also has an effect on the counseling relationship and plays an important role in the ultimate outcome of counseling. Little attention has been directed, however, to the relationships among abnormal personality, career development, and interventions in career counseling and guidance (Kjos, 1995). Of 10 personality disorders, the *Diagnostic and Statistical Manual of Mental Disorders* (4th ed., *DSM-IV*; American Psychiatric Association, 1994) specifically links nine with occupational difficulties or impairment in occupational functioning. These include paranoid, schizoid, schizotypal, borderline, narcissistic, avoidant, dependent, obsessive, and compulsive. A personality disorder exists only when a grouping of traits or behaviors causes either "significant distress or impairment in social, occupational, or other important areas of functioning" (p. 633).

The school counselor's recognition of personality disorders and consideration of the needs of differing styles in treatment planning, including the selection and use of interventions and appraisal techniques, enhance the effectiveness of counseling and student–counselor satisfaction. Work activities and work settings are of more importance than actual occupation titles. Thus, a specific personality disorder should not be considered indicative of a specific job fit (Kjos, 1995).

Throughout the process of career counseling, it is important for the school counselor to encourage the student's sense of ability to function independently by using language that affirms the student's ability to make choices and the student's responsibility for those choices (Kjos, 1989). Finally, because personality influences interpersonal relationships, the counselor should be aware of his or her own responses to students, especially when their responses may interfere with effective treatment (Kjos, 1995).

Students with mental disabilities. Researchers have investigated the relationship between intelligence test scores and aptitude tests for students who are mentally challenged (e.g., Kohring & Tracht, 1978; J. T. Miller, 1978) and the relationship between intelligence and the occupational functioning among students who are learning challenged (e.g., Faas & D'Alonzo, 1990; Humes, 1992; Webster, 1974). Students with neurological impairment are also included within this category.

Morris and Levinson's (1995) review of research on exceptional populations has suggested some patterns in the relationship between intelligence and occupational factors. These suggestions include the following (p. 510):

1. Intelligence, when subdivided into ranges, has been predictive of which mentally retarded individuals, when released from institutions and selectively placed into occupations, might experience success.
2. Intelligence has a limited relationship with planned occupational placements among individuals who are mentally retarded and more

so with actual outcomes if reassessments are periodically completed throughout the rehabilitative process.

3. Individuals with higher intelligence are more likely to find and keep jobs as long as they do not exhibit deficits in behavioral, social, and attitudinal skills.
4. With all exceptional populations, performance, intelligence, or a combination of performance subtests has been predictive of success in low-level occupations.

Learning disabled. Career planning for this population, as with other populations, is intertwined with the need for better assessment of two important variables impinging on career success: personality and interests. Certainly, career planning for this subpopulation can be a productive activity, but one must obviously factor in the additional variables of intellect, motivation, and socioeconomic status (Humes, 1992). Research Emphasis 9.1 offers additional information on the appraisal of this population.

Students with behavioral or emotional disabilities. A number of research efforts have been aimed at students with emotional challenges (e.g., Warren & Gardner, 1981; Webster, 1979). Institutionalized psychiatric patients are within this category. School counselors should not overreact to the behavioral or emotional behaviors of these students. If the behaviors are intrusive to the immediate school situation, the counselor can take the student out of that setting and attempt to determine the student's needs using concrete and direct questions (Parette & Hourcade, 1995). Counselors should not assume that potential violence is associated with unusual behaviors. If aggressive behavior is observed, notification of security personnel is warranted.

Siblings of Students With Disabilities

A student population that has been woefully neglected is evidenced in siblings of students with disabilities. The few studies that have explored career choices of siblings of individuals with a developmental challenge seem to support Holland's (1963) trait-and-factor theory of career choice. Results seem to suggest that the experience of having a sibling with a developmental challenge may indeed affect career choice (Konstam et al., 1993). The combination of welfare goals and fatalism found in these siblings can possibly account for the high incidence of sisters of siblings with challenges in the helping professions (Farber, 1963). A critical variable for future study may be the identification and further understanding of factors that mediate the impact of a sibling with a developmental disability on his or her siblings.

Research Emphasis 9.1
Career Planning for Learning Disabled High School Students

Humes (1992) studied the personality and interests of 141 (101 male, 40 female) high school students (14 to 18 years old) in Learning Disabled (LD) resource room programs. These students were given the Myers–Briggs Type Indicator—Abbreviated Version (MBTI–AV) and the Self-Directed Search–Easy (SDS-E) for the purposes of career planning. Results indicated the efficacy of these instruments.

Personality
The LD students placed predominantly along the Extraversion–Perception (EP) MBTI-AV continuum. EPs are active, energetic, sociable, and always seeking new experiences. In the general population, 55% to 60% prefer Judging; in this sample, 67% preferred Perception, which is a reversal.

Interests
- The male LD students displayed realistic interests with Realistic–Investigative and Realistic–Enterprising predominant.
- The female LD students displayed a preference for conventional pursuits with Social–Artistic, Conventional–Social, Social–Enterprising, and Social–Conventional as the preferred codes.

The research indicates that career planning with this population can be productive with these instruments. However, the additional variables of intellect, motivation, and socioeconomic status must be considered. Career planning may also be dependent on a counselor's familiarity with the MBTI and the SDS.

SOURCE: From "Career Planning Implications for Learning Disabled High School Students Using the MBTI and SDS-E," by C. W. Humes, 1992, *The School Counselor, 39,* 362–368. Copyright 1992 by the American Counseling Association. Adapted with permission.

F. Grossman (1972) found that college students with siblings with mental retardation were more inclined to do volunteer work in human services than those who did not have such a sibling. Konstam et al. (1993) found that no research in the past decade had built on Farber's (1963) and F. Grossman's (1972) research efforts. In fact, Konstam et al. discovered no significant difference in career choice between two sets of siblings.

Models of stress and coping seem to predict well-being in these families; potential mediators include parental attitudes, family social support, and family social environment (L. Dyson, Edgar, & Crnic, 1989). A sibling's self-concept was best predicted by parental stress and resources. Future research that uses alternative instruments to measure value orientation might prove fruitful. In addition, a larger sample representing a more diverse population may yield different results.

The school counselor can be effective by creating a sensitive, open milieu in which the siblings of an individual with a disability can explore career options and academic choices that acknowledge the impact of having a sibling with a developmental disability (Konstam et al., 1993).

GUIDANCE AND COUNSELING IMPLICATIONS

In counseling students with disabilities for career assistance, school counselors must (a) have an understanding of various disabilities and their career implications; (b) be knowledgeable about appropriate resources, training, and career opportunities; and (c) be sensitive, supportive, and, concurrently, realistic (R. L. Gibson & Mitchell, 1995). School counselors must be prepared to assist students with disabilities in personal adjustment, self-concept development, career development, and job placement. School counselors may also play the role of advocates for this student population as they seek access to education, other training, or the workplace itself.

Omizo and Omizo (1992) emphasized the importance of the school counselor combining data on career/vocational interests, aptitude, and work-related adaptive habits with data generated from psychological, educational, economic, and sociocultural appraisals in helping students with disabilities to plan for the future. School counselors need to be effective consultants as well as advocates for students with disabilities. They need to provide useful information to employers participating in cooperative education programs on how to work effectively with students with disabilities. Regular education teachers and parents who may be involved also need accurate and appropriate information (Elksnin & Elksnin, 1990).

In addition, school counselors need to address with their students the issues of competence and the ethical standard that requires counselors to function within the limits of their defined role, training, and technical competence (Hosie, 1979; Hosie, Patterson, & Hollingsworth, 1989; Nadolsky, 1986). Up-to-date curricula are vitally important in the preparation of school counselors (Nadolsky, 1986). Obsolescent resources restrict the delivery of appropriate services and can be detrimental or counterproductive to appropriate service. Hosie (1979) proposed 14 competency areas for school counselors that remain, with some modification, relevant. School counselors need those competencies to provide comprehensive services to this population (see Something to Consider 9.1).

The inability of students with disabilities to compete adequately for jobs in their communities clearly indicates their need for more appropriate career-vocational preparation prior to leaving the secondary school (Omizo & Omizo, 1992). School counselors can become valuable members of the multidiscipline team responsible for the development of career-vocational educational-training program placement and planning decisions, because they have specific skills (e.g., interviewing techniques) that can contribute significantly to the collection, coordination, and implementation of career-vocational

Something to Consider 9.1
School Counselor Competencies in Providing Services to Students With Disabilities

1. Knowledge of current federal and state legislation, program guidelines, and policies relating to the broad spectrum of federal, state, and local services for people with disabilities.
2. Knowledge of the rights of individuals with disabilities (both youths and adults) and their families, and the skills necessary to advise them of their rights and advocate on their behalf or to refer them to appropriate advocacy agencies or groups.
3. Knowledge of state program guidelines for classification and eligibility determination, current diagnostic tools and their limitations, and the skills necessary to relate these to learning and training characteristics and their remediation or correction.
4. Knowledge of formal and informal assessment and observational procedures, and the skills necessary to relate these to the special learning strategies of individuals with various types of disabilities.
5. Knowledge of individual growth and development processes, and the interaction of these processes with various types of disabling conditions, as well as the skills necessary to relate this knowledge to developmental learning objectives when applicable.
6. Knowledge of physical, mental, and emotional disabilities, including sensory impairments, speech disorders, communication deficits, and their effect on diagnostic and remediation methodologies, as well as aids and assistive devices, and the skills necessary to overcome or lessen their effect in learning, training, counseling, and employment settings.
7. Knowledge of input, structure, and purposes of Individualized Education Programs, Individualized Transition Programs, and Individualized Written Rehabilitation Programs, and the skills necessary to consult on their development or assist in their construction, implementation, and evaluation.
8. Knowledge of ability, learning rates, modes of learning, and impediments to learning of people with disabilities, and the skills necessary to identify unsuccessful achievement and to change methods and learning objectives when necessary.
9. Knowledge of ethnic, cultural, and language factors related to people with disabilities, as well as attitudinal biases held by teachers, employers, and others, and the skills necessary to modify these attitudes.
10. Knowledge of environmental and architectural barriers that prevent individuals with disabilities from full participation in society, and the skills to consult with appropriate individuals to alleviate these barriers.
11. Knowledge of learning disorders, social and emotional behavioral problems of persons with disabilities, and the skills necessary to instruct or consult with teachers and potential employers, using behavioral modification and management principles to enhance learning and social behavior.
12. Knowledge of the psychological and sociological impact of disability on individuals with congenital, as well as adventitious, disabilities and the impact on the family, and the skills necessary to consult, counsel, and/or provide information to individuals with disabilities and their families or significant others to alleviate myths and stereotypes and facilitate their understanding.
13. Knowledge of the impact of disability on the career decision-making process and the skills to assist individuals with disabilities in career decision making and development.
14. Knowledge of the roles and skills of other personnel within and outside rehabilitation and educational institutions, and the skills to appropriately refer individuals with disabilities and their families.

SOURCE: From "School and Rehabilitation Counselor Preparation: Meeting the Needs of Individuals With Disabilities," by T. W. Hosie, J. B. Patterson, and D. K. Hollingsworth, 1989, *Journal of Counseling & Development, 68,* 171–176. Copyright by the American Counseling Association. Adapted with permission.

appraisal information (Omizo & Omizo, 1992). See Something to Consider 9.2 for additional information.

Robinson and Mopsik (1992) provided viable suggestions on establishing and maintaining an appropriate environment for counseling students with disabilities and creating appropriate experiential situations for the student. Their guidelines have applicability across developmental levels and suggest that school counselors use multisensory approaches and structured tasks in a nondistracting environment. School counselors need to communicate concretely, avoiding verbal generalities and abstract relationships, and to use concise, explicit sentences with consistent repetitions. The school counselor may have to deal with a lack of family support and self-confidence as well and must monitor the student closely until adjustment to the training or work setting is ensured.

As career education terminology subsided in the 1980s, a new term that closely resembled the career education concept was introduced and is applicable to students with disabilities. The term *transition* was defined as an outcome-oriented process involving a broad array of services that lead to employment (Super, 1990). The transition period includes high school graduation, postsecondary education or adult services, and the initial years of employment. Examples of transitional strategies include

---

Something to Consider 9.2
Multidiscipline Career-Vocational Appraisal of Students With Disabilities

---

Career-vocational appraisal of students with disabilities should be conducted along with other forms of assessment (i.e., medical, social, cultural, educational, and psychological). Without school counselors' involvement, students with disabilities will continue to be mediocre (E. M. Levinson, 1987). Information collected through various career-vocational appraisals can be used to help students with disabilities in the following ways.

- To determine the student's interests, strengths, and needs as they relate to future roles of being a family member, citizen, employee, and social-recreational participant
- To gain knowledge of the student's ability to learn from career-vocational instruction
- To reveal the need for instructional modification and accommodations and optimal teaching methods
- To obtain more detailed information about the student's individual characteristics
- To make an informed decision regarding suitable career-vocational education-training program placement alternatives
- To indicate needed support services
- To improve the responsiveness of career and vocational development programs and planning decisions (e.g., Individualized Education Plans)

SOURCE: From "Career and Vocational Assessment Information for Program Planning and Counseling for Students With Disabilities," by S. A. Omizo and M. M. Omizo, 1992, *The School Counselor, 40*, 32–39. Copyright 1992 by the American Counseling Association. Adapted with permission.

vocational training, work adjustment programs, traditional employment programs, on-the-job training, job placement, and job restructuring. A number of transitional strategies are widely used to help individuals with disabilities adjust from school or training to work.

Transition must be planned effectively, and individual transition plans developed for the students and interagency agreements must be negotiated (Heal, Copher, & Rusch, 1990). The transition concept, like career education, requires interdisciplinary cooperation in the schools and with community service agencies and employers, as well as meaningful parent involvement (Brolin & Gysbers, 1989). Collaboration is essential to a successful transition-oriented program so students receive planned, appropriate, and nonduplicated services (Chadsey-Rusch, Rusch, & Phelps, 1989).

Too many schools depend on other agencies to provide for the career development needs of students with disabilities. However, in reality, most do not have the time, staff, or money to provide quality services. Perhaps, school-based rehabilitation counselors would improve this student population's transition into the world of work (Szymanski & King, 1989; Szymanski, King, Parker, & Jenkins, 1989). Otherwise, until educators come to grips with how to effect systemwide change, the struggle will continue as it has in the past (Knowlton & Clark, 1987). School counselors also assist in the placement of their students with disabilities in peer support groups with other similarly disabled students (R. L. Gibson & Mitchell, 1995). As with so many other educational and social services, ethnic minority students have not proportionally availed themselves of rehabilitation counseling. Dziekan and Okocha (1993) commented:

> It is only possible to speculate about reasons for lower acceptance rates for minority clients, and a number of factors might have contributed. Lower proportions of minority individuals applying for services may have actually met agency eligibility criteria. Lower proportions of minority clients may have chosen not to follow through with the acceptance process because of their frustrations with the steps and delays involved. Alternatively, biases in the perceptions of rehabilitation counselors determining eligibility for services may have resulted in inaccurate assessments and underestimations of rehabilitation potential. (p. 187)

An increasingly popular intervention in the delivery of career development to students with disabilities is the Life-Centered Career Education curriculum approach developed by Brolin (1978, 1983, 1989) that has been implemented in many school districts across the country (e.g., Arizona, California, Colorado, Minnesota, Michigan, and Missouri). This curriculum emphasizes 22 major competencies that students need to succeed in daily living, personal-social, and occupational areas after they leave school. These 22 competencies are further subdivided into 97 subcompetencies that relate to one or more of four important career roles that constitute a total worker. These four career roles consist of the work of an employee, the work that is done in the home, volunteer work, and productive avocational activities. This curriculum is designed to facilitate the student's individual growth and development for all the major roles, settings, and events that constitute a person's total life career development. It is a K–12+ approach built on the four stages of career awareness, exploration, preparation, and assimilation and requires a close and meaningful partnership between educators, the family, and community agencies, employers, and other resources. This collaborative and multifaceted approach is reported to be an effective curriculum that fuses daily living skills instruction with an employability skills focus (Hoyt & Shylo, 1989).

Appraisal Issues

Appraisal is an important phase of career guidance and counseling for students with disabilities. Career guidance and counseling of special populations are usually the mission of special education programs in the schools and rehabilitation services in the public and private sector. Berven (1986) emphasized that a wide variety of sources and types of appraisal data are used. He noted four main types of procedures: the interview, the use of tests and inventories, simulated and real work experiences, and the use of functional assessment scales. Chapter 12 details appraisal from a multicultural emphasis and offers suggestions for appropriate appraisal instruments for special populations.

Gifted and Talented Students

Differences exist between gifted and talented male and female students in their career and educational aspirations, in terms of prestige, gender traditionality (i.e., masculinity vs. femininity), and field of interest. Whether such differences begin in the early or later age periods, however, is not clear.

Leung, Conoley, and Scheel (1994) investigated career aspirations of 194 (69 male, 125 female) gifted and talented high school juniors from a retrospective format. These students responded to the Occupations List (Leung & Harmon, 1990) from age periods of 8 years and younger, 9 to 13 years, and 14 years of age and older. Their research yielded the following results.

1. These students often explore occupations of higher prestige with increasing age.
2. Little change exists in the average gender traditionality of career aspirations with age, but the acceptable range of gender tradition-

ality decreased significantly from the first life period to the second, then increased significantly in the third period.

3. No gender differences were found in the prestige level of career aspirations.

4. Female students were less likely than were male students to aspire to a doctoral or professional degree, yet more likely to aspire to a master's or bachelor's degree.

Gassin, Kelly, and Feldhusen (1993) studied 766 former and current enrichment youths and accelerated learning experiences for high-ability youths in Grades 4 through 12. These students either had a tested intelligence of at least 130 or had scored at the 95th percentile or above on two subsections of a standardized achievement test. These researchers found that gifted female students were more certain than gifted male students about their talents and career plans in elementary school. This difference, however, was not shown in the junior high and high school groups. This result may reflect the tendency for gifted female adolescents to adopt career myths (e.g., the irrational career belief that family vocational goals are incompatible with the adolescent; see Herring, 1990a) and to deny their talents and alter career plans owing to the tension between sex and ability expectations (B. A. Kerr, 1985). Gifted male students, however, displayed relatively constant career certainty throughout junior and senior high school.

Gassin et al.'s (1993) study suggests that sex differences in the career development of gifted youths are age specific and are not uniform for all career variables. Gifted youths, male and female, may need different types of career education at different points in their educational experiences.

Gifted and talented students should collect and assimilate information that will enable them to consider the advantages and disadvantages of particular careers. For example, comparing how different types of engineers or physicians view their careers is vital because students can think about jobs and how jobs relate to a variety of important conditions. Considering the multiple talents that these students have and getting information that helps them to consider what they want from a work situation may have long-term benefits (Good & Brophy, 1995). Something to Consider 9.3 presents recommendations and strategies to helping professionals in counseling this population.

Students With Mental Challenges

Morris and Levinson (1995) suggested that school counselors may wish to confine their use of intelligence test data (in combination with other data generated in a comprehensive psychoeducational evaluation) to generating recommendations for vocational training. They also may wish to weigh performance intelligence test scores more heavily than

Something to Consider 9.3
Gifted and Talented Students

The following recommendations and strategies are suggested to helping professionals in counseling gifted and talented students.

Recommendation	Strategy
1. Recognize the internal and external pressures for gifted and talented students to pursue high-prestige occupations and encourage them to free themselves of some unnecessary assumptions about prestige attainment, so that they can participate in a process of full exploration.	Explore occupations of different prestige levels.
2. Thorough exploration of a wide range of occupational alternatives is particularly important for individuals who possess multiple talents.	Explore occupations regardless of gender composition.
3. Encourage students not to give up their high career and educational aspirations.	Implement a systematic longitudinal program.
4. Recognize the internal gender role conflicts that a female student may experience as a result of being a gifted student and a woman.	Use approaches to increase the self-efficacy of students in taking multiple roles and not to perceive them as conflicting roles. Seek out accurate information.
5. Gifted and talented students may not be aware of the educational commitment needed for certain occupations.	
6. Although prestige and gender type preferences are formed in the early years and are resistant to change, a great deal of vocational exploration happens after the first 10 years of life.	Use multiple and varied inventories.
7. Recognize that although being gifted and talented is often an asset for a student, it can also become a source of confusion, especially for female students.	Explore and clarify the dynamics behind the confusion so that decisions are made in accordance with the giftedness and talent of the student.

verbal or full-scale intelligence tests scores when using these scores for this purpose. Moreover, school counselors must recognize that intelligence test scores may actually increase as a function of such training.

Schmitt, Growick, and Klein (1988) developed a model to assist students with learning disabilities in their transition from school to employment, and from adolescence to adulthood. These students have difficulty in making the adjustment and are not as directed toward the future opportunities in their career and education as their nondisabled peers. These authors delineated their comprehensive delivery plan with the following steps:

- Development of an individualized transition plan that is based on a comprehensive assessment of vocational, academic, and interpersonal functioning
- Evaluations that will identify the individualized learning styles resulting in the maximum use of program information and facilitate planning and delivery of services
- Vocational exploration and career education that include a planned career exploration using an interactive computer program and counseling services
- Employability training skills that address the vocational, social, and emotional skills necessary to enter the training step of the model. The interpersonal skills include listening, problem exploration, goal setting, problem solving, and decision making. Assertiveness training and conflict management skills are also provided to youths with learning disabilities
- Interpersonal skills including a variety of behavioral, cognitive, and cognitive–behavioral skills such as self-instruction, cognitive restructuring, cognitive rehearsal, cognitive modeling, imagery, and stress testing experiences
- Extrapersonal skills including the development of skills to gain access to and effectively use community resources
- Supported job search and placement follow-up that includes job-seeking skills, job clubs, and business/industry linkages
- Parent and agency cooperation and involvement that includes active, structured involvement and participation of parents and schools, agencies, and business/industry

Case Study 9.1 presents the profile of a student who is visually disabled. Review the data and respond to Question 4 in the Experiential Activities section.

Elite Athletes

Elite athletes represent another special population that receives insufficient attention. In 1988 the United States Olympic Committee initiated a unique program, the Career Assistance Program for Athletes (CAPA), to assist Olympic athletes in making the transition out of

Case Study 9.1
Profile of a Student With a Visual Disability

Name: Rasheen Smith
Age: 16 years
Grade: 11
School: Robeson County High School

Background

Rasheen, an African American male 11th-grade student, was placed in a learning disabilities class in the 2nd grade. He was diagnosed as having a severe reading disability because of visual processing and visual perceptions problems. He is an auditory learner with good listening and verbal skills. For example, he scores higher in a test if the test is read to him than if he has to read the test himself. His resource teacher has recommended that he be given oral tests as an accommodation for his disability. This accommodation is part of his written individual education plan.

Because Rasheen has good verbal and listening skills, his disability is not apparent in most settings. He has developed excellent coping strategies in reading and processing visual information. These coping strategies have presented problems for Rasheen because some of his teachers expected him to achieve the same as a nondisabled student based on his verbal skills.

Appraisal Information

The results of an intelligence test indicated that Rasheen's overall level of intellectual functioning on the Weschler Intelligence Scale for Children was in the low-average range (IQ = 85, Verbal = 92, Performance = 79). Rasheen's adaptive behavior on the Adaptive Behavior Scale was average for his age. The results of the Stanford Achievement Test from last year were as follows:

Subtest	Percentile Rank
Word Reading	27
Reading Comprehension	18
Word Study Skills	22
Number Concepts	47
Math Computations and Applications	52
Spelling	30
Vocabulary	35
Listening Comprehension	52
Reading	21
Total Reading	23
Total Math	50
Total Auditory	53

Educational Placement and Goals

Rasheen is mainstreamed for his mathematics, science, physical education, and business education classes. He receives special instruction in English and learning strategies in a resource room for students with learning disabilities. His grades in English and math are Cs; in science, Ds and Fs. Rasheen plans to enroll in a high school work-study program during his senior year. This will involve placement in a part-time job in which he will leave school early each day to go to work. Rasheen has had no previous work experience.

(continues)

Case Study 9.1 (continued)

Classroom Behavior

Rasheen's classroom behavior and emotional development appear normal. His behavior is satisfactory except for three incidents of misbehavior in science classes. During an informal interview, one of his teachers (a European American female) indicated concern about Rasheen's self concept and felt that he may have a low sense of self-worth due to academic frustration. His parents have reported that Rasheen sometimes indicates his frustration with school by saying things such as 'I'm dense" and "I won't ever get it." Another of his teachers (an African American female) also observed that Rasheen is attentive in class but is usually one of the last students to finish his work.

---

active sport competition. In addition, CAPA is exploring ways to target younger athletes who are participating in the various elite junior programs. This proactive approach is consistent with the life span developmental philosophy that drives CAPA. If younger athletes can be assisted in understanding and identifying their transferable skills, they may experience increases in feelings of personal competence and be better able to meet the challenges of future transitions (Petitpas, Danish, McKelvain, & Murphy, 1992). It is also possible that by reducing anxieties over future career concerns, young athletes may be better able to mobilize their energies to reach current performance goals.

This life span developmental approach offers three types of interventions: enhancement of coping skills, social support, and counseling. In a 1-day workshop, three main topics can be covered: (a) managing the emotional and social impact of transitions; (b) increasing understanding and awareness of personal qualities relevant to coping with transitions and career development; and (c) introducing information about the world of work.

The athletic dream or the desire to pursue super-stardom and mobility through sports has become a major liability for many male students, especially African American male students. The African American male athlete has special needs because of the perception of limited opportunity by traditional means and that athletics are an easy, and often the only way, to achieve upward mobility (Parmer, 1994). Parmer's research demonstrated the efficacy of the results management process as a prevention model. Results management is a system involving a manager and individuals from different organizational levels who convene in a joint work effort to set personal goals and objectives. The program is appropriate for schools because the counselor can be easily integrated into a program with the counselor serving as the manager.

CONSIDERATIONS FOR THE FUTURE

Szymanski et al. (1989) recommended five directions for future developments in the delivery of career development to students with disabilities.

1. Academic training will become the predominant thrust in education for all students, resulting in less time available for career and vocational education.
2. Professionals need to view students with disabilities in the perspective of modification and individual attention rather than in stereotypic and limiting manners.
3. Too many schools depend on other agencies to provide for the career development needs of students with disabilities. Perhaps school-based rehabilitation counselors are one solution to providing some of the students with a specialized transition service if they need it.
4. Schools must become more flexible and willing to change their programs to meet the real needs of their students.
5. Schools must break away from traditional practices so that comprehensive career education and guidance programs are truly implemented in schools in the United States. (pp. 70–77)

SUMMARY

School counselors generally allow special education teachers to implement guidance and counseling services to special populations. However, many special education teachers have received no formal training in guidance and counseling techniques. The major purpose of career guidance and counseling with special populations is to assist these students to enhance their self-concepts and self-esteems. Concurrently, the students need assistance in making appropriate career and educational decisions. School counselors need to be familiar with the legal rights of special populations and be proactive advocates for these populations.

In addition, school counselors are required to ensure that all students are welcomed in the school setting. Disability etiquette is not a typical component of many counselor education programs (Parette & Hourcade, 1995). Yet, these courtesies are mandated by the Americans With Disabilities Act.

EXPERIENTIAL ACTIVITIES

1. Have students name characters from their favorite TV shows who either fit or contradict a common stereotype. How might their per-

ceptions of other people be influenced by what they see on TV? (adapted from Aronson, 1994).

2. Make a file of agencies and individuals who provide career counseling for special populations.

3. Interview several resource room and special education teachers. Find out how they approach career education in their work with special populations. Interview a school counselor and find out what type of career guidance program is conducted for special needs students.

4. Review Case Study 9.1 and respond to these questions.

   a. How would you work with this student as a career counselor in terms of your theoretical approach and philosophy of intervention?

   b. What additional information would you need to obtain to provide career counseling services? How would you obtain the information quickly and efficiently?

   c. How can the appraisal information that is provided be used? Is additional appraisal information needed? If so, what?

   d. How should learning style and coping strategies be implemented in career counseling?

   e. What types of career counseling services would be most beneficial to this student?

   f. What types of part-time jobs would best fit this student's needs?

   g. This student is a junior. When should he receive career counseling?

   h. How does career counseling for students with disabilities differ from services for nondisabled students?

   i. Are ethnic and/or cultural influences apparent in this case?

10

Familial Influences
on Career Development

What families have in common the world around is that they are
the place where people learn who they are and how to be that way.

Jean Illset Clarke

Career development literature has largely ignored the role that family dynamics may play in the career decision making of individuals. Vocationally mature adolescents use information from home and the community to make curriculum choices and to contemplate future involvement in the world (DeRidder, 1990). They are able to cope with developmentally appropriate tasks with respect to career matters. The primary career developmental task for adolescents is exploration, an attempt to satisfy curiosity about occupations. Exploration helps adolescents to develop their feelings of autonomy as they realize that they can control their activities and plan their futures (Super, 1990).

Parents are the most important sociocultural factors influencing career development, especially in areas such as expectations for achievement and teaching about the world of work (Santrock, 1993). Among the earliest observations that children make are observations about their parent's or parents' jobs (Morrow, 1995). School counselors may want to take a closer look at the family environment of students who are not able to articulate career goals (Seligman, Weinstock, & Owings, 1988).

This chapter identifies the most salient influences that families have on the children's career development and decision making. Selected familial influences are the effects of socioeconomic status (SES), dysfunctional family behaviors, community involvement, predominantly ethnic-dissimilar schools, gay and lesbian family members, family members with disabilities, and unemployment. In addition, suggestions are presented relating to the addressing of these issues by school counselors.

FAMILY SOCIOECONOMIC STATUS

The student characteristic having the most significant impact on the school counseling process is SES, or social class (Hannon, Ritchie, & Rye, 1992). Government statistics regarding socioeconomic conditions in the United States indicate that racial and ethnic minority families are overrepresented among the poor. For example, citing U.S. census data for 1987, Ponterotto and Casas (1991) reported that whereas only 11% of European American families live in poverty, approximately 31% of African Americans, 28% of Mexican Americans, and 39% of Puerto Ricans are poor. Other government statistics summarized by Herring (1997a) document that Native American Indians have the highest unemployment and the lowest average income of any ethnic minority group in this nation.

SES affects the school counseling process, the quality of the relationship that is established, and the value placed on the counseling process itself by the poor student. For example, a knowledgeable school counselor would not destroy positive accomplishments by displaying signs of one-upmanship to a low-SES ethnic minority student (Herring, 1990b). Selected minority statuses are presented for the reader's edification.

MINORITY STATUSES

Some children are born and raised in advantaged families, whereas others are born and raised in disadvantaged families (Otto, 1996). The advantages and disadvantages include a wide range of economic considerations, including parental occupational, educational, and income statuses. The more the advantages, the better the chance that young people can pursue the education and training that prepares them for advantaged occupations and incomes. The lower the family social status, the lower the probabilities the children will have access to resources that assure education and training. In the case of ethnic minorities, there is the added consideration that they do not get the same return on their education and training investments as do members of the majority culture.

Parental education. Ethnic minority families are disadvantaged on each status dimension: education, occupation, and income. For example, 82% of African Americans completed 4 years of high school in 1992, but the corresponding figure for European Americans is 87% (U.S. Department of Education, 1994a). The difference in educational attainment is more apparent at the college level. The proportion of African Americans with a college education is 12%, half as high as European Americans (24%; U.S. Department of Education, 1994b).

Parental occupation status.   Lower levels of parental education suggest that the levels of parent occupational status will be lower, too. Large numbers of African American men work as operators, fabricators, laborers, janitors, cleaners, or cooks. As a group, African Americans are employed in low-level occupations, and they are located in a narrow range of occupations. In 1992, the unemployment rate for male African Americans 16 years and older was 15%, more than twice the corresponding unemployment rate for male European Americans, which was 7% (U.S. Department of Commerce, 1993b). See Research Emphasis 10.1 for a multicultural intervention for ethnic families.

Family income.   Education, occupation, and income interrelate, and lower levels of family income would be expected to follow from lower levels of parental education and occupations. In 1991, the median income for African American families was $21,550, whereas

---

Research Emphasis 10.1
Career Awareness for Chinese and Korean American Parents

The Career Awareness Program for Chinese and Korean American parents has been a successful, culture-specific effort in educating and informing groups of Chinese and Korean American parents and students of career opportunities. It is possible to replicate this program or aspects of it in a variety of institutional settings and with other ethnic or culturally similar groups. The most useful strategy in implementing such programs seems to be the concept of the bilingual role model. It is also recommended that written materials be prepared in the native language of the target group. Linkage with community organizations of the special target population is also critical to the success of such a program.

The program consists of 3-hour workshops that incorporate the following:

1. Deliver an overview of career choices, decision-making strategies, and financial aid.
2. Role model those professions for which the audience has great respect as well as less known professions.
3. Use college professionals to explain the concept of the community college both as a vehicle for acquiring job skills and for rapid absorption into the job market.
4. Use a question-and-answer format.

SOURCE: From "Career Awareness Program for Chinese and Korean American Parents," by P. O. Evanoski and F. W. Tse, 1989, *Journal of Counseling & Development, 67,* 472–474. Copyright 1989 by the American Counseling Association. Adapted with permission.

the median income for European American families was $37,780 (U.S. Department of Commerce, 1993a, 1993b). That's a difference of $16,230 per year, $1,352 per month, or $45 per day. The median income of African American married-couple families was $33,310; for male-headed families it was $24,510; and for families maintained by women with no spouse present, it was $11,410—which means the family lives on $32 per day!

Poverty.   Another gauge of the economic well-being of families is the poverty rate. In 1991, 12% of families lived in poverty (U.S. Department of Commerce, 1993a). But of families maintained by a woman with no spouse present, 36% were poor. Among woman-headed families with no spouse present and living in poverty, the proportion of ethnic minority families was especially high: 51% of African American and 50% of Hispanic families, compared with 28% of European American families. Woman-headed families with no spouse present represent 78% of all poor African American families and 46% of poor Hispanic families. Fourteen percent of all persons live in poverty, but 33% of African Americans live in poverty. But what happens when specific interventions fail to improve the lives of families in poverty?

For example, TV personality Oprah Winfrey guaranteed to finance a program to move 100 families in Chicago out of public housing, off public aid, and into better lives. The program was called Families for a Better Life, and no experiment in shifting people from welfare to work had a better chance to succeed than this one.

Families for a Better Life began with the promise of $3 million and the freedom to spend it without government red tape. Chicago's best-known social services agency, Jane Addams Hull House Association, was in charge. The agency even handpicked the first group of families for their likelihood to make it: no drug users, no alcoholics, nobody who lacked motivation. But almost 2 years and $1.3 million later, only five families have completed the program, and the project itself was on hold. What happened?

Several causative factors prohibited the success of this project:

- The lives of the poor were so chaotic and infused with a "mind frame of entitlement" that they defied even this program specifically designed to overcome these obstacles.
- From an administrative perspective, officials spent excessive time and money to determine who would get money.
- Candidates chosen for their drive struggled with attitudes that caused them to focus on issues that had little effect on their lives.
- The course often was detoured by the paradox that crisis may be the only constant in the lives of the poor, and each crisis threatened to plunge them into a financial and emotional abyss.

- Finally, adults who did not have high school education or any significant job experience had so much trouble finding and keeping work that the program could not set them firmly on their feet within a time frame designed to quickly foster self-sufficiency.

SELECTED FAMILIAL INFLUENCES
ON CAREER DEVELOPMENT

Most students are very concerned about issues relating to their families. Virginia Satir estimated that 96% of all families are dysfunctional to some degree (Watkins, 1989). Nichols (1984) cited a growing disturbance and instability in family life since the 1960s.

Demographic data provide quantitative documentation for the decline in the quality of family life in this nation. The following statistics are synthesized from the research literature as mitigating familial influences on children (Costa & Stiltner, 1994; Fine & Holt, 1981; Ryan & Sawatzky, 1989):

- Divorce rates are currently 50% for first marriages and 60% for second marriages.
- Two-thirds of all mothers are in the workforce.
- One out of four children is being reared by a single parent.
- One-third of all children born in the past decade will live with a stepfamily before the age of 18.
- Stepchildren are more likely to have developmental, emotional, and behavioral problems than children in intact families.
- Stepchildren are more likely to be victims of child abuse, especially sexual abuse, than children in intact families.
- Effects of parental divorce on children do not dissipate over time without intervention.
- Students read poorly because this activity is not emphasized at home.
- Students speak out of turn because they come from chaotic impulse-laden home environments.
- Students have short attention spans because they are not given breakfast.

The following discussion focuses on selected examples of negative familial influences on students' career development.

Influences of Dysfunctional Family Behaviors

Seligman et al. (1988) reported that elementary school children with positive family orientations received encouragement and information about their parents' activities. They concluded that understanding the role of the father and the father–child relationship is necessary for understanding children's career development. Children who perceive their fathers as powerful, important, and approachable linked career aspirations with power and competence.

Penick and Jepson (1992) supported the salience of family behavior as a factor in career development. Perceptions of family functioning explained more variance in vocational identity than achievement, gender, or SES. The failure of adolescents to engage in meaningful career exploration can be symptomatic of dysfunction within the family behavior dimensions of cohesion and adaptability (Morrow, 1995). If the family is rigidly organized and does not change to satisfy needs for more autonomy, difficulties in adolescent career development may result (Penick & Jepsen, 1992).

Family Enmeshment

The term *enmeshment* refers to a familial environment in which members are undifferentiated from overdependence on each other (S. Minuchin, Montalvo, Guerney, Rosman, & Schumer, 1967). *Individuation* (or differentiation) is the process whereby individuals extricate themselves from parental dominion and develop autonomous self-identities. The opposite of individuation is *fusion*. *Triangulation* is a more noxious form of fusion that involves three people, where one, usually the child, has the sense of being pulled in two different directions by the other two members of the triangle (Kinnier, Brigman, & Noble, 1990). Frequently, the result of such familial dysfunction is career indecision by the children. Indecisiveness has repeatedly been linked to the personality characteristics of poor identity formation, low self-esteem, external locus of control, and anxiety (Lopez & Andrews, 1987).

The relationship between career indecision and enmeshment will be better understood when a more efficacious measure of enmeshment is developed. The *Personal Authority in the Family System Questionnaire (PAFS-Q;* Williamson, Bray, & Malone, 1982) currently appears to be the best instrument available. This self-report aims to assess inter- and intragenerational familial relationship. The 132 items measure eight aspects (i.e., scales) of self-differentiation: spousal fusion/individuation, intergenerational fusion/individuation, spousal intimacy, intergenerational intimacy, nuclear family triangulation, intergenerational triangulation, intergenerational intimidation, and personal authority. Although useful, further development and refinement are needed (Kinnier et al., 1990).

Influences of the Family and Community

Family and community are inalienable components of ethnic minority existence. Hernandez (1995) suggested the use of the career trinity concept as a powerful connection for family, community, and self-concept as mediators in the development of a personal concept of career for the participants and for their subsequent career development and decision-making process. The implications of this intervention are:

1. An understanding of the frustration and powerlessness that affect these students' career decision making is critical to effective counseling. An awareness of the social causative factors will allow them to verbalize these feelings, become more self-aware, and eventually empower themselves.
2. School counselors must recognize the student's hierarchy of values and the values placed on familial and community counsel.

Impact of Predominantly Ethnic-Dissimilar Schools

For many European American families, sending their children to schools where students are predominantly ethnic minority children requires surrendering a privileged status gained by virtue of their skin color (McIntosh, 1988). For example, "If the mix is one-third African American, one-third Hispanic, and one-third European American, European American parents see the school as two-thirds non-European American" (Jervis, 1995, p. 561). Even in a school that is respectful of ethnic and cultural diversity, it takes time-consuming, committed, moral leadership to develop a school community based on the agreement that everyone is a citizen in this society together.

Integration must be built on something other than a European American, middle-class model for the benefits of European Americans, as many African American families are now charging (Ladson-Billings, 1994). Veteran European American teachers and counselors may have thought about educating the increasing numbers of ethnic minority students, albeit often in terms of assimilating them into European American middle-class norms (Jervis, 1995). European American educational personnel's blindness to ethnicity clouds their ability to notice what students are really saying about themselves and their identities.

Families With Gay or Lesbian Members

If society's greatest desire, despite a begrudging "tolerance" of homosexuality, is "that gay people *not* exist" (Sedgwick, 1991, p. 4), how do parents and siblings shape a pedagogy that thrives on the tension of multiple, conflicting differences?

Several studies have examined the experiences of educators with alternative lifestyle parents and parents of gay and lesbian students (e.g., Casper, Cuffaro, Schultz, Silin, & Wickens, 1995; Casper, Schultz, & Wickens, 1992). Common features include the connections among feeling different, of translating that feeling into a broad respect for diversity in general, and the fact that the way people experience, think, and talk about the world changes over time. Perspectives can be personal and idiosyncratic, and concurrently shaped by cultural and social dynamics.

Jackson (1992) emphasized that an individual's early experiences and subsequent memories may affect his or her contemporary self in ways that often seem mysterious. The mystery comes in the difficulty and sometimes impossibility of putting a finger on the particular event or interaction behind one's actions, thinking, and understanding. Some educators who learn that they have students with gay, lesbian, bisexual, or transgender (GLBT) parents may be also dealing with the issue of sexual orientation for the first time in their own lives and may be struggling to fit it into their current worldview (Casper et al., 1995).

In the 1960s, homosexuality was still considered a matter of deviance and a topic of family discussions. Today national organizations (e.g., the Gay, Lesbian and Straight Teachers Network), local projects that advocate for GLBT youths (e.g., the Hetrick-Martin Institute in New York City), and family support groups (e.g., Lesbian and Gay Parents Coalition International) are available for support services. An increasing literature for children about gay and lesbian lives and curriculum materials is also evident (e.g., Chapman, 1992; Heron, 1994).

Early childhood educators have relied on conceptual and empirical research that distances children from adults and from their material worlds (Casper et al., 1995). Developmental psychologists have frequently underestimated children's abilities to understand complex social issues (Short, 1991). Teachers and parents want to protect children from knowledge of the social world that they themselves find discomforting (Silin, 1995). Adults forget that what represents change to them does not necessarily represent change for children. Many children have never known a world without lesbian and gay families.

Families of Students With Disabilities

School counselors may find themselves facilitating family support for the efforts of students with disabilities. The family support system is important at all ages, of course, and with children it is important in many ways, not the least of which is the influencing of how they feel about themselves (R. L. Gibson & Mitchell, 1995). Gilbride (1993, p. 149) reported the results of a study that suggest that parents' attitudes, apart from their actual instrumental capacity, may influence attitudes and expectations of their child's success. Something to Consider 10.1 offers some suggestions for dealing with parents of children with disabilities.

Unemployment Effects

The effects of long-term unemployment have an impact not only on the unemployed worker but also on the family system (Schliebner & Peregoy, 1994). Insufficient attention has been addressed to these

Something to Consider 10.1
Counseling Tips With Parents of Children With Disabilities

1. Understand that these parents deal with a lot on a day-to-day basis. Be patient—changes take time.

2. Communicate positive things to the parents about their children. Try to maintain regular contact with them.

3. Make the parents part of the team. Their support is essential. Join with the special education or general education teacher to suggest ideas for helping the children, and accept ideas from them. Make the education of their child a joint endeavor.

4. Be honest. Do not be afraid to tell the parents if plans that they have for their child are unrealistic. Attempt to redirect them toward more realistic goals. Some parents remain in a state of denial and need positive counseling to enable them to see a different way.

5. On the other hand, do not assume that just because a child has a physical disability that he or she is mentally retarded. Many children with physical disabilities have average or above-average intelligence. Be willing to assist the child in obtaining the necessary adaptations and support that are needed for his or her success in school.

6. Encourage parents to form parents' support groups that are organized and run by parents.

7. Be available and listen to their concerns.

8. Realize that while you may not be able to identify with the frustrations faced by parents of children with disabilities, your objective and professional viewpoint can help.

9. Treat students with disabilities as "normally" as possible—meet with them to set up their schedules, future vocational goals, and other things that you would do with any other student.

10. Familiarize yourself with available resources to assist parents (e.g., Medicaid waiver, respite care services, other assistance).

11. Accept the fact that statistically, there are approximately 20% of families that are not going to change. Be an advocate for the child.

effects, and this lack of focus has resulted in numerous concerns and unanswered questions. Unemployment and its emotional effects have been compared with a roller coaster's ups and downs—continually lower and lower swings at the emotional bottom (Amundson & Borgen, 1982).

Large plant closings can affect many families in a single community. For example, the closing of the General Motors plant in Ypsilanti, Michigan, has affected 4,014 workers and their families; and the closing of the North Tarrytown, New York, plant has affected 3,456 workers and their families (Standish, 1992). The school represents an ideal venue to help youths from these homes.

Children, particularly adolescents, have difficulty envisioning their own future in the world of work. Witnessing a parent's frustration and futile attempts to secure employment, children begin to view access to employment out of their control (Schliebner & Peregoy, 1994). This feeling leads to a lack of confidence in self, in the parent seeking employment, and even in the economic system itself (Isralowitz & Singer, 1986). If adolescents maintain this view of the world of work, it is expected that they will experience difficulties such as increased anxiety and depression, a less subjective well-being, and low self-esteem (Pautler & Lewko, 1987).

Not only is the view of the world of work affected but also the adolescent may experience a decline in academic performance (Flanagan, 1990). This academic decline may in turn manifest itself in a reduction of educational aspirations and opportunities. Girls, as compared with boys, tend to have lowered aspirations and job expectations that seem to be correlated to the father's pessimistic outlook. This pessimism was reflected by an adolescent girl whose parents had both lost their jobs (McLoyd, 1990):

> The future stinks. You're supposed to spend your childhood preparing for the real life of being an adult. But what if that real life is no good? What's the sense? Look at my parents. They always did everything the way you're supposed to. Now look at them—nobody will give them a job. . . . What's the sense of trying in school. There's no jobs for my dad or mom. Why should I believe there will be jobs for me when I get out [of school]? (p. 299).

When adolescents maintain this perspective, they are more likely to be low risk takers "who are not prepared to work hard and who do not believe they are capable of getting a job" (Pautler & Lewko, 1987, p. 30).

COUNSELING IMPLICATIONS FOR MULTICULTURAL FAMILIES

Parents are among the most important sociocultural factors influencing career development, especially in areas such as expectations for achievement and teaching about the world of work (Santrock, 1993). Career development difficulties can occur when families do not provide adolescents the opportunities to test roles and shape values (Munson, 1992). The effects of dysfunctional families on children result in low self-esteem and increasing behavior problems that interfere with learning and create tough challenges for counselors and other personnel (Costa & Stiltner, 1994).

A most visible discussion about the "what is counseling?" question can be found in the proliferation of literary efforts proposing that school counselors provide family counseling (e.g., Hinkle, 1993; Nicoll,

1992; Peeks, 1993). Paisley and Borders (1995) synthesized the lead-ing research into the advocates and the opponents of family counsel-ing in school settings. Advocates of family counseling in the schools note the unarguable contribution that parents and family problems often make to students' in-school problems and cite research support-ing the effectiveness of family interventions in improving students' academic and behavioral problems. Opponents emphasize the over-whelming list of tasks and responsibilities assigned to school coun-selors and ask which of these family counseling is to replace.

School counselors are not trained to be family therapists nor are they expected to be family therapists. However, some descriptions of family counseling in the schools are quite similar to descriptions of consultation with parents, a function that has been a part of the school counselor's role for some time (Paisley & Borders, 1995). However the question about family counseling is answered, it is a critical one in light of predictions that schools of the future will function as "family centers" that offer a variety of family services, from medical clinics to satellite counseling and from recreation centers to retraining career programs for adults (Cetron, 1985).

In reality, school counselors must respond in some manner to these issues so that optimal learning can occur. Whether their response is evidenced in student support groups or family education sessions, the needs of students at risk from dysfunctional families must be addressed. This section presents selected suggestions for counseling implications for multicultural families.

Appraisal

School counselors will need to solicit information directly from the family, searching for pertinent family life experiences. Because culture plays a significant role in career development, counselors must be aware of their own cultural boundaries and worldviews and be sensi-tive to the experiences of the families with whom they are working (Fouad, 1993). Some racial-ethnic groups, for example, place a higher value on familial or group decisions than others.

Fouad (1993) offered three suggestions for gathering information that may be useful in the appraisal process: family observation and interview, a family lifeline, and family homework. First, school coun-selors must be allowed to observe family interaction patterns directly. Family individuals tend to bring their own typical and most salient behaviors to the interview (Krathwohl, 1993). Observations during the interview about who is involved directly in the interview and at the periphery offer clues about the quality of family commitment and closeness.

Second, the family lifeline helps family members to review periods or events that are significant markers in the family's development and allows the family members to evaluate family experiences (Goldman, 1990). Third, students can interview their parents about their work experiences. This homework assignment appraises parental levels of interest in their children's career development while providing a complementary exploration relationship between parent and child. "When a counselor is working with a student who is having difficulty making a career decision, inquiry concerning family or origin issues may help to clarify the situation" (Kinnier et al., 1990, p. 311).

Language Barriers

In many instances school counselors may confront language barriers in working with ethnic families, especially if English is not spoken, or is spoken hesitantly, in the home. Axelson (1985) provided an excellent example of the dialogue between a career counselor and a Vietnamese father to illustrate how the language barrier presents a viable concern (see Case Study 10.1).

The school counselor can help students who have limited English proficiency in several ways (Keyes, 1989):

- Arrange for a bilingual translator, either through contacts with the school or with community organizations such as United Way and American Red Cross.
- Provide a support system for the student, including teachers and peers.
- Reduce cultural conflict by helping both the culturally different student and other students to understand cultural variations.

The school counselor will note that second- and third-generation students with educated and successful parents probably will have fewer language problems than first-generation learners of lower SES (Baruth & Manning, 1991).

Generational Conflicts

Generational conflicts between parents and their adolescents in the United States reflect two central issues: the ongoing acculturation process or the rejection of parental career aspirations for their children. These conflicts can significantly influence the career development of adolescents. Whether this influence is negative or positive is basically dependent on the parameters of the individual situation.

The effects of evolving acculturation are found in many first-generation immigrants to this country. For example, many Asian

Case Study 10.1
Language Barriers With A Vietnamese Family

Counselor:	How are things going now that you and your family have settled into your new apartment?
Client:	Yes. (Smiles and glances down)
Counselor:	Sometimes moving into a strange neighborhood and new home brings problems.
Client:	Many things for Kien fix up, work hard . . . need stove, one [burner] only work, but cos' so much. Friends [sponsors] help get good price, and get TV.
Counselor:	A TV?
Client:	Yes, they get good education, get better life. Can no teach English Kim and Van, school help . . . (pauses) . . . worry abou' Lan. Change so much, go far from Vietnamese way. She have American boyfriend. Want be like American. (Smiles, and becomes very quiet, looks at floor, seems embarrassed by what she has said.)
Counselor:	You seem sad.
Client:	(Grins and laughs) My father tell me take care of Lan. My brothers all made dead by soldiers . . . only me left to watch Lan . . . (pauses) . . . our boat ge' Thai pirates. Lan and me make face black, hide in boat . . . no see us! (Laughs and begins to sob quietly) Oh, excuse me.
Counselor:	That's OK. I know it's difficult to talk about those past days and the things that hurt you. And it's a big responsibility to look out for Lan. It's all right to show how you feel to me. I won't take it as being impolite to me and I'll try to help you in any way I can—including listening and caring for how you feel about something that hurts or makes you sad or angry. It's my job to help you with things that are difficult for you.
Client:	Oh (faint smile) so many problems wan' to please father; help Kien . . .
Counselor:	Yes, that's all important to you. How is Kien's job training going for him?
Client:	Kien in Vietnam, big navy officer . . . now nothing feel bad, but training good . . . become computer-electronic man. That good for him, get job, more money, feel better.
Counselor:	Yes, that's a good thing for your family.
Client:	Thank you.
Counselor:	Let's talk now about the work that you want. You said before that you like to sew. That's a skill that you have that you can use right now to add to the family income.
Client:	Yes, make clothes for children, men Kien's shirt.
Counselor:	I know. You showed me some of the good work you have done. There's a job that I'd like to see you try at the store. It will be to alter clothes that customers buy.
Client:	Oh . . . speak little English, so har' for me, makes others feel bad . . . no way go store . . . can't find . . . where bus?

SOURCE: From *Counseling and Development in a Multicultural Society,* by J. A. Axelson and P. McGrath. Copyright 1998, 1993, 1985 Brooks/Cole Publishing Company, Pacific Grove, CA 93950, a division of International Thomson Publishing Inc. By permission of the publisher.

American (i.e., second-generation children) adolescents experience a dislike for their own culture, especially in their social life (Sue & Sue, 1990). Many Asian American adolescents may view Western personality characteristics as more admirable than traditional Asian characteristics. A recent study indicated that Chinese American adolescents' tendency to date students of other ethnic and cultural groups can result in considerable generational conflict.

A study of 29 Hmong high school youths further illustrates the conflicts that many Asian American youths experience in the United States (Rick & Forward, 1992). According to this study, Hmong youths perceive themselves as being more acculturated than their parents to the United States. Second, increasing levels of student acculturation are associated with increasing perceived intergenerational differences, but this relationship is dependent on the number of years students have been in U.S. schools. Third, acculturation with respect to traditional behaviors, family relationships, value changes, and decision making predicted increased perceived intergenerational differences.

The second factor influencing generations is evidenced in the adolescents' rejection of parental career aspirations for them. In some instances, this rejection may be an example of adolescent identity development and desire for autonomy. This factor can be found in all ethnic groups and immigrant families.

Counseling implications.   School counselors need to be aware of these intergenerational conflicts, as well as the degree of acculturation of individual students. Both factors may appear as separate counseling concerns or as an integrated presenting difficulty. Yao (1988) noted several factors that should be considered in devising appropriate strategies in working effectively with Asian immigrant parents:

- Asian parents are often depicted as quiet, submissive, and cooperative.
- Asian parents' lack of knowledge about U.S. society and customs results in insecurities and confusion.
- Asian parents' problems with language hamper their communication with teachers and other school officials.
- Asian parents often set high goals for their children. Pressure from parents can be detrimental to the children's emotional and social development.

The importance of considering acculturation as a variable that differentiates among subgroups of ethnic groups cannot be underestimated. Acculturation levels have been shown to affect mental health status, level of social support, level of social deviance, various health behaviors, political and social attitudes, alcoholism, and drug use (Herring, 1997a, 1997b).

Unemployment and Poverty Issues

Previous discussion has highlighted the negative effects of economic factors such as low SES, unemployment, and poverty. School counselors may be limited by workload demands and institutionally imposed limits for outreach activities; however, the group experience affords them the opportunity for students to share problems and conflicts with other students in similar circumstances. The group members can learn coping skills from one another and see themselves through the perspective of another person (Morris-Van, 1981). The group setting can also give students an opportunity to see how other students view the world of work. Their daydreams, desires, and fears can be challenged and explored with other students who may view things differently.

In conjunction with individual and group counseling, career counseling and cooperative education programs are suggested as potential concurrent interventions (Schliebner & Peregoy, 1994). Research has emphasized the impacts and consequences for youths in career planning, including the influence on their view of the future in the world of work (Flanagan, 1990; Isralowitz & Singer, 1986; McLoyd, 1990; Work, Parker, & Cowen, 1990). This perceived future is characterized by the students' development of an external locus of control and their perceptions of an employer as fair, honest, and understanding becoming distorted (Pautler & Lewko, 1987).

Counseling Implications

These perceptions combined with lower self-esteem have implications for career and personal counseling. Career counseling can alleviate feelings of hopelessness and confusion by encouraging students to explore their interests, abilities, and options for future education and employment. Alternative interventions such as group work and community support networks must be identified and used to meet the needs of newly unemployed persons and their families. An intervention strategy that includes all components of long-term unemployment must be developed so that efficacious interventions can be used. "Unemployment can no longer be viewed as an individual problem. . . . Its effects are felt in the family, community, and nation" (Schliebner & Peregoy, 1994, p. 371).

Grandparents Rearing Grandchildren

Children and adolescents are being reared by grandparents in greater numbers than would be expected by choice or by chance. Historically, the assumption of a parenting role by the grandparents has been connected to life events, such as death, divorce, or abandonment; the parent was no longer around and the grandparent stepped in to care for the dependent children (Pinson-Millburn, Fabian, Schlossberg, & Pyle, 1996). Within the last decade, there has been a 40% increase in these households across the United States (Minkler, Driver, Roe, & Bedeian, 1993), with a disproportionate presence among African American families. These grandparents are faced with multiple problems: their own declining health, the incapacity of their children, and the possibility that their grandchildren could be disabled or dysfunctional (Pinson-Millburn et al., 1996). An additional concern is the effect this parenting style will have on the career development of the grandchildren.

A study announced by the American Association of Retired Persons' (AARP, 1994) Women's Initiative confirmed that these caregivers must also face bureaucratic obstacles. It also emphasized that grandparents are continually at war with unfriendly laws and officials in their search for the most basic entitlements for their grandchildren (e.g., access to food stamps or Medicaid). That study reported that in those households headed by grandparents, about 33% have no parent present and reflect an estimated 723,000 midlife and older adults caring for grandchildren.

Many of these grandparents have volunteered for these roles without realizing the stresses of rearing children in the 1990s. Child management problems, combined with their own aging, exert unexpected pressures, with social isolation, financial difficulty, and health problems becoming primary concerns (Pinson-Millburn et al., 1996).

A number of factors are frequently cited as causes for the biological parent's "disappearance" from this household. These factors have important implications for counselors. The following characteristics are associated with the creation of grandparent–grandchildren households:

1. An increase in drug abuse (particularly, crack cocaine) by young mothers and a parallel decrease in funding of treatment programs have created a catch-22: Infants with serious developmental problems are now being reared by their grandparents and young mothers remain vulnerable to their addiction (Davis, 1995).
2. Children born to young parents who are unable to care for them and children born out of wedlock to parents of any age are more likely to be a part of these households (Downey, 1995).
3. Reasons given by grandparents for the formation of these families are parental substance abuse (44%), child abuse/neglect (28%), teenage pregnancy or parent failure to handle children (11%), death of parent (5%), unemployment of parent (4%), divorce (4%), and other reasons (4%), including HIV/AIDS (Centers for Disease Control and Prevention, 1995).

In studying this population, Pinson-Millburn et al. (1996) observed this paradox: the necessity of understanding an increasing number of grandparents rearing grandchildren and the difficulty of categorizing such a diverse group of adults. For example:

1. Some grandparents are 40 years old, others 50, some 80—there is no single age pattern.
2. No single pattern of household arrangements is evident. To illustrate, more than 1 million households are headed by single grandparents with a median income of $18,000 a year. Many more grandparents are part-time caretakers or live in three-generation families. Some grandparents have legal custody; others have no legal rights. Some grandparents are poor, but others have financial resources.
3. This caregiving has no specific time frame. For some, it is for life. For others, it is intermittent or short-lived.
4. Ethnic composition of these households shows that 12% of all African American children are living with grandparents, with 6% of Hispanic children and 4% of European American children similarly situated. Each ethnic group has different expectations about caregiving and different sets of experiences. And, individuals within each ethnic group have different sets of expectations.

Counseling implications.   No intervention strategy should avoid consideration from a multicultural perspective. C. C. Lee and Richardson (1991) noted that the range of problem solutions increases with multiple cultures and ethnic groups being represented. Direct interventions include assessment and outreach, teaching new coping strategies, and teaching new skills. In supportive interventions, counselors' roles frequently involve coordination or collaboration. Such interventions include creating grandparent support groups, family support groups, a "Grandparents' Day" at school, and appropriate referrals to agencies that serve "seniors" or grandparents such as the local senior center or the local AARP chapter. Multiple strategies are described in greater detail in a resource manual available from the National Institute of Mental Health (Center of Human Services Department, 1995).

From a career development perspective, school counselors need to be alert to the possible career immaturity and career misinformation evidenced by youths from these households. The generational disparity may result in these youths being exposed to outdated career information. These youths deserve special treatment because of their multiple problem situation. In addition, activities need to be generated to enhance the career awareness of the grandparents.

Additional Suggested Interventions

School counselors are beginning to appreciate the enormous influence of family culture on the behavior of their students. The chapter has previously presented numerous root causes of common educational problems that relate to the family. See Research Emphasis 10.2 for an example of family change counseling.

Family systems-oriented school counseling. Widerman and Widerman (1995) stressed the efficacy of family systems counseling, using the interactional game metaphor, to intervene in many of the problems common in school settings. They emphasized that negative response or physical punishment, often evoked by frustrated parents

---

Research Emphasis 10.2
A Family Change Counseling Group

Costa and Stiltner (1994) conducted a family change group with seven junior high students, 2 male and 5 female. All were referred by a parent, teacher, peer, or self. Parental permission was obtained. The group met for a total of eleven 50-minute sessions over 14 weeks. All of the students had been involved in at least three different parental marriages. Additional experiences included mental illness and hospitalization of a parent, parental substance abuse, numerous relocations, physical abuse of a child or parent, and the assumption of parental roles by the child.

Goals: To Assist Participants in:
1. Understanding and appropriately expressing feelings about family change
2. Gaining a realistic awareness of the family situation
3. Listening to and understanding the feelings of others in similar situations
4. Developing strategies for adjusting to family change
5. Understanding loss and separation
6. Enhancing self-esteem

Group Guidelines
1. Listen to what others had to say
2. Avoid put-downs
3. Take turns talking
4. Keep information shared in the group confidential
5. Come to group on time
6. Offer help to others

Sessions
1. Introduction and Guidelines
2 & 3. Continued Introduction and Lifelines
4. Values Clarification
5. Bibliotherapy
6. Continued Bibliotherapy
7. Review of Bibliotherapy
8. Family Coat of Arms
9 & 10. Empathic Assertion
11. Summary and Wrap-Up

(continues)

Research Emphasis 10.2 (continued)

Emergent Issues
1. Crises: life-threatening events such as suicide, the diagnosis and hospitalization of a parent for major mental illness, violence and physical abuse, and shelter in a safe house.
2. Less crisis-oriented issues: clarification of family relationships and family roles, and adjusting to a new stepparent or meeting a biological parent.
3. Student expressed needs: to sort out and understand complex issues such as multiple marriages, affairs, divided loyalties, visitation, custody and legal matters, diffuse boundaries, parental alcohol abuse, parental depression and unpredictable moods, and "parentification" of a child.

Results
- Overall, students received support and encouragement from others with similar concerns.
- They were able to learn from one another as well as from the counselors.
- Students received concrete suggestions for decision making and conflict resolution, crisis intervention, and stress management.
- Students improved their coping ability and developed more realistic expectations about growing up in a dysfunctional family and about their own future marriages.
- Students increased their awareness and appreciation of the potential benefits of counseling and therapy, not only in crisis intervention but also for prevention.

SOURCE: From "Why Do the Good Things Always End and the Bad Things Go on Forever: A Family Change Counseling Group," by L. Costa and B. Stiltner, 1994, *The School Counselor, 41*, 300–304. Copyright 1994 by the American Counseling Association. Adapted with permission.

and school personnel, is not only ineffective but results in perpetuating unintended family and school interaction patterns.

The ways in which school students of all ages interact with others in their environment can be better understood by using the metaphor of *interactional games*. This concept captures the fact that behavioral responses are learned from birth within the family or home (Selvini Palazzoli, Cirillo, Selvini, & Sorrentino, 1989). Imber-Black (1988) and Madanes (1990) saw family myths, beliefs, and rituals as important types of games as well. The reader is encouraged to consult the references for an in-depth discussion of this intervention.

The school counselor's responsibility is to clarify the interactional games and prescribe courses of action when particular strategies seem to reduce incongruity. Generally, a short-term orientation to school-based counseling is to assure parental attendance. The counselor will remember that no one ideal interactional pattern exists for any given family system and that patterns are constantly evolving (Widerman & Widerman, 1995).

Family-oriented, systemic, school-based counseling replaces the individual student with the entire family system as the unit of analysis and relocates the locus of change to the classroom and the home, with the family system conceptualized as the source of learning and construction of interactional games (Widerman & Widerman, 1995). School counselors can become more adept at systemic strategy by reading and studying the works of strategic family therapists. They can also seek out consultation and training opportunities or refer to a family therapist.

SUMMARY

When it comes to planning and preparing for careers, what youths want is important; but what they want reflects the expectations parents and other people have for them. Young people are influenced over the long term by as few as four or five other people who are especially important to them, and as few as two or three others may be particularly influential over their early years when it comes to career plans. Parents figure prominently among the most influential others. And the way parents influence their children's career outcomes the most is by the level of education and training they expect, encourage, and provide (Otto, 1996). Parents should provide their children with good education and training, because the better their education and training, the better their employment prospects; and the better their jobs, the better their income.

The need for family change groups in the schools to ameliorate problems that interfere with learning is clearly evident (Costa & Stiltner, 1994). School-based groups can be an effective method of intervention for students at risk from dysfunctional families (Watkins, 1989). Family change groups can also be an effective prevention-intervention strategy to support students and to enhance learning in school environments.

EXPERIENTIAL ACTIVITIES

1. Have students draw a family "coat of arms" depicting their families. Students can then share their similarities and differences in their perceptions of their families. You can ask students to use the following adjectives to describe their family: "depressing," "demented," "fun," "mixed up," "miserable," "boring," "cool," and "very very weird."
2. What is the rate of unemployment in your community? Have students of unemployed parents been identified as at-risk? If so, what is being done for them? If not, why not?
3. Does your school have any first- or second-generation students with non-English-speaking parents? What has been done with these students to enhance their career development?

4. Generate other ideas that can facilitate career development with families.
5. What are your thoughts on school counselors doing family counseling? Distinguish family therapy, family counseling, and family education efforts.
6. Select an Asian American or Hispanic American family with multiple-age siblings and an extended family. Do an interview and discern if intergenerational conflicts are inherent.

Part IV

Cogent Areas of Career Development

PART IV CONSIDERS areas of career development that cross all developmental levels. The effectiveness of any career counseling and guidance program is hinged on the efficacy of these
important components. Chapter 11 describes the
delivery of career information and the methods
by which to acquire and implement an appropriate delivery service. Chapter 12 stresses the need
for unbiased appraisal resources and accommodations. Chapter 13 concludes this section with
commentary on future directions of career counseling and guidance in schools.

11

Delivery of Career Information Services

The best career advice given to the young is
"Find out what you like doing best and get someone to pay
you for doing it."

Katherine Whitehorn

A primary purpose of school counselors is to assist students with educational and career planning. To choose appropriate strategies in helping students address career issues, school counselors receive training in career development theories and information services. Having a broad view of the importance of career planning enables counselors to encourage teachers to incorporate career guidance into daily instruction across subject areas of the curriculum (Schmidt, 1996). For example, in English classes, teachers can explore careers that rely on language and communication skills. Likewise, science teachers can incorporate ways that scientific discovery affects countless career choices.

Knowledge and implementation of information services are important to school counselors, especially secondary school counselors, in providing students with the most recent information about career trends and educational requirements. A current knowledge of career resources, college requirements, technical training programs, vocational interest inventories, and other materials enables school counselors to guide students and parents accurately.

DEVELOPMENTAL FOCUS

For review purposes, early elementary grades (i.e., the primary Grades 1–3) emphasize career awareness and the upper elementary grades (Grades 4–6) focus on career exploration. These developmental stages involve the expansion of career awareness activities in the classroom and special events (e.g., field trips) as well as the careful selection of books, films/videos, and other media that are void of sexual and cultural stereotyping. The middle grades incorporate career classes rather than infusing career precepts in the curricula. The high school years involve special career events and individual or small-group career counseling. In addition, high school classroom teachers should incorporate career aspects of their subject areas into daily lessons. Comprehensive programs of counseling, consulting, coordinating, and appraising activities enable all students to develop their fullest potential, achieve academic success, and select appropriate career goals (Schmidt, 1996). Gysbers and Henderson (1994) described this as the "life career development" perspective (p. 61). For example, students who understand the interrelatedness of school experiences and aspirations for future career success view these experiences as a relatively short-term challenge when compared with their lifelong ambitions (Schmidt, 1996). Something to Consider 11.1 further explores this perspective.

Something to Consider 11.1
Life Career Development

The life career development perspective involves four areas of student growth and development.

Focus Area	Goal
1. Self-knowledge and interpersonal skills	To increase students' self-awareness and acceptance of others through individual and small-group sessions emphasizing appropriate communication and problem-solving skill development.
2. Life roles, settings, and events	To emphasize the interrelatedness of various life roles (e.g., learner, citizen, and consumer), settings (e.g., home, school, work, and community), and events (e.g., job entry, marriage, retirement) in which students participate over the life span.
3. Life career planning	To help students master decision-making skills with which to explore various career interests, match those interests with their abilities and characteristics, and make decisions accordingly.
4. Basic studies and occupational preparation	To integrate all the learning objectives inherent to a school's curriculum.

SOURCE: From *Developing and Managing Your School Guidance Program* (2nd ed.), by N. C. Gysbers & P. Henderson, 1994. Copyright 1994 by the American Counseling Association. Adapted with permission.

EFFECTIVE USE OF INFORMATION

Simple exposure to career information does not mean that the information will be used or, if used, that it will be done so effectively. To increase the probability that career information will be effectively used, counselors must consider aspects of motivation, quality of the data, and how the data are assimilated (Herr & Cramer, 1996).

Motivation

Counselors must place an emphasis on motivation, readiness, and the establishment of a learning set in their students. To become motivated, students must be assisted to see how their needs are met by whatever information is delivered (Herr & Cramer, 1996). Peterson, Sampson, and Reardon (1991, p. 197) perceived the effective use of career information as a learning event consisting of three components:

1. An objective; that is, the capability to be acquired;
2. An intervention to bring about the desired capability; and
3. An evaluation to ascertain whether the objective was obtained.

These authors advise the use of a CASVE (communication, analysis, synthesis, valuing, and execution) decision-making process in which learning is the foundation for decision making and information is required in each phase of the learning process. For example, *communication* (identifying a need) is a description of the personal/family issues that women face in returning to work (information) in a videotaped interview of currently employed women (medium); *analysis* (interrelating problem components) comprises explanations of the basic requirements for degree programs (information) in college catalogs (medium); *synthesis* (creating alternatives) is a presentation of nontraditional careers for women (information) at a career seminar for women (medium); *valuing* (prioritizing alternatives) is an explanation of how the roles of parent, spouse, citizen, leisurite, and homemaker would be affected by a worker role (information) in an adult version of a computer-assisted career guidance system (medium); and *execution* (forming means–ends strategies) is a description of a resume emphasizing transferable skills, followed by creating a resume (information) on an computer-assited employability skills system (medium).

Readiness and motivation are requisite to the effective use of occupational information at any intervention point in one's life (Herr & Cramer, 1996). Readiness assumes that school counselors can accurately appraise the level of a student's occupational information. Chapter 12 describes some instruments available to measure the frequency and variety of vocational information-seeking behavior.

Quality of the Information

A second aspect in the effective use of information is the quality of the information. One important criteria is the source of the information. For example, some material is produced for recruitment and may be misleading. Other important criteria are the currency, validity, and applicability of the information.

The National Career Development Association's Career Information Review Service periodically publishes reviews of career and occupational information materials based on guidelines determined by the profession. These reviews are usually printed in the *Career Development Quarterly* with both general guidelines and content guidelines that cover the following areas (adapted from Herr & Cramer, 1996, p. 625):

General Guidelines
Accuracy of information: current and nonbiased
Format: clear, concise, and interesting
Vocabulary: appropriate to target group
Bias and stereotyping: gender-, ethnic-, and religion-free information
Graphics: current and nonstereotyped
Dating and revisions: frequent revisions required
Credits: who and where

Content Guidelines
Duties and nature of the work: purpose, activities, skills, specializations, and so on
Work settings and conditions: physical activities and work environment
Personal qualifications: specific to a particular occupation
Social and psychological factors: satisfiers/limiters associated with an occupation; lifestyle implications
Preparation required: length and type, cost, difficulty of entry
Special requirements: physical, personal, licensing, and so on
Methods of entering: typical and alternative approaches
Earnings and other benefits: current ranges
Usual advancement possibilities: typical career ladders
Employment outlook: short and long range
Opportunities for experience and exploration: part-time, summer, volunteer, and so on
Related occupations: alternative possibilities
Sources of education/training: schools, agencies, and so on
Sources of additional data: where to go, whom to see

Considerable agreement exists among scholars and practitioners regarding the criteria of what constitutes "good" career information (e.g., Bloch & Kinnison, 1989a, 1989b). School counselors need to keep abreast of these criteria. Outdated and misleading information can be as damaging as no information. Students deserve the best information that is available to them.

Use of Information

The way students assimilate, process, and accept or reject information in their career-related decision making is generally complex and idiosyncratic. However, expanding occupational information has been found not to lead to an increase in vocational differentiation, that is, the number of different judgments and more cognitively complex processes used by the student (Herr & Cramer, 1996). New information given to students that disconfirms their prior career expectations *increases* vocational differentiation, whereas confirming information *decreases* vocational differentiation (Moore, Neimeyer, & Marmarosh, 1992). In addition, men tend to have higher vocational differentiation than do women (Parr & Neimeyer, 1994).

The school counselor should personalize career information for each student. In addition, the counselor should appraise the level of a student's information processing so the type of intervention can be determined (Rounds & Tracey, 1990). Such matching enhances the career information process. Career information results when a student attaches personal meaning to information (Herr & Cramer, 1996).

TYPES OF CAREER DECISION INFORMATION

Research has not yet identified one single method of career exploration that is significantly better than others. The rapidly changing world of work and technological advances anticipated in the future make it unlikely that any single method or approach will emerge as a dominant theme (Gysbers, 1990). The most common types of career decision information are discussed briefly.

Printed Forms

The most common type of career decision information is in a printed format. The most pervasive examples of printed material include pamphlets, brochures, books, periodicals, journals, magazines, newspapers, and encyclopedias. The counselor will need to generate appropriate means of dissemination and storage. Detailed descriptions of how to handle these forms can be found in S. T. Brown and Brown (1990).

Audiovisuals

Audiovisual materials include movies, slides, CD-ROMs, and videotapes. A wide variety of both commercially produced and uncommercially produced materials is readily available. Many of these materials can be obtained free or inexpensively. Professional organizations and many corporations offer free orientations to individuals and groups relating to potential career opportunities in specific areas.

Computer-Assisted Career Guidance

Computer-assisted career guidance (CACG) is now a common resource in the delivery of career guidance counseling in schools (Sampson, Shahnasarian, & Reardon, 1987). The core elements of most CACG systems are dissemination of occupational and educational information, generation of occupational alternatives, and self-assessment (Sampson, Peterson, & Reardon, 1989). Although the information component provides users with occupational data, the guidance element provides more personalized exploration and assessment of career possibilities (Hinkle, 1992). For example, the computer database can supply vast amounts of information about jobs (including training) and educational opportunities, different types of universities and technical schools, available scholarships and financial aid, costs for tuition and residence, potential salaries, and a specified occupational outlook. Research Emphasis 11.1 presents teenagers' perspectives relating to technology.

Research Emphasis 11.1
The Nintendo Generation: Wired for the Future

Princeton Survey Research Associates interviewed 508 teenagers, ages 12–17. The survey was conducted by telephone March 12–16, 1997. The margin of sampling error is ± 5 percentage points. The survey discovered that school students are using computers regularly in class and increasingly at home to get on-line. Other interesting results include the following:

- 71% think the V-chip is a "good idea."
- 89% use computers at least several times a week.
- 61% surf the Net (boys = 66%, girls = 56%).
- 50% think the best thing about the Net is that it is like a library, a place to find information.
- 33% think it is better as a shopping mall, where you can hang out and meet friends.
- 14% admit to having seen or done something they "wouldn't want their parents to know about."
- 92% think computers will improve their educational opportunities.
- 28% believe technology is not helping—or, worse, actually harms—the environment.
- 71% want to talk to, rather than type into, their computers.
- 98% credit technology for making a positive difference in their lives (boys = 57%, girls = 46%).

SOURCE: From "Teenagers and Technology," *Newsweek*, April 28, 1997, p. 86. Copyright 1997 by Newsweek Inc. All rights reserved. Reprinted with permission.

The interactive capabilities of the computer allow the student to explore personal values, interests, abilities, and decision-making styles. Additional CACG systems components include orientation to the career decision-making process, orientation to the world of work, means of dealing with barriers to career choice, and the development of strategies for such a choice (Sampson et al., 1989).

As a counseling technology, CACG is becoming widely accessible, cost effective, and reasonably easy to use (Hinkle, 1992). Computer software is available to assist elementary students in their search of occupational options, to aid in the exploration of occupational choices in middle school and junior high programs and in the decision making and job placement in high schools (Schmidt, 1996). Zunker (1994) noted, however, these three areas of career focus are not limited to any single level of education or development.

Career information systems. Computed-assisted career information systems are supported by the availability of grants from the U.S. Department of Labor and the National Occupational Information Coordination Committee (NOICC), which offer local and regional data and information. These resources are supplemented by state branches of NOICC (SOICCs). The Guidance Information System, published by the Time Share Corporation of West Hartford, Connecticut, and the C-Elect from Chronicle Guidance Publications, Moravia, New York, offer CACG programs to enhance student awareness and orientation activities and services. The constantly changing field of computer technology and software development requires consistent monitoring in order for counselors to remain current.

Career guidance. The second type of CACG programs tend to have a broader focus than simply the dissemination of information. These programs venture into areas including self-assessment processes, instructional modules, planning activities, and decision-making steps. For example, the two most popular CACG programs are the System of Interactive Guidance and Information (SIGI-Plus) from Educational Testing Services, Princeton, New Jersey, and the Discover II from the American College Testing Program, Iowa City, Iowa (Gladding, 1991; Zunker, 1994). SIGI-Plus provides five components to assist students and their school counselors in (a) self-assessment, (b) identification of possible occupational choices, (c) comparison of pertinent occupational information, (d) review of educational preparation for occupations, and (e) evaluation of the risks and rewards of particular occupations, including consideration of the consequences of particular career choices. The Discover II is an interactive CACG system designed to provide (a) self-assessment, (b) opportunity to explore the world of work, (c) strategies to identify occupations of interest, (d) detailed information about different occupations, (e) and educational requirements to assist in career planning. However, Baker (1992) noted that this increasing popularity of computer technology in school counseling programs has raised several issues, including the question of the effectiveness of CACG programs.

Special Events

School counselors have used special events in career development for years. The more popular examples include career fairs and guest speakers. Job shadowing and other similar procedures provide students an opportunity to observe a specific job realistically. Field trips are a common method of gaining occupational and educational information. They can be accomplished on a group or individual basis. In addition, they can be videotaped and incorporated into local workshops. By observing a career in situ, the student acquires necessary career information and is an active participant in the process (Herr & Cramer, 1996).

Modeling Interventions

Several authors have emphasized the efficacy of modeling as a career intervention and have also hypothesized that modeling of nontraditional career choices increases the range of occupations perceived by students to be available (e.g., Sauter, Seidl, & Karbon, 1980). Successful career modeling occurs when career behaviors are acquired or existing interests are enhanced as a result of observing the consequences of another person's career behavior (Van Buren, Kelly, & Hall, 1993).

The use of visual media to model nontraditional careers has affected positively the career decision-making skills of young women (Foss & Slaney, 1986). However, little empirical evidence supports modeling of nontraditional careers to increase interests basic to nontraditional career choice for women and men. Neither Foss and Slaney (1986) nor Little and Roach (1974) found that their participants expressed greater interest in nontraditional careers after viewing a videotape regarding nontraditional career choices for women and men.

Van Buren et al. (1993) studied the effects of an 18-minute videotape promoting nontraditional career choices of 986 eighth-grade and eleventh-grade girls and boys from rural and urban schools (469 treatment group, 517 control group; 508 girls, 478 boys; 592 rural, 394 urban). Models were women and men in occupations traditionally held by the opposite sex. Posttreatment realistic, investigative, and social interests of the treatment group that viewed the videotape were compared with a control group that received a minimal intervention. A main effect for the brief videotape was not found. Boys in the treatment group expressed significantly higher social interests at posttest than did control group boys. Findings indicated that brief interventions promoting nontraditional careers have limited impact.

SOURCES OF CAREER INFORMATION

Many sources of career and educational information are available for counselors and students. Drummond and Ryan (1995) suggested that counselors design and implement a community survey to obtain firsthand information on the cost, time of training, financial aid available, time of programs, entry requirements, and contact individuals for the availability and the type of anticipated vacancies in different occupations.

School counselors also need to conduct a student needs survey to determine what their educational and career aspirations are. Then student expectations can be matched with available opportunities. State departments of labor, state manpower commissions, and the U.S. Department of Labor provide projections of needs in all occupational areas for a 5- to 10-year period. In addition, follow-up surveys of graduates can provide valuable information about current employment and career avenues. A secondary purpose of follow-ups is to obtain data about the school's success rate of graduates and fulfillment of student postsecondary expectations.

Career Centers

Many schools have career centers for student use. Two specific functions of such centers are program activities and material development. Program activities include speakers, tours, career counseling, in-service training, outreach functions, and staff training. Material development includes briefs, curriculum guides, research reports, and staff materials. Additional functions include research and development, worker needs, projection and trends, and translation functions.

The terms *career resource center, educational information center,* or *career information center* are most often used for this concept. The primary purpose of a career center (for school counselors) is to enhance the use of career-related information by gathering together in one place within a school or school district all educational, occupational, and financial aid information (Herr & Cramer, 1996). The center provides students with help in using the information and allows a physical space for students to meet with representatives of educational/ training institutions, potential employers, and community resource people. The emphasis is placed on facilitating easy accessibility for student users.

These centers facilitate the acquisition, storage, retrieval, and dissemination of career-related information. They may be housed in a separate structure or within the guidance and placement offices. Examples of their components include microfilm and microfiche viewers, view-decks, books, pamphlets, occupational files, reference and resource volumes, catalogues, brochures, computers, video and audio tapes, and convenient spaces for students to use the information. At the elementary school level, it is sometimes labeled a *guidance learning center*.

A career education center that is conveniently located, attractively arranged, facilitative to users, and adaptable will be used more frequently than one that is not (S. T. Brown & Brown, 1990). Mamarchev and Pritchett (1978) outlined eight required steps in establishing a career resource center:

1. To plan thoroughly after conducting a needs assessment and to include immediate, intermediate, and long-range goals.
2. To consider the physical design carefully.
3. To determine the staff needs and role of each staff member.
4. To determine how the resource materials and information sources will be cataloged and arranged.
5. To develop a plan for publicizing the availability of the center.
6. To assist individuals in their career planning, decision making, and personal appraisal.
7. To have a plan of evaluation in place to assess the effectiveness of the program and to demonstrate the accountability of the center.
8. To provide fiscal budget for the center's operation.

Zunker (1998) identified several additional needs for the developers of career resource centers to consider. These needs are as follows:

1. Recognize the importance of identifying the needs that users have and ensure that activities and materials meet those needs.
2. Be flexible with the hours in which the center will be accessible (e.g., before and after school and work hours).
3. Incorporate simple procedures for coding and organizing materials.
4. Determine whose responsibility it is to develop and maintain the center.
5. Coordinate the center's operation with teachers, administrators, counselors, and media specialists to ensure a collaborative effort.
6. Determine the operating policies of the center.

In many incidences, the career resource center might be part of the library or media center of a school, so it is usually the media specialist's responsibility to develop and maintain the center. Frequently, however, the career resource center is located in the guidance and counseling complex. In this case, it is the school counselor's role to develop and operate the center. In reality, the variance in size, staff, and materials of a center is quite large. Students deserve to have access to some kind of career information regardless of size of school or availability of funds. Suggestions for the setting up and evaluating of a career center are available (e.g., S. T. Brown & Brown, 1990; Zunker, 1986).

Major Federal Sources

The U.S. Department of Labor is the major source of labor market information. The Bureau of Labor Statistics publishes the *Occupational Outlook Handbook*, the *Occupational Outlook Quarterly*, the *Occupational Projections and Training Data*, the *Occupational Employment Statistics Survey Operations Manual*, and the *Occupational Employment Statistics Dictionary of Occupations*. The Employment and Training Administration section of the U.S. Department of Labor publishes the *Dictionary of Occupational Titles*, *Guide for Occupational Exploration*, and *Selected Characteristics of Occupations Defined in the Dictionary of Occupational Titles*.

Additional publications useful to career decision making are the *Military Career Guide: Employment and Training Opportunities in the Military* and the *Military Occupational and Training Data*, published by the U.S. Department of Defense Division on Manpower Installations and Logistics. The U.S. Department of Commerce's International Trade Administration publishes the *U.S. Industrial Outlook*, a source of projected growth. The Bureau of Census publishes the *U.S. Census of Population, 1990: Alphabetical Index of Occupations and Industries* and *U.S. Census of Population, 1990: Classified Index of Industries and Occupations*. Several of the major governmental publications are listed and summarized in Something to Consider 11.2.

NOICC.   NOICC provides guidance to each states' career, occupational, and labor market. NOICC operates as a facilitator among various agencies that produce and use occupational information. This agency also provides funds and assistance to the states for developing systems of using and disseminating career information.

The American School Counselor Association (ASCA) and NOICC have developed the "Get A Life" career development portfolio. The portfolio is intended for educational settings and is a personalized sequential planning journal. It is designed to help students relate education to career interests and aptitudes. The portfolio, available from ASCA, includes a Facilitator's Manual and user-friendly software.

The Occupational Data Analysis System (ODAS).   A second example of networking is the ODAS, sponsored by the Vocational Technical Education Consortium of States. ODAS is a computer-based

Something to Consider 11.2
Selected Governmental Career Information Sources

Source	Description	Counseling Uses
Occupational Outlook Handbook	Contains detailed information on about 200 occupations including descriptions on working conditions, employment, training, other qualifications, advancement, job outlook, earnings, and related occupations	Good readable reference source
Occupational Outlook Quarterly	Contains articles on new occupations, job and labor market, training opportunities, and studies completed by the Bureau of Labor Statistics	Good readable reference source
U.S. Industrial Outlook	Contains reviews and forecasts as well as current situations for 250 industries	Excellent source for identifying growth industries and nongrowth industries and understanding trends in industry
Military Career Guide	Contains 134 clusters of occupations common to the military services and describes typical work tasks, work environment, physical demands, training, and civilian counterpart	Good guide to explore career fields within the military services and how they are reflected in civilian life
Dictionary of Occupational Titles	Contains definitions and classifications for about 20,000 occupations using a nine-digit code number	Good source for types of tasks, job functions, and groups of related jobs
Vocational Preparation and Occupations	Contains explanation of classification systems and crosswalk tables for eight vocational areas	Good source to identify which programs to enroll in and which occupational skills to acquire

SOURCE: From Drummond and Ryan (1995).

system and uses three sources of data: catalogs of performance objectives related to the *Dictionary of Occupational Titles,* key-word descriptors designed by the Job Service of the U.S. Department of Labor, and vocational preparation and occupations designed by NOICC. The system describes skill requirements of jobs and the level of education and training required, describes skills required in training programs, and identifies skills required by new and emerging occupations, among other functions. The system's primary use is in vocational-technical schools, 2-year colleges, adult education programs, high schools, vocational rehabilitation centers, and business and industry. Target populations include youths and adults in and out of school; unemployed, displaced, or dislocated workers; vocational rehabilitation clients; and women who reenter the job market. Applications are in curriculum development, assessment and training of displaced workers, placement and guidance, and so on. A terminal and a telephone modem are required.

State Sources

Employment and labor market data are also available from federal agencies for each state relating to historical, contemporary, and projected information on employment, unemployment, and occupational trends. Agency reports emphasize the composition of the labor market and include statistics on the characteristics of those unemployed, the economically disadvantaged, and special groups (Drummond & Ryan, 1995). These publications disseminate information valuable to counselors in their mission to provide students with updates on labor trends.

All states have a state occupational coordinating committee (SOICC), comprising representatives from the state employment security agency, state employment and training council, vocational rehabilitation, economic development, education, human services, and corrections (Drummond & Ryan, 1995). A group within SOICC is charged with designing and implementing a state career information delivery system with five objectives (National Occupational Information Coordinating Committee, 1990b):

1. To inform students about various career opportunities available now and in the future.
2. To help students develop an awareness of occupations they would find satisfying.
3. To encourage adolescents to seek out career information on their own.
4. To provide students information about the educational and training opportunities available for careers or jobs that interest them.
5. To be a resource base for career education, career and employment counseling, employment and training, and educational decision making.

School counselors who deal with career development issues need to know the resources provided by their SOICC, which may be listed in governmental directories. A list of SOICCs is available as an appendix to the *Occupational Outlook Handbook* and in NOICC's annual report, "Status of the NOICC/SOICC Network." For more information, write to the Executor Director, NOICC, Suite 156, 2100 M Street, NW, Washington, DC 20037.

Nongovernmental Sources

Numerous nongovernmental agencies, professional organizations, private organizations, local organizations, and foundations develop and distribute career information. Most of this resource material is free or nominally priced. The school counselor can consult the yellow pages, chambers of commerce, and other media sources for this type of information. Word-of-mouth is always a source of information regardless of its lack of empirical support.

Periodicals

A variety of professional journals and popular periodicals emphasize career development and career education. Some of the governmental periodicals include *Monthly Labor Review* (U.S. Department of Labor), *Occupational Outlook Quarterly* (U.S. Department of Labor), and *American Education* (U.S. Department of Education). The more popular magazines include *Career World, Glamour, Mademoiselle, Seventeen,* and *Reader's Digest.*

Technical and Trade Schools

Guides are available on technical and trade schools. Some technical and trade schools are not accredited, and many are for-profit operations. Examples of these guides are the following:

American Trade School Directory. Queens Village, NY: Corner Publications.
Directory of the National Association of Trade and Technical Schools. Washington, DC: National Association of Trade and Technical Schools.
Directory of Post-Secondary Schools With Occupational Programs, Public and Private. Washington, DC: U.S. Government Printing Office.
Lovejoy's Career and Vocational School Guide. New York: Simon & Schuster.
Technical, Trade, and Business School Data Handbook (by geographic region). Concord, MA: Orchard House.

Colleges and Universities

A large variety of sources of information can be discovered about colleges and universities. College and university catalogs are available in most libraries and counselor offices. Many directories are also available, including the following:

The College Blue Book. New York: Macmillan.
The College Handbook. Princeton, NJ: Educational Testing Service.

Barron's Profiles of American Colleges. Hauppaugy, NY: Barron's Educational Series.

Lovejoy's College Guide. New York: Simon & Schuster.

Peterson's Annual Guides to Graduate Study. Princeton, NJ: Educational Testing Service.

College Admission Index of Majors and Sports. Concord, MA: Orchard House.

Media Sources

A multitude of media materials are available for school counselors. Media approaches appeal to visual learners, to adults, as well as to low-motivated students and clients (Drummond & Ryan, 1995). Media sources include posters, slides, films, records, cassettes, microfilm, microfiche, transparencies, and videos on career fields, career awareness, and self-awareness topics. The Educators' Guide to Free Guidance Materials lists free films, filmstrips, slides, and tapes. Modern Talking Picture Services, Inc. (Scheduling Center, 5000 Park Street, N., St. Petersburg, FL 33709-2254) is an example of film and video libraries that provide career and educational videos and films frees for a given show date. Some films and videos are produced by governmental organizations such as the Peace Corps, the National Science Foundation, and the National Oceanic and Atmospheric Administration.

Other Sources

Career information can also be found in other sources. Commercial publishers offer a variety of printed materials that include biographies and autobiographies, fiction or novels about people in career fields, career encyclopedias and books about specific careers, directories, and how-to books. Many professional organizations publish and distribute career and educational information. In addition, industries and businesses publish recruiting and promotional materials for specific careers. Most educational and training organizations provide brochures and booklets on types of programs, entry requirements, costs, whom to contact, and how to apply.

Bibliographies and indexes are available to help counselors keep informed. Some are published by professional organizations (e.g., National Vocational Guidance Association), others by public service organizations (e.g., the B'nai B'rith Career and Counseling Service), and others by commercial publishers (e.g., Chronicle Guidance Publications). The ERIC Counseling and Student Services Clearinghouse publishes numerous periodicals and monographs. School counselors should avail themselves of all of these potential resources, especially for free information.

GENDER AND RACIAL/ETHNIC EQUITY

Although gender, racial/ethnic, and socioeconomic differences are discussed in other chapters, student performance and career development are associated with multiple effects of gender, race or ethnic identification, and socioeconomic status (SES). Educators may disagree about the broad issues involved in defining gender or ethnic equity, but most would probably agree that certain current educational practices are unfair and should be corrected (H. Grossman & Grossman, 1994). For example, few educators would support such practices as using textbooks that only reflect the interests or contributions of one gender or one ethnicity, or providing students of one gender or ethnicity less assistance when they need help. Even though educators have conflicts about the cause or causes of gender and ethnic differences and different comfort levels with the status quo, most would probably agree that schools should provide equitable information services to their students. Research Emphasis 11.2 presents specific guidelines for the equitable delivery of career information in the classroom.

Recently the American Association of University Women (1992) presented evidence that female students are not participating equally in the U.S. educational system. The report offered 40 recommendations that schools should act on to improve education for female stu-

---

Research Emphasis 11.2
Guidelines for Gender and Racial/Ethnic/Cultural Equity in the Classroom

---

Scott and McCollum (1993) offered the following ideas for making classroom gender-appropriate and race/ethnic/culture-appropriate:

- Actively challenge misconceptions of race, culture, and gender through class lectures and discussions.
- Model sex-equitable behavior.
- Physically organize classrooms so students are not segregated by race or ethnicity, culture, or gender.
- Eliminate the assignment of sex-stereotyped tasks (e.g., male students dissect the frog, female students record procedures).
- Use instructional materials that are culture fair and gender fair (e.g., allow students to see active role models from a variety of professions, history from multiple viewpoints).
- Encourage female students to use equipment typically reserved for male students (computers, basketballs).
- Provide opportunities for cooperative learning activities to occur across gender, cultural, and racial/ethnic lines.

SOURCE: From "Making It Happen: Gender Equitable Classrooms," by E. Scott & H. McCollum, 1993. In S. Biklen & D. Pollard (Eds.), *92nd Yearbook of the National Society for the Study of Education: Part 1. Gender and Education* (pp. 174–190). Copyright 1993 by the University of Chicago Press. Adapted with permission.

dents (see Appendix 1 of the report for the full list of recommendations). Something to Consider 11.3 presents a synthesis of these recommendations.

The AAUW report (1992) conveys data from the National Education Longitudinal Study of eighth graders from 1988 and from the High School and Beyond Study for 1980. These studies compared grades, test scores, and postschool plans of the major ethnic groups including European Americans. Student performance and career plans often vary by race or ethnicity. Many of the differences narrow considerably when students from the same SES are compared. Again, such data emphasize that SES is more powerful than any other variable in predicting educational outcomes (Reinolds, 1996).

Many counselors and parents believe that students are not receiving equitable career information delivery services. Title IX may make the implementation of certain recommended approaches illegal or at least difficult. For example, single-sex instruction, defeminizing schools, introducing more male tutors into elementary school classrooms, emphasizing active learning, and stressing field-independent teaching techniques have been proposed to increase gender-equitable services. Because accommodating to gender or racial stereotypes can

---

Something to Consider 11.3
Improving Education for Female Students

The American Association of University Women maintains that:
- The reinforcement of Title IX must be strengthened.
- Teachers, administrators, and counselors must bring gender equity and awareness to every aspect of schooling.
- The formal school curriculum must include the experiences of women and men from various aspects of life. Young women and men must come to see women and girls as valued in the materials they study.
- Young women must be encouraged to understand that mathematics and the sciences are important and relevant to their lives.
- Attention must be paid to gender equity in vocational educational programs.
- Testing and assessment must serve as stepping stones, not terminal points. In particular, new testing techniques must accurately reflect the abilities of women and men.
- Women must play a central role in educational reform: the experiences, strengths, and needs of girls from every race, ethnicity, culture, and social class must be considered if excellence and equity are to be provided for all U.S. students.
- A critical goal of educational reform must be to enable students to consider effectively the realities of their lives, particularly in areas such as health and sexuality.

SOURCE: From *AAUW Report: How Schools Shortchange Girls,* by American Association of University Women, 1992. Copyright 1992 by the AAUW Educational Foundation, Washington, DC. Adapted with permission.

have negative as well as positive results, counselors and educators might consider both possibilities before choosing a course of action.

CAREER INDECISIVENESS

School counselors frequently encounter students who seem unable to make a career decision. Even though the counselor may have done his or her best by providing students with career information, interest inventories, ability appraisals, and other interventions, many students still are not closer to a career decision (Bansberg & Sklare, 1986). These students present difficult and often frustrating challenges to the counselor.

The traditional model of career counseling has typically approached a career decision problem as a need for self- or occupational information (Larson, Busby, Wilson, Medora, & Allgood, 1994). Many quality career counseling instruments are available to assist students with learning more about their interests, work values, abilities, and career alternatives. These include interest inventories, ability assessments, and computerized career guidance systems.

Research, however, strongly suggests that career decisions involve more than just obtaining information (Bansberg & Sklare, 1986). An earlier discussion emphasized the importance of motivation in the effective use of career information (Herr & Cramer, 1996; Peterson et al., 1991). Various intrapersonal motivations or problems can interfere with career decision making. Examples include anxiety, an external locus of control, lack of self-awareness, and other "personality problems" (Bansberg & Sklare, 1986; Hartman, Fuqua, & Blum, 1985).

Psychological blocks may be affective, cognitive, or behavioral (Bansberg & Sklare, 1986). Decision anxiety is an affective psychological block that inhibits career decision making by immobilizing the individual (Hartman et al., 1985). It may be due to unrealistic expectations, fear of success or failure, fear of change, or intermodal conflicts experienced when an individual possesses two strong but opposite vocational personality traits (e.g., creativity and conventionality; Holland & Holland, 1977).

In contrast, a lack of life or goal awareness may be categorized as a cognitive psychological block to career decision making (Bansberg & Sklare, 1986). It may be due to unresolved identity issues; a lack of purpose, mission, or goals; or an unawareness of needs (Hartman et al., 1985). Authority orientation and a luck-and-fate orientation to career decision making reflect both cognitive and behavioral blocks. Students with both tend to accept uncritically the values and beliefs of others (often a parent or significant other), have low self-esteem, and avoid responsibility (Bansberg & Sklare, 1986).

Secondary gain motivation is another psychological block that could best be described as cognitive and behavioral. The individual is motivated not to choose a career because of perceived disadvantages, such as "If I choose a career in art instead of medicine, my parents will never forgive me" (Larson et al., 1994). Thus, the best perceived alternative may be not to make a choice. Students may be nonconformists or may be manipulating the system to avoid employment and still receive benefits.

The psychometric qualities of the *Career Decision Diagnostic Assessment (CDDA)* justify it as an instrument worthy of continued study by school counselors for further verification of its validity and reliability (Bansberg & Sklare, 1986). The *CDDA* provides information about the psychological causes of career indecision that other instruments also provide (i.e., decision anxiety and life/goal awareness). The unique areas assessed by the *CDDA* include authority orientation, luck-and-fate orientation, and secondary gain motivation. The *CDDA* seems to have the potential of joining the ranks of the few valid and reliable appraisal instruments for career decision problems.

The Career Decision Scale (CDS; Osipow, 1987; Osipow, Carney, Winer, Yanico, & Koschier, 1976) has also generated considerable research. Much of the research has attempted to obtain a more differential measure of the antecedents of career indecision and in developing a typology of indecision (F. W. Vondracek, Schulenberg, & Hostetler, 1989). In addition, deleting some items out of Holland's (1987) Self-Directed Search may produce a "cleaner" set of subscales for indecision (F. W. Vondracek, Hostetler, Schulenberg, & Shimizu, 1990).

SUMMARY

The delivery of career information services facilitates career development and decision making. School counselors are required to be cognizant of the various sources of career and educational information. School counselors also must know the biases, weaknesses, and strengths of those sources. They must be prepared for student queries about career information and be able to direct students to the appropriate resource.

The delivery of career information services must be equitable and available to all students, regardless of their individual and group dissimilarities. The United States is increasingly evolving into a nation of ethnic minorities. In addition, the continually advancing world of technology is contributing new career opportunities and is requiring more specificity from training programs. The constantly shrinking world is creating additional opportunities for international careers. These increases augment the need for effective information delivery services.

EXPERIENTIAL ACTIVITIES

1. Are you likely to encourage male students more than female students to go to college? Why or why not?
2. Conduct a career guidance needs assessment with your students and design your data-gathering instrument, pilot it, and analyze the results.
3. Interview several career or school counselors and have them identify the information sources that they find are the most valuable to them.
4. How would you arrange a career resource center? What criteria for the selection of resources would you set? What staff and budget would you need?
5. Develop a personal intervention for dealing with a student's indecisiveness about careers and the world of work.
6. Brainstorm ideas for maintaining a current inventory of available vocational and career information on the local, state, and national levels.

12

Appraisal From a Multicultural Focus

First of all, the most successful instruments are those that
fill a need,
and that are of tangible value to those who use them
or to those who benefit from their use.

F. W. Vondracek, 1991, p. 327

Appraisal is an integral part of the educational process as it provides information that counselors and other educational personnel need to determine whether students have acquired the knowledge, skills, abilities, and other objectives of the curriculum. Because the U.S. society is so diverse, until recently, assessment procedures, particularly standardized instruments, were not very accurate when used with many ethnic and low-income students.

Assessment instruments are often criticized as being biased and unfair when they are used in the assessment of ethnic minority students. They are also criticized for being inattentive to students' socioeconomic, linguistic, contextual, and gender characteristics and their conditions of disability. If that is the case, millions of school-age youths are being improperly served, especially in the area of career development and guidance. This chapter addresses some of these concerns and attempts to enlighten school counselors about those concerns. In addition, attention is given to the more popular appraisal devices and how they "stack up" on the issue of multicultural efficacy. The chapter also suggests how school counselors can avoid discriminatory appraisals by adapting their efforts to students' characteristics and selecting appropriate nonbiased, nonsexist appraisal materials and procedures. The discussion begins with a review of various standards for multicultural assessment, as adapted from Drummond (1996).

STANDARDS FOR MULTICULTURAL ASSESSMENT

The Association for Assessment in Counseling (1993) identified 34 standards with multicultural relevance from their standards. These 34 standards included 10 concerning the selection of assessment instruments according to content; 9 related to the use of reliability, validity, and norming; 4 involving scoring and administration; and 11 addressing the use and interpretation of the results of assessment. As can be easily ascertained, the major theme permeating these standards is the selection process.

Content Appropriateness

The *Code of Fair Testing Practices in Education* (American Psychological Association [APA], 1988) included two standards in the area of content. The first emphasizes the need to define the purpose of assessment and the population to be assessed. Once those two concerns are considered, then selecting an appropriate instrument is begun. The second standard addresses the need to evaluate the appraisal instrument for any potentially insensitive or inappropriate content and language.

The *Responsibilities of Users of Standardized Tests* (American Association for Counseling and Development & Association for Measurement and Evaluation in Counseling and Development [hereinafter, AACD], 1989) included four standards regarding content appropriateness. The test interpreter has the responsibility to (a) determine the limitations to testing created by the test taker's age, ethnic/racial, sexual, and cultural characteristics; (b) ascertain how the assessment instrument addresses variation of motivation, pace of work, linguistic issues, and test-taking experience of the test taker; (c) ascertain whether one common or several different assessments are necessary for accurate measurement of special populations; and (d) determine whether individuals of dissimilar language groups need assessment in either or both languages.

The *Standards for Educational and Psychological Testing* (American Education Research Association, American Psychological Association, & National Council on Measurement in Education [hereinafter APA], 1985) adopted four multiculturally appropriate standards. An appraisal instrument's publisher should provide the information necessary for appropriate use and interpretation when recommending an appraisal instrument for linguistically diverse test takers. School and career counselors must review the interpretive materials to ensure that stereotypical and traditional roles are not depicted in case studies or examples. The type and content of the items should be congruent with the backgrounds and experiential base of the population. The item differences should be researched to avoid inappropriateness regarding age, gender, ethnic, and cultural factors. All in all, appraisal instruments and their contents need to be unbiased and appropriate to the test takers' characteristics.

Technical Appropriateness

The *Code of Fair Testing Practices in Education* (APA, 1988) and the *Responsibilities of Users of Standardized Tests* (AACD, 1989) require test interpreters to validate that content and normative data are congruent with test takers from diverse backgrounds. School counselors need to review the manual to see previous performance by test takers of dissimilar ethnic/racial, cultural, and gender backgrounds. This search should include the viability of reliability and validity indicators as well. Special attention is needed to ensure that normative groups represent sufficient numbers.

Standards for Educational and Psychological Testing (APA, 1985) stresses the value of reviewing the criterion-related evidence of validity when recommending decisions having an actuarial and clinical influence. The simple translation of an appraisal instrument from one language to another language does not necessarily transfer the validity and reliability indexes. In addition, one must review any research studies exploring the magnitude of predictive bias due to differential prediction for groups for which previous research has established a substantial prior probability of differential prediction for the type of appraisal in question (see Case Vignette 12.1).

Considerations of Administration and Scoring

The *Responsibilities of Users of Standardized Tests* (AACD, 1989) stresses the need for test interpreters to demonstrate verbal clarity, calmness, empathy, and impartiality toward all test takers. Test interpreters need to also consider potential effects of examiner–examinee dissimilarity in

---

Case Vignette 12.1
Kim: A Korean American Youth

Kim, a 6-year-old Korean American girl, entered first grade but was having academic difficulties and was referred for a multifactor evaluation by the school's multidisciplinary team. The mother refused to allow her daughter to be tested until she could examine the tests that would be used. The psychologist met with the mother to explain why the tests would be given and to discuss what tests would be given.
1. What factors were involved?
2. What test standards were involved in the case?
3. What was the ethical responsibility of the psychologist?

ethnic, cultural, and linguistic backgrounds, attitudes, and value systems. *Standards of Educational and Psychological Testing* (APA, 1985) advises test interpreters to ensure that linguistic modification recommended by test publishers are described in detail in the test manual. Test administrations should be designed to minimize threats to reliability and validity that can arise from language differences.

Use and Interpretation

Test interpreters must take into consideration differences between the norms and the scores of test takers in their score interpretations (APA, 1988). Parents and legal guardians also deserve to know their rights and the procedures for appeal if necessary. Socioeconomic status, gender, inappropriate application of norms, and other influences can affect test performance as well (AACD, 1989). In addition, test administrators and consumers need to ensure their competencies in dealing with special populations in regard to their academic training or supervised experience (APA, 1985).

Multicultural Counseling Competencies and Standards (Sue, Arredondo, & McDavis, 1992) included three standards related to multicultural assessment. In April 1995, the Executive Board adopted these competencies (Arredondo et al., 1996, pp. 71–73).

1. Culturally skilled counselors must be aware of the potential bias of assessment instruments and when interpreting findings keep in mind the client's cultural and linguistic characteristics.
2. They also need an awareness and understanding of how culture and ethnicity may affect personality formation, vocational choices, manifestations of psychological disorders, help-seeking behavior, and the appropriateness of counseling approaches.
3. Counselors not only must understand the technical aspects of the instruments, they must also be aware of the cultural limitations.

The American Counseling Association's (1995) *Code of Ethics* also revised its standards to ensure counselors are providing specific orientation or information to the test takers before and after test administration so that the results of assessment may be placed in proper perspective with other relevant factors such as the effects of socioeconomic, ethnic, and cultural factors on test scores.

INSTRUMENT BIAS

Bias in appraisal processes can be a complex and frustrating concern. The major concern during the 1970s and 1980s emphasized racial, ethical, and cultural bias inherent to appraisal instruments and testing (Valencia & Aburto, 1991). Jensen (1980), on the other hand, purported that test fairness or unfairness results from moral philosophy, not psychometrics. He believed that appraisal items are biased if empirical data establish that the items are more difficult for one group member than another, the general ability level of the two groups is held constant, and no reasonable rationale exists to explain group differences on the same items. Consider Case Vignette 12.2.

Six areas of appraisal instrument bias have been suggested: inappropriate content, inappropriate standardization samples, examiner and language bias, inequitable social consequences, measurement of different constructs, and differential predictive validity. In particular, bilingual and ESL (English as a Second Language) students have difficulty with oral and written instructions in addition to the vocabulary and the syntax of items (Drummond, 1996). In addition, these students may also have difficulty giving appropriate verbal responses and understanding verbal instructions or questions.

TEST TAKER BIAS FACTORS

Students require adaptations in the appraisal process to avoid bias. This section describes and evaluates suggestions for adapting the appraisal process to these differences. School counselors must avoid overgeneralizations and stereotypical statements about students. The ethnic, socioeconomic, and gender differences discussed in this chapter are meant to make school counselors aware of and sensitive to differences that may possibly characterize students, not to encourage them to judge students by their ethnic background, name, skin color, conditions of disability, gender, or lifestyle preference. The most common test taker bias factors are test wiseness and text motivation or anxiety.

Case Vignette 12.2
Darryl: An African American Youth

Darryl is a 14-year-old African American boy. Assessment using Gardner's Typology (1987) indicated he had high musical and kinesthetic intelligence. His family moved to the city from a suburban area because of his father's transfer. He attends an inner-city high school with a magnet program in engineering and mathematics because his parents did not want him to be bused to another school. The school he last attended had limited programs in fine arts and music and few resources. One of Darryl's friends was shot by a gang, and another classmate overdosed and died. Darryl began to withdraw, showing signs of depression. He became sick on school days. His parents want you to test Darryl and counsel him.
1. What type of appraisal procedures and instruments would you use with Darryl?
2. What factors and issues do you feel need to be addressed?
3. What additional information would you like to have about Darryl?

Familiarity With the Appraisal Process

The test administrator cannot assume that all students are test wise. Not all students are accustomed to being appraised, especially in a one-to-one situation (H. Grossman, 1995). Students who are unfamiliar with appraisal procedures often become anxious when they are appraised (Dao, 1991). Research indicates that a small amount of anxiety can interfere with their performance. As Hill (1980) described this anxiety,

> The way many standardized tests are composed and given do, in fact, elicit or at least allow strong debilitating motivational dynamics such as test anxiety to operate. Such motivational test bias will cause many children to perform well below their optimal level of functioning in the test situation, thereby invalidating their results if one is interested in what the children have learned, as opposed to whether they can demonstrate that learning under heavy testing pressure. (p. 4)

Immigrant and refugee students who have never been appraised, especially on a one-to-one basis, are likely to be anxious during the appraisal process (Dao, 1991). Considerable evidence also indicates that African American and low-income students are more anxious in appraisal procedures compared with European American and middle-class students (Hill, 1980). For example, some Hispanic American students come from countries where students are seldom appraised individually as they are in the United States (H. Grossman, 1984). "The strangeness and unfamiliarity of this situation may make Hispanic American students anxious to the point that their anxiety interferes with their ability to demonstrate their achievement and potential" (p. 175).

Students come to the appraisal process with different test-testing skills. Their test wiseness and their capacity to use the characteristics and format of an appraisal procedure or the appraisal situation to solve the problems included in an appraisal procedure affect their ability to perform up to their actual level (H. Grossman, 1995). Students who have not acquired test-taking skills may be unable to demonstrate what they actually know and can do. For example,

> Many Native American Indian students fail to exhibit successful test-taking behaviors due to a multiplicity of underlying causes. Cultural beliefs in some tribes may bar competitive behaviors in an academic setting. The student may underestimate the seriousness of the test or fail to adopt a successful response strategy which may involve selective scanning for known items, techniques of using partial information to guess correct answers, or efficient time use. (Brescia & Fortune, 1988, p. 101)

Research has consistently indicated that improving students' test-taking skills, including those of African American, Hispanic American,

Native American Indian, and low-income students, also improves their scores on appraisal procedures (e.g., Brescia & Fortune, 1988; Haladyna, Nolen, & Hass, 1991). Haladyna et al. (1991) suggested that ethical and unethical ways exist to prepare students for standardized tests. The school counselor or test administrator must be alert to these ethical considerations.

Motivation

All students are not equally motivated to do their best when they are appraised. Some students may not realize that the appraisal being conducted is designed to evaluate them. This is especially true of Hispanic American, Native American Indian, and Southeast Asian American students, who come from cultures in which they are not evaluated in the same way (H. Grossman, 1995). For example, Native American Indian students who have not been exposed to a great deal of testing in reservation schools tend to view a test as a game. Therefore, they do not try to do as well as they might if they understood the significance of the situation (Deyhle, 1987; see Something to Consider 12.1).

When attempting to motivate students to do their best when they are appraised, it is also helpful to know whether individual recognition

---

Something to Consider 12.1
Cooperative Appraisal Environments

As the following citations attest, ethnic minority students tend to prefer cooperative environments.
- Cooperative learning is essential for Central Americans. Cooperation and collectivity are always regarded as essential values, whereas in the United States what is valued is individualism and competition (National Coalition of Advocates for Students, 1988).
- Because of their belief that it is bad manners to try to excel over others, some Hispanic students may not volunteer answers or they may even pretend not to know the correct answer when called on (H. Grossman, 1990, p. 358).
- There is evidence that Hawaiians are seldom concerned with the pursuit of success for the purely personal satisfaction involved. . . . Hawaiians apparently derive little personal pleasure from competing successfully against others and, in fact, avoid individual competition. . . . As an illustration, many children in Hawaiian schools refused to accept material rewards (e.g., cokes or candy) for high grades or successful competition unless the rewards could be shared with their friends (Slogett, 1971, pp. 55–56).
- Native American Indian parents desire their children to be successful, just as any other parents, but in a manner that is consistent with the cooperative and non-competitive tribal, community, and family values and aspirations (Burgess, 1978, p. 46).

or anonymity is stressed in their culture (H. Grossman, 1995). Chamberlain and Medinos-Landurand (1991) emphasized that

> In American society, students who do not value or are not skilled in competition are at a serious disadvantage in the testing process. These students do not understand or accept the concept of doing their "best" and working to do better than others during a test. (p. 118)

The test administrator must consider the attitudinal characteristics of students and encourage them to do their best in test situations. See Case Vignette 12.3.

Other Potential Factors

In addition to test wiseness and motivational concerns, test taker bias can derive from additional cultural factors that may include student perception of test administrators, variance in communication style, different learning styles, individual activity levels, pace, and response styles. Ethnic and cultural minority students may come from restricted environments in relation to expectations, language experiences, formal and informal learning experiences, and socialization. In addition, students' ability to understand and communicate in English is extremely important.

TEST ADMINISTRATOR AND EXAMINER BIAS FACTORS

The test administrator and examiner may introduce bias to the test setting. They must recognize personal bias and how it may influence interpretation of test results (Drummond, 1996). The main concern is to ensure that each student is treated with dignity and respect and that their best interests are ensured. Baruth and Manning (1991, pp. 121–145) identified the following most common obstacles to effective multicultural counseling.

Case Vignette 12.3
Rosita: A Latina Youth

Rosita is a 14-year-old bilingual Latina who was referred to the child study team because of her truancy, lack of motivation, and negative attitude toward her teachers and school. She was placed in an ESL class with many students who had negative motivation and poor skills. She told her parents she was going to school, but would skip and go to the local mall. She did well academically when she was in class. One of her teachers said, "She is like all of the other problem students we have in this program: no interest, no discipline, and no motivation."

1. What type of tests would you give and why?
2. What factors might tend to bias Rosita's test results?
3. What additional information about Rosita would you want to have?

---

1. The counselor makes erroneous assumptions about cultural assimilation.
2. Differences do exist in class and cultural values.
3. Language differences and both cultural and socioeconomic class misunderstandings exist.
4. The counselor believes in stereotypes about culturally different people.
5. The counselor fails to understand the culture.
6. Little understanding of the student's reasoning structures is evidenced.
7. A lack of cultural relativity exists among counselors.

APPRAISAL MATERIALS AND PROCEDURES

In dealing with ethnic minority and culturally different students, test administrators and examiners must have basic knowledge of the trends and issues related to the treatment of these students, the culture of those being tested, tests and appraisal procedures appropriate for the students, and agency and institutional sources of referral and support for the students being appraised (Drummond, 1996). As each student is unique, test administrators, examiners, and counselors need to be alert to important behavioral signals. Certain behaviors may affect the reliability and validity of the test. Appropriate examiner responses are summarized in Table 12.1.

In trying to adapt instruments for counseling in general, Osipow (1991) made several relevant points: (a) Cross-cultural adaptation is extremely difficult; (b) reliance on judges' ratings of items has inherent difficulties; and (c) theoretical notions on which to build instruments must be clear and must be made operational. With those thoughts in mind, this section addresses several of the most viable considerations in the selection of ethnically and culturally appropriate appraisal materials and procedures.

Etic/Emic Perspectives

Another way of viewing the appraisal of dissimilar ethnic and cultural students exists in the differentiation of the examiner's perspective. The terms *emic* and *etic* are often used to describe the phenomena that have culture-specific (culturally localized) or universal (culturally generalized) application (Atkinson, Morten, & Sue, 1993; S. D. Johnson, 1990). Viewing a culture as represented by individuals could be described as taking an idioemic perspective (i.e., examining a particular manifestation of the emic). Thus, emic, etic, and idioemic are categor-

Table 12.1
Critical Behavior Indicators and Possible Examiner Responses

Student Behavior	Response
Is silent	Establish rapport. Give nonverbal and performance test first. Get other indexes of individual behavior.
Says "don't know"	Don't assume student cannot respond.
Is shy and reserved, lowers eyes	Observe student in other situations, spend time establishing rapport, start with nonverbal and untimed tests, provide reinforcement, and try to motivate student.
Uses wit or popular language	Be firm and positive. Be sure student knows why the test/instrument is being used.
Interrupts the test or questions	Be firm but allow some dialogue and be sure the student knows the purpose of the test.
Is inattentive and restless	Structure test environment and keep student involved.
Is uncertain about how to respond	Rephrase question and make meaning clear.
Watches the examiner rather than listens to the question	Be firm, be sure questions are clear, and be sure there are no distractions in test situation.
Performs poorly on timed tests	Recognize a culture not oriented to the value of time. Avoid drawing conclusions about individual performance until untimed measures have been tried.
Shows poor knowledge of vocabulary	Try other ways of measuring the student's expressive vocabulary and question student in primary language.
Is unmotivated to take test	Explain purpose and value of test to student and family. Try techniques to motivate student performance.
Scores poorly on information items	Recognize that some items might be biased and not a part of the student's culture. Ask student to clarify any unusual responses.
Is afraid of embarrassing or dishonoring family	Initiate testwise session, practice session, or some type of warm-up.
Is quiet and does not ask questions or interact	Establish rapport. Explain examiner's role and purpose of the test. Ask student to repeat the question if no answer is given or the answer is inappropriate.
Is afraid of a male examiner	Observe student and establish rapport before testing.

ically related, as they are all classes of context, and none replicates the other exactly (Johnson, 1990).

More specifically, an etic perspective stresses the universal qualities among ethnic groups by examining and comparing many cultures from a position external to those cultures. Conversely, an emic perspective is culture-specific and examines behavior from within a culture, using criteria relating to the internal characteristics of that culture (Dana, 1993). From the etic perspective, appraisal involves comparing students' scores to a normative population and comparing different students from different cultures on a construct that is assumed to be universal across all cultures.

Dana (1993) included as etic measures a broad spectrum of instruments to measure psychopathology, personality measures, and major tests of intelligence and cognitive functioning. Examples of etic personality instruments are the California Psychological Inventory and the Eysenck Personality Questionnaire. Examples of etic intelligence/ cognitive functioning instruments are the Wechsler Intelligence Scales, System of Multicultural Pluralistic Assessment, Kaufman Assessment Battery for Children, McCarthy Scales of Children's Abilities, and Stanford–Binet Intelligence Scale. Other single-construct tests for identification of psychopathology are the State–Trait Anxiety Scale, Beck Depression Inventory, Michigan Alcoholism Screening Test, and Minnesota Multiphasic Personality Inventory. All of these tests have been translated into other languages.

Emic appraisal instruments include observations, case studies, studies of life events, picture story techniques, inkblot techniques, word association, sentence completion, and drawings (Drummond, 1996). Most of these methods are classified as protective. These tests can generate a personality description of the individual that reflects the data and mirrors the culture and ethnic group (Dana, 1993). The analysis requires more knowledge of the culture by the test examiner but enhances the understanding of the individual student in a cultural context (Drummond, 1996). An excellent example of the use of holistic and indigenous appraisal techniques for Native American Indian and Alaska Native students, especially in gifted and talented appraisal, can be reviewed in Herring (1997b). Thematic apperception test versions are also available. Examples of such tests are the following (Drummond, 1996):

- *Thompson Modification of the TAT*: 10-card version for African Americans.

- *Themes Concerning Blacks Test*: 20 charcoal drawings depict aspects of African American culture and lifestyle.
- *Tell Me a Story Test* (TEMAS): designed for Spanish-speaking populations.
- *Michigan Picture Story Test*: designed for use with Hispanic American and African American children and adolescents.

Sentence completion methods have been used with many different cultures. The items can be designed to appraise the social norms, roles, and values of students from different cultures. Examples of some of the items are:

- The thing I like most/worst about the United States is _____.
- European Americans (Whites) are _____.
- If I could be from another culture or ethnic group, I _____.
- I am of mixed race but I prefer to be called _____.

One caution to the reader is that formal scoring systems for emic tests are not always available or consistently reliable.

Degree of Culturation

Culturation (whether enculturation or acculturation) is a major and complex construct (Domino & Acosta, 1987). The concept describes "the changes in behaviors and values made by members of one culture as a result of contact with another culture" (Burnam, Telles, Hough, & Escobar, 1987, p. 106). The *ac-* or *en-* prefixes denote the voluntariness (*acculturation*) or coerciveness (*enculturation*) of that action. The degree of culturation to mainstream society (i.e., the Protestant, European American, masculine-dominated middle class) and the extent to which the original culture has been retained provide valuable information in interpreting appraisal results (Drummond, 1996).

Dana (1993) developed a checklist to record culturation information that included two relevant items. One item relates to the phase of the culturation process and has five levels: precontact, contact, conflict, crisis, or adaptation. Another item related to the mode and had four categories: assimilation, bicultural, traditional, and marginal. Dana also addressed group membership, that is, whether the group consists of native peoples, immigrants, refugees, ethnic groups, or sojourners. The sociocultural pattern is also recorded by looking at settlement patterns, status, status mobility, support network, and group acceptability.

Two instruments can provide information on the moderating variables that affect appraisal interpretation: the Developmental Inventory of Black Consciousness (DIB-C) and the Racial Identity Attitude Scale

(RIAS). The DIB-C has four stages: preconsciousness, confrontation, internalization, and integration. The RIAS also has four: preencounter, encounter, immersion–emersion, and internalization. Another useful scale is the African Self-Consciousness Scale, which has four dimensions: (a) awareness of Black identity; (b) recognition of survival priorities and affirmative practices, customs, and values; (c) active participation in defense of survival, liberation, and the like; and (d) recognition of racial/ethnic oppression (Baldwin & Bell, 1985).

Interpretation of Data

School counselors might profitably investigate new and innovative graphic approaches to demonstrate to students what their multivariate profiles mean (Strahan & Kelly, 1994). Students frequently do not "see" what are in data depicted in forms such as bars, stanines, percentiles, and plots. Creative visual displays could accompany data from a variety of interest inventories and simplify interpretations of the often complex information appraisal that results generate.

SELECTED APPRAISAL INSTRUMENTS

The top three inventories currently in use are the Strong–Campbell Interest Inventory (SCII; D. P. Campbell & Hanson, 1981), the Myers–Briggs Type Indicator (I. B. Myers & McCaulley,1985), and the Wechsler Adult Intelligence Scale (Wechsler, 1981). What are the multicultural implications of these and other appraisal instruments? For example, Haviland and Hanson (1987) found that the SCII has adequate criterion validity for Native American Indian college students. This section discusses selected appraisal instruments and their applicability for multicultural student populations.

Students With Disabilities

Although vocational training and career counseling for students with disabilities are mandated, appraisal of vocational potential has continued to be incongruent with placement outcomes (Vandergoot, 1987). Federal support for research and demonstration projects emphasizing transition of youths with disabilities from school to work has promoted community-referenced appraisal procedures, relegating psychometric tests and traditional vocational evaluations to a "nonfunctional assessment tools" category (Rusch, 1986, p. 9). Appraisal strategies that can survive such charges of invalidity must meet these criteria: Assessment should consist of multiple components and be included in multiple settings by multiple assessors over a period of time (Guidubaldi, Perry, & Walker, 1989). A continuum of assessment components is beginning to emerge that relate to the environments in which students with disabilities are expected to live and work (Daniels, 1987).

A variety of appraisal instruments are available for students with various disabilities. In addition, the *Standards for Educational and Psychological Testing* (APA, 1985) has explicit standards for the appropriate use and interpretation of standardized tests that school counselors and other appraising professionals need to know. Table 12.2 lists a number of appraisal instruments for this population.

Assessment and Treatment of Abnormal Behavior

The discussion of abnormal behavior is important to career counseling. Frequently, ethnic minority students are misdiagnosed as manifesting symptoms of pathology. Such misappraisal results in these students being labeled and assigned to educational programs that potentially limit their career choices in life.

Assessment of abnormal behavior involves identifying and describing an individual's symptoms "within the context of his or her overall level of functioning and environment" (Carson, Butcher, & Coleman, 1988, p. 531). The tools and methods of assessment should be sensitive to ethnic, cultural, and other environmental influences on behavior and functioning. The literature involving standard assessment techniques, however, indicates that problems of bias and insensitivity exist when psychological tests and other methods developed in one cultural-ethnic context are used to assess behavior in other cultures (Nystul, 1993).

The definition and expression of abnormal behavior may vary within and across cultures. Traditional tools of clinical assessment,

---

Table 12.2
Examples of Appraisal Instruments With Special Populations

USES Nonreading Aptitude Test Battery—United States Employment Service

This test is designed for use with disadvantaged and semiliterate students, Grades 9 to 12. It measures intelligence, verbal, numerical, spatial, form perception, clerical perception, motor coordination, finger dexterity, and manual dexterity.

Wide Range Achievement Test—Jastak Assessment Systems

This test can be administered to individuals 5 years of age to adults. It measures spelling, arithmetic, and reading. It is best used in a clinical setting as a screening device to determine approximate educational achievement levels.

Reading-Free Vocational Interest Inventory—Elbern Publications

This test is designed to provide information about the vocational preferences for persons with mental retardation and learning disabilities through the use of pictorial illustrations of individuals engaged in various occupational tasks.

however, are primarily based on a standard definition of abnormality and use a standard set of classification criteria for evaluating problematic behavior. Therefore, the tool may have little meaning in cultures with varying definitions, however well translated they are into the native language, and they may mask or fail to capture culturally specific expressions of disorder (Marsella, DeVos, & Hsu, 1979).

For example, standard diagnostic instruments to measure depressive disorder may also miss important cultural expressions of the disorder in African Americans (Neighbors, 1991) and Native American Indians (Manson, Shore, & Bloom, 1985). In two extensive studies of depression among Native American Indians (Manson & Shore, 1981; Manson et al., 1985), the American Indian Depression Schedule was developed to assess and diagnose depressive illness. The investigators found that depression among the Hopi Indians includes symptoms not measured by standard measures of depression such as the Diagnostic Interview Schedule and the Schedule for Affective Disorders and Schizophrenia. These measures, based on diagnostic criteria found in the *Diagnostic and Statistical Manual of Mental Disorders* (4th ed.; American Psychiatric Association, 1994), failed to capture the short but acute dysphoric moods sometimes reported by the Hopi (Manson et al., 1985).

In reviewing the limitations of standard assessment techniques, several authors (Higginbotham, 1979; Lonner & Ibrahim, 1989; Marsella et al., 1979) have offered guidelines for developing measures to be used in cross-cultural assessment of abnormal behavior. They suggested that sensitive assessment methods examine sociocultural norms of healthy adjustment as well as culturally based definitions of abnormality. Higginbotham (1979) suggested the importance of examining culturally sanctioned systems of healing and influence on abnormal behavior. Evidence shows that people whose problems match cultural categories of abnormality are more likely to seek folk healers (Left, 1986). Failure to examine indigenous healing systems would thus overlook some expressions of disorders. Assessment of culturally sanctioned systems of cure should also enhance the planning of treatment strategies, one of the major goals of traditional assessment (Carson et al., 1988).

The Interdomain Model

Unless an occupation requires exclusively intellectual abilities, career appraisals should encompass multiple patterns of ability, not just variable patterns of intellectual aptitude. Appraising only intellectual or cognitive factors is generally limiting (Lowman, 1993). In addition, unless a counselor is dealing with a well-defined problem, it is professionally poor practice to use a single-test approach to career appraisal.

Career behavior is heavily influenced, among other factors, by a variety of psychological, individual-difference factors including (but not limited to) those variables in the three separate but overlapping domains of vocational interests, abilities, and personality characteristics (Lowman, 1993). Career appraisal, like any kind of psychological appraisal, requires theory derived from, and theory-relevant testing instruments validated for, career and work arenas. Derivative theory and test instrumentation may or may not prove efficacious for new undertakings. At least, measures developed in other settings must be renormed and revalidated when directed to a new purpose (Lowman, 1993).

Extensive literature exists on the career implications of abilities and interests (e.g., Holland, 1985a; Lowman, 1991). An emerging literature on occupationally relevant personality characteristics is available as well (e.g., Hough, Eaton, Dunnette, Kamp, & McCloy, 1990; Lowman, 1991). A primary reason for the popularity of occupational interests is that they may represent less potential for bias than do abilities and interests (Spokane & Hawks, 1990). The potential sources of bias in the triple-domain appraisal model are troublesome. Although this model might work for middle-class European American males, ability-interest-personality maps might be very different for African Americans, other European Americans, Hispanic Americans, and especially for females (Betz & Fitzgerald, 1987).

However, Lowman's (1991, 1993) interdomain contention is not without its critics. Barak's (1981) thorough critical review of research on the relationship between interests and ability concluded that the history of research on the relationship between abilities and interests suggested little overlap unless complex mediators are considered: "there are no correlations between interests and actual (tested) relevant abilities and performance" (p. 7). Attempts to combine interests, abilities, and personality without references to the cognitive process involved in their interaction are not likely to result in a satisfactory representation of the actual relationships involved (Barak, Shiloh, & Haushner, 1992). Additional research and theory are needed on how individuals encode, store, and retrieve the information they are presented with or scan on their own (Spokane, 1993).

Lowman (1993) never mentioned measurement bias, sufficient attention to lifestyle considerations (Gysbers & Moore, 1987), cultural robustness (Carter & Cook, 1992), or the risk status of members of ethnic minority groups (Spokane & Hawks, 1990). These variables are crucial in determining careers (Spokane, 1993). Counselors are also advised to use measures of career maturity (e.g., Super, 1990), self-efficacy, or decisional status (Chartrand & Camp, 1991). Fitting the intervention to the student is more efficacious for the practicing counselor than a rigid formula proposed by Lowman (Rounds & Tracey, 1990; Spokane, 1993).

The Career-Development Assessment and Counseling Model

The Career-Development Assessment and Counseling Model (C-DAC; McDaniels, 1989) recognizes that, in an age of increasingly rapid cultural and economic change, no simple process of matching people and jobs can adequately meet the needs of individuals and society. Developmental career counseling initially involves sharing with students an understanding of the normal sequence and nature of life stages and of life space (Super, Osborne, Walsh, Brown, & Niles, 1992). The Life Career Rainbow is, for this purpose, a good teaching device (Super, 1990).

The Life Career Rainbow (Super, 1990, 1992) portrays the development or unfolding of the life career of an individual from birth until death. The two outside arcs of the Rainbow show, one, the name of the life stages and, two, the approximate ages of transition from one stage to another. The Rainbows depict the person's career in terms of life span and life space, formed by nine major roles played, first as a child, then with the other roles of pupil-student, leisurite, citizen, worker, spouse, homemaker, parent, and pensioner (Super et al., 1992).

The C-DAC model offers a marriage between the best of differential methods and an implementation of the developmental theories of career choice (Super et al., 1992). This model is actually based on three models: career development, maturity and adaptability importance, and determinants. The career development model is based on the Life Career Rainbow (Super, 1990). Maturity and adaptability importance indicates the salience of various roles in an individual's life and is a relatively recent area of investigation. Determinants combine the trait–factor approach in incorporating many of the variables central to that method.

The Personal Styles Inventory

The Personal Styles Inventory (PSI; Kunce, Cope, & Newton, 1986a, 1986b, 1989) is an empirically derived, self-report instrument designed to measure enduring, common-place personality characteristics. The inventory is based on the personal styles model of personality (Kunce & Cope, 1987), which uses a circumplex format to integrate data on personality characteristics in relation to two basic bipolar dimensions: (a) *extroversion* versus *introversion* and (b) the need for *stability* versus *change*. The 24 PSI scales relate to either one or both of these two dimensions. Style scores indicate strength of a characteristic only; scores are unrelated to either mental health or psychopathology. The adaptive and maladaptive implications of an individual's personal styles are determined by environmental circumstances and the psychological state of the individual.

In regard to career counseling, the PSI is used to evaluate the "fit" of an individual's personal styles with job roles and expectations (Kunce, Cope, & Newton, 1991)). The use of the PSI differs from interest inventories, which are designed to assist in the selection of occupations (e.g., engineering vs. medicine). The results of the PSI can be used to "fine tune" an individual's selection of a specific position within an occupation (Kunce et al., 1991).

Some correspondence exists between four global PSI personality types and career choice (Kunce et al., 1991). For example, Change-Oriented Extroverts tend to choose jobs in which public contact and verbal expressiveness are job requirements; Stability-Oriented Extroverts prefer jobs in which human services are a major activity; Change-Oriented Introverts prefer jobs with investigative activities; and Stability-Oriented Introverts prefer jobs involving technical-type activities.

A major advantage is that the results themselves do not imply either adjustment or maladjustment (Kunce at al., 1991). Schauer (1991) concluded that additional assets of the PSI are its reliability and validity, the use of precise language, and a variety of available interpretive tools. Limitations include the lack of reliability and validity data on the PSI-120 or short form and computerized narratives (Kunce et al., 1991). The test manuals need to include research results, and the test itself needs to be more readily available for use and evaluation. Schauer (1991) pointed out the lack of linkage to a theoretical model; the test's interpretive complexity; and, assuming normality, the omission of a clear-cut check on the validity of a person's responses.

Holland's Typology Appraisals

John Holland has developed many appraisal instruments for determining career interests by individuals. For the purposes of this text, the instrument most applicable to school settings is emphasized. Holland's (1994a) Self-Directed Search (SDS) is considered the most widely used career interest inventory in the world. The SDS family of career appraisal tools provides complete and accurate career guidance for students and adults. These easy-to-use instruments are self-administered and self-scored. The SDS system helps students explore their interests and competencies, discovering careers and occupations that best match the characteristics of their own personalities. Three basic forms of the SDS are available for school counseling: Form R (high school students), Form E (high school students with limited education or reading ability), and the Career Explorer (middle and junior high students). These instruments are offered in English, Spanish, English Canadian, and French Canadian languages. A companion software system is also available.

Scores from the SDS yield a three-letter summary code (Form E derives a two-letter summary code) that designates the three personality types a student most closely resembles. With this code, test takers use the revised Occupations Finder to discover those occupations that best match their personality types, interests, and skills. This comprehensive booklet lists over 1,300 occupational possibilities—more than any other career interest inventory. The Occupations Finder also provides the educational development level each occupation requires and the associated *Dictionary of Occupational Titles* (U.S. Department of Labor, 1996) codes.

The SDS is based on Holland's theory and extensive research that assert that most individuals can be categorized as one of six personality types: Realistic, Investigative, Artistic, Social, Enterprising, or Conventional. As presented more thoroughly in Chapter 2, Holland (1985a) hypothesized that satisfaction with an educational environment is related to specific personality types. The greater congruence between a student's personality pattern and the educational environment, the more satisfying the interactions will be. For example, students respond more positively to teachers and counselors whose personality patterns reflect their own. Student dissatisfaction, attribution, and delinquency may be a function not only of poor academic skills but also of a failure in empathy and understanding "for teachers are largely S's and dropouts are largely R's—opposites in the hexagon model" (Holland, 1985a, p. 56).

The normative sample for the *Self-Directed Search (SDS) Form R Assessment Booklet* (4th ed.; Holland, 1994b) was composed of 2,602 students and working adults. The sample included 1,600 female and 1,002 male participants ranging in age from 17 to 65 years ($M = 23.5$), with 75% European Americans, 8% African Americans, 7% Hispanics, 4% Asian Americans, 1% Native American Indians/Alaskan Natives, and 5% from other ethnic backgrounds. The data were collected in 10 high schools, 9 community colleges, 19 colleges or universities, and a variety of other sources throughout the United States.

Few studies are available that used Native American Indians students for a personality-type educational satisfaction study. Such a study could support or prevent the use of this hypothesis with a cultural minority population. It could also provide school and career counselors with comparison data about the distribution of Native American Indian students' personality types and about their satisfaction with education.

Gade, Fuqua, and Hurlburt (1988) examined this relationship, using a sample of 596 Native American Indian high school students (321 female, 275 male) enrolled in eight schools in Manitoba, Canada. The SDS (Holland, 1985b) was used to determine personality typologies and the Teacher Approval and Education Acceptance scales of the Survey of Study Habits and Attitudes—Form H (W. Brown & Holtzman, 1967) to measure educational satisfaction. Results of analysis of variance showed that students with an Investigative or Social personality type code had significantly higher scores on educational satisfaction than students with a Realistic type code. These results are in the direction hypothesized by Holland and provide support for the generalizability of this hypothesis to a Native American Indian population.

Additional support for the use of the congruence-educational satisfaction is the fact that all other major studies have found teachers, counselors, principals, and superintendents to be predominantly Social type personalities (Holland, 1985a, 1985b). These results should also be useful in comparing data about the Holland congruence model of a cultural minority with the results from many studies of congruence conducted with the dominant European American culture. Additional studies using such criteria as academic achievement may also help answer questions about the generalizability of the Holland congruence-achievement hypothesis to the Native American Indian high school population. Case Vignette 12.4 presents another case.

Qualitative Evaluation

Researchers and scientist-practitioners often neglect the use of qualitative measures in their evaluations of career awareness and career maturity. This omission serves to infer that only quantitative procedures are useful. Most objective researchers contend that both modes

---

Case Vignette 12.4
Jamie Redhorse: A Native American Indian Student

Jamie Redhorse, a 12-year-old Native American Indian girl of the Paiute tribe, was referred to a multidisciplinary team by her guidance counselor and teachers for evaluation of her avoidant behavior and appraisal of her intellectual potential. She had participated in her reading group, cried often, and usually failed to follow directions. Her teacher said Jamie isolated herself from others in the class and refused to participate. Her mother indicated that the other students made fun of Jamie.
1. What advice would you give to the psychologist before he meets with Jamie?
2. What important professional standards for multicultural appraisal should be considered in this case?
3. What appraisal techniques and procedures would you use in this case?

of data discovery are needed to obtain a total picture of career education and guidance.

One study aimed to provide high school juniors with the opportunity for career exploration and planning and to address language arts and English skills, including research and writing (Hughey, Lapan, & Gysbers, 1993). All juniors from a midwestern public high school, located in a university town, participated in this study. Teachers selected 10 of their students whom they felt would benefit from this activity. Twenty-five juniors, four counselors, and four English teachers were interviewed using a structured format. See Research Emphasis 12.1 for additional data.

In a similar study, 166 high school juniors (including both honors and nonhonors students) attending a suburban midwestern public high school participated in a joint guidance and language arts (writing skills) unit (Lapan, Gysbers, Hughey, & Arni, 1993). This population included European American (86% male, 90% female), African American (11.7% male, 6.6% female), and Asian American (2.1% male,

---

Research Emphasis 12.1
A Qualitative Approach to Cooperative Career Guidance

Hughey, Lapan, and Gysbers (1993) provided high school juniors with the opportunity for career exploration and planning and to address language arts and English skills through a Guidance-Language Arts Career Unit. The unit stressed the cooperation between teachers and counselors.

1. English teachers emphasized the following skills:
   a. Selecting and using various references.
   b. Organizing information for personal use.
   c. Summarizing information.
2. The Guidance-Language Arts Career Unit provided opportunities to:
   a. Explore possible careers and the world of work.
   b. Explore several different careers in areas of interest.
   c. Improve knowledge of how to prepare for a career.
   d. Develop some tentative plan after graduation.
   e. Improve understanding of how abilities are related to certain career choices.
   f. Improve understanding of the role of women in today's workforce.
   g. Understand opportunities to enter careers traditionally held by members of the opposite sex.
   h. Improve knowledge about various colleges and what they offer.
   i. Gain insight into choosing colleges to prepare for a career.
   j. Gain insight into the careers that complement certain college majors and into the future.
   k. Possess a better understanding of vocational interests, aptitudes, and abilities.

SOURCE: From "Evaluating a High School Guidance-Language Arts Career Unit: A Qualitative Approach," by K. F. Hughey, R. T. Lapan, and N. C. Gysbers, 1993, *The School Counselor, 41,* 96–101. Copyright 1993 by the American Counseling Association. Reprinted with permission.

2.6% female) students. Results indicated that for a wide range of students, participation in the program led to the achievement of specific guidance competencies. Changes in perceived mastery of guidance competencies predicted positive changes in vocational identity and attainment of higher English grades for female students. Results also indicated that certain professional development benefits accompanied the counselors' participation in evaluating the unit. First, gathering data on and appraising change in the tests used led to both a better understanding of some scales and different ways of interpreting results to students. Second, opportunities for counselor networking became more obvious.

A key element of this cooperative guidance and language arts career unit was that students learned the career process even though they may not have made a definite decision. Cooperative activities can be effective in addressing needs of students and involving others in the guidance delivery service (Herring, 1995; Herring & White, 1995). Cooperative activities also appeal to ethnic minority youths, especially Native American Indians and Hispanic Americans (Herring, 1997a).

Multiple Interventions

School counselors play varied roles in the appraisal of their students. In most instances, the specific roles are decided by noncounselors (e.g., principals and supervisors). However, when they are projecting the role of career counselor, counselors need to be mindful of the availability of, and need for, multiple interventions. For example, the singular use of videotape modeling is a relatively ineffectual intervention to increase nontraditional career interests (Van Buren, Kelly, & Hall, 1993). Van Buren et al.'s study demonstrated the need to use more intensive and multiple interventions.

A variety of modes and tests can be used, ranging from nonverbal culture-free tests in the language of linguistic minorities to tests in standard English. The student's level of culturation into the mainstream culture is important to know. Understanding the student's educational level and background, language facility, and receptive and expressive vocabulary can also help guide test selection (Drummond, 1996).

Self-Efficacy Measurement

One of the major limitations of past research on career self-efficacy, and a serious drawback for self-efficacy applications to career counseling, has been the absence of a general measure useful under a variety of circumstances (Hackett, 1991). Osipow and Rooney's (1989) Task-Specific Scale of Occupational Self-Efficacy is an example of one sound assessment for this emphasis. In addition, Osipow's (1991) work represents a substantive advance in the development of instruments to be used in counseling.

SUMMARY

Many factors can bias the appraisal of multicultural student groups and individuals, leading to possible sources of misinterpretation. Ethical and legal standards are in place to ensure these students are not appraised inappropriately. In developing an action plan to increase their multicultural understanding, school and career counselors can use research on the multicultural counseling process, case studies in the literature, experiences of other counseling colleagues, their own personal experiences with culturally different individuals, and other firsthand experiences with various ethnic and cultural groups (Draguns, 1989; Nutall, Romero, & Kalesnik, 1992).

The first step for school and career counselors is to develop greater self-awareness and comprehension of their own cultural group. They also need to develop an awareness of the ethnic and cultural groups with which students are identifying or encountering (Herring, 1997b). In general, they must develop perceptual sensitivity toward students' personal beliefs and values (Baruth & Manning, 1991). Then, school and career counselors can internalize the advice of this chapter's opening quote (F. W. Vondracek, 1991), "First of all, the most successful instruments are those that fill a need, and that are of tangible value to those who use them or to those who benefit from their use"(p. 327).

EXPERIENTIAL ACTIVITIES

1. Describe yourself in terms of the student characteristics discussed in this chapter. Then ask a few of your peers whose backgrounds are different to do the same. Do you observe any similarities or dissimilarities among individuals from different backgrounds?
2. How have your professors evaluated you over the years? Have they used a multicultural, multiple approach to assess students? Is there one format that you prefer?
3. Review the case vignettes in this chapter and respond to the corresponding questions.

13

Future Directions: Where Do We Go Now and How Do We Do It?

The world is round and the place which may seem
like the end may also be only the beginning.

Ivy Baker Priest

An essential part of every young person's development includes his or her success in planning, choosing, and following a satisfying career (Schmidt, 1996). Adler wrote that the three main tasks in life include contributions through work, successful sharing with others, and satisfying love relationships (Dinkmeyer, Dinkmeyer, & Sperry, 1987). Each of these three tasks relates to the other two, but of the three, the success people achieve in their careers most strongly influences their social achievements and loving relationships (Schmidt, 1996).

FUTURE CHANGES IN SCHOOL GUIDANCE/COUNSELING PROGRAMS AND PERSONNEL

The following discussion addresses three of the more important future changes in the implementation of comprehensive school guidance and counseling programs: the changing world of work, the impact of guidance and counseling programs on career development, and the future roles and functions of the school counselor. Policymakers and practitioners can use these examples to guide their actions and decisions as they endeavor to respond to the career developmental needs of contemporary and future students.

The Changing World of Work

R. L. Gibson and Mitchell (1995) noted the aspects of the changing nature of the world of work that have particular meaning for school counselors. These authors stressed the diversity of vocational occupations, the dangers of gender and cultural stereotyping, the relationship between education and career development, and the future of occupational opportunities. In observing these aspects, they offered these symptoms of "the changing nature of the world of work" (p. 310):

1. Career development is a process of many opportunities and probabilities.
2. Gender and cultural stereotyping in career selection is over.
3. Higher formal education will not necessarily equate to greater career satisfaction.
4. The present will no longer predict the future.
5. Career development is an interactive process.

In addition, analysis of labor trends through the year 2000 indicates a major shift from goods-producing to service-producing industries (Van Buren, Kelly, & Hall, 1993). Service jobs such as sales clerk and janitor, which pay significantly less than the skilled trades, will be most available to new workers (Hoyt, 1989).

Impact of Guidance and Counseling Programs

Policymakers, administrators, and school counselors need to ensure that schools implement a comprehensive guidance and counseling program in their school systems (Borders & Drury, 1992). Such implementation prevents school counselors from becoming "marginalized" (Watkins, 1994) and places them in the center of the school's mission to meet critical educational objectives. Comprehensive guidance and counseling programs provide school counselors with their own subject-matter content, thereby making guidance more than an ancillary, support service in the schools (Aubrey, 1973; Sprinthall, 1971).

A commitment to serving the career needs of all students has become a central component in comprehensive guidance and counseling programs (Gysbers & Henderson, 1994; Hotchkiss & Vetter, 1987). Gysbers (1988) concluded that developmental guidance interventions could positively affect career goals, career planning skills, and attendance. Evaluation research has tried to develop practical means to evaluate the impact of guidance classroom activities on career development competencies (Lapan, Gysbers, Multon, & Pike, 1997; Multon & Lapan, 1995).

In one research effort to discover interactions among a fully implemented guidance and counseling program and increased availability of career information to students, student and school counselor survey data were analyzed from the Missouri School Improvement Program from 1992 to 1995 (Lapan, Gysbers, & Sun, 1997). The sample population included 22,964 students (11% were ethnic minority; 24% received free or reduced lunches) from 236 Missouri high schools. The majority of the school counselors were European American (92.8), female (60%), and held master's degrees (86%); 95% of the total sample of school counselors had earned a specialist, master's, or doctoral degree. The mean years of work experience was 18.5 (SD = 8.1) with a mean salary of $34,188 per year ($SD$ = $9,647).

This study found positive roles for more fully implemented guidance programs in promoting student academic achievement, career development, and more supportive school climates. The results corroborated and extended previous research on school counselor effectiveness (Hughey, Lapan, & Gysbers, 1993; Lapan, Gysbers, Hughey, & Arni , 1993; R. S. Lee, 1993). Findings also indicated differences in academic achievement and differences in school attitudes for young women, ethnic minorities, and lower socioeconomic status students that were neither positively nor negatively affected by level of implementation of the guidance program. Positive effects for comprehensive guidance programs were found across all schools despite the negative differences associated with these factors. Results emphasized the need for school counselors and university counselor educators to redirect their endeavors on developing and systematically implementing guidance program strategies that help to reduce differences between students (Lapan et al., 1997).

In addition, the availability of career and college information was found to be highly valued by the sample's student respondents. Students linked availability with higher grades and a more positive school climate and attitude toward school, and they believed that their schools were more adequately preparing them for their future. These findings clearly support the vision of early advocates for infusing career development activities across curricula and guidance programs (Enderlein, 1976; Herr, 1969; Hoyt, 1976).

Role of the School Counselor

The social strata to which people belong, the personal relationships they establish, and the economic successes they achieve are among many factors related to career choices made over a lifetime. For this reason, schools have the responsibility to help students use their knowledge and skill to develop realistic and self-satisfying career goals. School counselors help with this process by (a) providing students with accurate information about the world of work and existing career opportunities;

(b) appraising students' interests and abilities and sharing these findings to enable students to make appropriate career choices; and (c) encouraging students to broaden their options as a precaution to future changes in career opportunities and the job market (Schmidt, 1996). In addition, counselors must ensure the implementation of comprehensive guidance and counseling programs that monitor the infusion of career development across curricula (Lapan et al., 1997).

Welch and McCarroll (1993) provided a description of the roles and functions of the school counselor as they appear now and provided a description of what shifts need to be made to move into the future. Something to Consider 13.1 illustrates these role shifts for school counselors in the future.

Many additional issues remain to be addressed: leadership roles, middle schools, special education, the role of higher education, counselor training, community–school relations, and lifelong learning. The school counselor of the future may well be a community resource specialist who assesses needs within the school and community and who matches resources with needs as a counselor-teacher-administrator. The infusion of career concerns into these role shifts is a cogent mission. Brief summaries of more specific potential future needs and changes for school counselors are presented in the following discussions.

Something to Consider 13.1
Future Role Shifts for School Counselors

The Past and Present	The Future
The counselor is a primary provider of direct services (supplier, furnisher, caterer, purveyor, provider).	The counselor is a conduit between needs and resources (passage, passageway, channel).
The counselor is in a closed system.	The counselor is a community resource specialist.
The counselor provides individual counseling.	The counselor provides family and group counseling.
The counselor is perceived as an "ex-teacher."	The counselor is perceived as a teacher.
The counselor is an administrator or teacher.	The counselor is a teacher, counselor, and administrator.
The "line and staff" model prevails.	The "systems" model comes into play.
Power (perceived or real) is a political necessity.	Power (perceived or real) is an educational tool.
Self-development is assumed.	Self-development is planned.

SOURCE: From "The Future Role of School Counselors," by I. R. Welch and L. McCarroll, 1993, *The School Counselor, 41,* 48–53. Copyright 1993 by the American Counseling Association. Adapted with permission.

Supply and demand.   A "new wave" of school counselors will be
needed as many of the National Defense Education Act-trained counselors of the 1960s move into retirement. This projection, coupled with
the increased national demand for elementary school counselors,
could result in an acceleration in employment opportunities for school
counselors (R. L. Gibson & Mitchell, 1995). Moreover, the need for
more ethnic and cultural minority school counselors remains an ongoing concern.

School counselors or career counselors.   The industrialism of the
late 1800s altered working conditions and vocational needs of society
rapidly and immensely (Zunker, 1994). In addition, the interaction
among educational planning, personal development, career choices,
and successful living has become clearer. These relationships are
affected by a number of technological, industrial, social, and political
changes that are rapidly sweeping the globe (Herr & Cramer, 1996:
Hoyt, 1988).

Throughout its history and development, the school counseling
profession has been closely associated with vocational guidance and
career development. Some counselors specialize in vocational or
career counseling and use the title "career counselor" or "vocational
counselor" to identify their particular role in the school, especially
large high schools (R. L. Gibson & Mitchell, 1995). In reality, however,
most school counselors are charged with a wide range of responsibilities, including career counseling.

Professional competency.   Revised training and certification
requirements are occurring in many states. A major force behind such
revisions is witnessed in an increasing multicultural society. Schools
will increasingly be charged with providing appropriate educational
opportunities for a diverse student population. A second force exists in
the ever-changing world of technology. School counselors need to
become computer literate to use current and future technological aids
for counseling and guidance activities. Many states are also offering
alternative certification programs for school counselors-in-training
who do not possess a teaching or educational background.

Interaction with the family.   Chapter 10 emphasized the role of
the family in the career development and career decision making of
children and adolescents. The interactions between school counselors
and families will increase in the future. The rapidly developing field of
family therapy will also influence school counseling in future decades.
Peeks (1993) wrote:

> The changes occurring in the fields of counseling and education are tra-
> versed within the walls of U.S. public schools. As counseling has made a
> shift toward the systems paradigm, the student is viewed as a part of a

larger unit, his [her] family. As education makes a shift toward expanded effectiveness, parents are viewed as an important and integral part of the educational process. Both of the changes acknowledge the importance of a student's extended social unit to the success of his or her education. Students are first members of a family. (p. 248)

School counselors will also be called upon in the near future to direct more attention to family lifestyles and their impact on school youths. Peeks (1993) predicted:

The increasing changes in education and the expanded counseling function will bring counseling and education closer together within the context of the schools. It is predicted that the schools of the future will become family centers (Cetron, 1985), where family health and employment services are offered for stress-laden families. A typical school district may provide training for students ages 3 to 21 years and for adults 21 to 80-plus years. These expanded services will be offered either through satellites or widely expanded professional staffs. Schools will need programs to protect children against the ravages of social disorganization and family collapse (London, 1987). The establishment of such programs will necessitate family involvement in the context of the school by school counselors who understand the powerful systemic connection between the student and family. Parent involvement in the school in almost any form seems to produce measurable gains in student achievement (Henderson, 1988). (p. 249)

The relationships between family systems and birth-order dynamics as the basis for career decision making among students have been addressed in the literature (e.g., Bradley & Mims, 1992; Kinnier, Brigman, & Noble, 1990). This research supports the use of family systems theory as a viable perspective for research and practice in career counseling (Kinnier et al., 1990). Cogently, the Adlerian concept of striving for significance has merit as children adopt a role identity that incorporates certain attributes. This concept may help children to recognize that certain siblings may assume particular roles. The strive for significance develops in unique ways, and children may consider their reactions to such sibling roles. For example, it is common for a first-born child to be assigned a role of caregiver. If the child was good at this role, it may have implications for career decision making.

Effects of dual-career families. In addition, by 1998 the vast majority of homes in the United States with children will be either dual-career or single-parent homes (R. L. Gibson & Mitchell, 1995). The implications of such models of family life are many, not the least of which will be "what happens to the children?" So far, little planning has ensued to provide for these "latchkey" youths. The failure to make adequate provisions guarantees disastrous consequences to both the child and society. School counseling programs must take the lead in developing effective and comprehensive programs for all school youths.

THE CHANGING NEEDS IN CAREER DEVELOPMENT AND EDUCATION

As the twenty-first century approaches, career development needs will undergo a dramatic shift from the historical "one person, one career" approach. The future will present a century in which individuals entering the workforce (with the exception of the professions) can anticipate at least three distinctly different careers over their working life time. Career changes will result from returning to educational settings, adapting to advanced technologies, and moving to different geographic locations (R. L. Gibson & Mitchell, 1995). The most acute of these changes are presented in the following discussions.

Career Theory

Some career theories have addressed current trends but have remained static because they fail to reflect the fabric of society and the changes occurring in the labor market (see Chapter 2). Cross-disciplinary approaches and cross-cultural models must be developed so that researchers from disciplines such as biology, economics, anthropology, sociology, psychology, counseling, education, business, and medicine are all involved in theory development and inquiry (Drummond & Ryan, 1995). Whereas in the past, career theories emphasized traits and factors, life roles, and developmental stages, future career theories will need to be more holistic and allow for more worldview differentiation. Continued advancements in technological knowledge and artificial intelligence will also undoubtedly be a major force in the revision and updating of career development and choice theories.

Meeting Student Needs

School career education programs must prepare students for both adaptability and flexibility (R. L. Gibson & Mitchell, 1995). School counselors must ensure that youths are prepared for tomorrow's career world rather than yesterday's. This urgency is compounded by an ethnic minority population that exceeds 25% of the population and is projected to increase to 32% by the year 2010 and 47% by the year 2050 (U.S. Bureau of the Census, 1993). The elimination of prejudice and the substitution of respect and understanding in human relations must begin in the school setting (R. L. Gibson & Mitchell, 1995). To achieve this goal, school counselors must themselves be models of awareness, understanding, and acceptance.

Occupational Wellness

Traditionally, career counseling has been viewed by many critics as either "test and tell" or "three interviews and a cloud of dust" (Crites, 1981). Researchers and practitioners must generate more creative conceptualizations of the career development and career counseling process. For example, is occupational wellness a reflection of integrated career and personal identity, or does the understanding of self in relationship to the family system serve as the antecedent to career satisfaction and occupational wellness? Career counseling as an intervention will need to be enhanced in terms of demonstrating to students the quality of their individual lives, assisting students in developing more appreciation for the emotional components that contribute to the selection or avoidance of career options, and demonstrating how these emotional components can and do have relevance to overall wellness (Dorn, 1992).

Although some progress has occurred in moving away from the "test and tell" approach, Dorn (1992) observed that counselors still need more assistance with how to do career counseling. Phillips, Friedlander, Kost, Specterman, and Robbins (1988) noted:

> Our results [indicated that] career counseling should probably be undertaken by more experienced counselors, if client satisfaction is to be achieved. Strict adherence to vocational content, such as might be found in counseling that follows the trait–factor approach, apparently facilitates the practitioner's perception of positive outcome, but does not seem to have a greater impact on the client's perspective. (p. 172)

Increasing Ethnic Minority Counselors

The lack of sufficient numbers of ethnic minority counselors in the field of career planning and placement often leaves ethnic minority students without the option of interacting with an ethnic-similar counselor (N. K. Campbell & Hadley, 1992). Research suggests that a significant percentage of ethnic minority students, particularly African American students, prefer counselors of the same ethnic group (e.g., Bernstein, Wade, & Hofmann, 1987). To increase the pool of ethnic minorities in career planning and placement significantly, however, multiple programs and strategies will need to be initiated (N. K. Campbell & Hadley, 1992).

Improvement Through Evaluation

Comprehensive school guidance and counseling programs require periodic internal and external evaluations to ensure the appropriate delivery of services. Gysbers, Hughey, Starr, and Lapan (1992) recommended that evaluation practices should answer five basic questions:

1. Are the program's contents, structure, and resources in place in the school?
2. Are counselors supervised and evaluated based on their job descriptions?
3. Are procedures used to measure students' mastery of guidance competencies?
4. Are procedures used to measure the impact of the program on the climate and goals of the school?
5. Are the individuals served by the program and the community satisfied with the program?

The information gained from these inquiries will determine to what extent the career counseling and guidance program is comprehensive, the status of its efficacy of delivery services, and reactions from the program's service population.

CAREER COUNSELING INTERVENTIONS FOR THE FUTURE

In addition to the previously addressed changes in the role of school counselors, school guidance and counseling programs, and career development, counselors will need to adapt their intervention efforts to appropriately match these changes. The following discussions accentuate selected areas of emphasis for tomorrow's youths.

Poverty

Reports indicate that the percentage of youths in poverty rose from approximately 14% to about 17% in 1980, and then to 20% in 1990. At this rate, more than 25% of youths will live in economically disadvantaged homes by the year 2000. As a result of poverty, a high percentage of youths will suffer from poor nutrition, lack of health care, familial and neighborhood problems, and other deficiencies that will inhibit their education and development.

Ethnic Diversity

Current predictions are that the United States will more closely reflect the cultural and racial balance of the globe by the end of the next century (Ibrahim, 1991; P. Lee, 1995). Mitigating factors that may alter these forecasts include immigration policies, worldwide economic depression, and unexpected changes in birth rates (Schmidt, 1996). By the year 2000, ethnic minorities will account for more than 25% of all U.S. workers and 33% of all new entrants into the labor force (Tidwell, 1992).

Little argument can be made that helping ethnic and cultural minorities' career development is one of the most serious challenges facing the counseling profession (Hoyt, 1989). Numerous researchers have echoed Osipow's (1983) earlier contention that the assumptions inherent in traditional theories of career development fail to accommodate non-Eurocentric perspectives (Arbona, 1990; Cheatham, 1990; Cook, 1991). In addition, despite a variety of documented ethnic differences in career development, a 20-year retrospective of vocational behavior research included the charge that responding to ethnic and cultural differences through appropriate strategies has represented an all-too-empty stage in career development literature (Arbona, 1990; Leong, 1991; London & Greller, 1991).

Special Education Students

More research is needed to examine the career development of special education students. Chapter 9 emphasized the career needs of special needs students. Future research must develop a linkage between the career development of exceptional youths and current theoretical models of career development (Leung, Conoley, & Scheel, 1994). In particular, more emphasis on career opportunities is needed for students in the tails of normal distribution.

Nontraditional Career Choices and Gender Equity

Counseling professionals have demonstrated great interest in reducing occupational sex stereotyping. Although progress is occurring (Fullerton, 1987; Hodgkinson, 1985; National Organization for Women, 1985), occupational segregation continues to produce harmful effects for women (Shaffer, 1986). For example, 75% of the higher paying occupations are held by men (Ehrhart & Sandler, 1987). In addition, women who are college educated earn less, in general, than do men with a high school education (U.S. Department of Labor, 1985), about 64% of what full-time male workers earn (U.S. Department of Labor, 1986).

By the year 2000, four in every five women ages 25–54 years will be employed (Hoyt, 1988) and will account for 47% of the total labor force (Kutscher, 1987). Although the majority of women are currently working, gender equity in the labor force has not been achieved (Bartholomew & Schnorr, 1994). They remain concentrated in low-paying, traditionally female-dominated occupations (e.g., clerical and retail sales), whereas the majority of jobs in the higher paying, and often math- and science-related fields, are held by men (Sadker & Sadker, 1994; Sadker, Sadker, & Donald, 1989). The majority of adult and young women continue to plan to enter career areas that are traditionally dominated by women (Eccles, 1987; Gerstein, Lichtman, & Barokas, 1988).

One important explanation for the perpetuation of gender inequity is the internalization of gender role stereotypes and cultural expectations of women and men (Bartholomew & Schnorr, 1994). If young women's awareness and perceptions of occupations available to them are limited, they may not realize their true potential. Gender bias still pervades the school system through the curricula, the instruction, and the role models that it provides for students (Sadker & Sadker, 1994; Sadker et al., 1989).

Counselor awareness and confrontation of gender stereotypes will help to influence young women's decisions and to achieve equity in the workforce. Career counseling and guidance programs that desire to expand career options for young women must include the following efforts (Bartholomew & Schnorr, 1994, pp. 245–255):

- Enhance counselor awareness of gender role and stereotyping.
- Breakdown women's gender roles and occupational stereotypes.
- Help young women overcome math and science stereotypes.
- Improve and enhance young women's self-esteem and self-confidence.
- Address young women's fear-of-success issues.
- Help female students formulate realistic family and life-planning goals.
- Examine young women's parental and peer influences.
- Develop support systems.

Appraisal

Accountability mandates will demand increased counselor knowledge in the areas of measurement and standardized testing (R. L. Gibson & Mitchell, 1995). School counselors of the next century will be expected to be more professionally competent in appraising different environments (i.e., community and school) and their impact on students. Walz (1991) stated that "there is a pressing need for research that establishes the credibility of schools, colleges, and agencies continuing to offer it" (i.e., appraisal; p. 72).

In addition, advancements in and new adaptations of appraisal instruments will be available. For example, an extension of Holland's (1985a) hexagon model is currently under consideration. The hexagon can provide an overview of a work world comprising thousands of occupations and can help school counselors identify occupational choices that are congruent with their students' personal characteristics (Prediger, Swaney, & Mau, 1993). An expanded model can also provide school counselors and researchers with ways (visual and numerical) to communicate similarities and differences among occupations—not just six broad groups of occupations or abstract, three-letter code lists (Strahan & Kelly, 1994). The World-of-Work Map (American College Testing, 1988) illustrates one way to extend the hexagon.

Other congruence indexes have been devised to assess agreement between pairs of three-letter codes. Holland (1987) recommended an index developed by Iachan (1984). However, this index and a popular alternative (Zener & Schnuelle, 1976) do not take relationships among Holland's types into account (Prediger et al., 1993) and "use arbitrary, unanchored scales" (p. 428). The procedure for extending Holland's hexagon appears to address the concerns of Holland and his colleagues (N. S. Cole, Whitney, & Holland, 1971), who expressed concern "when occupations have divergent interest patterns," even though they found "few cases of this kind" (p. 5). The procedure provides a synthesis of divergent interest patterns—a common way of addressing inconsistencies in counseling and research. The nature of this synthesis can be seen by applying M. J. Miller's (1985) mapping procedure to a three-letter code. Each letter in the code influences the code's location.

Computer-Assisted Career Guidance

Unfortunately, the majority of counselor education programs present research as an isolated activity, poorly integrated within the curriculum (e.g., Hoshmand, 1989; D. Martin & Martin, 1989). As a result, few school counselors engage in research, and they do not realize that the purpose of research is to improve practice. Computer-assisted career guidance programs can remediate this problem by applying single-subject research designs and strategies within a scientist–practitioner framework (Hinkle, 1992). Such application provides three primary roles for school counselors: scientific consumer of new research findings, data-producing researcher, and an evaluator of personal interventions to increase accountability.

More research is needed concerning the benefits from computerized self-help programs investigating actual student samples. One possible future direction would be to use the Holland variables in conjunction with superiority and goal instability as predictors in a similar study (Kivlighan, Johnston, Hogan, & Mauer, 1994). It is also important to develop a clearer picture of who can be assigned self-help as the sole treatment, who needs counselor contact in addition to self-help, and for whom self-help is contraindicated. Only research that varies student and treatment variables within the same study can ultimately address this important question (Kivlighan et al., 1994).

Discrimination and Technology

The approaching decade will witness even more technological advancements that will bring additional societal changes. However, technological advancement itself does not create special adjustment problems for ethnic and cultural minority groups. On the other hand, technological equity is a political matter. All ethnic and cultural groups need access to new technologies and equal opportunities to learn about them (e.g., scholarships, loans, and information). If school counselors cannot help, then any other help may be irrelevant (Hilliard, 1985).

The psychological damage that emanates from discrimination has yet to be adequately explored. If this lack of sufficient data is not considered in technological training programs or dealt with in service delivery programs, counseling will have little meaning for the real world (Hilliard, 1985). School counselors have the mission to ensure that all students exist in a nondiscriminating environment. Concurrently, school counselors must provide equitable and appropriate career education and information in relation to new technology to all students.

RESEARCH NEEDS FOR THE FUTURE

Herr and Cramer (1996) presented an excellent reference relating to future research needs, especially in relevant journals such as the *Annual Review of Psychology, Career Development Quarterly, Journal of Vocational Behavior,* and *The Counseling Psychologist.* Selected highlights of their reviews are summarized in this section.

For example, Bartol (1981) professed nearly two decades ago:

> As greater emphasis is placed on the work life of individuals after initial occupational choices are made, researchers on vocational behavior and career development will increasingly find it necessary to synthesize research findings from the areas of industrial/organizational psychology, organizational sociology, and organizational behavior and theory. . . . In any event, the broadening base of relevant research, while challenging, also is an exciting development with rich potential for increased knowledge of vocational behavior. (p. 151)

Historically, researchers have emphasized environmental and organizational variables as major factors in career development (Fretz & Leong, 1982). A different perspective of this view contends that both industrial psychology and counseling psychology are centrally concerned with vocational behavior (Slaney & Russell, 1987). Advocates of this perspective argue for discussions on specific topics in which collaboration would be most beneficial to both perspectives. They ask:

> Would it be productive for I/O (industrial/organization) psychologists to examine closely the research on career interventions in developing programs to aid the career development of employees? Conversely, would it make sense for counselors who deal with reentry women or retired persons to have a greater awareness of what provisions are made by employers for helping persons reenter the employment market, on the one hand, or depart successfully from paid employment, on the other? (Slaney & Russell, 1987, p. 157)

In addition, four classic analyses of continuing research needs in career theory and practice are those suggested by Holland, Magoon, and Spokane (1981) in their thorough review of career interventions;

by Osipow (1986) in his lecture; by L. S. Gottfredson (1990) in her analysis of the future of Holland's theory and the status of research in career behavior in general; and by Fouad (1994) in her review of research in vocational choice, decision making, appraisal, and intervention.

Holland et al. (1981) suggested the following:

- More rigorous evaluations of all forms of vocational interventions are still required.
- More analytical evaluations in which client goals are linked to treatments are needed to acquire a comprehensive knowledge of client treatment interaction and related outcomes.
- More potent treatments should be developed by incorporating the influential characteristics of past treatments.
- The ordering effects of treatment chains should be investigated.
- The neglected but painfully relevant topics of job finding, placement strategies, and vocational adaptation require more attention.
- The classification research should be more completely exploited. (pp. 298–300)

Osipow (1986) advised that several issues influence the life span practice and research agenda for the future:

Issues such as unemployment, underemployment, serial careers, the problems of part-time and temporary workers, disability and compensation, rehabilitation, labor force shifts, and working conditions have rarely been studied from a life-span perspective. (p. 164)

Osipow concluded his analysis of research issues with an observation that integrates demographics, development, and research. He stated:

Much of this anticipated research agenda is stimulated by the aging population. The baby boom has been a prime factor in determining the research agenda on career development since the 1950s. When the "boomers" were young, education and career entry were major needs for assistance; as they have aged, a variety of other services have been emphasized. The professional and research agenda will continue to be defined by this population bulge as it goes through the life span. (p. 166)

L. S. Gottfredson (1990) suggested four areas for research and several admonitions for improved research designs. Her suggestions included increasing research efforts on self-efficacy expectation in career behavior, effects studies that benefit school counselors, better designs with simple but efficacious parameters, and appraising appropriate demographic populations.

Fouad (1994) provided a variety of important observations and recommendations. She stated:

We now have abundant evidence that men and women differ, that whites differ from minority groups members, and that minority group members differ from each other . . . but implicit in much of this research is a standard from which special populations deviate. That standard is based on research on white heterosexual males. . . . We must move to exploring reality for women as their own referent [not in comparison to white men] and do the same for minority group members and lesbians and gays. This must include within-group studies, but also include awareness of individual differences that are not due to ethnicity, gender, or sexual orientation. (p. 157)

Fouad (1994, pp. 160–161) also identified priority areas for research that include the following:

1. Factors that influence male choices of nontraditional careers.
2. Understanding how successful minority group members differ from those that society considers to be nonsuccessful, and how cultural values interact with societal expectations to shape career choices.
3. The role of sexual orientation in vocational choice and examination of the ways in which heterosexual counselors can work effectively with homosexual clients.
4. A better operationalization of vocational identity is needed.
5. How families influence vocational choice.
6. How information processing occurs in vocational decision making.
7. The role of self-efficacy expectations in influencing career choices throughout the developmental process.
8. The process of career counseling.
9. The effectiveness of treatment interventions.

Although the four sets of research priorities just presented blend across some areas, they nevertheless establish the broad parameters of needed research in career theory and practice (Herr & Cramer, 1996). From the perspective of the school counselor, constant vigilance is necessary to keep abreast of the literature as research efforts are directed in these critical areas. School counselors do not generally deal with topics such as career midlife crisis and vertical mobility. However, they surely need to be open to innovations and creative theoretical precepts as they are generated and perhaps, ultimately, implemented in comprehensive school counseling and guidance career programmatic components.

SUMMARY

This chapter presented only a few of the issues and trends that will need to be addressed into the next century. As Drummond and Ryan (1995) surmised, the one dimension that can be predicted with accuracy is the predictability of change. School counselors must present themselves as change agents, among their various other roles. With that role, however, school counselors must also develop the ability to adapt to change.

Perhaps, from a multicultural perspective, the most pervasive change for the next century will be evidenced in the demographics of the United States. The realization that European Americans are rapidly becoming an ethnic minority is only just beginning to be comprehended. This change in one ethnic group's domination of the U.S. socioeconomic and political society will have extensive ramifications for student career development. School counselors must be prepared for this onslaught and may be so if the following tasks are followed (Schmidt, 1996):

1. Develop a broader knowledge of human development throughout the life span.
2. Adapt to new technology (e.g., computer-assisted learning, interactive media, and voice-to-print capability).
3. Increase the use of group processes, including teachers and parents.
4. Expand their professional development.
5. Measure the outcome of their services.

EXPERIENTIAL ACTIVITIES

1. What significant changes have you observed in careers and the world of work in your life? What changes may be anticipated in other regions of the United States?
2. Discuss the growth of specialty areas in the counseling profession (i.e., marriage and family, sports, gerontology, etc.). Are there other areas of counseling specialization that you see emerging in the next 25 years?
3. What issues and trends listed in the chapter do you accept? Do not accept?
4. How far do you think that technology can be extended, in relation to the world of work and career development?
5. Interview several school counselors and ask them what they think are the major future issues in career counseling?
6. Review Something to Consider 13.1. What are some ways in which the delivery of career development will be affected by these role shifts?

Part V

Practical Applications

PART V CONCLUDES this book with several examples of practical applications of the information presented in the text. Chapter 14 will present 10 selected vignettes that depict career dilemmas. Examples represent all developmental levels and influences of families. The reader is encouraged to attempt an appraisal of the presenting problems and compare that analysis with another reader's perspective. It may be noted that most of these vignettes can be adapted or modified to represent diverse student clients.

14
Selected Career Vignettes
for Consideration

For most children only two places exist where they can gain
a successful
identity and learn to follow the essential pathways. These
places are
the home and the school . . . if the home is successful, the
child may succeed
despite the school, but that is too big an if to rely upon. We
must ensure that
the child's major experience in growing up, the most
constant and important
factor in his [her] life, school, provides within it the two
necessary pathways: a
chance to give and receive love and a chance to become
educated and therefore worthwhile.

William Glasser, 1969

This chapter presents selected career vignettes that will allow the school counselor or counselor-in-training opportunities to apply synergetic principles effectively in the career guidance and counseling of diverse students. The reader is cautioned that his or her analyses may not be congruent with other interpretations. Many theoretical orientations may be applied to these career vignettes. The question remains, however, whether those theoretical modalities consider influences of history and environment as well as ethnicity, gender, class, culture, lifestyle, and conditions of disability.

These career vignettes were adapted from professional cases and from the literature or compilations thereof.

PRIMARY AND ELEMENTARY SCHOOLS

Career Vignette 1: Girl Engineers?

"Designing and building space stations sounds like a very exciting job," Susan, an African American third-grade student commented. Before she could continue, Sam, a European American classmate, said, "Girls do not become engineers. They need us men. We know more science and math."

Vignette questions to consider:

1. Should the school counselor or teacher interrupt the discussion and make some comments? Why or why not?
2. How could a school counselor discourage sex stereotyping and encourage consideration by students of nontraditional career fields?
3. What, if any, ethnic factors are embedded in this vignette? If they are present, how would you handle an appropriate discussion?

Career Vignette 2: Boring Field Trips

The school counselor is walking down the hall and overhears the conversation of a third-grade Japanese American male student who says, "To the fire station again. All we ever do is take trips to the same stupid places."

Vignette questions to consider:

1. Should the school counselor inquire why the student did not like the field trips?
2. Should any ethnic factors be involved in this vignette? How can they be addressed?
3. How could the school counselor work with teachers to make field trips more exciting and include career preparation objectives?

Career Vignette 3: Jorge in Trouble

The school counselor is asked by a classroom teacher to have a conference with a Latino student and his mother. Jorge is from a single-parent family whose father recently deserted Jorge's mother for another woman. Jorge refuses to do any homework, and his mother works two jobs to make ends meet. He is left alone at home part of the time while his mother works. Jorge feels rejected and has also developed a negative identity at school because he is failing his reading and math in second grade. He received S's (satisfactory) and P's (passing) on his report card the year before. He scored in the average range on the annual Stanford Achievement Test.

Vignette questions to consider:

1. What additional information might be needed to help Jorge?
2. How could the school counselor help Jorge develop a positive identity and meet the goals at this stage of development?
3. Are any multicultural factors present in this vignette? If so, what are they? How might they be addressed?

MIDDLE AND JUNIOR HIGH LEVELS

Career Vignette 4: Profile of a Potential Dropout

Name: Rosita Lopez
Age: 12 years
Grade: 6
School: Carver Middle School

Background.   Rosita, A Mexican American student, is currently attending Carver Middle School. She lives with her mother and grandmother. Her mother is 31 years of age and on public assistance. Rosita had an excellent attendance record through Grade 5; however, her attendance record in Grade 6 is poor and she frequently misses several days within a week of school. Her grandmother works part time for a bakery and her mother is unemployed.

Her grades in school range from D's to B's. Rosita makes C's and D's in her math and science classes and C's in reading and language arts. She makes B's in physical education and fine/practical arts classes. The school does not have an ESL (English as a Second Language) program.

Appraisal information.   Rose took the Otis Lennon Scholastic Ability Test in sixth grade and had a score of 98. Her sixth-grade scores on the Differential Aptitude Test were as follows:

Verbal	35%
Numerical	5%
Abstract	25%
Spatial	35%
Mechanical	5%
Sentence	28%
Spelling	55%
Clerical speed	85%

At Carver Middle School, Rosita was administered The Culture Free Self-Concept Scale. She scored 35% on the General Self Scale, 75% on the Social Self, 48% on the School Self, and 15% on the Personal Self Scale. When asked what she would like to be when she finishes school, she says pediatrician or gynecological nurse.

Vignette questions to consider:

1. What additional types of information would be useful to a counselor?
2. How can the appraisal information be used most effectively? Are addition appraisal data required? If so, what data are needed?
3. What type of career guidance/counseling services and interventions are the most applicable in Rosita's situation?
4. How could career theories be used in analyzing Rosita's stages of development?
5. How should a school counselor handle her unrealistic career aspirations?

Career Vignette 5: The Shoplifter

The administrators of Littlefield Junior High School have requested that all students who desire to participate on school-sponsored field trips bring money to purchase school insurance. Phillip Crazy Horse, an Oglala Sioux ninth grader, does not want to admit to his teacher that he can't ask his mother for the money. A woman has left her purse on a store counter. Phillip slips the money into his wallet and calmly walks out the door. However, he is caught by the store clerk.

Vignette questions to consider:

1. How would you have handled the problem?
2. What would you do if you had this problem?
3. If you were the injured party in this case, how would you explain your feelings to your best friend?
4. How do issues of ethnicity affect or not affect this vignette?

Career Vignette 6: The Troublemaker

Edgar, a European American seventh grader, comes to class, takes out paper, and draws cartoons. He obviously is not listening to the teacher's assignment, and his teacher is becoming annoyed. She has requested him to put his cartoons aside but he continues to ignore her. Now she tells him again to stop drawing and pay attention. Reluctantly, he puts his paper into his desk and begins to whistle softly. At this point his teacher orders Edgar out of the room and to the principal's office.

Vignette questions to consider:

1. What are the possible causative factors in this conflict, and how could they be identified and resolved?
2. How could Edgar have prevented this conflict?

HIGH SCHOOL GRADES

Career Vignette 7: Profile of a Disadvantaged Youth

Name: Randy Edwards
Age: 16 years
Grade: 10
School: Hall High School

Background. Randy, an African American student, is from an economically disadvantaged family. He repeated third grade because of excessive absences (his family had moved in the middle of the school year). His grades have been at the C and D level, but Randy can get better grades when he tries. Standardized achievement test scores show that Randy has the ability to achieve. This year, unfortunately, Randy has been failing most of his academic subjects.

Appraisal information. The results of a group intelligence test indicated that Randy's overall level of intellectual functioning was in the above-average range (IQ 118). The results of the Stanford Achievement Test from last year were as follows:

Subtest	Percentile Rank
Word reading	43
Reading comprehension	37
Number concepts	60
Math computations and applications	52
Spelling	50
Vocabulary	45
Listening comprehension	22
Reading	40
Total reading	41
Total math	52
Total auditory	21

Randy was identified as a potential dropout after missing school frequently during the 9th grade. Randy was placed in vocational education in the 9th grade and then put in a special dropout prevention vocational education program in the 10th grade. This program features a work-study program in which students arrange their schedules so that they can leave school early to go to work. The students receive assistance in obtaining employment and follow-up help after placement.

Randy was fired from his initial work-study job and arrangements have been made for him to be placed in another. Randy told one of his teachers that he was "going to quit school and get his own job." He said that he "could make more money and wouldn't have to hassle with school no more."

Classroom behavior.   Randy's classroom behavior and emotional development appear normal. His behavior in school is satisfactory except for his extreme passivity and lack of interest in school this year. He has stopped doing all of his homework and participating in class, and he doesn't try to finish his class work or tests.

Vignette questions to consider:

1. How could a school counselor, acting as a career counselor, work with this student in terms of theoretical approach and philosophy of intervention?
2. What additional appraisal and other information are needed to provide career counseling services? How could this information be obtained expeditiously?
3. What type of career testing would be appropriate to give to Randy? How could the results be used?
4. What are some specific techniques for motivating students who miss school frequently?
5. Why is career counseling an important educational service in this situation?
6. What multicultural variables are present in this vignette? How might they be addressed and resolved?

Career Vignette 8: The Hard Worker

Hans, a German American high school senior, had his first job with his father, who was a building contractor. The father loved to work and received pleasure from creating the buildings he completed. Hans had to work afternoons and weekends, beginning at age 15. Hans had to lift 75- and 100-pound bags of cement and plaster, mix mortar and plaster, and carry it when needed. He helped rake concrete when it was being poured. It was hard work and Hans hated it. However, the job provided money for movies and dates when time was available, such as rainy days and holidays.

Vignette questions to consider:

1. What type of work ethic is being illustrated in Hans's situation?
2. How is work defined?
3. What is the role of job satisfaction in this vignette? Dissatisfaction?

4. How does Hans's job influence his social needs? Self-esteem needs? Physical needs?
5. What additional multicultural aspects are apparent in this career vignette?

Career Vignette 9: The Big Picture

Tom, a 10th grader, came into the career resource center and said: "I want to research what I am going to do after I graduate. I know I should have done something before now but I have just kept putting it off. I am interested in psychology because it deals with people's minds. I really like stuff like that. I have read that there is a tight job market for psychology majors. I know that I will do well in college and will have competencies employers are looking for. I think that I need to get the big picture and find out what jobs are out there and whether they match what I want to do."

Vignette questions to consider:

1. What sources of information would you use in this situation?
2. What additional information is needed?
3. What counseling strategies/approaches would you use with this student?

THE FAMILY

Career Vignette 10

Robert Elk, a 16-year-old male, has Native American Indian ancestry. His family has resided on a Lakota Sioux reservation for generations. The family exists in an impoverished area, and having enough money is a constant concern for the family. Robert has been raised in the traditional way. One of the basic values of their tradition is not to depend on others for their needs.

Robert has been attending a Bureau of Indian Affairs school on the reservation, which is 90% Native. The faculty, however, is European American with the exception of several Native paraprofessionals. The European American counselor has held career workshops and small-group discussions to encourage the students to aspire to less traditional ways of earning a living. Robert is beginning to accept the advice of the counselor, but he is not encouraged by his family. He is beginning to think about postsecondary options that will necessitate his leaving reservation life.

Vignette questions to consider:

1. What intergenerational conflicts may be present in this vignette?
2. Has the counselor advised the Native students appropriately?

3. Depending on Robert's ultimate decision, what family conflicts can he expect to experience?
4. How do traditional values affect this vignette?
5. What options does Robert have regarding his postsecondary education plans?
6. What potential effects will Robert's decisions have on his future as a Native person?

References

Allen, J. E., Jr. (1970, February). *Conference for all as the goal for secondary education.* Paper presented at the meeting of the National Association of Secondary School Principals, Washington, DC.

American Association for Counseling and Development & Association for Measurement and Evaluation in Counseling and Development. (1989, May). The responsibilities of users of standardized tests. *AACD Guideposts,* 12–28.

American Association of Retired Persons. (1994). Barriers to raising grandchildren. *AARP Bulletin, 35*(9), p. 3.

American Association of University Women. (1992). *AAUW report: How schools shortchange girls.* Washington, DC: AAUW Educational Foundation.

American College Testing. (1988). *Interim psychometric handbook for the 3rd edition ACT Career Planning Program.* Iowa City, IA: Author.

American College Testing. (1989). *State and national trend data for students who take the ACT Assessment.* Iowa City, IA: Author.

American Counseling Association. (1995). *Code of ethics.* Alexandria, VA: Author.

American Educational Research Association, American Psychological Association, & National Council on Measurement in Education. (1985). *Standards for educational and psychological testing.* Washington, DC: American Psychological Association.

American Psychiatric Association. (1994). *Diagnostic and statistical manual of mental disorders* (4th ed.). Washington, DC: Author.

American Psychological Association (Joint Committee on Testing Practices). (1988). *Code of fair testing practices in education.* Washington, DC: Author.

American School Counselor Association. (1977, August). *The unique role of the middle/junior high school counselor* [Position paper]. Alexandria, VA: Author.

American School Counselor Association. (1980). Human sexuality and sex education. *The School Counselor, 27,* 317.

American School Counselor Association. (1984a). ASCA position statement: School counselors and military recruitment. *The School Counselor, 32,* 73–75.

American School Counselor Association. (1984b). The role of the school counselor in career guidance: Expectation and responsibilities. *The ASCA Counselor, 21*(5), 8–10.

American School Counselor Association. (1985). The role of the school counselor in career guidance: Expectations and responsibilities. *The School Counselor, 32,* 164–168.

Americans With Disabilities Act of 1990, 42 U.S.C.A. § 12101 *et seq.* (West 1993).

Amundson, N. E., & Borgen, W. A. (1981). The dynamics of unemployment: Job loss and job search. *Personnel and Guidance Journal, 60,* 562–564.

Arbona, C. (1990). Career counseling research and Hispanics: A review of the literature. *The Counseling Psychologist, 18*, 300–323.

Aronson, D. (1994). Changing channels. *Teaching Tolerance, 3*(2), 28–31.

Arredondo, P., Toporek, R., Brown, S. P., Jones, J., Locke, D., Sanchez, J., & Stadler, H. (1996). Operationalization of the multicultural counseling competencies. *Journal of Multicultural Counseling and Development, 24*, 42–78.

Association for Assessment in Counseling. (1993). *Standards for assessment in counseling.* Washington, DC: Author.

Astin, H. S. (1984). The meaning of work in women's lives: A sociopsychological model of career choice and work behavior. *The Counseling Psychologist, 112*, 117–126.

Atkinson, D. R., Morten, G., & Sue, D. W. (1993). *Counseling American minorities: A cross-cultural perspective* (4th ed.). Dubuque, IA: William C. Brown.

Aubrey, R. F. (1973). Organizational victimization of school counselors. *The School Counselor, 20*, 346–354.

Aubrey, R. F. (1978). *Career development needs of thirteen year olds: How to improve career development programs.* Washington, DC: National Advisory Council for Career Education.

Axelson, J. A. (1985). *Counseling and development in a multicultural society.* Monterey, CA: Brooks/Cole.

Axelson, J. A. (1993). *Counseling and development in a multicultural society* (2nd ed.). Pacific Grove, CA: Brooks/Cole.

Axelson, J. A., & McGrath, P. (1998). *Counseling and development in a multicultural society* (3rd ed.). Pacific Grove, CA: Brooks/Cole.

Bachhuber, T. (1992). 13 ways to pass along real information to students. *Journal of Career Counseling and Development, 52*, 66–69.

Baker, S. B. (1992). *School counseling for the twenty-first century.* New York: Merrill.

Baker, S. B., & Popowicz, C. L. (1983). Meta-analysis as a strategy for evaluating effects of career education interventions. *Vocational Guidance Quarterly, 31*, 178–186.

Baldwin, J. A., & Bell, Y. R. (1985). The African Self-Consciousness Scale: An Africentric personality questionnaire. *Western Journal of Black Studies, 9*(2), 65–68.

Bandura, A. (1977). *Social learning theory.* Englewood Cliffs, NJ: Prentice Hall.

Bansberg, B., & Sklare, J. (1986). *The career decision diagnostic assessment.* Monterey, CA: CTB/McGraw-Hill.

Barak, A. (1981). Vocational interests: A cognitive view. *Journal of Vocational Behavior, 19*, 1–14.

Barak, A., Shiloh, S., & Haushner, O. (1992). Modification of interests through cognitive restructuring: Test of a theoretical model in preschool children. *Journal of Counseling Psychology, 39*, 490–497.

Bartholomew, C. G., & Schnorr, D. L. (1994). Gender equity: Suggestions for broadening career options of female students. *The School Counselor, 41*, 245–255.

Bartol, K. M. (1981). Vocational behavior and career development, 1980: A review. *Journal of Vocational Behavior, 19*, 123–162.

Baruth, L. G., & Manning, M. L. (1991). *Multicultural counseling and psychotherapy: A life span perspective.* New York: Merrill.

Baumgardner, S. R. (1977). Vocational planning: The great swindle. *Personnel and Guidance Journal, 56,* 17–22.

Beale, A. V., & Nugent, D. G. (1996). The pizza connection: Enhancing career awareness. *Elementary School Guidance and Counseling, 30,* 294–303.

Beauvais, F. (1992). Trends in Indian adolescent drug and alcohol use. *American Indian and Alaska Native Mental Health Research Journal, 5,* 1–12.

Benvenutti, A. C. (1986, November). *Assessing and addressing the special challenge of gay and lesbian students for high school counseling programs.* Paper presented at the 65th Annual Meeting of the California Educational Research Association, San Jose, CA.

Bernstein, B. L., Wade, P., & Hofmann, B. (1987). Students' race and preferences for counselor's race, sex, age, and experience. *Journal of Multicultural Counseling and Development, 15,* 60–70.

Berven, N. C. (1986). Assessment practices in rehabilitation counseling. In T. F. Riggar, D. R. Maki, & A. W. Wolf (Eds.), *Applied rehabilitation counseling* (pp. 21–33). New York: Springer.

Berzon, B. (1979). Developing a positive gay identity. In B. Berzon (Ed.), *Positively gay: New approaches in gay and lesbian life* (pp. 1–14). Los Angeles: Mediamix.

Berzon, B. (1988). *Permanent partners: Building gay and lesbian relationships that last.* New York: Dutton.

Betz, N. E., & Fitzgerald, L. F. (1987). *The career psychology of women.* Orlando, FL: Academic Press.

Bhaerman, R. D. (1977). *Career education and basic academic achievement: A descriptive analysis of the research.* Washington, DC: U.S. Office of Education.

Birk, J. M., & Blimline, C. A. (1984). Parents as career development facilitators: An untapped resource for the counselor. *The School Counselor, 31,* 310–317.

Blau, P. M., Gustad, J. W., Jessor, R., Parnes, H. S., & Wilcox, R. S. (1956). Occupational choices: A conceptual framework. *Industrial Labor Relations Review, 9,* 531–543.

Bloch, D. P., & Kinnison, J. F. (1989a). A method for rating computer-biased career information delivery systems. *Measurement and Evaluation in Counseling and Development, 21,* 177–187.

Bloch, D. P., & Kinnison, J. F. (1989b). Occupational and career information components: A validation study. *Journal of Studies in Technical Careers, 11,* 101–109.

Blocher, D. H. (1989). *Career actualization and life planning.* Denver, CO: Love.

Bonett, R. M. (1994). Marital status and sex: Impact on career self-efficacy. *Journal of Counseling & Development, 73,* 187–190.

Borders, L. D., & Drury, S. M. (1992). Comprehensive school counseling programs: A review for policy makers and practitioners. *Journal of Counseling & Development, 70,* 487–498.

Bordin, E. S., Nachmann, B., & Segal, S. J. (1963). An articulated framework for vocational development. *Journal of Counseling Psychology, 10,* 107–116.

Boudreau, F. A. (1986). Education. In F. A. Boudreau, R. S. Sennott, & M. Wilson (Eds.), *Sex roles and social patterns* (pp. 1–27). New York: Praeger.

Boy, A. V., & Pine, G. J. (1963). *Client-centered counseling in the secondary school.* Boston: Houghton Mifflin.

Bradley, R. W., & Mims, G. A. (1992). Using family systems and birth order dynamics as the basis for a college career decision-making course. *Journal of Counseling & Development, 70,* 445–448.

Brescia, W., & Fortune, J. C. (1988). *Standardized testing of American Indian students.* Las Cruces: New Mexico State University.

Brindis, C. (1997). Adolescent pregnancy prevention for Hispanic youth. *The Prevention Researcher, 4,* 8–9.

Brolin, D. E. (1978). *Life-centered career education: A competency-based approach.* Reston, VA: Council for Exceptional Children.

Brolin, D. E. (1983). *Life-centered career education: A competency-based approach.* Reston, VA: Council for Exceptional Children.

Brolin, D. E. (1989). *Life-centered career education: A competency-based approach.* Reston, VA: Council for Exceptional Children.

Brolin, D. E., & Gysbers, N. C. (1989). Career education for students with disabilities. *Journal of Counseling & Development, 68,* 155–159.

Brooks, J. S., Whiteman, M., Persach, E., & Deutsch, M. (1974). Aspiration levels of and for children: Age, race and socioeconomic correlates. *Journal of Genetic Psychology, 124,* 2–16.

Brophy, J. E. (1985). Interaction of male and female students with male and female teachers. In L. C. Wilkinson & C. B. Marrett (Eds.), *Gender influences in classroom interaction* (pp. 23–46). New York: Academic Press.

Brown, D. (1990a). Summary, comparison, and critique of the major theories. In D. Brown, L. Brooks, & Associates (Eds.), *Career choice and development* (2nd ed., pp. 338–363). San Francisco: Jossey-Bass.

Brown, D. (1990b). Trait and factor theory. In D. Brown, L. Brooks, & Associates (Eds.), *Career choice and development* (2nd ed., pp. 13–36). San Francisco: Jossey-Bass.

Brown, D. (1995). A values-based model for facilitating career transitions. *Career Development Quarterly, 44,* 4–11.

Brown, D. (1996). Brown's values-based, holistic model of career and life-role choices and satisfaction. In D. Brown, L. Brooks, & Associates (Eds.), *Career choice and development* (3rd ed., pp. 337–372). San Francisco: Jossey-Bass.

Brown, D., Brooks, L., & Associates. (1990). *Career choice and development, applying contemporary theories to practice* (2nd ed.). San Francisco: Jossey-Bass.

Brown, D., Brooks, L., & Associates. (1996). *Career choice and development, applying contemporary theories to practice* (3rd ed.). San Francisco: Jossey-Bass.

Brown, D., Minor, C. W., & Jepsen, D. A. (1992). Public support for career development activities in America's schools: Report of the 1989 NCDA survey. *The School Counselor, 39,* 257–262.

Brown, F., & Tooley, J. (1989). Alcoholism in the Black community. In G. W. Lawson & A. W. Lawson (Eds.), *Alcoholism and substance abuse in special populations* (pp. 115–128). Rockville, MD: Aspen.

Brown, S. T., & Brown, D. (1990). *Designing and implementing a career information center.* Garrett Park, MD: Garrett Park Press.

Brown, W., & Holtzman, W. (1967). *Manual, survey of study habits and attitudes.* New York: Psychological Corporation.

Browning, C., Reynolds, A. L., & Dworkin, D. (1991). Affirmative psychotherapy for lesbian women. *The Counseling Psychologist, 19,* 177–196.

Burgess, B. J. (1978). Native American learning styles. In L. Morris, G. Sather, & S. Scull (Eds.), *Extracting learning styles from social/cultural diversity: A study of five American minorities* (pp. 37–51). Norman, OK: Southwest Teacher Corps Network.

Burnam, M. A., Telles, C. A., Hough, R. L., & Escobar, J. I. (1987). Measurement of acculturation in a community population of Mexican Americans. *Hispanic Journal of Behavioral Science, 9,* 105–130.

Campbell, D. P., & Hanson, J. I. C. (1981). *Manual for the SVIB–SCII Strong–Campbell Interest Inventory* (3rd ed.). Stanford, CA: Stanford University Press.

Campbell, N. K., & Hadley, G. B. (1992). Creating options: A career development training program for minorities. *Journal of Counseling & Development, 70,* 645–647.

Campbell, R. E., Connel, J. B., Boyle, K. K., & Bhaerman, R. (1983). *Enhancing career development: Recommendations for action.* Columbus: Ohio State University, National Center of Research in Vocational Education.

Canale, J. R., & Dunlap, L. L. (1987). *Factors influencing career aspirations of primary and secondary grade students.* Ann Arbor: University of Michigan. (ERIC Document Reproduction Service No. ED 288 164)

Capintero, H. (1994). Some historical notes on scientific psychology and its professional development. *Applied Psychology: An International Review, 43,* 131–150.

Carkhuff, R. R., Alexik, M., & Anderson, S. (1967). Do we have a theory of vocational choice? *Personnel and Guidance Journal, 46,* 335–345.

Carson, R. C., Butcher, J. N., & Coleman, J. C. (1988). *Abnormal psychology and modern life* (8th ed.). Glenview, IL: Scott, Foresman.

Carter, R. T., & Cook, D. A. (1992). A culturally relevant perspective for understanding the career paths of visible racial/ethnic group people. In Z. Leibowitz & D. Lea (Eds.), *Adult career development: Concepts, issues, and practices* (2nd ed., pp. 192–217). Alexandria, VA: National Career Development Association.

Casper, V., Cuffaro, H. K., Schultz, S., Silin, J., & Wickens, E. (1995). Toward a most thorough understanding of the world: Sexual orientation and early childhood education. *Harvard Educational Review, 66*(2), 271–293.

Casper, V., Schultz, S., & Wickens, E. (1992). Breaking the silences: Lesbian and gay parents and the schools. *Teachers College Record, 94,* 109–137.

Cayleff, S. E. (1986). Ethical issues in counseling gender, race, and culturally distinct groups. *Journal of Counseling & Development, 64,* 345–347.

Center of Human Services Department. (1995). *Grandparent caregiving households: An informational and training manual for school and community counselors.* College Park: University of Maryland.

Centers for Disease Control. (1990). Progress toward achieving the 1990 objectives for the nation for sexually transmitted diseases. *Morbidity and Mortality Weekly Report, 39,* 53–57.

Centers for Disease Control and Prevention. (1995). U.S. HIV and AIDS cases reported through December, 1994. *HIV/AIDS Surveillance Report, 6*(2).

Cetron, M. J. (1985). *Schools of the future: How American business and education can cooperate to save our schools.* New York: McGraw-Hill.

Chadsey-Rusch, J., Rusch, F. R., & Phelps, L. A. (1989). Analysis and synthesis of transition issues. In D. E. Berkell & J. M. Brown (Eds.), *Transition from school to work for persons with disabilities* (pp. 227–241). New York: Longman.

Chamberlain, K. P., & Medinos-Landurand, P. (1991). Practical considerations for the assessment of LEP students with special needs. In E. V. Hamayan & J. S. Damico (Eds.), *Limiting bias in assessment of bilingual students* (pp. 83–101). Austin, TX: PRO-ED.

Chapman, S. (1992). *The power of children's literature: A rationale for using books on gay and lesbian headed families.* Unpublished master's thesis, Bank Street College of Education, New York City.

Chartrand, J. M., & Camp, C. C. (1991). Advances in the measurement of career development constructs: A 20-year review. *Journal of Vocational Behavior, 39,* 1–39.

Chassler, S. (1997, February 2). What teenage girls say about pregnancy. *Parade Magazine,* 4–5.

Chavez, E. L., Oetting, E. R., & Swaim, R. C. (1994). Dropout and delinquency: Mexican-American and Caucasian non-Hispanic youth. *Journal of Clinical Child Psychology, 23,* 47–55.

Chavez, E. L., & Swaim, R. C. (1992). An epidemiological comparison of Mexican-American and White non-Hispanic eighth- and twelfth-grade students' substance use. *American Journal of Public Health, 82,* 445–447.

Cheatham, H. E. (1990). Africentricity and career development of African Americans. *Career Development Quarterly, 38,* 334–346.

Chojnacki, J. T., & Gelberg, S. (1995). The facilitation of a gay/lesbian/bisexual support-therapy group by heterosexual counselors. *Journal of Counseling & Development, 73,* 352–354.

Christensen, C. P. (1989). Cross-cultural awareness development: A conceptual model. *Counselor Education and Supervision, 28,* 270–287.

Ciborowski, P. (1978). Guidelines for armed services recruiters. *The School Counselor, 25,* 285–286.

Ciborowski, P. (1980). In-school military recruiting: A counseling perspective. *The School Counselor, 28,* 22–25.

Ciborowski, P. (1994). Choosing the military as a career: A group counseling program that addresses issues not presented by recruiters. *The School Counselor, 41,* 305–309.

Claes, R., Martin, G., Coetsier, P., & Super, D. E. (1995). Homemakers and employed women in Belgian Flanders and the Southeast United States. In D. E. Super, B. Sverko, & C. M. Super (Eds.), *Life roles, values, and careers: International findings of the Work Importance Study* (pp. 201–252). San Francisco: Jossey-Bass.

Clark, G. M., Carlson, B. C., Fisher, S., Cook, I. D., & D'Alonzo, B. J. (1991). Career development for students with disabilities in elementary schools. A position statement of the division of career development for exceptional individuals. *Career Development for Exceptional Individuals, 14,* 109–120.

Clement, S. (1987). The self-efficacy expectations and occupational preferences of females and males. *Journal of Occupational Psychology, 60,* 257–265.

Coates, S. (1985). Extreme boyhood femininity: Overview and new research findings. In Z. DeFries, R. Friedman, & R. Conn (Eds.), *Sexuality: New perspectives* (pp. 101–129). Westport, CT: Greenwood Press.

Cole, J. (1975). *A study of person–environment interactions in a school system.* Unpublished master's thesis, University of Melbourne, Melbourne, Australia.

Cole, N. S., Whitney, D. R., & Holland, J. L. (1971). A spatial configuration of occupations. *Journal of Vocational Behavior, 1,* 1–9.

Coleman, E., & Remafedi, G. (1989). Gay, lesbian, and bisexual adolescents: A critical challenge to counselors. *Journal of Counseling & Development, 68,* 36–40.

Coleman, J. S. (1974). *Youth: Transition to adulthood.* Chicago: University of Chicago Press.

Collin, A., & Young, R. A. (1986). New directions for theories of career. *Human Relations, 39,* 837–853.

Columbia Broadcasting System. (1993, April 4). *Sixty minutes: The rainbow curriculum.* Author.

Comas-Diaz, L. (1990). Hispanic/Latino communities: Psychological implications. *Journal of Training and Practice in Professional Psychology, 4*(1), 14–35.

Cook, E. P. (1991). Annual review: Practice and research in career counseling and development, 1990. *Career Development Quarterly, 40,* 99–131.

Cosse, W. J. (1992). Who's who and what's what? The effects of gender on development. In B. R. Wainrib (Ed.), *Gender issues across the life cycle* (pp. 121–153). New York: Springer.

Costa, L., & Stiltner, B. (1994). Why do the good things always end and the bad things go on forever? A family change counseling group. *The School Counselor, 41,* 304.

Cramer, S. H., Wise, P. S., & Colburn, E. D. (1977). An evaluation of a treatment to expand the career perceptions of high school girls. *The School Counselor, 25,* 125–129.

Crites, J. O. (1978). *Career maturity inventory.* Monterey, CA: CTB/McGraw-Hill.

Crites, J. O. (1981). *Career counseling.* New York: McGraw-Hill.

Croteau, J. M., & Thiel, M. J. (1993). Integrating sexual orientation in career counseling: Acting to end a form of the personal–career dichotomy. *Career Development Quarterly, 42,* 174–179.

Curtis, P. A. (1990). The consequences of acculturation to service delivery and research with Hispanic families. *Child and Adolescent Social Work, 7,* 147–159.

Damico, S., & Scott, E. (1988). Behavior differences between Black and White females in desegregated schools. *Equality and Excellence, 23,* 63–66.

Dana, R. H. (1993). *Multicultural assessment perspectives from professional psychology.* Boston: Allyn & Bacon.

Daniels, J. L. (1981). World of work in disabling conditions. In R. M. Parker & C. E. Hansen (Eds.), *Rehabilitation counseling* (pp. 169–199). Boston: Allyn & Bacon.

Daniels, J. L. (1987). Transition from school to work. In R. M. Parker (Ed.), *Rehabilitation counseling: Basics and beyond* (pp. 283–317). Austin, TX: PRO-ED.

Dao, M. (1991). Designing assessment procedures for educationally at-risk Southeast Asian-American students. *Journal of Learning Disabilities, 24,* 594–601.

Davidson, G. C., & Friedman, S. (1981). Sexual orientation stereotyping in the distortion of clinical judgement. *Journal of Homosexuality, 6,* 37–44.

Davis, E. (1995, March). [Untitled presentation to Mini-White House Conference on Grandparents Raising Grandchildren]. College Park: University of Maryland, University College.

Dawis, R. V. (1996). The theory of work adjustment and person–environment-correspondence counseling. In D. Brown, L. Brooks, & Associates (Eds.), *Career choice and development* (3rd ed., pp. 75–120). San Francisco: Jossey-Bass.

Dawis, R. V., England, G. W., & Lofquist, L. H. (1964). A theory of work adjustment. *Minnesota Studies in Vocational Rehabilitation, XV,* 1–27.

Deaux, K. (1984). From individual differences to social categories: Analysis of a decade's research on gender. *American Psychologist, 39,* 105–116.

Deisher, R. W. (1989). Adolescent homosexuality: Preface. *Journal of Homosexuality, 17,* xiii–xv.

Della Face, L. R. (1974). Success values: Are they universal or class-differentiated. *American Journal of Sociology, 80,* 153–169.

del Pinal, J. H., & DeNavas, C. (1990). *The Hispanic population in the United States: March 1989* (Series P-20, No. 444). Washington, DC: U.S. Department of Commerce.

Demographer sees a 2050 U.S. of 383 million, only 53% White. (1992, December 4). *Arkansas Democrat-Gazette,* p. 5A.

DeRidder, L. (1990). *The impact of parents and parenting on career development.* Ann Arbor: University of Michigan. (ERIC Document Reproduction Service No. ED 325 769)

Deyhle, D. (1987). Learning failure: Tests as gatekeepers and the culturally different child. In H. E. Trueba (Ed.), *Success or failure?* (pp. 21–40). Rawley, MA: Newbury House.

Diamant, L. (1993). *Homosexual issues in the workplace.* Washington, DC: Taylor & Francis.

Dillon, C. (1986). Preparing college health professionals to deliver gay-affirmative services. *Journal of the Academy of College Health, 36,* 36–40.

Dinkmeyer, D., Dinkmeyer, D., Jr., & Sperry, L. (1987). *Adlerian counseling and psychotherapy* (2nd ed.). Columbus, OH: Charles E. Merrill.

Division of Career Development of the Council for Exceptional Children. (1987). *Position paper on career education.* Washington, DC: Author.

Domino, G., & Acosta, A. (1987). The relation of acculturation and values in Mexican Americans. *Hispanic Journal of Behavior Science, 9,* 191–250.

Dorn, F. J. (1987). Dispelling career myths: A social influence approach. *The School Counselor, 34,* 263–267.

Dorn, F. J. (1992). Occupational wellness: The integration of career identity and personal identity. *Journal of Counseling & Development, 71,* 176–178.

Downey, T. (1995, March). [Untitled presentation to Mini-White House Conference on Grandparents Raising Grandchildren]. College Park: University of Maryland, University College.

Draguns, J. G. (1989). Dilemmas and choices in cross-cultural counseling: The universal versus the culturally distinctive. In P. B. Pedersen, J. G. Draguns, J. Lonner, & J. E. Trimble (Eds.), *Counseling across cultures* (3rd ed., pp. 3–21). Honolulu: University of Hawaii Press.

Drummond, R. J. (1996). *Appraisal procedures for counselors and helping professionals* (3rd ed.). Columbus, OH: Charles E. Merrill.

Drummond, R. J., & Hansford, S. G. (1992). *Career aspirations of pregnant teens* (Report from *Journal of Adolescence Health: Vol. 1. Summary and policy options,* 1991). Washington, DC: Congress of the United States, Office of Technology Assessment.

Drummond, R. J., & Ryan, C. W. (1995). *Career counseling: A developmental approach.* Columbus, OH: Charles E. Merrill.

Dudley, G. A., & Tiedeman, V. D. (1977). *Career development: Exploration and commitment.* Muncie, IN: Accelerated Development.

Dulaney, D., & Kelly, J. (1982). Improving services to gay and lesbian clients. *Social Work, 27,* 178–183.

Dunham, K. L. (1989). *Educated to be invisible: The gay and lesbian adolescent.* Ann Arbor: University of Michigan Press. (ERIC Document Reproduction Service No. ED 336 676)

Durkin, K. (1987). Social cognition and social context in the construction of sex differences. In M. A. Baker (Ed.), *Sex differences in human performance* (pp. 206–246). Chichester, England: Wiley.

Dyson, A. H. (1996). Cultural constellations and childhood identities: On Greek gods, cartoon heroes, and the social lives of school children. *Harvard Educational Review, 66*(2), 471–495.

Dyson, L., Edgar, E., & Crnic, K. (1989). Psychological predictors of adjustment by siblings of developmentally disabled children. *American Journal on Mental Retardation, 94,* 292–302.

Dziekan, K. I., & Okocha, A. A. G. (1993). Accessibility of rehabilitation services: Comparison by racial-ethnic status. *Rehabilitation Counseling Bulletin, 36,* 183–189.

Eccles (Parsons), J. S. (1984). Sex differences in mathematics participation. In M. Steinkamp & M. Maehr (Eds.), *Women in science* (pp. 101–133). Greenwich, CT: JAI Press.

Eccles, J. S. (1987). Gender roles and women's achievement-related decisions. *Psychology of Women Quarterly, 11,* 135–172.

Eccles, J. S., Adler, T. F., & Meece, J. L. (1984). Sex differences in achievement: A test of alternate theories. *Journal of Personality and Social Psychology, 46,* 26–43.

Eccles, J. S., Midgley, C., Wigfield, A., Buchanan, C. M., Reuman, D., Flanagan, C., & Maciver, P. (1993). Development during adolescence: The impact of stage–environmental fit on young adolescents' experiences in schools and families. *American Psychologist, 48,* 90.

Eggen, P., & Kauchak, D. (1997). *Windows on classrooms* (3rd ed.). Columbus, OH: Charles E. Merrill.

Ehrhart, J., & Sandler, B. (1987). *Looking for more than a few good women in traditional male fields: Project on the status and education of women.* Washington, DC: U.S. Department of Labor.

Eisen, V., & Hall, I. (1996). Youth voices. *Harvard Educational Review, 66,* 173–197.

Elkind, D. (1980). Child development and counseling. *Personnel and Guidance Journal, 58,* 353–355.

Elksnin, L. K., & Elksnin, N. (1990). Using collaborative consultation with parents to promote effective vocational programming. *Career Development for Exceptional Individuals, 13,* 135–142.

Elliott, J. E. (1993). Career development with lesbian and gay clients. *Career Development Quarterly, 41,* 210–226.

Enderlein, T. (1976). *A review of career education evaluation studies.* Washington, DC: U.S. Department of Health, Education and Welfare, Office of Education, Office of Career Education. (ERIC Document Reproduction Service No. 159 445)

Erikson, E. H. (1963). *Childhood and society* (2nd ed.). New York: Norton.

Erikson, E. H. (1968). *Identity: Youth and crisis.* New York: Norton.

Evanoski, P. O., & Tse, F. W. (1989). Career awareness program for Chinese and Korean American parents. *Journal of Counseling & Development, 67,* 472–474.

Evans, J. H., Jr., & Burck, H. D. (1992). The effects of career education interventions on academic achievement: A meta-analysis. *Journal of Counseling & Development, 71,* 63–68.

Evans, K. M., & Herr, E. L. (1991). The influence of racism and sexism in the career development of African American women. *Journal of Multicultural Counseling and Development, 19,* 130–135.

Evans, R. N., & Herr, E. L. (1978). *Foundations of vocational education* (2nd ed.). Columbus, OH: Charles E. Merrill.

Faas, L. A., & D'Alonzo, B. (1990). WAIS–R scores as predictors of employment success and failure among adults with learning disabilities. *Journal of Learning Disabilities, 23,* 311–316.

Farber, B. (1963). Interaction with retarded siblings and life goals of children. *Marriage and Family Living, 25,* 96–98.

Farley, J. E. (1982). *Majority–minority relations.* Englewood Cliffs, NJ: Prentice Hall.

Farmer, H. (1978). Why women choose careers below their potential. In L. S. Hansen & R. S. Rapoza (Eds.), *Career development and counseling of women* (pp. 31–54), Springfield, IL: Charles C Thomas.

Federal Register. (1978, May 4). Washington, DC: Government Printing Office.

Felix-Ortiz, M., & Newcomb, M. D. (1992). Risk and protective factors for drug use among Latino and White adolescents. *Hispanic Journal of Behavioral Sciences, 14,* 291–309.

Fennema, E., & Peterson, P. L. (1986). Teacher student interactions and sex-related differences in learning mathematics. *Teaching and Teacher Education, 2*(1), 19–42.

Fine, M., & Holt, P. (1981, August). *The family–school relationship: A systems perspective.* Paper presented at the 89th Annual Convention of the American Psychological Association, Los Angeles.

Fischer, L., & Sorenson, G. P. (1991). *School law for counselors, psychologists, and social workers* (2nd ed.). New York: Longman.

Fisher, I. (1989). *Midlife change.* Unpublished doctoral dissertation, Teachers College, Columbia University.

Fitzgerald, L. F., & Betz, N. E. (1994). Career development in a cultural context: The role of gender, race, class, and sexual orientation. In M. L. Savickas & R. W. Lent (Eds.), *Convergence in career development theories: Implications for science and practice* (pp. 103–117). Palo Alto, CA: Consulting Psychologists Press.

Fitzgerald, L. F., & Crites, J. O. (1980). Toward a career psychology of women: What do we know? What do we need to know? *Journal of Counseling Psychology, 27,* 44–62.

Flanagan, C. A. (1990). Change in the family work status: Effects on parent–adolescent decision making. *Child Development, 61,* 163–177.

Florida State Department of Education. (1988). *Florida blueprint for career preparation.* Tallahassee, FL: Author.

Foss, C. J., & Slaney, R. B. C. (1986). Increasing nontraditional career choices in women: Relation of attitudes toward women and responses to a career intervention. *Journal of Vocational Behavior, 28,* 191–202.

Fossey, R. (1996). School dropout rates: Are we sure they are going down? *Phi Delta Kappan, 78,* 140–144.

Fouad, N. A. (1993). Cross-cultural vocational assessment. *Career Development Quarterly, 42,* 4–13.

Fouad, N. A. (1994). Annual review 1991–1993: Vocational choice, decision-making, assessment, and intervention. *Journal of Vocational Behavior, 45,* 125–176.

Fouad, N. A., & Bingham, R. (1995). Career counseling with racial/ethnic minorities. In W. B. Walsh & S. H. Osipow (Eds.), *Handbook of vocational psychology* (2nd ed., pp. 110–123). Hillsdale, NJ: Erlbaum.

Fraser, S. (1995). *The bell curve wars: Race, intelligence, and the future of America.* New York: Basic Books.

Fretz, B. R., & Leong, F. T. L. (1982). Vocational behavior and career development, 1981: A review. *Journal of Vocational Behavior, 21,* 123–163.

Friends of Project Inc. (1991). *Project 10 handbook: Addressing lesbian and gay issues in our schools. A resource directory for teachers, guidance counselors, parents and school-based adolescent care providers* (3rd ed.). Ann Arbor: University of Michigan. (ERIC Document Reproduction Service No. 337–567)

Fullerton, H., Jr. (1987, September). *Projections 2000: Labor force projections—1986 to 2000 (Monthly Labor Review).* Washington, DC: U.S. Department of Labor.

Gade, E. M., Fuqua, D., & Hurlburt, G. (1988). The relationship of Holland's personality types to education satisfaction with a Native American high school population. *Journal of Counseling Psychology, 35,* 183–186.

Gade, E. M., Hurlburt, G., & Fuqua, D. (1992). The use of the Self-Directed Search to identify American Indian high school dropouts. *The School Counselor, 39,* 311–315.

Gallup Organization, Inc. (1987). *Career development survey* (conducted for National Career Development Association). Princeton, NJ: Author.

Gardner, H. (1987). Developing the spectrum of human intelligence. *Harvard Education Review, 57*(1), 187–193.

Gassin, E. A., Kelly, K. R., & Feldhusen, J. F. (1993). Sex differences in the career development of gifted youth. *The School Counselor, 41,* 90–96.

Gelatt, H. B. (1962). Decision-making: A conceptual frame of reference for counseling. *Journal of Counseling Psychology, 9,* 240–245.

Gelso, C. J., & Fretz, B. R. (1992). *Counseling psychology.* Orlando, FL: Holt, Rinehart & Winston.

Gerstein, M., Lichtman, M., & Barokas, J. U. (1988). Occupational plans of adolescent women compared to men: A cross-sectional examination. *Career Development Quarterly, 36,* 222–230.

Gerstel, C. J., Feraios, A. J., & Herdt, G. (1989). Widening circles: An ethnographic profile of a youth group. *Journal of Homosexuality, 17,* 75–92.

Ghiselli, E. E. (1966). *The validity of occupational aptitude tests.* New York : Wiley.

Gibbs, J. T. (1990). Mental health issues of Black adolescents: Implications for policy and practice. In A. R. Stiffman & L. E. Davis (Eds.), *Ethnic issues in adolescent mental health* (pp. 21–52). Newbury Park, CA: Sage.

Gibbs, J. T., & Hines, A. M. (1992). Negotiating ethnic identity: Issues for Black–White biracial adolescents. In M. P. P. Root (Ed.), *Racially mixed people in America* (pp. 23–238). Newbury Park, CA: Sage.

Gibson, P. (1989). *Gay male and lesbian youth suicide* (Report of the DHHS Secretary's task force on youth suicide). Washington, DC: U.S. Department of Health and Human Services.

Gibson, J. T., & Associates. (1991). Youth and culture: A seventeen nation study of perceived problems and coping strategies. *International Journal for the Advancement of Counselling, 14,* 203–216.

Gibson, R. L. (1972). *Career development in the elementary school.* Columbus, OH: Charles E. Merrill.

Gibson, R. L., & Mitchell, M. H. (1995). *Introduction to counseling and guidance* (4th ed.). Englewood Cliffs, NJ: Merrill.

Gibson, R. L., Mitchell, M. H., & Basile, S. K. (1993). *Counseling in the elementary school.* Boston: Allyn & Bacon.

Gilbert, M. J. (1989). Alcohol use among Latino adolescents: What we know and what we need to know. *Drugs and Society, 3,* 39–57.

Gilbert, P. (1994). "And they lived happily ever after": Cultural storylines and the construction of gender. In A. H. Dyson & C. Genishi (Eds.), *The need for story: Cultural diversity in classroom and community* (pp. 124–144). Urbana, IL: National Council Teachers of English.

Gilbride, D. D. (1993). Parental attitudes toward their child with a disability: Implications for rehabilitation counselors. *Rehabilitation Counseling Bulletin, 36,* 139–150.

Ginsburg, H., & Operr, S. (1988). *Piaget's theory of intellectual development* (2nd ed.). Englewood Cliffs, NJ: Prentice Hall.

Ginzberg, E. (1972). Toward a theory of occupational choice: A restatement. *Vocational Guidance Quarterly, 20,* 169–176.

Ginzberg, E. (1984). Career development. In D. Brown & L. Brooks (Eds.), *Career choice and development* (pp. 281–355). San Francisco: Jossey-Bass.

Ginzberg, E., Ginsburg, S. W., Axelrad, S., & Herma, J. L. (1951). *Occupational choice: An approach to general theory.* New York: Columbia University Press.

Gladding, S. T. (1991). *Group work: A counseling specialty.* New York: Harper & Row.

Glasser, W. (1969). *Schools without failure.* New York: Harper & Row.

Goldenberg, H., & Goldenberg, I. (1994). *Counseling today's families* (2nd ed.). Pacific Grove, CA: Brooks/Cole.

Goldman, L. (1990). Qualitative assessment. *The Counseling Psychologist, 18,* 205–213.

Goleman, D. (1990, July 10). Homophobia: Scientists find clues to its roots. *The New York Times,* pp. C1, C11.

Gollnick, D., & Chinn, P. (1994). *Multicultural education in a pluralistic society* (4th ed.). New York: Merrill/Macmillian.

Gonsiorek, J. C. (1988). Mental health issues of gay and lesbian adolescents. *Journal of Adolescent Heath Care, 9,* 114–122.

Good, T., & Brophy, J. (1995). *Contemporary educational psychology* (5th ed.). White Plains, NY: Longman.

Gottfredson, G. D., Holland, J. L., & Ogawa, D. K. (1982). *Dictionary of Holland occupational codes.* Palo Alto, CA: Consulting Psychologists Press.

Gottfredson, L. S. (1981). Circumscription and compromise: A developmental theory of occupational aspirations. *Journal of Counseling Psychology, 28,* 545–579.

Gottfredson, L. S. (1983). Creating and criticizing theory. *Journal of Vocational Behavior, 23,* 203–212.

Gottfredson, L. S. (1984). *The role of intelligence and education in the division of labor* (Center for Social Organization of Schools Report No. 355). Baltimore: Johns Hopkins University Press.

Gottfredson, L. S. (1986). Special groups and the beneficial use of vocational interest inventories. In W. B. Walsh & S. H. Osipow (Eds.), *Advances in vocational psychology: Vol. 1. Assessment of interests* (pp. 140–176). Hillsdale, NJ: Erlbaum.

Gottfredson, L. S. (1990, December 6). When job-testing "fairness" is nothing but a quota. *The Wall Street Journal,* p. 23.

Gould, R. (1978). *Transformations.* New York: Simon & Schuster.

Gould, S. J. (1994, November 28). Curveball. *The New Yorker,* 11–16.

Gramick, J. (1983). Homophobia: A new challenge. *Social Work, 28,* 137–141.

Grant, L. (1985). Black females' "place" in desegregated classrooms. *Sociology of Education, 57,* 98–110.

Green, L. B., & Parker, H. J. (1965). Parental influence upon adolescents' occupational choice: A test of an aspect of Roe's theory. *Journal of Counseling Psychology, 12,* 379–383.

Green, R. (1987). *The "sissy boy" syndrome and the development of homosexuality.* New Haven, CT: Yale University Press.

Greenlee, S. P., Damarin, F. L., & Walsh, W. B. (1988). Congruence and differentiation among Black and White males in two non-college-degreed occupations. *Journal of Vocational Behavior, 32,* 298–306.

Gross, J. (1996, January 14). Groups encourage redefining America's view of race. *Arkansas Democrat Gazette,* p. 12A.

Grossman, F. (1972). *Brothers and sisters of retarded children: An exploratory study.* New York: Syracuse University Press.

Grossman, H. (1984). *Educating Hispanic students: Cultural implications for instruction, classroom management, counseling, and assessment.* Springfield, IL: Charles C Thomas.

Grossman. H. (1990). *Trouble free teaching: Solutions to behavior problems in the classroom.* Mountain View, CA: Mayfield.

Grossman, H. (1995). *Teaching in a diverse society.* Boston: Allyn & Bacon.

Grossman, H., & Grossman, S. H. (1994). *Gender issues in education.* Boston: Allyn & Bacon.

Guidubaldi, J., Perry, J. D., & Walker, M. (1989). Assessment strategies for students with disabilities. *Journal of Counseling & Development, 68,* 160–165.

Gysbers, N. C. (1988). Career guidance: A professional heritage and future challenge. In G. R. Walz (Ed.), *Building strong school counseling programs* (pp. 99–122). Alexandria, VA: American Association for Counseling and Development.

Gysbers, N. C. (1990). *Comprehensive guidance programs that work.* Ann Arbor: University of Michigan. (ERIC/CAPS Document Reproduction Service No. ED 314 660).

Gysbers, N. C., & Henderson, P. (1994). *Developing and managing your school guidance program* (2nd ed.). Alexandria, VA: American Association for Counseling and Development.

Gysbers, N. C., Hughey, K., Starr, M., & Lapan, R. T. (1992). Improving school guidance programs: A framework for program, personnel, and results evaluation. *Journal of Counseling & Development, 70,* 565–570.

Gysbers, N. C., & Moore, E. J. (1975). Beyond career development—Life career development. *Personnel and Guidance Journal, 53,* 647–652.

Gysbers, N. C., & Moore, E. J. (1987). *Career counseling: Skills and techniques for practitioners.* Englewood Cliffs, NJ: Prentice Hall.

Haase, R. F., Reed, C. F., Winer, J. L., & Bodden, J. L. (1979). Effect of positive, negative, and mixed occupational information on cognitive and affective complexity. *Journal of Vocational Behavior, 15,* 294–301.

Hackett, G. (1991). Career-efficacy measurement: Reactions to Osipow. *Journal of Counseling & Development, 70,* 330–331.

Hackett, G., & Betz, N. E. (1981). A self-efficacy approach to the career development of women. *Journal of Vocational Behavior, 18,* 326–339.

Haladyna, T. M., Nolen, S. B., & Hass, N. S. (1991). Raising standard achievement scores and the origins of test score pollution. *Educational Researcher, 20*(5), 2–7.

Hallinan, M. T., & Sorensen, A. B. (1987). Ability grouping and sex differences in mathematics achievement. *Sociology of Education, 60*(2), 63–72.

Hamburg, D. A., & Takaniski, R. (1989). Preparing for life: The critical transition of adolescence. *American Psychologist, 44,* 825–827.

Hannon, J. E., Ritchie, M. R., & Rye, D. A. (1992, September). *Class: The missing dimension in multicultural counseling and counselor education.* Paper presented at the Association for Counselor Education and Supervision National Conference, San Antonio, TX.

Hansen, L. S., Klaurens, M. K., & Tennyson, W. W. (1972). *Life styles and work: A career education resource guide.* St. Paul: Minnesota Department of Education, Pupil Personnel Services Section.

Hansen, L. S., & Tennyson, W. W. (1975). A career management model for counselor involvement. *Personnel and Guidance Journal, 53,* 638–646.

Harrington, T. F., & O'Shea, A. J. (1982). *Career Decision-Making System manual.* Circle Pines, MN: American Guidance Service.

Harry, J. (1991). Sexual identity issues: In L. Davidson & M. Linnoila (Eds.), *Risk factors for youth suicide* (pp. 115–122). New York: Hemisphere.

Hartman, B. W., Fuqua, D. R., & Blum, C. R. (1985). A path-analytic model of career indecision. *Vocational Guidance Quarterly, 33,* 231–240.

Havighurst, R. J. (1964). Youth in exploration and man emergent. In H. Borow (Ed.), *Man in a world of work* (pp. 215–236). Boston: Houghton Mifflin.

Havighurst, R. J. (1972). *Developmental tasks and education* (3rd ed.). New York: David McKay.

Haviland, M. G., & Hanson, J.-I. C. (1987). Criterion validity of the Strong–Campbell Interest Inventory for American Indian college students. *Measurement and Evaluation in Counseling and Development, 20,* 196–201.

Haycock, K. (1991). Reaching for the year 2000. *Childhood Education, 67,* 276–279.

Hayes-Bautista, D. E., & Chapa, J. (1987). Latino terminology: Conceptual bases for standardized terminology. *American Journal of Public Health, 77,* 61–68.

Heacock, D. R. (1990). Suicidal behavior in Black and Hispanic youth. *Psychiatric Annals, 20,* 134–142.

Heal, L. W., Copher, J. L., & Rusch, F. R. (1990). Interagency agreements (IAAs) among agencies responsible for the transition education of students with handicaps from secondary schools to post school settings. *Career Development for Exceptional Individuals, 13,* 121–128.

Hearn, J. C., & Moos, R. H. (1978). Subject matter and classroom climate: A test of Holland's environmental propositions. *American Educational Research Journal, 15,* 111–124.

Heinz, K. (1987). An examination of sex occupational role presentations of female characters in children's picture books. *Women's Studies in Communication, 11,* 67–78.

Helwig, A. A. (1984). Increasing vocational self-awareness in high school students. *The School Counselor, 32,* 61–66.

Henderson, A. (1988). Best friends. *Phi Delta Kappan, 70,* 149–153.

Herbert, T. P. (1991). Meeting the affective needs of bright boys through bibliography. *Roeper Review, 13,* 207–212.

Herek, G. M. (1990). Gay people and government security clearances. *American Psychologist, 45,* 1035–1042.

Hernandez, T. J. (1995). The career trinity: Puerto Rican college students and their struggle for identity and power. *Journal of Multicultural Counseling and Development, 23,* 103–115.

Heron, A. (Ed.). (1994). *Two teenagers in twenty: Writings by gay and lesbian youth.* Boston: Alyson.

Herr, E. L. (1969). *Unifying an entire system of education around a career development theme.* Washington, DC: U.S. Department of Health, Education, and Welfare, Office of Career Education, Bureau of Adult Education. (ERIC Document Reproduction Service No. ED 045 860)

Herr, E. L. (1977). Vocational planning: An alternative view. *Personnel and Guidance Journal, 56,* 25–27.

Herr, E. L. (1978). *Research in career education: The state of the art.* Columbus, OH: ERIC Clearinghouse for Career Education.

Herr, E. L. (1990, August). *Counseling for personal flexibility in a global economy.* Plenary paper presented at the 14th World Congress, Counseling in a Global Economy, of the International Association for Educational and Vocational Guidance, Montreal, Quebec, Canada.

Herr, E. L. (1994, July). *The role of schools, universities, and enterprises in human resource development of the work force for the 21st century.* Paper presented at the XVI International Conference on Human Resources, Guidance and Labour, Madrid, Spain.

Herr, E. L., & Cramer, S. H. (1984). *Career guidance and counseling through the life span: Systematic approaches.* Boston: Little, Brown.

Herr, E. L., & Cramer, S. H. (1987). *Controversies in the mental health professions.* Muncie, IN: Accelerated Development.

Herr, E. L., & Cramer, S. H. (1996). *Career guidance and counseling through the life span: Systematic approaches* (5th ed.). New York: Harper Collins.

Herring, R. D. (1990a). Attacking career myths among Native Americans: Implications for counseling. *The School Counselor, 38,* 13–18.

Herring, R. D. (1990b). Nonverbal communication: A necessary component of cross-cultural counseling. *Journal of Multicultural Counseling and Development, 18,* 172–179.

Herring, R. D. (1995). Creating culturally compatible classrooms: Roles of the school counselor. *North Dakota Journal of Counseling and Development, 1,* 28–33.

Herring, R. D. (1997a). *Counseling diverse ethnic youth: Synergetic strategies and interventions for school counselors.* Fort Worth, TX: Harcourt Brace.

Herring, R. D. (1997b). *Multicultural counseling in schools: A synergetic approach.* Alexandria, VA: American Counseling Association.

Herring, R. D., & Walker, S. S. (1993). Synergetic counseling: Toward a more holistic model with a cross-cultural specific approach. *Texas Counseling Association Journal, 22,* 38–53.

Herring, R. D., & White, L. (1995). School counselors, teachers, and the culturally compatible classroom: Partnerships in multicultural education. *Journal for the Professional Counselor, 34,* 52–64.

Hershenson, D. B. (1974). Vocational guidance of the handicapped. In E. L. Herr (Ed.), *Vocational guidance and human development* (pp. 478–501). Boston: Houghton Mifflin.

Hetherington, C., Hillerbrand, E., & Etringer, B. (1989). Career counseling with gay men: Issues and recommendations for research. *Journal of Counseling & Development, 67,* 452–454.

Hetherington, C., & Orzek, A. (1989). Career counseling and life planning with lesbian women. *Journal of Counseling & Development, 68,* 52–57.

Hetrick, E. S., & Martin, A. D. (1987). Developmental issues and the irresolution for gay and lesbian adolescents. *Journal of Homosexuality, 14,* 13–24.

Higginbotham, H. N. (1979). Culture and mental health services. In A. J. Marsella, G. DeVos, & F. L. K. Hsu (Eds.), *Perspectives on cross-cultural psychology* (pp. 307–332). New York: Academic Press.

Hill, K. T. (1980). *Eliminating motivational causes of test bias* (Final report, October 1, 1976, through March 31, 1980). Ann Arbor: University of Michigan. (ERIC Document Reproduction Service No. ED 196–936)

Hilliard, A. G., III. (1985). Multicultural dimensions to counseling and human development in an age of technology. *Journal of Non-White Concerns, 13*(1), 17–27.

Hinkle, J. S. (1992). Computer-assisted career guidance and single-subject research: A scientist–practitioner approach to accountability. *Journal of Counseling & Development, 70,* 391–395.

Hinkle, J. S. (1993). Training school counselors to do family counseling. *Elementary School Guidance and Counseling, 27,* 252–257.

Hispanic Research Center. (1991). *Background and demand for engineering training and need for professional engineers in South Texas.* San Antonio: University of Texas Press.

Ho, M. K. (1992). *Minority children and adolescents in therapy.* Newbury Park, CA: Sage.

Hoar, W. (1992, April). *Title II of the Americans With Disabilities Act.* Paper presented by the Disability Rights, Education and Defense Fund, Little Rock, AR.

Hodgkinson, H. (1985). *All one system: Demographics of education, kindergarten through graduate school.* Washington, DC: Institute for Educational Leadership.

Hoffman, L. R., & McDaniels, C. (1991). Career development in the elementary schools: A perspective for the 1990s. *Elementary School Guidance and Counseling, 25,* 163–171.

Holahan, W., & Gibson, S. A. (1994). Heterosexual therapists leading lesbian and gay therapy groups: Therapeutic and political realities. *Journal of Counseling & Development, 72,* 591–594.

Holland, J. L. (1963). Explanation of a theory of vocational choice: Vocational images and choices. *Vocational Guidance Quarterly, 11,* 232–239.

Holland, J. L. (1966). *The psychology of vocational choice.* Waltham, MA: Blaisdell.

Holland, J. L. (1970). *Self-directed search.* Palo Alto, CA: Consulting Psychologists Press.

Holland, J. L. (1973). *Making vocational choices: A theory of careers.* Englewood Cliffs, NJ: Prentice Hall.

Holland, J. L. (1984, August). *A theory of careers: Some new developments and revisions.* Paper presented at the 92nd Annual Convention of the American Psychological Association, Toronto, Ontario, Canada.

Holland, J. L. (1985a). *Making vocational choices: A theory of vocational personalities and work environments* (2nd ed.). Englewood, Cliffs, NJ: Prentice Hall.

Holland, J. L. (1985b). *The Self-Directed Search professional manual.* Palo Alto, CA: Consulting Psychologists Press.

Holland, J. L. (1987). *1987 manual supplement for the Self-Directed Search.* Odessa, FL: Psychological Assessment Resources.

Holland, J. L. (1994a). *Self-Directed Search (SDS) Form R* (4th ed.). Odessa, FL: Psychological Assessment Resources.

Holland, J. L. (1994b). *Self-Directed Search (SDS) Form R assessment booklet* (4th ed.). Odessa, FL: Psychological Assessment Resources.

Holland, J. L. (1996). *Professional manual Self-Directed Search.* Odessa, FL: Psychological Assessment Resources.

Holland, J. L., Daiger, D. C., & Power, P. G. (1980). *My vocational situation.* Palo Alto, CA: Consulting Psychologists Press.

Holland, J. L., Fritzsche, B. A., & Powell, A. B. (1994). *Technical manual for the self-directed search.* Odessa, FL: Psychological Assessment Resources.

Holland, J. L., & Gottfredson, G. D. (1990). *An annotated bibliography for Holland's theory of vocational personality and work environment.* Baltimore: Johns Hopkins University Press.

Holland, J. L., & Holland, J. E. (1977). Distributions of personalities within occupations and fields of study. *Vocational Guidance Quarterly, 25,* 226–231.

Holland, J. L., Magoon, T. M., & Spokane, A. R. (1981). Counseling psychology: Career interventions, research, and theory. *Annual Review of Psychology, 32,* 279–300.

Homma-True, R., Greene, B., Lopez, S. R., & Trimble, J. E. (1993). Ethnocultural diversity in clinical psychology. *The Clinical Psychologist, 46,* 50–63.

Hope, S. K., & Martin, H. W. (1986). Patterns of suicide among Mexican-Americans and Anglos, 1960–1980. *Social Psychiatry, 21,* 83–88.

Hoppock, R. (1976). *Occupational information.* New York: McGraw-Hill.

Horn, L. (1990, April). *Trends in high school math and science course taking: Effects of gender and ethnicity.* Paper presented at the annual meeting of the American Educational Research Association, Boston, MA.

Hoshmand, L. L. S. T. (1989). Alternate research paradigms: A review and teaching proposal. *The Counseling Psychologist, 17,* 3–79.

Hosie, T. W. (1979). Preparing counselors to meet the needs of the handicapped. *American Personnel and Guidance Journal, 59,* 271–275.

Hosie, T. W., Patterson, J. B., & Hollingsworth, D. K. (1989). School and rehabilitation counselor preparation: Meeting the needs of individuals with disabilities. *Journal of Counseling & Development, 68,* 171–176.

Hotchkiss, L., & Vetter, L. (1987). *Outcomes of career guidance and counseling.* Columbus, OH: National Center for Research in Vocational Education.

Hough, L. M., Eaton, N. K., Dunnette, M. D., Kamp, J. D., & McCloy, R. A. (1990). Criterion-related validity of personality constructs and the effect of response distortion on those validities. *Journal of Applied Psychology Monograph, 75,* 581–595.

House, R. M. (1991). Counseling gay and lesbian clients. In D. Capuzzi & D. R. Grow (Eds.), *Introduction to counseling: Perspectives for the 1990s* (pp. 56–81). Boston: Allyn & Bacon.

Hoyt, K. B. (1976). *Refining the career education concept.* Washington, DC: U.S. Department of Health, Education and Welfare, Office of Education, Office of Career Education. (ERIC Document Reproduction Service No. ED 132 367)

Hoyt, K. B. (1978). *Refining the concept of collaboration in career education: Monographs on Career Education.* Washington, DC: U.S. Office of Education.

Hoyt, K. B. (1980). *Evaluation of K–12 career education: A status report.* Washington, DC: U.S. Office of Career Education.

Hoyt, K. B. (1984). Career education and career guidance. *Journal of Career Education, 10,* 148–157.

Hoyt, K. B. (1985). Career guidance, educational reform, and career education. *Vocational Guidance Quarterly, 34*(1), 6–14.

Hoyt, K. B. (1988). The changing work force: A review of projections—1986–1990. *Career Development Quarterly, 37,* 31–39.

Hoyt, K. B. (1989). The career status of women and minority persons: A 20-year retrospective. *Career Development Quarterly, 37,* 202–212.

Hoyt, K. B., & Lester, J. N. (1995). *Learning to work: The NCDA Gallup survey.* Alexandria, VA: National Career Development Association.

Hoyt, K. B., & Shylo, K. R. (1989). *Career education in transition: Trends and implications for the future.* Columbus, OH: National Center for Research in Vocational Education.

Huang, L. N. (1994). An integrative view of identity formation: A model for Asian Americans. In E. P. Salett & D. R. Koslow (Eds.), *Race, ethnicity, and self-identity in multicultural perspective* (pp. 42–61). Washington, DC: National MultiCultural Institute.

Hughey, K. F., Lapan, R. T., & Gysbers, N. C. (1993). Evaluating a high school Guidance-Language Arts Career Unit: A qualitative approach. *The School Counselor, 41,* 96–101.

Humes, C. W. (1992). Career planning implications for learning disabled high school students using the MBTI and SDS–E. *The School Counselor, 39,* 362–368.

Hummel, D. L., & McDaniels, C. (1982). *Unlock your child's potential.* Washington, DC: Acropolis.

Hurlburt, G., Schulz, W., & Eide, L. (1985). Using the Self-Directed Search with American Indian high school students. *Journal of American Indian Education, 25*(1), 34–41.

Huston, A. C. (1983). Sex-typing. In E. M. Hetherington (Ed.), *Handbook of child psychology: Vol. 4. Socialization, personality, and social development* (4th ed., pp. 183–217). New York: Wiley.

Hyde, J., & Fennema, E. (1990, April). *Gender differences in mathematics performance and affect: Results of two meta-analyses.* Paper presented at the annual meeting of the American Educational Research Association, Boston, MA.

Iachan, R. (1984). A measure of agreement for use with the Holland classification system. *Journal of Vocational Behavior, 24,* 133–141.

Ibrahim, F. A. (1991). Contribution of cultural worldview to generic counseling and development. *Journal of Counseling & Development, 70,* 13–19.

Imber-Black, E. (1988). *Families and larger systems: A family therapist's guide through the labyrinth.* New York: Guilford Press.

Iowa State Department of Education. (1986). *Iowa K–12 career guidance curriculum: Guide for student development.* Des Moines, IA: Author. (ERIC Document Reproduction Service No. ED 273 873)

Isaacson, L. E., & Brown, D. (1993). *Career information, career counseling, and career development* (5th ed.). Boston: Allyn & Bacon.

Isralowitz, R. E., & Singer, M. (1986). Unemployment and its impact on adolescent work values. *Adolescence, 21*(81), 145–158.

Jackson, P. (1992). *Untaught lessons.* New York: Teachers College Press.

James, A. (1993). *Childhood identities: Self and social relationships in the experience
of the child.* Edinburgh, Scotland: Edinburgh University Press.

Jensen, A. R. (1980). *Bias in mental testing.* New York: Free Press.

Jepsen, D., Dustin, R., & Miars, R. (1982). The effects of problem-solving training on adolescents' career exploration and career decision-making. *Journal
of Counseling & Development, 61,* 149–153.

Jervis, K. (1995). "How come there are no brothers on that list?": Hearing
the hard questions all children ask. *Harvard Educational Review, 66*(3),
546–576.

Johnson, R. H., & Myrick, R. D. (1971). MOLD: A new approach to career
decision making. *Vocational Guidance Quarterly, 21,* 48–53.

Johnson, S. D. (1990). Toward clarifying culture, race, and ethnicity in the
context of multicultural counseling. *Journal of Multicultural Counseling and
Development, 18,* 41–50.

Jones, A. J. (1945). *Principles of guidance.* New York: McGraw-Hill.

Jones, A. J. (1970). *Principles of guidance* (6th ed., revised and updated by
B. Stefflre and N. R. Stewart). New York: McGraw-Hill.

Jones, E. E., Kanouse, D. E., Kelley, H. H., Nisbett, R. E., Valins, S., & Weiner,
B. (Eds.). (1971). *Attribution: Perceiving the causes of behavior.* Morristown, NJ:
General Learning Press.

Jones, E. E., Krupnick, J. L., & Kerig, P. K. (1987). Some gender effects in a
brief psychotherapy. *Psychotherapy , 24,* 373–352.

Jones, L. K. (1983). Occ-U-Sort Kit: Educational and career guidance through
the library. *Personnel and Guidance Journal, 61,* 628–631.

Jones, L. K. (1990). *The career key.* Raleigh, NC: Author. (Original work published 1987)

Jones, L. K. (1993). Two career guidance instruments: Their helpfulness to students and effect on student's career exploration. *The School Counselor, 40,*
191–200.

June, L. N., & Pringle, G. D. (1977). The concept of race in the career development theories of Roe, Super, and Holland. *Journal of Non-White Concerns,
6,* 17–24.

Karraker, M. W. (1991). *Predicting adolescent females' plans for higher education:
Race and socioeconomic differences.* Ann Arbor: University of Michigan. (ERIC
Document Reproduction Service No. ED 337 517)

Katz, J. H. (1985). The sociopolitical nature of counseling. *The Counseling Psychologist, 13,* 615–624.

Kelly, A., & Smail, B. (1986). Sex stereotypes and attitudes to science among
eleven-year-old children. *British Journal of Educational Psychology, 56,*
158–168.

Kelly, K. R., & Cobb, S. J. (1991). A profile of the career development characteristics of young gifted adolescents: Examining gender and multicultural
differences. *Roeper Review, 13,* 202–206.

Kerr, B. A. (1985). *Smart girls, gifted women.* Columbus, OH: Ohio Psychology
Publishing.

Kerr, G., & Colangelo, N. (1988). College plans of academically talented students. *Journal of Counseling & Development, 67,* 42–48.

Keyes, K. L. (1989). The counselor's role in helping students with limited English proficiency. *The School Counselor, 37,* 144–148.

Kiernan, L. (1996, September 6). From welfare to work: A first experiment. *Arkansas Democrat Gazette,* p. 3A.

Kimmel, D. C., & Weiner, I. B. (1985). *Adolescence: A developmental transition.* Hillsdale, NJ: Erlbaum.

King, S. (1989). Sex differences in a causal model of career maturity. *Journal of Counseling & Development, 68,* 208–215.

Kinloch, G. (1979). *The sociology of minority group relations.* Englewood Cliffs, NJ: Prentice Hall.

Kinnier, R. T., Brigman, S. L., & Noble, F. C. (1990). Career indecision and family enmeshment. *Journal of Counseling & Development, 68,* 309–312.

Kiser, J. D. (1996). Travelmates used in career education across the curriculum. *Elementary School Guidance and Counseling, 30,* 259–263.

Kivlighan, D. M., Jr., Johnston, J. A., Hogan, R. S., & Mauer, E. (1994). Who benefits from computerized career counseling? *Journal of Counseling & Development, 72,* 289–292.

Kjos, D. (1989). Understanding and meeting the needs of the career undecided. *IACD Quarterly, 115,* 17–23.

Kjos, D. (1995). Linking career counseling to personality disorders. *Journal of Counseling & Development, 73,* 592–597.

Kleinberg, J. L. (1976). Adolescent correlates of occupational stability and change. *Journal of Vocational Behavior, 9,* 219–232.

Knapp, R. R., & Knapp, L. (1977). *Interest changes and the classification on occupations.* Unpublished manuscript, EdITS, San Diego, CA.

Knapp, R. R., & Knapp, L. (1984). *COPS Interest Inventory technical manual.* San Diego, CA: EdITS.

Knapp, R. R., & Knapp, L. (1985). *California Occupational Preference System: Self-interpretation profile and guide.* San Diego, CA: EdITS.

Knowlton, H. E., & Clark, G. M. (1987). Transition issues for the 1990s. *Exceptional Children, 53,* 562–563.

Kochenberger-Stroeher, S. (1994). Sixteen kindergartners' gender-related views of careers. *Elementary School Journal, 95,* 95–103.

Kohlberg, L. A. (1966). A cognitive developmental analysis of children's sex-role concepts and attitudes. In E. Maccoby (Ed.), *The development of sex differences* (pp. 82–173). Stanford, CA: Stanford University Press.

Kohring, C., & Tracht, V. S. (1978). A new approach to a vocational program for severely handicapped high school students. *Rehabilitation Literature, 39,* 138–146.

Konstam, V., Drainoni, M., Mitchell, G., Houser, R., Reddington, D., & Eaton, D. (1993). Career choices and values of siblings of individuals with developmental disabilities. *The School Counselor, 40,* 287–292.

Korchin, S. J. (1980). Clinical psychology and minority problems. *American Psychologist, 35,* 262–269.

Krathwohl, D. R. (1993). *Methods of educational and social science research: An integrative approach.* New York: Longman.

Krumboltz, J. D. (1979). A social learning theory of career decision making. In A. Mitchell, G. B. Jones, & J. D. Krumboltz (Eds.), *Social learning and career decision making* (pp. 19–49). Cranston, IL: Caroll Press.

Krumboltz, J. D. (1983). *Private rules in career decision making*. Columbus: Ohio State University, National Center for Research in Vocational Education.

Krumboltz, J. D., Mitchell, A. M., & Gellat, H. G. (1975). Applications of social learning theory of career selection. *Focus on Guidance, 8*(3), 1–16.

Krumboltz, J. D., Mitchell, A. M., & Jones, G. B. (1976). A social learning theory of career selection. *The Counseling Psychologist, 6*, 71–81.

Krysiak, G. J. (1987). A very silent and gay minority. *The School Counselor, 34*, 304–307.

Kunce, J. T., & Cope, C. S. (1987). Personal styles analysis. In N. C. Gysbers & E. J. Moore (Eds.), *Career counseling: Skills and techniques for practitioners* (pp. 100–130). Englewood Cliffs, NJ: Prentice Hall.

Kunce, J. T., Cope, C. S., & Newton, R. M. (1986a). *The Personal Styles Inventory*. Columbia, MO: Educational & Psychological Consultants.

Kunce, J. T., Cope, C. S., & Newton, R. M. (1986b). *Personal Styles Inventory: Manual for counselors and clinicians*. Columbia, MO: Educational & Psychological Consultants.

Kunce, J. T., Cope, C. S., & Newton, R. M. (1989). *Personal Styles Inventory: Interpretation guide and scoring directions*. Columbia, MO: Educational & Psychological Consultants.

Kunce, J. T., Cope, C. S., & Newton, R. M. (1991). Personal Styles Inventory. *Journal of Counseling & Development, 70*, 334–341.

Kutscher, R. (1987, September). *Projections 2000: Overview and implications of the projections to 2000 (Monthly Labor Review)*. Washington, DC: U.S. Department of Labor.

Ladson-Billings, G. (1994). *The dreamkeepers: Successful teachers of African American children*. San Francisco: Jossey-Bass.

Lapan, R. T., Gysbers, N., Hughey, K., & Arni, T. J. (1993). Evaluating a guidance and language arts unit for high school juniors. *Journal of Counseling & Development, 71*, 444–451.

Lapan, R. T., Gysbers, N. C., Multon, K. D., & Pike, G. R. (1997). Developing guidance competency self-efficacy scales for high school and middle school students. *Measurement and Evaluation in Counseling and Development, 30*(1), 4–16.

Lapan, R. T., Gysbers, N. C., & Sun, Y. (1997). The impact of more fully implemented guidance programs on the school experiences of high school students: A statewide study. *Journal of Counseling & Development, 75*, 292–302.

Larsen, P., & Shertzer, B. (1987). The high school dropout: Everybody's problem? *The School Counselor, 34*, 163–169.

Larson, J. H., Busby, D. M., Wilson, S., Medora, N., & Allgood, S. (1994). The multidimensional assessment of career decision problems: The Career Decision Diagnostic Assessment. *Journal of Counseling & Development, 72*, 323–328.

Lawson, G. W., & Lawson, A. W. (1989). *Alcoholism and substance abuse in special populations*. Rockville, MD: Aspen.

Layton, P. L. (1984). Self-efficacy, locus of control, career salience, and women's career choice. *Dissertation Abstracts International, 45*, 2672B.

Lee, C. C. (1985). An ethnic group–gender comparison of occupational choice among rural adolescents. *Journal of Non-White Concerns, 13,* 28–37.

Lee, C. C. (Ed.). (1995a). *Counseling for diversity: A guide for school counselors and related professionals.* Boston: Allyn & Bacon.

Lee, C. C. (1995b). Multicultural literacy imperatives for culturally responsive school counseling. In C. C. Lee (Ed.), *Counseling for diversity: A guide for school counselors and related professionals* (pp. 191–198). Boston: Allyn & Bacon.

Lee, C. C., & Richardson, B. (Eds.). (1991). *Multicultural issues in counseling: New approaches to diversity.* Alexandria, VA: American Counseling Association.

Lee, P. (1995). *Super Saiyan and the secrets of life: On the role of animation in Asian-American children's social and composing worlds.* Unpublished manuscript, University of California, Berkeley.

Lee, R. S. (1993). Effects of classroom guidance on student achievement. *Elementary School Guidance and Counseling, 27,* 163–171.

Lefstein, L. M., & Lipsitz, J. (1986). *3:00 to 6:00 p.m.: Program for young adolescents.* Chapel Hill: University of North Carolina, Center for Early Adolescence.

Left, J. (1986). The epidemiology of mental illness. In J. L. Cox (Ed.), *Transcultural psychiatry* (pp. 23–36). London: Croom Helm.

Leifer, A. D., & Lesser, G. S. (1976). *The development of career awareness in young children* (NIE Papers on Education and Work, No. 1). Washington, DC: National Institute of Education.

Lent, R. W., Brown, S. D., & Hackett, G. (1994). Toward a unified theory of career and academic interests, choice, and performance. *Journal of Vocational Behavior, 45,* 79–122.

Lent, R. W., & Hackett, G. (1987). Career self-efficacy: Empirical status and future directions. *Journal of Vocational Behavior, 30,* 347–382.

Leonard, G. E., Jeffries, D., & Spedding, S. (1974). Career guidance in the elementary school. *Elementary School Guidance and Counseling, 9,* 48–51.

Leong, F. T. L. (1991). Career development attributes and occupational values of Asian Americans and White American college students. *Career Development Quarterly, 39,* 221–230.

Leong, F. T. L. (1993). The career counseling process with racial-ethnic minorities: The case of Asian Americans. *Career Development Quarterly, 42,* 26–40.

Lester, J. N., & Frugoli, P. (1989). Career and occupational information: Current needs, future directions. In D. Brown & C. A. Minor (Eds.), *Working in America: A status report on planning and problems* (pp. 60–81). Alexandria, VA: National Career Development Association.

Leung, S. A., Conoley, C. W., & Scheel, M. J. (1994). The career and educational aspirations of gifted high school students: A retrospective study. *Journal of Counseling & Development, 72,* 298–303.

Leung, S. A., & Harmon, L. W. (1990). Individual and sex differences in the zone of acceptable alternatives. *Journal of Counseling Psychology, 37,* 153–159.

Levinson, D. J., Darrow, C. N., Klein, E. B., Levinson, M. H., & McKee, B. (1978). *The seasons of a man's life.* New York: Knopf.

Levinson, E. M. (1987). Vocational assessment and programming of students with handicaps: A need for school counselor involvement. *The School Counselor, 35,* 6–8.

Liddle, B. J. (1996). Therapist sexual orientation, gender, and counseling practices as they relate to ratings of helpfulness by gay and lesbian students. *Journal of Counseling & Development, 43,* 394–401.

Liptak, J. J. (1989). Irrational expectations in the job search process. *Journal of Employment Counseling, 26,* 35–40.

Little, D. M., & Roach, A. J. (1974). Videotape modeling of interest in nontraditional occupations for women. *Journal of Vocational Behavior, 5,* 133–138.

Liu, W. T., Yu, E. S. H., Chang, C. F., & Fernandez, M. (1990). The mental health of Asian American teenagers: A research challenge. In A. R. Stiffman & L. E. Davis (Eds.), *Ethnic issues in adolescent mental health* (pp. 92–112). Newbury Park, CA: Sage.

Lockheed, M. E., & Harris, A. M. (1984). Cross-sex collaborative learning in elementary classrooms. *American Educational Research Journal, 21,* 275–294.

Loganbill, C., Hardy, E., & Delworth, V. (1982). Supervision: A conceptual model. *The Counseling Psychologist, 10,* 1.

Lombana, J. H. (1992). *Guidance of handicapped students.* Springfield, IL: Charles C Thomas.

London, M., & Greller, M. M. (1991). Demographic trends and vocational behavior: A twenty year retrospective and agenda for the 1990s. *Journal of Vocational Behavior, 38,* 125–164.

London, P. (1987). Character education and clinical intervention: A paradigm shift for U.S. schools. *Phi Delta Kappan, 69,* 211–215.

Lonner, W. J., & Ibrahim, F. A. (1989). Assessment in cross-cultural counseling. In P. B. Pedersen, J. Draguns, W. J. Lonner, & J. E. Trimble (Eds.), *Counseling across cultures* (3rd ed., pp. 299–334). Honolulu: University of Hawaii Press.

Lopez, F. G., & Andrews, S. (1987). Career indecision: A family systems perspective. *Journal of Counseling & Development, 65,* 304–307.

Lowman, R. L. (1991). *The clinical practice of career assessment: Interests, abilities, and personality.* Washington, DC: American Psychological Association.

Lowman, R. L. (1993). The Inter-Domain Model of career assessment and counseling. *Journal of Counseling & Development, 71,* 549–554.

Luchins, A. S. (1960). Influences of experiences with conflicting information and reactions to subsequent conflicting information. *Journal of Social Psychology, 5,* 367–385.

Lueptow, L. B. (1984). *Adolescent sex roles and social change.* New York: Columbia University Press.

Lunneborg, P. W. (1981). *The Vocational Interest Inventory (VII) manual.* Los Angeles: Western Psychological Services.

Maccoby, E., & Jacklin, C. (1974). *The psychology of sex differences.* Stanford, CA: Stanford University Press.

MacFarland, R. (1997). Summary of adolescent pregnancy research: Implications for prevention. *The Prevention Researcher, 4,* 5–7.

Madanes, C. (1990). *Sex, love, and violence.* New York: Norton.

Mahan, J. M., & Rains, F. V. (1990). Inservice teachers expand their cultural knowledge and approaches through practice in American Indian communities. *Journal of American Indian Education, 29,* 11–23.

Mahoney, F. E. (1992). Adjusting the interview to avoid cultural bias. *Journal of Career Planning and Employment, 52*(23), 41–43.

Malinowitz, H. (1995). *Textual orientations: Lesbian and gay students and the making of discourse communities.* Portsmouth, NH: Heinemann.

Malone, T. E. (1986). *Report of the Secretary's task force on Black and minority health: Vol. V. Homicide, suicide, and unintentional injuries* (GPO Publication No. 491-313/44710). Washington, DC: U.S. Government Printing Office.

Mamarchev, H. L., & Pritchett, B. (1978). *Career resource centers.* Ann Arbor: University of Michigan, ERIC Counseling & Personnel Services Clearinghouse.

Manaster, G. J., Chan, J. C., & Safady, R. (1992). Mexican-American migrant students' academic success: Sociological and psychological acculturation. *Adolescence, 27*(105), 124–135.

Manson, S. M., & Shore, J. H. (1981). Psychiatric epidemiological research among American Indian and Alaska Natives: Some methodological issues. *White Cloud Journal, 2,* 48–56.

Manson, S. M., Shore, J. H., & Bloom, J. D. (1985). The depressive experience in American Indian communities: A challenge for psychiatric theory and diagnosis. In A. Kleinman & B. Goods (Eds.), *Culture and depression: Studies in the anthropology and cross-cultural psychiatry of affect and disorder* (pp. 331–368). Berkeley: University of California Press.

Marin, G., & Marin, B. V. (1991). *Research with Hispanic populations.* Newbury Park, CA: Sage.

Marjoribanks, K. (1984). Occupational status, family environments, and adolescents' aspirations: The LAOSA model. *Journal of Educational Psychology, 76,* 690–700.

Marjoribanks, K. (1985). Ecological correlates of adolescents' aspirations: Gender-related differences. *Contemporary Educational Psychology, 10,* 329–334.

Marsella, A. J., DeVos, G., & Hsu, F. L. K. (Eds.). (1979). *Perspectives on cross-cultural psychology.* New York: Academic Press.

Martin, A. D. (1982). Learning to hide: Socialization of the gay adolescent. *Adolescent Psychiatry, 10,* 52–65.

Martin, A. D., & Hetrick, E. S. (1988). The stigmatization of the gay and lesbian adolescent. *Journal of Homosexuality, 15,* 163–183.

Martin, D., & Martin, M. (1989). Bridging the gap between research and practice. *Journal of Counseling & Development, 67,* 481–482.

Maruyama, M. (1978). Psychotherapy and its applications to cross-disciplinary, cross-professional, and cross-cultural communication. In R. E. Holloman & S. A. Arutiunov (Eds.), *Perspectives on ethnicity* (pp. 131–156). The Hague, The Netherlands: Mouton.

Maslow, A. H. (1954). *Motivation and personality.* New York: Harper & Row.

Mayhovich, M. K. (1976). Asian Americans—quiet Americans? In H. A. Johnson (Ed.), *Ethnic American minorities: A guide of media and materials* (pp. 24–47). New York: Bowler.

McCarty, D. (1993). Travelmates: Geography for kids (and stuffed pets). *Teaching PreK–8, 23*(7), 32–35.

McDaniels, C. (1978). The practice of career guidance and counseling. *INFORM, 7,* 1–2, 7–8.

McDaniels, C. (1989). *The changing workplace.* San Francisco: Jossey-Bass.

McFarland, W. P. (1993). A developmental approach to gay and lesbian youth. *Journal of Humanistic Education and Development, 32,* 17–29.

McGowan, B. G., & Kohn, A. (1990). Social support and teen pregnancy in policy and practice. In A. R. Stiffman & L. E. Davis (Eds.), *Ethnic issues in adolescent mental health* (pp. 189–207). Newbury Park, CA: Sage.

McIntosh, P. (1988). *White privilege and male privilege: A personal account of coming to see correspondences through work in women's studies* (Working Paper No. 189). Wellesley, MA: Wellesley College Center for Research on Women.

McLoyd, V. C. (1990). Socialization and development in a changing economy: The effects of paternal job and income loss on children. *American Psychologist, 44,* 293–302.

Meece, J. L. (1987). The influence of school experiences on the development of gender schemata. *New Directions for Child Development, 38,* 57–73.

Meir, E. I. (1975). *Manual for the Ramak and Courses Interest Inventories.* Tel Aviv, Israel: Tel Aviv University, Department of Psychology.

Meir, E. I., & Shiran, D. (1979). The Occupational Cylinder as a means for vocational maturity enhancement. *Journal of Vocational Behavior, 14,* 279–283.

Mercier, L., & Berger, R. (1989). Social service needs of lesbian and gay adolescents: Telling it their way. *Journal of Social Work and Human Sexuality, 8,* 75–95.

Miller, A. W. (1968). Learning theory and vocational decisions. *Personnel and Guidance Journal, 47,* 18–23.

Miller, D. C., & Form, W. H. (1951). *Industrial sociology.* New York: Harper & Row.

Miller, J. T. (1977). *Career development with nine-year-olds: How to improve career development programs.* Washington, DC: National Advisory Council for Career Education.

Miller, J. T. (1978). A study of WISC subtest scores as predictors of GATB occupation aptitude patterns for EMH students in a high school occupational course. *Dissertation Abstracts International, 38*(12-A), 7272.

Miller, J. V. (1984). Career development programs and practices in schools. In N. C. Gysbers & Associates (Eds.), *Designing careers* (pp. 443–457). San Francisco: Jossey-Bass.

Miller, M. F. (1974). Relationship of vocational maturity to work values. *Journal of Vocational Behavior, 5,* 367–371.

Miller, M. J. (1985). Counseling Region 99 clients. *Journal of Employment Counseling, 22,* 70–77.

Miller, M. J. (1988). Career counseling for the middle school youngster: Grades 6–9. *Journal of Employment Counseling, 25,* 172–179.

Miller, M. J. (1989). Career counseling for the elementary school child: Grades K–5. *Journal of Employment Counseling, 26,* 169–177.

Miller, M. J., Springer, T. P., & Wells, D. (1988). Which occupational environment do Blacks prefer? Extending Holland's typology. *The School Counselor, 36,* 103–106.

Miller, M. J., & Stanford, J. Y. (1987). Early occupational restriction: An examination of elementary school children's expression of vocational preferences. *Journal of Employment Counseling, 24,* 115–121.

Miller-Tiedeman, A. L. (1980). Explorations of decision making in the expansion of adolescent personal development. In V. L. Erickson & J. M. Whiteley

(Eds.), *Developmental counseling and teaching* (pp. 103–152). Pacific Grove, CA: Brooks/Cole.

Miller-Tiedeman, A. L., & Tiedeman, D. V. (1990). Career decision-making: An individualistic perspective. In D. Brown & L. Brooks (Eds.), *Career choice and development* (2nd ed., pp. 308–337). San Francisco: Jossey-Bass.

Minkler, M., Driver, D., Roe, K., & Bedeian, K. (1993). Community interventions to support grandparent caregivers. *The Gerontologist, 33,* 807–811.

Minuchin, P. P. (1977). *The middle years of childhood.* Monterey, CA: Brooks/Cole.

Minuchin, S., Montalvo, B., Guerney, B. G., Rosman, B. C., & Schumer, F. (1967). *Families of the slums.* New York: Basic Books.

Mitchell, L. K., & Krumboltz, J. D. (1990). Social learning approach to career decision making: Krumboltz's theory. In D. Brown, L. Brooks, & Associates (Eds.), *Career choice and development* (2nd ed., pp. 145–196). San Francisco: Jossey-Bass.

Mitchell, T. (1990). Project 2000 gateway to success for some Black males. *Black Issues in Higher Education, 7*(18), 49–50.

Money, J., & Ehrhardt, A. (1972). *Man and woman, boy and girl: The differentiation and dimorphism of gender identity from conception to maturity.* Baltimore: Johns Hopkins University Press.

Money, J., & Russo, A. (1979). Homosexual outcome of discordant gender identity role in childhood: Longitudinal follow-up. *Journal of Pediatric Psychology, 4,* 29–41.

Moore, M. A., Neimeyer, G. J., & Marmarosh, C. (1992). Effects of informational valiance and occupational favorability on vocational differentiation: A test of the disconfirmation hypothesis. *Journal of Counseling Psychology, 39,* 335–341.

Morris, T. W., & Levinson, E. M. (1995). Relationship between intelligence and occupational adjustment and functioning: A literature review. *Journal of Counseling & Development, 73,* 503–514.

Morris-Van, A. (1981). *Group counseling for children whose parents are unemployed.* Southfield, MI: Aid-U Publishing.

Morrow, M. R. (1995). The influence of dysfunctional family behaviors on adolescent career exploration. *The School Counselor, 42,* 311–316.

Muller, A. (1987). Retrospective distortion in homosexual research. *Archives of Sexual Behavior, 9,* 523–531.

Mullet, E., Neto, F., & Henry, S. (1992). Determinants of occupational preferences in Portuguese and French high school students. *Journal of Cross-Cultural Psychology, 23,* 521–531.

Multon, K. D., & Lapan, R. T. (1995). Developing scales to evaluate career and personal guidance curricula in a high school setting. *Journal of Career Development, 21,* 293–306.

Munch, G. R. (1993). *Getting it together, the practical job search.* Baltimore: Genmet.

Munson, W. W. (1992). Self-esteem, vocational identity, and career salience in high school students. *Career Development Quarterly, 40,* 361–368.

Murphy, P. P., & Burck, H. D. (1976). Career development of men at midlife. *Journal of Vocational Behavior, 9,* 337–343.

Myers, H. F. (1989). Urban stress and mental health of Afro-American youth: An epidemiologic and conceptual update. In R. L. Jones (Ed.), *Black adolescents* (pp. 123–152). Berkeley, CA: Cobbs Henry.

Myers, I. B., & McCaulley, M. H. (1985). *Manual: A guide to the development and use of the Myers–Briggs Type Indicator.* Palo Alto, CA: Consulting Psychologists Press.

Nadolsky, J. M. (1986). Preparing for quality in rehabilitation education. *Journal of Rehabilitation, 52*(2), 7–10.

Nash, S. C. (1975). The relationship among sex-role stereotyping, sex-role preferences, and the sex difference in spatial visualization. *Sex Roles, 1,* 15–32.

National Black Child Development Institute. (1990). *The status of African American children: Twentieth anniversary report.* Washington, DC: Author.

National Career Development Association. (1987). *Planning for and working in America: Report of a national survey.* Alexandria, VA: Author.

National Career Development Association. (1991). *Position paper approved by the Board of Directors.* Columbus, OH: Author.

National Center for Educational Statistics. (1984). *High school seniors: A comparative study of the classes of 1972 and 1980.* Washington, DC: U.S. Government Printing Office.

National Center for Educational Statistics. (1995). *Digest of education statistics 1995.* Washington, DC: U.S. Department of Education.

National Coalition of Advocates for Students. (1988). *New voices: Immigrant students in U.S. public schools.* Boston: Author.

National Institute on Drug Abuse. (1988). *National household survey on drug abuse: Main finding 1985* (DHHA Publication No. ADM 88-1565). Washington, DC: U.S. Government Printing Office.

National Occupational Information Coordinating Committee. (1988). *The National Career Counseling and Development Guidelines—Postsecondary Institutions.* Washington, DC: Author.

National Occupational Information Coordinating Committee. (1990a, January 11). *Almost two thirds of Americans would seek more information about career options if they had it to do over again, new survey finds* (Press release). Washington, DC: Author.

National Occupational Information Coordinating Committee. (1990b). Status of NOICC/SOICC Network 1989: Administrative report 14. Washington, DC: Author.

National Opinion Research Center. (1995). *National education longitudinal study of 1988.* Chicago: University of Chicago Press.

National Organization for Women Legal Defense and Education Fund. (1985). *Facts on women as entrepreneurs.* Washington, DC: Author.

National Research Council. (1980). *Science and engineering doctorates in the United States.* Washington, DC: National Academy of Sciences.

Neighbors, H. W. (1991). Mental health. In J. S. Jackson (Ed.), *Life in Black America* (pp. 221–237). Newbury Park, CA: Sage.

Nemerowicz, G. M. (1979). *Children's perceptions of gender and work roles.* New York: Praeger.

Neukrug, E. S., Barr, C. G., Hoffman, L. R., & Kaplan, L. S. (1993). Developmental counseling and guidance: A model for use in your school. *The School Counselor, 40,* 356–358.

Nevill, D. D. (1995). Perceptions and expectations of the worker and homemaker roles in Australia, Portugal, and the United States. In D. E. Super, B. Sverko, & C. M. Super (Eds.), *Life roles, values, and careers: International findings of the Work Importance Study* (pp. 139–143). San Francisco: Jossey–Bass.

Newman, B. (1989). Including curriculum content on lesbian and gay issues. *Journal of Social Work Education, 3,* 202–211.

Newman, K. S. (1988). *Falling from grace: The experience of downward mobility in the American middle class.* New York: Free Press.

Nichols, M. (1984). *Family therapy: Concepts and methods.* Boston: Allyn & Bacon.

Nicoll, W. G. (1992). A family counseling and consultation model for school counselors. *The School Counselor, 39,* 351–361.

Nutall, E. V., Romero, J., & Kalesnik, J. (1992). *Assessing and screening preschoolers: Psychological and educational dimensions.* Boston: Allyn & Bacon.

Nystul, M. S. (1993). *The art and science of counseling and psychotherapy.* New York: Merrill.

O'Dell, F. L., & Eisenberg, S. (1989). Helping students make important decisions. *The School Counselor, 36,* 286–292.

Odell, K. S. (1989). Gender differences in the educational and occupational expectations of rural Ohio youth. *Research in Rural Education, 5*(3), 37–44.

O'Hara, R. P. (1968). A theoretical foundation for the use of occupational information in guidance. *Personnel and Guidance Journal, 46,* 636–640.

O'Key, J. L., Snyder, L. M., Jr., & Hackett, G. (1993). The broadening horizon project: Development of a vocational guidance program for eighth-grade students. *The School Counselor, 40,* 218–222.

Oliver, L. W., & Spokane, A. R. (1988). Career-intervention outcome: What contributes to client gain? *Journal of Counseling Psychology, 35,* 447–462.

Omizo, S. A., & Omizo, M. M. (1992). Career and vocational assessment information for program planning and counseling for students with disabilities. *The School Counselor, 40,* 32–39.

Ormiston, W. (1996). Stone Butch celebration: A transgender-inspired revolution in academia. *Harvard Educational Review, 66*(2), 198–215.

Ormrod, J. E. (1995). *Educational psychology: Principles and applications.* Englewood Cliffs, NJ: Prentice Hall.

Orzek, A. M. (1992). Career counseling for the gay and lesbian community. In S. H. Dworkin & F. J. Gutierrez (Eds.), *Counseling gay men and lesbians: Journey to the end of the rainbow* (pp. 23–24). Alexandria, VA: American Association for Counseling and Development.

Osipow, S. H. (1975). The relevance of theories of career development to special groups: Problems. Needed data and implications. In J. S. Picou & R. E. Campbell (Eds.), *Career behavior of special groups* (pp. 137–167). Westerville, OH: Merrill.

Osipow, S. H. (1977). The great expose swindle: A reader's reaction. *Personnel and Guidance Journal, 56,* 23–24.

Osipow, S. H. (1983). *Theories of career development* (3rd ed.). Englewood Cliffs, NJ: Prentice Hall.

Osipow, S. H. (1986). Career issues through the life span. In M. S. Pallak & R. Perloff (Eds.), *Psychology and work: Productivity, change and employment* (pp. 137–168). Washington, DC: American Psychological Association.

Osipow, S. H. (1987). *Manual for the Career Decision Scale* (Rev. ed.). Odessa, FL: Psychological Assessment Reserves.

Osipow, S. H. (1991). Developing instruments for use in counseling. *Journal of Counseling & Development, 70,* 322–326.

Osipow, S. H., Carney, C. G., Winer, J., Yanico, B., & Koschier, M. (1976). *The Career Decision Scale.* Odessa, FL: Psychological Assessment Resources.

Osipow, S. H., & Fitzgerald, L. F. (1996). *Theories of career development* (4th ed.). Boston: Allyn & Bacon.

Osipow, S. H., & Rooney, R. (1989). *The task-specific scale of occupational self-efficacy.* Columbus, OH: Author.

Otto, L. B. (1996). *Helping your child choose a career: A book for parents, teachers, counselors, and (even) students* (Rev. ed.). Indianapolis, IN: JIST Works.

Otto, L. B., & Call, Y. A. (1985). Parental influences on young people's career development. *Journal of Career Development, 9,* 65–69.

Paisley, P. O., & Borders, L. D. (1995). School counseling: An evolving specialty. *Journal of Counseling & Development, 74,* 150–153.

Paisley, P. O., & Hubbard, G. T. (1994). *Developmental school counseling programs: From theory to practice.* Alexandria, VA: American Counseling Association.

Parette, H. P. (1992). *Helping people with disabilities: The ADA and service accessibility.* Little Rock, AR: Arkansas Easter Seal Society.

Parette, H. P., Jr., & Hourcade, J. J. (1995). Disability etiquette and school counselors: A common sense approach toward compliance with the Americans With Disabilities Act. *The School Counselor, 42,* 224–232.

Parker, L. O. (1992). Easing the graduation transition: Career seminars for seniors. *The School Counselor, 39,* 394–398.

Parmer, T. (1994). The athletic dream and the Black male student: Primary prevention implications for counselors. *The School Counselor, 41,* 333–337.

Parsons, F. (1909). *Choosing a vocation.* Boston: Houghton Mifflin.

Parr, J., & Neimeyer, J. (1994). Effects of gender, construct type, occupational information, and career relevance on vocational differentiation. *Journal of Counseling Psychology, 41,* 27–33.

Paul, G. (1967). Strategy of outcome research in psychotherapy. *Journal of Consulting Psychology, 31,* 109–118.

Pautler, K. J., & Lewko, J. H. (1987). Children's and adolescent's views of the work world in times of economic uncertainty. In J. H. Lewko (Ed.), *New directions for child development* (No. 5, pp. 21–31). San Francisco: Jossey-Bass.

Peatling, J. H., & Tiedeman, D. V. (1977). *Career development: Designing self.* Muncie, IN: Accelerated Development.

Peeks, B. (1993). Revolutions in counseling and education: A systems perspective in the schools. *Elementary School Guidance and Counseling, 27,* 245–251.

Penick, N. I., & Jepson, D. A. (1992). Family functioning and adolescent career development. *Career Development Quarterly, 40,* 208–221.

Perls, F., Hefferline, R., & Goodman, P. (1951). *Gestalt therapy.* New York: Dell.

Perrone, P. A. (1973). A longitudinal study of occupational values in adolescent. *Vocational Guidance Quarterly, 22,* 116–123.

Peterson, G. W., Sampson, J. P., & Reardon, R. C. (1991). *Career development and services: A cognitive approach.* Pacific Grove, CA: Brooks/Cole.

Peterson, G. W., Sampson, J. P., Reardon, R. C., & Lenz, J. G. (1996). A cognitive information processing approach to career problem solving and decision making. In D. Brown, L. Brooks, & Associates (Eds.), *Career choice and development* (3rd ed., pp. 423–473). San Francisco: Jossey-Bass.

Petitpas, A., Danish, S., McKelvain, R., & Murphy, S. (1992). A career assistance program for elite athletes. *Journal of Counseling & Development, 70,* 383–386.

Phillips, S. D., Friedlander, M. L., Kost, P. P., Specterman, R. V., & Robbins, E. S. (1988). Personal versus vocational focus in career counseling: A retrospective outcome study. *Journal of Counseling & Development, 67,* 169–173.

Phinney, J. S., & Alipuria, L. L. (1990). Ethnic identity in college students from four ethnic groups. *Journal of Adolescence, 13,* 171–183.

Phinney, J. S., Lochner, B. T., & Murphy, R. (1990). Ethnic identity development and psychological adjustment in adolescence. In A. R. Stiffman & L. E. Davis (Eds.), *Ethnic issues in adolescent mental health* (pp. 53–72). Newbury Park, CA: Sage.

Pinson, N. M. (1980). School counselors as interpreters for and of the community: New roles in career eduction. In F. E. Burtnett (Ed.), *The school counselor's role in career education* (pp. 123–149). Falls Church, VA: APGA Press.

Pinson-Millburn, N. M., Fabian, E. S., Schlossberg, N. K., & Pyle, M. (1996). Grandparents raising grandchildren. *Journal of Counseling & Development, 74,* 548–554.

Ponterotto, J. G., & Casas, J. M. (1991). *Handbook of racial/ethnic minority counseling research.* Springfield, IL: Charles C Thomas.

Pope, M. (1995). The "salad bowl" is big enough for us all: An argument for the inclusion of lesbians and gays in any definition of multiculturalism. *Journal of Counseling & Development, 73,* 301–304.

Postrado, L. T., Weiss, F. L., & Nicholson, H. J. (1997). Prevention of sexual intercourse for teen women aged 12 to 14. *The Prevention Researcher, 4,* 10–11.

Powell, D. H. (1957). Careers and family atmosphere: An empirical test of Roe's theory. *Journal of Counseling Psychology, 4,* 212–217.

Powell, R. (1987). Homosexual behavior and the school counselor. *The School Counselor, 34,* 202–208.

Prediger, D., Swaney, K., & Mau, W. C. (1993). Extending Holland's hexagon: Procedures, counseling applications, and research. *Journal of Counseling & Development, 71,* 422–428.

Pryor, R. G. L. (1985). Toward exorcising the self-concept from psychology: Some comments on Gottfredson's circumscription/compromise theory. *Journal of Counseling Psychology, 32,* 154–158.

Pugh, N. (1986). *Occupations: A unit designed for Grades 4 to 5.* Ann Arbor: University of Michigan. (ERIC Document Reproduction Service No. ED 272 445).

Purcell, P., & Stewart, L. (1990). Dick and Jane 1989. *Sex Roles, 22,* 177–185.

Reeb, M. (1974). The perception of occupational structure, an intervening variable in vocational behavior. *Journal of Vocational Behavior, 4,* 125–137.

Reinolds, C. (1996, June 20). Study: Income, not race, fuels education gap. *Arkansas Democrat Gazette,* pp. 1A, 11A.

Remafedi, G. (1987). *Homosexuality: The adolescent's perspective. Six lesbian and gay adolescents discuss their experiences* [Videotape]. (Available from University of Minnesota, Media Distribution, Box 734 UMHC, 420 Delaware St. SE, Minneapolis, MN 55455)

Remer, P., & Schrader, L. A. (1981). Gestalt approach to classroom guidance. *Elementary School Guidance and Counseling, 16,* 15–23.

Rice, F. P. (1993). *The adolescent: Development, relationships, and culture.* Boston: Allyn & Bacon.

Richardson, R. C., & Evans, E. T. (1991, August). *Empowering teachers to eliminate corporal punishment in the schools.* Paper presented at the annual conference of the National Black Child Development Institute, Washington, DC.

Richmond, L. J., Johnson, J., Downs, M., & Ellinghaus, A. (1983). Needs of non-Caucasian students in vocational education: A special minority group. *Journal of Non-White Concerns, 12,* 13–18.

Rick, K., & Forward, J. (1992). Acculturated and perceived intergenerational differences among Hmong youth. *Journal of Cross-Cultural Psychology, 23*(1), 85–94.

Rivers, R. Y., & Morrow, C. A. (1995). Understanding and treating ethnic minority youth. In J. F. Aponte, R. Y. Rivers, & J. Wohl (Eds.), *Psychological interventions and cultural diversity* (pp. 164–180). Boston: Allyn & Bacon.

Robinson, D., & Mopsik, W. (1992). An environmental experimental model for counseling handicapped children. *Elementary School Guidance and Counseling, 27,* 73–78.

Robinson, K. E. (1991). Gay youth support groups: An opportunity for mental health intervention. *Social Work, 36,* 458–459.

Robinson, K. E. (1994). Addressing the needs of gay and lesbian students: The school counselor's role. *The School Counselor, 41,* 326–332.

Roe, A. (1956). *The psychology of occupations.* New York: Wiley.

Roe, A. (1957). Early determinants of vocational choice. *Journal of Counseling Psychology, 4,* 212–217.

Roe, A. (1972). Perspectives on vocational development. In J. M. Whiteley & A. Resnikoff (Eds.), *Perspectives on vocational development* (pp. 102–161). Washington, DC: American Personnel and Guidance Association.

Roe, A., & Lunneborg, P. W. (1990). Personality development and career choice. In D. Brown & L. Brooks (Eds.), *Career choice and development* (2nd ed., pp. 68–101). San Francisco: Jossey-Bass.

Rofes, E. (1989). Opening up the classroom closet: Responding to the educational needs of gay and lesbian youth. *Harvard Educational Review, 59*(3), 444–453.

Rohner, R. P., Hahn, B. C., & Koehn, U. (1992). Occupational mobility, length of residence, and perceived maternal warmth among Korean immigrant families. *Journal of Cross-Cultural Psychology, 23,* 366–376.

Ross-Reynolds, G. (1982). Issues in counseling the "homosexual" adolescent. In J. Grimes (Ed.), *Psychological* approaches to problems of children and adolescents (pp. 123–153). Des Moines, IA: Iowa State Department of Public Instruction, Division of Special Education.

Rotter, J. B. (1966). Generalized expectations for internal versus external control of reinforcement. *Psychological Monographs, 80*(1, Whole No. 609).

Rounds, J. B., Jr., & Tracey, T. J. (1990). From trait-and-factor to person–environment fit counseling: Theory and process. In W. S. Walsh & S. H. Osipow (Eds.), *Career counseling: Contemporary topics in vocational psychology* (pp. 1–44). Hillsdale, NJ: Elbaum.

Ruble, D. N. (1988). Sex-role development. In M. H. Bornstein & M. E. Lamb (Eds.), *Developmental psychology: An advanced textbook* (2nd ed., pp. 76–101). Hillsdale, NJ: Erlbaum.

Ruhland, D. J., Brittle, M., Norris, S., & Oakes, R. (1978). *Determinants of career goals in junior and senior high school women.* Ann Arbor: University of Michigan. (ERIC Document Reproduction Service No. ED 185 356)

Rusch, F. (1986). *Competitive employment issues and strategies.* Baltimore: Paul H. Brooks.

Russell, D. M. (1988). Language and psychotherapy: The influences of nonstandard English in clinical practice. In L. Comas-Diaz & E. E. H. Griffith (Eds.), *Clinical guidelines in cross-cultural mental health* (pp. 33–68). New York: Wiley.

Ryan, B., & Sawatzky, D. (1989). Children's school problems and family system processes. *International Journal for the Advancement of Counselling, 12,* 215–222.

Sadker, M., & Sadker, D. (1994). *Failing at fairness: How America's schools cheat girls.* New York: Scribner.

Sadker, M., Sadker, D., & Donald, M. (1989). Subtle sexism at school. *Contemporary Education, 60,* 204–212.

Salomone, P. R., & Slaney, R. B. (1978). The applicability of Holland's theory to nonprofessional workers. *Journal of Vocational Behavior, 13,* 63–74.

Sampson, J. P., Jr., Peterson, G. W., & Reardon, R. C. (1989). Counselor intervention strategies for computer-assisted career guidance: An information-processing approach. *Journal of Career Development, 16,* 139–154.

Sampson, J. P., Jr., Shahnasarian, M., & Reardon, R. C. (1987). Computer-assisted career guidance: A national perspective on the use of DISCOVER and SIGI. *Journal of Counseling & Career Development, 65,* 416–419.

Sandler, S. B. (1989). Teaching job search skills to eighth grade students: A preview of the world of work. *The School Counselor, 36,* 219–223.

Santrock, J. W. (1993). *Adolescence: An introduction* (5th ed.). Madison, WI: Brown & Benchmark.

Sauter, D., Seidl, A., & Karbon, J. (1980). Counseling experience and attitudes toward women's roles on traditional or nontraditional career choice. *Vocational Guidance Quarterly, 28,* 241–249.

Savage, J., Stearns, A., & Friedman, P. (1979). Relationship of internal–external locus of control, self-concept, and masculinity–femininity to fear of success in Black freshmen and senior college women. *Sex Roles, 5,* 373–383.

Schauer, A. H. (1991). Reaction: Personal Styles Inventory. *Journal of Counseling & Development, 70,* 342–343.

Schliebner, C. T., & Peregoy, J. J. (1994). Unemployment effects on the family and the child: Interventions for counselors. *Journal of Counseling & Development, 72*, 368–371.

Schmidt, J. J. (1991). *A survival guide for the elementary/middle school counselor.* West Nyack, NY: Center for Applied Research in Education.

Schmidt, J. J. (1996). *Counseling in schools: Essential services and comprehensive programs* (2nd ed.). Boston: Allyn & Bacon.

Schmitt, P., Growick, B., & Klein, M. (1988). Transition from school to work for individuals with learning disabilities: A comprehensive model. In S. E. Rubin & N. M. Rubin (Eds.), *Contemporary challenges to the rehabilitation counseling profession* (pp. 93–110). Baltimore: Paul H. Brooks.

Schmitz, T. J. (1988). Career counseling implications with the gay and lesbian population. *Journal of Employment Counseling, 25*, 51–56.

Schmuck, R. A., & Schmuck, P. A. (1997). *Group processes in the classroom* (7th ed.). New York: McGraw-Hill.

Schrock, L. L. (1981). The relationship of adolescent females' career choices to locus of control and perceptions of femininity. *Dissertation Abstracts International, 42*, 1015A. (University Microfilms No. 8118712)

Scott, E., & McCollum, H. (1993). Making it happen: Gender equitable classrooms. In S. Biklen & D. Pollard (Eds.), *92nd yearbook of the National Society for the Study of Education: Part 1. Gender and education* (pp. 174–190). Chicago: University of Chicago Press.

Scott, T. B., Dawis, R. V., England, G. W., & Lofquist, L. H. (1960). A definition of work adjustment. *Minnesota Studies in Rehabilitation, No. X*, 1–68.

Sears, S. J. (1982). A definition of career guidance terms: A national guidance association perspective. *Vocational Guidance Quarterly, 31*, 137–143.

Sedgwick, E. K. (1991). How to bring your kids up gay. *Social Text, 9*(4), 4.

Seligman, L. (1980). *Assessment in developmental career counseling.* Cranston, RI: Carroll Press.

Seligman, L., Weinstock, L., & Heflin, E. N. (1991). The career development of 10 year olds. *Elementary School Guidance and Counseling, 25*, 172–181.

Seligman, L., Weinstock, L., & Owings, N. (1988). The role of family dynamics in career development of 5-year-olds. *Elementary School Guidance and Counseling, 22*, 222–230.

Selvini Palazzoli, M., Cirillo, S., Selvini, M., Sorrentino, A. (1989). *Family games.* New York: Norton.

Sewell, W. H., & Shah, V. P. (1968). Social class, parental encouragement, and educational aspirations. *American Journal of Sociology, 73*, 559–572.

Shaffer, S. (1986). *Gifted girls: The disappearing act* (The report card no. 6). Washington, DC: Mid-Atlantic Center for Sex Equity.

Shannon, J. W., & Woods, W. J. (1991). Affirmative psychotherapy for gay men. *The Counseling Psychologist, 19*, 197–215.

Sheffey, M. A., Bingham, R. P., & Walsh, W. B. (1986). Concurrent validity of Holland's theory for college-educated Black men. *Journal of Multicultural Counseling and Development, 14*, 149–156.

Shertzer, B. E., & Stone, S. C. (1980). *Fundamentals of counseling* (3rd ed.). Boston: Houghton Mifflin.

Short, G. (1991). Children's grasp of controversial issues. In M. Woodhead, P. Light, & R. Carr (Eds.), *Growing up in a changing society* (pp. 333–351). New York: Routledge.

Siegel, R. G., Galassi, J. P., & Ware, W. B. (1985). A comparison of two models for predicting mathematics performance: Social learning versus math aptitude-anxiety. *Journal of Consulting Psychology, 32,* 531–538.

Silin, J. (1995). *Sex, death and the education of children: Our passion for ignorance in the age of AIDS.* New York: Teachers College Press.

Siltanen, J. (1994). *Locating gender: Occupational segregation, wages, and domestic responsibilities.* London: University College London Press.

Simpson, A. W., & Erickson, M. T. (1983). Teachers' verbal and nonverbal communication patterns as a function of teacher race, student gender, and student race. *American Educational Research Journal, 20,* 183–198.

Slaney, R. B. (1983). Influence of career indecision on treatments exploring the vocational interests of college women. *Journal of Counseling Psychology, 30,* 55–63.

Slaney, R. B., & Russell, J. E. A. (1987). Perspectives on vocational behavior: 1986: A review. *Journal of Vocational Behavior, 31,* 111–173.

Slogett, B. B. (1971). Use of group activities and team rewards to increase individual classroom productivity. *Teaching Exceptional Children, 3*(2), 54–66.

Smith, E. J. (1983). Issues in racial minorities' career behavior. In W. B. Walsh & S. H. Osipow (Eds.), *Handbook of vocational psychology: Vol. 1. Foundations* (pp. 170–198). Hillsdale, NJ: Erlbaum.

Smith, J., & Russell, G. (1984). Why do males and females differ? Children's beliefs about sex differences. *Sex Roles, 11,* 1111–1120.

Sodowsky, G. R., Kwan, K. K., & Pannu, R. (1995). Ethnic identity of Asians in the United States. In J. G. Ponterotto, J. M. Casas, L. A. Suzuki, & C. M. Alexander (Eds.), *Handbook of multicultural counseling* (pp. 123–154). Thousand Oaks, CA: Sage.

Solomon, D., Scheinfeld, D. R., Hirsch, J. G., & Jackson, J. C. (1971). Early grade school performance of inner city Negro high school high achievers, low achievers and dropouts. *Developmental Psychology, 4,* 482.

Sowell, T. (1995). Ethnicity and IQ. In S. Fraser (Ed.), *The bell curve wars: Race, intelligence, and the future of America* (pp. 70–79). New York: Basic Books.

Splete, H., & Freeman-George, A. (1985). Family influences on the career development of young adults. *Journal of Career Development, 9,* 55–64.

Spokane, A. R. (1991). *Evaluating career interventions.* Englewood Cliffs, NJ: Prentice Hall.

Spokane, A. R. (1993). Are career counselors really guilty of malpractice? *Journal of Counseling & Development, 71,* 555–557.

Spokane, A. R. (1996). Holland's theory. In D. Brown, L. Brooks, & Associates (Eds.), *Career choice and development* (3rd ed., pp. 33–74). San Francisco: Jossey-Bass.

Spokane, A. R., & Hawks, B. K. (1990). Annual review: Practice and research in career development and counseling: 1989. *Career Development Quarterly, 39,* 98–128.

Sprinthall, N. A. (1971). *Guidance for human growth.* New York: Van Nostrand Reinhold.

Stamm, M. L., & Nissman, B. S. (1973). The counselor's view of the middle school student. *The School Counselor, 21,* 34–38.

Standish, F. (1992, February 25). Plant closings to affect 16,000 workers. *The Denver Post,* p. 1.

Stein, A. H. (1971). The effects of sex-role standards for achievement and sex-role preferences on three determinants of achievement motivation. *Developmental Psychology, 4,* 219–231.

Stein, A. H., & Smithells, J. (1969). Age and sex differences in children's sex-role standards about achievement. *Developmental Psychology, 1,* 252–259.

Steinberger, E. (1991). Multicultural curriculum uncovers common bonds, individual strengths, fiery debate. *The School Administrator, 48*(4), 8–14.

Stockard, J., Schmuck, P. A., Kemper, K., Williams, P., Edson, S. K., & Smith, M. A. (1980). *Sex equity in education.* New York: Academic Press.

Stone, W. O. (1984). Servicing ethnic minorities. In H. D. Burck & R. C. Reardon (Eds.), *Career development interventions* (pp. 267–291). Springfield, IL: Charles C Thomas.

Stone, W. O., & Brooks, L. C. (1979). *Cross-cultural counseling: Practitioner training and methods.* Unpublished grant proposal submitted to the Fund for the Improvement of Postsecondary Education, Washington, DC.

Strahan, R. F., & Kelly, A. E. (1994). Showing clients what their profiles mean. *Journal of Counseling & Development, 72,* 329–331.

Street, S. (1994). Adolescent male sexuality issues. *The School Counselor, 41,* 319–325.

Strong, E. K., & Campbell, D. P. (1981). *Strong–Campbell Interest Inventory.* Stanford, CA: Stanford University Press.

Sue, D. W. (1978). World views and counseling. *Personnel and Guidance Journal, 56,* 458–463.

Sue, D. W., Arredondo, P., & McDavis, R. J. (1992). Multicultural counseling competencies and standards: A call to the profession. *Journal of Counseling & Development, 20,* 64–88.

Sue, D. W., & Sue, D. (1990). *Counseling the culturally different: Theory and practice* (2nd ed.). New York: Wiley.

SUNY study finds school management still white male dominated. (1990). *Black Issues in Higher Education, 7*(5), 23.

Super, D. E. (1951). Vocational adjustment: Implementing a self-concept. *Occupations, 30,* 88–92.

Super, D. E. (1953). A theory of vocational development. *American Psychologist, 8,* 189–190.

Super, D. E. (1957). *The psychology of careers.* New York: Harper & Row.

Super, D. E. (1969). The natural history of a study of lives and of vocations. *Perspectives on Education, 2,* 13–22.

Super, D. E. (1972). Vocational development theory: Persons, positions, and processes. In J. M. Whiteley & A. Resnikoff (Eds.), *Perspectives on vocational development* (pp. 56–101). Washington, DC: American Personnel and Guidance Association.

Super, D. E. (1974). *Measuring vocational maturity for counseling and evaluation.* Washington, DC: National Vocational Guidance Association.

Super, D. E. (1976). *Career education and the meaning of work* (Monographs on career education). Washington, DC: Office of Career Education, U.S. Office of Education.

Super. D. E. (1977). Vocational maturity in mid-career. *Vocational Guidance Quarterly, 25,* 297.

Super, D. E. (1980). A life-span, life-space approach to career development. *Journal of Vocational Behavior, 16,* 282–298.

Super, D. E. (1983). Assessment in career guidance: Toward truly developmental counseling. *Personnel and Guidance Journal, 61,* 555–562.

Super, D. E. (1984). Perspectives on the meaning and value of work. In N. C. Gysbers (Ed.), *Designing careers: Counseling to enhance education, work, and leisure* (pp. 1–34). San Francisco: Jossey-Bass.

Super, D. E. (1985). *New dimensions in adult vocational and career counseling* (Occupational Paper No. 106). Columbus, OH: National Center for Research in Vocational Education.

Super, D. E. (1990). A life-span, life-space approach to career development. In D. Brown & L. Brooks (Eds.), *Career choice and development* (2nd ed., pp. 197–261). San Francisco: Jossey-Bass.

Super, D. E. (1992). Toward a comprehensive theory of career development. In D. J. Montross & C. J. Shinkman (Eds.), *Career development: Theory and practice* (2nd ed., pp. 35–64). Springfield, IL: Charles C Thomas.

Super, D. E., Bohn, M. J., Forrest, D. J., Jordan, J. P., Lindeman, R. H., & Thompson, A. A. (1971). *Career Development Inventory.* New York: Columbia University, Teachers College.

Super, D. E., & Bowlsbey, J. A. (1979). *A guided career exploration.* New York: Psychological Corporation.

Super, D. E., & Crites, J. O. (1962). *Appraising vocational fitness.* New York: Harper & Brothers.

Super, D. E., Crites, J. O., Hummel, R. C., Moser, H. P., Overstreet, P. L., & Warnath, C. (1957). *Vocational development: A framework for research.* New York: Teachers College Press.

Super, D. E., & Kidd, J. M. (1979). Vocational maturity in adulthood: Toward turning a model into a measure. *Journal of Vocational Behavior, 14,* 255–270.

Super, D. E., Kowalski, R. S., & Gotkin, E. H. (1967). *Floundering and trial after high school.* New York: Teachers College, Columbia University.

Super, D. E., Osborne, W. L., Walsh, D. J., Brown, S. D., & Niles, S. G. (1992). Developmental assessment and counseling: The C-DAC model. *Journal of Counseling & Development, 71,* 74–80.

Super, D. E., & Overstreet, P. L. (1960). *The vocational maturity of ninth grade boys.* New York: Teachers College, Columbia University.

Super, D. E., Savickas, M. L., & Super, C. M. (1996). The life-span, life-space approach to careers. In D. Brown, L. Brooks, & Associates (Eds.), *Career choice and development* (3rd ed., pp. 121–178). San Francisco: Jossey-Bass.

Swaim, R. C., Oetting, E. R., Thurman, P. J., Beauvais, F., & Edwards, R. W. (1993). American Indian adolescent drug use and socialization characteristics: A cross-cultural comparison. *Journal of Cross-Cultural Psychology, 24,* 53–70.

Swaim, R. C., Thurman, P. J., Beauvais, F., Oetting, E. R., & Wayman, J. (1993). *Indian adolescent substance use as a function of number of risk factors.* Unpublished manuscript.

Swanson, J. L. (1993). Integrating a multicultural perspective into training for career counseling and programmatic and individual interventions. *Career Development Quarterly, 42,* 41–49.

Szymanski, E. M., & King, J. (1989). Rehabilitation counseling in transition planning and preparation. *Career Development for Exceptional Individuals, 12*(1), 3–10.

Szymanski, E. M., King, J., Parker, R. M., & Jenkins, W. M. (1989). The state–federal rehabilitation program: Overview and interface with special education. *Exceptional Children, 56,* 70–77.

Taylor, N. B., & Pryor, R. G. L. (1985). Exploring the process of compromise in career decision making. *Journal of Vocational Behavior, 27,* 171–190.

Teenagers and technology. (April 28, 1997). *Newsweek,* p. 86.

Testerman, J. (1996). Holding at-risk students: The secret is one-on-one. *Phi Delta Kappan, 77,* 364–365.

Thorndike, R. L., & Hagen, E. (1959). *10,000 careers.* New York: Wiley.

Tidwell, B. J. (1992). *The state of Black America 1992.* New York: National Urban League.

Tiedeman, D. V. (1961). Decision and vocational development: A paradigm and its implications. *Personnel and Guidance Journal, 40,* 15–20.

Tiedeman, D. V. (1979). *Career development: Designing our career machines.* Schenectady, NY: Character Research Press.

Tiedeman, D. V., & O'Hara, R. P. (1963). *Career development: Choice and adjustment.* Princeton, NJ: College Entrance Examination Board.

Tiedt, P. L., & Tiedt, I. M. (1995). *Multicultural teaching: A handbook of activities, information, and resources.* Boston: Allyn & Bacon.

Trebilco, G. R. (1984). Career education and career maturity. *Journal of Vocational Behavior, 25,* 191–202.

Trevino, F. (1987). Standardized terminology for Hispanic populations. *American Journal of Public Health, 77,* 69–72.

Tuckman, B. W. (1974). An age-graded model for career development education. *Journal of Vocational Behavior, 4,* 193–212.

U.S. Bureau of the Census. (1990). *Statistical abstracts of the United States: 1990* (110th ed.). Washington, DC: U.S. Government Printing Office.

U.S. Bureau of the Census. (1991). *Statistical abstracts of the United States: 1991* (111th ed.). Washington, DC: U.S. Government Printing Office.

U.S. Bureau of the Census. (1992). *Current population reports, P25-1092, Population projections of the United States by age, sex, race, and Hispanic origin 1992–2050.* Washington, DC: U.S. Government Printing Office.

U.S. Bureau of the Census. (1993). *Statistical abstract of the United States* (113th ed.). Washington, DC: U.S. Government Printing Office.

U.S. Congress. (1986). *Indian health care* (Report No. OTA-H-290). Washington, DC: U.S. Government Printing Office.

U.S. Department of Commerce. (1993a). *Population profile of the United States.* Washington, DC: U.S. Government Printing Office.

U.S. Department of Commerce. (1993b). *We, the American Blacks.* Washington, DC: U.S.Government Printing Office.

U.S. Department of Education. (1994a). *The condition of education, 1994.* Washington, DC: U.S. Government Printing Office.

U.S. Department of Education. (1994b). *Sixteenth annual report to Congress on the implementation of the Individuals With Disabilities Act.* Washington, DC: U.S. Government Printing Office.

U.S. Department of Justice. (1991). *Crime in the United States.* Washington, DC: U.S. Government Printing Office.

U.S. Department of Labor. (1977). *Dictionary of occupational titles* (4th ed.). Washington, DC: U.S. Government Printing Office.

U.S. Department of Labor. (1985). *Facts on working women: Earning differences between women and men workers* (Fact Sheet No. 85-7). Washington, DC: Department of Labor, Women's Bureau.

U.S. Department of Labor. (1986). *Twenty facts on working women* (Fact Sheet No. 86-1). Washington, DC: Department of Labor, Women's Bureau.

U.S. Department of Labor. (1996). *Dictionary of occupational titles* (5th ed.). Washington, DC: Author.

Valencia, R. R., & Aburto, S. (1991). The uses and abuses of educational testing: Chicanos as a case in point. In R. R. Valencia (Ed.), *Chicano school failure and success: Research and policy agendas for the 1990s* (pp. 121–154). Basingstoke, England: Falmer Press.

Van Buren, J. B., Kelly, K. R., & Hall, A. S. (1993). Modeling nontraditional career choices: Effects of gender and school location on response to a brief videotape. *Journal of Counseling & Development, 72,* 101–104.

Vandergoot, D. (1987). Review of placement research literature: Applications for practice. *Rehabilitation Counseling Bulletin, 30,* 243–272.

VanZandt, C. E., & Hayslip, J. B. (1994). *Your comprehensive school guidance and counseling program: A handbook of practical activities.* New York: Longman.

Villegas, A. (1991). *Culturally responsive pedagogy for the 1990s and beyond.* Princeton, NJ: Educational Testing Service.

Vincenzi, H. (1977). Minimizing occupational stereotypes. *Vocational Guidance Quarterly, 25,* 265.

Vondracek, F. W. (1991). Osipow on the Career Decision Scale: Some comments. *Journal of Counseling & Development, 70,* 327.

Vondracek, F. W., Hostetler, M., Schulenberg, J. E., & Shimizu, K. (1990). Dimensions of career indecision. *Journal of Counseling Psychology, 37,* 98–106.

Vondracek, F. W., Schulenberg, J., & Hostetler, M. (1989, March). *A typology of vocational indecision and implications for counseling.* Paper presented at the meeting of the American Educational Research Association, San Francisco.

Vondracek, S. I., & Kirchner, E. P. (1974). Vocational development in early childhood: An examination of young children's expressions of vocational aspirations. *Journal of Vocational Behavior, 5,* 251–260.

Warnath, C. F. (1975). Vocational theories: Direction to nowhere. *Personnel and Guidance Journal, 53,* 422–428.

Walsh, W. B., Hildebrand, J. O., Ward, C. M., & Matthews, D. F. (1983). Holland's theory and non-college-degreed working Black and White women. *Journal of Vocational Behavior, 22*, 182–190.

Walsh, W. B., Woods, W. J., & Ward, C. M. (1986). Holland's theory and working Black and White women. *Journal of Multicultural Counseling and Development, 14*, 116–123.

Walters, K. L., & Simoni, J. M. (1993). Lesbian and gay male group identity attitudes and self-esteem: Implications for counseling. *Journal of Counseling Psychology, 40*, 94–99.

Walz, G. R. (1991). Future focused generalizations on counseling. In G. R. Walz, G. M. Gazda, & B. Shertzer (Eds.), *Counseling futures* (pp. 71–78). Ann Arbor: University of Michigan Press.

Walz, G. R., & Benjamin, L. (1984). Systematic career guidance programs. In N. C. Gysbers & Associates (Eds.), *Designing careers* (pp. 336–361). San Francisco: Jossey-Bass.

Ward, C. M., & Bingham, R. P. (1993). Career assessment of ethnic minority women. *Journal of Career Assessment, 1*, 246–257.

Warren, S. A., & Gardner, D. C. (1981). Correlates of class rank of high school handicapped students in mainstream vocational educational programs. *Adolescence, 16*(62), 335–344.

Watkins, C. (1989). Student support groups: Help and healing through the education system. *Adolescent Counselor, 2*, 54–57.

Watkins, C. (1994). Whole-school guidance? *British Journal of Guidance and Counselling, 22*, 143–150.

Webster, R. E. (1974). Predictive applicability of the WAIS with psychiatric patients in a vocational rehabilitation setting. *Journal of Community Psychology, 2*, 141–144.

Webster, R. E. (1979). Utility of the WAIS in predicting vocational success of psychiatric patients. *Journal of Clinical Psychology, 35*, 111–116.

Wechsler, D. (1981). *WAIS–R manual–Wechsler Adult Intelligence Scale revised.* San Antonio, TX: Psychological Corporation.

Weeks, N. O., & Porter, M. P. (1983). A second look at the impact of nontraditional vocational role models and curriculum on the vocational role preferences of kindergarten children. *Journal of Vocational Behavior, 23*, 14–71.

Weeks, N. O., Wise, G. W., & Duncan, C. (1984). The relationship between sex-role attitudes and career orientations of high school females and their mothers. *Adolescence, 19*, 596–607.

Wehman, P. (Ed.). (1993). *The ADA mandate for social change.* Baltimore: Paul H. Brooks.

Weinrach, S. G. (1980). Have hexagon will travel: An interview with John Holland. *Personnel and Guidance Journal, 58*, 406–414.

Weinrach, S. G., & Srebalus, D. J. (1990). Holland's theory of careers. In D. Brown & L. Brooks (Eds.), *Career choice and development* (2nd ed., pp. 37–67). San Francisco: Jossey-Bass.

Welch, I. D., & McCarroll, L. (1993). The future role of school counselors. *The School Counselor, 41*, 48–53.

Werner, J. E. (1974). Effect of role choice on vocational high school students. *Journal of Vocational Behavior, 4*, 77–84.

Whelage, G. G., & Rutter, R. A. (Spring, 1986). Dropping out: How much do schools contribute to the problem? *Teachers College Record*, 374–391.

Widerman, J. L., & Widerman, E. (1995). Family systems-oriented school counseling. *The School Counselor, 43*, 66–73.

Wiggins, J. D., & Moody, A. H. (1987). Student evaluations of counseling programs: An added dimension. *The School Counselor, 34*, 353–361.

Wilcox-Matthew, L., & Minor, C. W. (1989). The dual career couples: Concerns, benefits, and counseling implications. *Journal of Counseling & Development, 68*, 194–198.

William T. Grant Foundation Commission on Work, Family and Citizenship. (1988). *The forgotten half: Noncollege youth in America: An interim report on the school-to-work transition.* Washington, DC: Author.

Williamson, D. S., Bray, J. H., & Malone, P. E. (1982). *Personal authority in the family system questionnaire.* Houston, TX: Houston Family Institute.

Williamson, E. G. (1939). *How to counsel students: A manual of techniques for clinical counselors.* New York: McGraw-Hill.

Williamson, E. G. (1949). *Counseling adolescents.* New York: McGraw-Hill.

Wilson, J., & Daniel, R. (1981). The effects of a career-options workshop on social and vocational stereotypes. *Vocational Guidance Quarterly, 30*, 341–349.

Wise, R., Charner, I., & Randour, M. A. (1978). A conceptual framework for career awareness in career decision–making. In J. Whitely & A. Resnikoff (Eds.), *Career counseling* (pp. 216–231). Monterey, CA: Brooks/Cole.

Wolfe, A. (1995). Has there been a cognitive revolution in America: The flawed sociology of *The Bell Curve*. In S. Fraser (Ed.), *The bell curve wars: Race, intelligence, and the future of America* (pp. 109–123). New York: Basic Books.

Wolfson, V. P. (1976). Career development patterns of college women. *Journal of Counseling Psychology, 23*, 119–125.

Woodill, G. (1987). Critical issues in the use of microcomputers by young children. *International Journal of Early Childhood, 19*, 50–57.

Work, W. C., Parker, G. R., & Cowen, E. L. (1990). The impact of life stresses on childhood adjustment: Multiple perspectives. *Journal of Community Psychology, 18*, 73–78.

Yao, E. (1988). Working effectively with Asian immigrants. *Phi Delta Kappan, 70*, 223–225.

Yawn, B. P., & Yawn, R. A. (1997). Adolescent pregnancy: A preventable consequence. *The Prevention Researcher, 4*, 1–4.

Yee, A. H., Fairchild, H. H., Weizmann, F., & Wyatt, G. E. (1993). Addressing psychology's problems with race. *American Psychologist, 48*, 1132–1140.

Young, J. L., Thomas, R. E., Hilliard, S. H., Shaw, H. S., IV, & Epstein, E. J. (1996). Anatomy of an academy: A career guidance unit. *Elementary School Guidance and Counseling, 30*, 304–312.

Zaccaria, J. (1970). *Theories of occupational choice and vocational development.* Boston: Houghton Mifflin.

Zane, N., & Sasao, T. (1992). Research on drug abuse among Asian Pacific Americans. In J. Trimble, C. Bolek, & S. Niemcryk (Eds.), *Ethnic and multicultural drug abuse* (pp. 181–209). Binghamton, NY: Harrington Park.

Zener, T. B., & Schnuelle, L. (1972). *An evaluation of the Self-Directed Search* (Center for Social Organization of Schools, Report No. 124). Baltimore: Johns Hopkins University Press.

Zener, T. B., & Schnuelle, L. (1976). Effects of the Self-Directed Search on high school students. *Journal of Counseling Psychology, 23,* 353–359.

Zucker, K. (1990). Psychosocial and erotic development in cross-gender identified children. *Canadian Journal of Psychiatry, 35,* 487–495.

Zunker, V. G. (1986). *Career counseling: Applied concepts of life planning.* Monterey, CA: Brooks/Cole.

Zunker, V. G. (1990). *Career counseling: Applied concepts of life planning* (3rd ed.). Pacific Grove, CA: Brooks/Cole.

Zunker, V. G. (1994). *Career guidance: Applied concepts of life planning* (4th ed.). Pacific Grove, CA: Brooks/Cole.

Zunker, V. G. (1998). *Career guidance: Applied concepts of life planning* (5th ed.). Pacific Grove, CA: Brooks/Cole.

Index